The Renaissance dialogue is the first full-length study of the use of the dialogue form in Italy from the early sixteenth century until Galileo. Drawing on a wide range of literary, philosophical and scientific sources, it examines the characteristics which determined the genre's unrivalled popularity in the period as a vehicle for polemic, debate, technical exposition and comic drama. Particular attention is paid to reception and to the place that the dialogue occupied within the evolving cultural economy of the Italian courts.

More than simply an account of the development of an individual literary genre, however, *The Renaissance dialogue* is a contribution to the broader social and cultural history of the period. As representations of conversation, miniature dramas of persuasion, the dialogues of the Italian Renaissance constitute an extraordinarily rich – and largely untapped – source of information about the ideals and practice of communication in the early modern age. *The Renaissance dialogue* draws on this evidence to trace a history of cultural dialogue, charting the effect of factors such as the cultural policies of the Counter-Reformation, the realignment of social and intellectual practice which came about with the consolidation of absolutist rule throughout Italy, and the gradual internalization of the psychological norms of a typographic culture.

CAMBRIDGE STUDIES IN RENAISSANCE
LITERATURE AND CULTURE 2

The Renaissance dialogue

Cambridge Studies in Renaissance Literature and Culture

General Editor
STEPHEN ORGEL
Jackson Eli Reynolds Professor of Humanities, Stanford University

Advisory Board
Anne Barton, *University of Cambridge*
Jonathan Dollimore, *University of Sussex*
Marjorie Garber, *Harvard University*
Jonathan Goldberg, *The Johns Hopkins University*
Nancy Vickers, *University of Southern California*

The last twenty years have seen a broad and vital reinterpretation of the nature of literary texts, a move away from formalism to a sense of literature as an aspect of social, economic, political and cultural history. While the earliest New Historicist work was criticized for a narrow and anecdotal view of history, it also served as an important stimulus for post-structuralist, feminist, Marxist and psychoanalytic work, which in turn has increasingly informed and redirected it. Recent writing on the nature of representation, the historical construction of gender and of the concept of identity itself, on theatre as a political and economic phenomenon and on the ideologies of art generally, reveal the breadth of the field. *Cambridge Studies in Renaissance Literature and Culture* is designed to offer historically oriented studies of Renaissance literature and theatre which make use of the insights afforded by theoretical perspectives. The view of history envisioned is above all a view of our own history, a reading of the Renaissance for and from our own time.

Opening titles

Drama and the market in the age of Shakespeare
DOUGLAS BRUSTER, University of Chicago

The Renaissance dialogue: literary dialogue in its social and political contexts, Castiglione to Galileo
VIRGINIA COX, University College London

The Renaissance dialogue

Literary dialogue in its social and political contexts, Castiglione to Galileo

Virginia Cox

Department of Italian, University College London

CAMBRIDGE
UNIVERSITY PRESS

CAMBRIDGE UNIVERSITY PRESS
Cambridge, New York, Melbourne, Madrid, Cape Town, Singapore, São Paulo

Cambridge University Press
The Edinburgh Building, Cambridge CB2 8RU, UK

Published in the United States of America by Cambridge University Press, New York

www.cambridge.org
Information on this title: www.cambridge.org/9780521405386

First published 1992
This digitally printed version 2008

A catalogue record for this publication is available from the British Library

Library of Congress Cataloguing in Publication data

Cox, Virginia.
The Renaissance dialogue: literary dialogue in its social and political contexts,
Castiglione to Galileo / Virginia Cox.
  p.   cm. – (Cambridge studies in Renaissance literature and culture: 2)
Includes bibliographical references and index.
ISBN 0–521–40538–6 (hardback)
1. Dialogues, Italian – History and criticism.
2. Italian literature – 16th century – History and criticism.
3. Italian literature – 17th century – History and criticism.
4. Renaissance – Italy.   5. Italy – Civilization – 1268–1559.
6. Italy – Civilization – 1559–1789.   I. Title II. Series.
PQ4183.D5C68   1992
850.9′26′09031 – dc20   91–46675   CIP

ISBN 978-0-521-40538-6 hardback
ISBN 978-0-521-06966-3 paperback

To my parents

Contents

Preface

Though it is generally acknowledged to be one of the most characteristic literary forms of the Renaissance, the dialogue remains curiously invisible in the literary history of the period. A small number of isolated masterpieces have, of course, attracted their share of attention, but there have been few attempts to grasp the phenomenon of literary dialogue as a whole, and what critical observation there has been has all too often been limited to vague diagnoses of the dialogic Zeitgeist of the age. It is as though this awkwardly hybrid genre – for Tasso, a union between poetry and dialectic – has slipped through the gap between philosophy and rhetoric which was already beginning to open up during the period in question and which is only now beginning to close.

Within this panorama of general neglect, a particularly untended area has been the social history of the dialogue. The concerns of most critics who have touched on the genre have tended to be either formal or epistemological; the dialogue is scrutinized as a work of art or a vehicle for thought. My aim in this book has been to examine the dialogue as an act of communication: to restore this most sociable of literary genres to the social matrix within which it was produced.

This book makes no claims to be a comprehensive history of the Italian dialogue in the period under consideration. Having started my research blithely unaware of the vastness of the field I was straying into, I rapidly realized that to attempt to say something about every use to which the dialogue was put in Renaissance Italy was to risk saying nothing very interesting about any of them at all. Substantial sections of Cinquecento dialogue production have consequently had to be ignored or passed over: most obviously, the flourishing humanistic and academic neo-Latin tradition, but also, significant areas of vernacular production. It is my good fortune, and the reader's, that Raffaele Girardi's *La società del dialogo*, which appeared while I was preparing my final draft, contains valuable discussions of several areas which have only been touched on here.

Another omission is more regrettable. With the single exception of an extended discussion of Castiglione's *Cortegiano* in chapter 5, the broad scope of material covered in this study has precluded any detailed analysis of individual dialogues. It is perhaps inevitable, in a work which attempts to sketch a picture as broad as this one does, that clarity of outline will take priority over detail. I am still uneasily conscious, however, of having dispatched in a sentence works to whose richness and complexity nothing but a monograph could really do justice.

My consolation must be that this book shares its provisional nature with the genre which it studies. The dialogue was conceived of by the humanists as a 'provocation' to the reader: a form of argumentation which deliberately eschewed the self-sufficiency of the treatise form, and actively challenged its readers and critics to pursue the quest it had begun. *The Renaissance Dialogue* will have served its purpose if its inadequacies and omissions provoke readers to venture into this much-neglected area for themselves.

Much of the fourth chapter of this book is taken up with a merciless deconstruction of the conventions of self-abasement which played such a prominent role in Cinquecento writers' presentation of their works. I hope this will not undermine readers' faith in the sincerity of my own *excusatio*, and, in particular, of my acknowledgments to the colleagues and friends who have played a more important role than some of them perhaps realize in the genesis and development of this book. My sincerest thanks are due to Frank Woodhouse and Conor Fahy for their patient and constructive readings of the various drafts of a work which was slow to take shape; to Jean-Louis Fournel, for his encouragement and advice, especially in the earlier and more wavering stages of the project; to John Woodhouse, for his valuable comments at a later stage and to Pat Boyde for his constant support and interest throughout. I would also like to thank the Master and Fellows of Sidney Sussex College, Cambridge, for providing much-needed financial support at a crucial stage in my writing and to Kevin Taylor, of Cambridge University Press, for his help in preparing the work for publication. Finally, my deepest gratitude to Tim Crane, who has borne the various practical and emotional strains which this book's composition has placed on him with the equanimity of a true philosopher.

Note on translations

All translations, unless otherwise stipulated, are my own. My aim has been to provide accurate and, above all, *comprehensible* translations, in a reasonable approximation to modern English. In certain cases, this has involved a significant departure from the syntax and phrasing of the original: obscure or elliptical passages have been expanded on or 'explained', and interminable periodic sentences cut down to a more manageable size. I realize that these liberties in my translations may disturb some readers, but this solution seemed preferable to the alternative of providing a word-for-word translation which, in many cases, would have been little more help than giving no translation at all.

1 Problems of method

> I will not here take notice of the several kinds of Dialogue, and the whole Art of it, which wou'd ask an entire Volume to perform. This has been a Work long wanted, and much desir'd, of which the Ancients have not sufficiently inform'd us; and I question whether any Man, now living, can treat it accurately.
>
> John Dryden, *Life of Lucian* (1711)[1]

Three centuries after Dryden wrote this passage, the work he refers to is still 'wanted' and the chief obstacle which confronts the student of any of the 'kinds' of literary dialogue remains the lack of any substantial and coherent theoretical discussion of the genre. As Dryden notes, the Ancients – and most significantly Aristotle – gave little indication of what form such a theory might take,[2] and subsequent critics have found themselves rather in the position of Northrop Frye's Renaissance doctors, who refused to take syphilis seriously because Galen had made no mention of it.[3] For a brief period in the sixteenth century in Italy, when the vogue for the literary dialogue was at its height, there was a sustained attempt to bring the dialogue into the fold of Aristotelian genre criticism.[4] But this initiative waned with the subsequent decline in the popular fortunes of the genre, and its provisional conclusion – that the dialogue was, in Tasso's formula, a fusion of dialectic and poetry – did not stand the dialogue in good stead in eras when poetry and non-poetry were ever more rigorously distinguished. Croce's extreme position, that such a 'forma sintetica filosofica-poetica' could not really be said to exist,[5] reflects a wide-spread unease with a genre whose status has always been subject to question.

In recent years, the blurring of the demarcation lines between the various academic disciplines and a renewed interest in rhetoric have opened the way for a far more sensitive appreciation of this 'non-existent' genre. It has come to be acknowledged, increasingly, in the field of intellectual history, that the literary form of a scientific or philosophical work is not mere 'verbal dressing', but an essential part of its message: that even those genres, like the academic monograph, which 'pretend disingenuously not to be genres' must be considered as rhetorical artefacts and not the parthenogenetic products of reason.[6] The dialogue, as a genre of exposition which wears its rhetorical heart on its sleeve, has inevitably been a beneficiary of this trend. Some of the first and most influential work in this field arose out of the study of the dialogues of Plato, and the fervid exploration of the philosophical significance of Plato's use of dialogue which has taken place, particularly over the last decade or so, has continued to produce insights of value for an understanding of the genre as a whole.[7]

One merit of this development has been to suggest a way out of the methodological *impasse* remarked on at the beginning of this chapter. Not least of the reasons why the dialogue has been so successful in eluding the net of traditional genre criticism is the sheer variety of different 'kinds' of writing encompassed by this most slippery of terms. A Renaissance work which calls itself a dialogue may be anything from a language-teaching primer to a comic verse exchange between animals; anything from a primitive catechism to a Ciceronian debate on the immortality of the soul. It may be safe to venture a definition of the dialogue as an exchange between two or more voices, but, beyond this unhelpfully low common denominator, even the most cautious generalizations are doomed to founder under the weight of the exceptions they create.[8] Given this bewildering heterogeneity, it is scarcely surprising that Dryden's 'whole art' has not been forthcoming and that most histories of the dialogue production of a particular nation or period have tended to splinter into unilluminating taxonomies of the various sub-species of the genre.[9]

It is here that critics working in the fields of philosophy or intellectual history are at an obvious advantage, since the nature of their work dictates the need for a narrower definition of the genre. The interest of the dialogue, for the historian of philosophy, lies in the philosophical import of the form: the answer to the question of what kind of thought 'thinks itself as a dialogue'?[10] Clearly, in such an enterprise, it can only be distracting to start from an inclusive definition of the dialogue, based on its formal characteristics. What matters is to be able to identify those – relatively few – works in the history of the genre which have made a meaningful use of the specifically philosophical, rather than the rhetorical or didactic, resources of dialogue. The essential distinction becomes that between 'true' dialogues and 'false' ones: dialogues which are genuinely dialectical and those which are monologues in disguise.

A particularly careful statement of this distinction – often left implicit or dealt with more perfunctorily – is offered by an article by David Simpson, on Hume's *Dialogues Concerning Natural Religion*. Simpson identifies two 'extreme alternatives' within the dialogue genre, although he acknowledges that, in practice, dialogues rarely correspond straightforwardly to one of these paradigms. One extreme is the purely 'ornamental' dialogue, typically used for didactic purposes, in which 'form and content do not in any organic sense interpenetrate'; where the content of the work may be 'varied' by the use of the dialogue form, but is 'not in any important sense modified or unsettled by it'. In Simpson's other extreme form of dialogue, by contrast, 'meaning itself becomes dramatic'. 'Poetic' elements like character and setting, rather than mere 'ornaments', become 'constitutive elements in any meanings which might be seen to emerge'. Most significantly, these truly dramatic dialogues give the reader a far more demanding role than is the case with their didactic counterparts. Reading a dialogue by, say, Plato or Hume, we are not relegated to the role of admiring spectators. We are participants in the dialogue: 'referees', 'actively engaged in the production of meaning' and implicated, with the author, in the peculiar 'instability' of the form.[11]

Of course, there is nothing new in this distinction between 'open' and 'closed' forms of dialogue and, to clarify its limitations, as well as its undoubted usefulness, it may be worth pausing a moment to consider its prehistory. The first clear statement of the distinction which I have encountered occurs in a treatise of the mid seventeenth century, by the Jesuit literary theorist and historian, Sforza Pallavicino. Like Simpson's, Pallavicino's division of dialogues is based on the criterion of what kind of role they confer on the reader. Some dialogues, he recognizes, like treatises, place their readers in the position of 'scolari', diligently absorbing their master's words, without making any contribution of their own. Another type of dialogue exists, however: 'a court-case conducted in the absence of a judge', where the reader takes on a far more challenging, arbitrational role.[12]

In Pallavicino, this distinction is neutral, rather than normative: indeed, in keeping with the spirit of his Order and his age, he shows a certain sympathy with the more authoritative forms of the genre. It is with the Enlightenment, in the following century, that the distinction takes on the evaluative slant whose resonances can still be detected in much dialogue criticism today. As one recent critic has observed, to an age imbued with the ideal of rational equality, the *ex cathedra* tones of dialogues like Malebranche's *Entretiens* 'would have seemed in some sense barbarous'.[13] Writers were warned against the temptation, in their dialogues, 'to make the Knight-Errant always beat the Giant',[14] and Lord Shaftesbury railed eloquently against the 'straw men' in contemporary polemical dialogues who, 'notwithstanding their seeming variance . . . collaborate in the most officious manner with the author towards the display of his own proper wit and the establishment of his private opinions and maxims'.[15] The true dialogue, for Shaftesbury as for Simpson, is one where 'the author is annihilated'; where the reader is forced to weigh the speakers' opinions for himself and 'judge coolly and with indifference of the sense delivered'.[16]

The distinction between 'dialogical' and 'monological' forms of the dialogue is a valuable one, and one of which I shall be making extensive use in the second part of this study. But it is nevertheless true that where it becomes evaluative – a means of dividing off the few sheep from the many goats in the genre – the distinction between didactic and non-didactic dialogues can have the effect of distorting our judgment of dialogues produced in eras, like the late sixteenth century in Italy, when the concept of authority carried great prestige and when didacticism had no negative connotations. The danger is a real one: Guido Baldassari, for example, in his otherwise exemplary article on Tasso's dialogue production, has surely allowed himself to be swayed by anachronistic standards when he states of what are, admittedly, two of Tasso's most 'monological' dialogues that 'they are not really "dialogues" in Tasso's sense of the word'.[17] In any case, the gulf which separates our perspective on the genre from that of post-Tridentine Italy is clearly revealed when we consider that Sforza Pallavicino recommends these same two dialogues as models for imitation precisely because 'in essi con gran chiarezza riluce l'opinione dello Scrittore e'l suo fondamento'.[18]

In a study like the present one, which aims to make sense of the dialogue production of an entire culture, over an extended period, it would be rash to start from anachronistic assumptions about what dialogues should or should not do. To do justice to the full range of factors which attracted writers to the dialogue form in Renaissance Italy, it will be necessary to develop a less prescriptive and more flexible approach than that adopted by historians of philosophy concerned with individual – and exceptional – texts. Nonetheless, one important aspect of the approach I have been examining may be retained and developed: its emphasis on the function of the dialogue, rather than its form. Even if the answers provided by critics like Simpson are of limited use for my purposes here, the questions they are asking are the right ones. The first problem to confront, if we are to understand the place of the dialogue in Renaissance culture is this: what is it that a dialogue can do which its closest rival, the treatise, does not?

The dialogue is unique among the familiar genres of argument and exposition, in that, at the same time as presenting a body of information or opinion, it also *represents* the process by which that information or opinion is transmitted to a particular audience, at a particular place and time. The degree of care with which this process is depicted varies considerably, of course, from one dialogue to the next: some dialogues – Plato's are the most obvious example – are meticulously crafted dramas of persuasion, while others provide only the most threadbare and half-hearted simulacrum of speech. But, even in the most formulaic of dialogues, an element of mimesis is present: even a catechistic interrogation between faceless figures labelled A and B, or Q and A, contains two voices and at least the skeleton of a dramatic exchange.

If the dialogue is a representation of a communicative process, it is also, like any text, a communication itself. The oral exchange depicted in a dialogue acts as a kind of fictional shadow to the literary transaction between the reader and the text, conveying at least some of the same information, with a similar intent. The relation between the two may be distanced by irony or intimate to the point of symbiosis. But the parallel between them remains: each word, each argument in a written dialogue is simultaneously part of a fictional conversation and an actual literary exchange. It is the contention of this study that this parallel, and the unlimited potential for self-reference it offers, has historically constituted much of the dialogue's appeal.

The relations between what it may be convenient to call the direct and fictional exchanges of the dialogue are too complex and protean to permit much useful generalization. In some dialogues, one speaker may be confidently identified as a spokesman for the author, another as a figure of the reader. In other works, the relation is more complex and the filter of the dialogue more opaque: the 'authorial' role may be splintered between a number of different speakers, or the role-division between 'authors' and 'readers' may be entirely broken down.[19] The precise function of the fictional exchange will vary according to whether it is dramatized or narrated, and, crucially, to whether it is presented as fiction or historical record.[20] The dialogue's double structure – or triple, or quadruple, if dialogues are narrated within dialogues – allows almost endless possibilities for creative manipulation of the relations between reader and text.

It will be the task of later chapters to explore some, at least, of these possibilities in detail. What I am concerned with here is one, very general point: that, by duplicating its primary communication with a fictional double, the dialogue has the effect of calling attention to the act of communication itself. In a genre like the manual, or the encyclopedia, the *personae* of persuasion – the 'addresser' and 'addressee' – are conventionalized to the maximum and, effectively, subsumed in the message.[21] In the dialogue, quite the opposite happens: the act of persuasion is played out before us, and we cannot simply absorb the message without reflecting on

the way in which it is being sent and received. Of the major argumentational genres, only the letter – a form whose affinities with the
dialogue were celebrated in the Cinquecento – insists to the same extent
on the reality of its addressee.[22] But the recipients of letters are silent and,
however solicitous their correspondents may be in anticipating their
responses, their presence is less real than that of even the most shadowy of
the speakers in a dialogue.

The effect of this foregrounding of the act of persuasion is that,
whatever the ostensible subject-matter of a dialogue, a secondary theme is
the problem of how to communicate this material successfully to an
audience. This is a crucial difference – perhaps *the* crucial difference –
between the dialogue and other argumentational forms. A manual on
falconry or car maintenance may give us the information we need to train
falcons or repair cars, but it will tell us little – at least, without some fairly
energetic semiotic decoding on our part – about what kind of people
possess this information and what kind might want to acquire it, or about
what type of rhetorical problems the former might encounter in attempting to share their expertise. A dialogue on the same subject, on the other
hand – however minimalist its *mise-en-scène* – is constrained to reflect on
the way in which it is going about its explanatory task. Galileo's *Dialogo
dei massimi sistemi* not only tells us something new about the universe,
but also tells us something about the way in which this information may
be communicated, and the reactions it will excite within the scientific
community and without.

The most fundamental distinguishing feature of the dialogue is a
concern with communication; with the problem of what people do with
language and what they do with knowledge. Every dialogue, from the
most vividly 'dialogical' to the most drably 'monological', shares the
generic trait of self-consciously embodying a conception of the relation
between language, social practice and cognition. It is the conceptions of
this relation which differ from one dialogue to another, and which
determine the vast gamut of formal differences between them. The 'dialogical' dialogue posits an open relation between utterance and knowledge,
while 'monological' dialogues reduce this relation to a strictly one-way
traffic. But all dialogues have at least something to say on the subject of
communication; and it is here that we should seek for the defining
characteristic of the genre, rather than in any tendency to privilege
dialectical models of thought.

What does this imply about those cultures which made the dialogue
form their own, like fifteenth- and sixteenth-century Italy or eighteenth-
century France? Of course, not all writers of dialogue show themselves
equally aware of the metacommunicational potential of the form and,

frequently, in these cultures, the choice of the dialogue form by individual authors must have been determined more by fashion and audience expectations than any more sophisticated intent. But it seems reasonable to assume that, when any age adopts on a wide scale a form which so explicitly 'stages' the act of communication, it is because that act has, for some reason, come to be perceived as problematic. The causes of this crisis in communication may be epistemological or sociolinguistic, or a combination of the two: the breakdown of traditional certainties, a failure of confidence in the concept of certainty itself, a major shift in the medium or audience of literary discourse.[23] Certainly, whatever they are, these causes will be complex, and any generalizations must be cautious ones. But it seems safe to suggest that the use of the dialogue form may be seen as a symptom of an unease with the conventions which govern the transmission of knowledge within a society, and a desire to reform them by returning to a study of the roots of persuasion. If a writer, or group of writers, can no longer recognize themselves in the conventionalized 'addresser' of the prevailing monological genres, it makes sense to bring addresser and addressee together out into the open and leave them to thrash out for themselves a new and more acceptable statute of discourse.[24]

What methodological implications do these reflections have for the study of the dialogue? If one function of the form is to portray and comment on the act of communication, then it will be necessary, in any study of the dialogue in a given society, to pay close attention to the conditions – material and social – in which communication took place in that society. In the case of the society and the period under consideration in the present study, this will involve an attempt to come to terms with the vast and quite unprecedented advance in information technology constituted by the advent of print. After about 1500, particularly, the Italian printing industry developed with a rapidity which left contemporaries gasping with wonder: by 1550, the proliferation of printed matter could already be figured as a 'selva inestricabile',[25] while, a century later, a commentator noted that there were now more people *writing* books than, a hundred and fifty years previously, had been capable of reading them.[26] The spread of printing affected everything from the way in which information was presented to the manner in which it was read, from the working patterns of writers to the language that they used.[27] It would be surprising if we did not see some reflection of these changes in communicative practices in the miniature drama of communication which is the literary dialogue.

Obviously, though, it would be misleading to attribute every characteristic of Renaissance dialogues to any one factor, however important. The very fact that, as my next chapter will show, the dialogue production of Renaissance Italy differed significantly from that of other European nations, should alert us to the need to take into account other characteristics of Italian cultural history in this period which affected the forms of communication enacted in contemporary dialogues. This will involve a consideration of factors like the social structure and communicational ideals of the Italian courts, the constitution of the new, vernacular audience for literature, the effects of the Counter-Reformation on the circulation of culture and the complex developments in pedagogical, dialectical and rhetorical theory. It is only by observing as closely as possible the way in which communication takes place in its natural habitat that we can learn to interpret the behaviour of this elusive beast in the dialogue, in the captivity of fiction.

Before going on to explore these questions, however, the most immediate problem is to establish some more accurate means of analysing the workings of the literary dialogue. I have stressed, in this chapter, that the most productive way to approach the dialogue is as a drama of communication: a practical embodiment of a communicative ideal. My task now is to begin examining the ways in which social ideals and values encode themselves in the formal structure of dialogical works.

2   History and invention in the dialogue

> ... recitaremo alcuni ragionamenti, i quali già passarono tra omini
> singularissimi a tale proposito ...
>
> Baldassare Castiglione, *Il libro del Cortegiano* (1528)[1]

A crucially important structural variable in dialogues, unaccountably neglected by critics, is the historical consistency of their fictional exchange. A dialogue which purports to be a transcription of a real conversation, between speakers whom the reader may plausibly even know, will clearly demand an entirely different kind of reception than one which presents a discussion undefined by place or time, peopled by puppets whose character and views are clearly defined by their role in the economy of the dialogue.

The extent to which historical consistency conditions our reading of a dialogue can be illustrated by looking at a work which exists in both a 'documentary' and a fictional version. In the original version of Torquato Tasso's *Malpiglio overo della corte* (1585), Tasso's discussion of courtiership gains a crucial level of meaning from the identity of the protagonists he chooses. The speakers are a father and son, Lorenzo and Giovanlorenzo Malpiglio, and the author himself, in his customary Platonic guise as a 'Neapolitan Stranger'. Giovanlorenzo is portrayed as a starry-eyed youth, besotted with the glamour of the Ferrarese court, and incapable of imagining a higher calling than the service of a prince. His father, Lorenzo, has misgivings about this: an exile from the fallen republic of Lucca, he is mindful of the family's past as members of an independent ruling élite. Tasso, finally, is a courtier with good reason to be disillusioned with the courts, but still courtier enough to express his criticisms with the utmost circumspection and tact. The different experiences of the three interlocutors, or the *lack* of experience, in one case, condition their perspective on the subject discussed, to considerable dramatic effect.[2]

In the French translation of the *Malpiglio* by Jean Badouin (1612), all these subtleties of *ethos* are lost, and the speakers become a faceless and interchangeable 'Tersandre', 'Cléon' and 'Ariste'.[3] This modification completely transforms the role of the reader of the dialogue. The tradition within which Tasso is working presupposes a reader trained in respecting the opacity of a 'documentary' fiction and in decoding the speakers' statements in the light of what he knows or can surmise of their opinions in life. In the case of Badouin's translation, on the other hand, such historicist zeal is uncalled for: the reader is encouraged to look through the transparent fiction of the work to the play of ideas behind it.

The distinction between 'documentary' and 'fictional' forms of dialogue has a peculiar importance for the present study, since it is the criterion of historical consistency, more than anything else, which serves to distinguish the dialogue production of Cinquecento Italy from that of the rest of Europe. That Badouin should have transposed Tasso's dialogues from a 'historical' to a 'fictional' format cannot be explained away as an eccentricity, or an expedient to prevent them from seeming foreign or dated.[4] His practice in this respect is consonant with his national tradition, just as Tasso's original practice was consonant with his. The most fundamental question which confronts the historian of the Italian Cinquecento dialogue is why it was only in Italy that a strong tradition of documentary dialogue developed, while elsewhere the vast majority of dialogues took a straightforwardly fictional form.[5]

Clearly, not all dialogues which employ contemporary figures as interlocutors do so in such an intelligent and self-conscious way as Tasso's do, and there were, as we shall see, more superficial motives which might prompt a writer to choose this form of dialogue rather than another.[6] Obviously, as well, the distinction between real and fictional characters is by no means clear-cut: the first-person 'Thomas More' of the *Utopia* has a somewhat different consistency from the 'More' of Ellis Heywood's commemorative dialogue, *Il Moro*, and neither, appearing as they do in the company of fictional figures, has the same historical solidity as, say, the interlocutors of Castiglione's *Cortegiano*.[7] Renaissance dialogue covers a bewildering variety of usage in this respect and a simple distinction between 'documentary' and 'fictional' dialogues is liable to prove misleading. In order to define our terms a little more closely, it may be useful at this point to examine the historical consistency of the fictional exchanges of classical Greek and Roman dialogues, and to form an idea of the range of possibilities which antiquity had bequeathed to the Renaissance.

The three great *auctores* of the classical dialogue, Plato, Lucian and Cicero, present three very different solutions to the problem of verisimilitude in the dialogue.[8] Of these, the most unequivocally fictitious is, of course, that represented by the Lucianic dialogue. With his boasted creation of the wholly new hybrid genre of the comic dialogue,[9] Lucian ushered into the genre, as companions to the 'vain, plodding speculative men'[10] of the Platonic tradition, a motley cast of interlocutors who share the purely fictional consistency of the protagonists of comedy: speaking animals, abstractions and personifications, sea-gods, nymphs and the dead. In such company, the historical figures Lucian occasionally introduces into his dialogues lose all their claims to reality. The Socrates of *The Dead Come Back to Life*, it has been observed, is not the Socrates of Plato's dialogues but merely 'le type du philosophe'.[11] Like the anonymous friend who acts as a foil to Menippus in the *Icaromenippus*, Lucian's Socrates is not a character with a life beyond the dialogue, but purely and simply a function of the argumentation of the work.

The author of a dialogue which takes this form makes no pretence of recording a conversation which has really taken place, and the work is presented quite simply as an unmediated production of fantasy. In many such dialogues, the reader is alerted to the interlocutors' role in the dialogue from the outset, by the more or less explicit tip-off of a characterizing name. The effect of this 'symbolisme onomastique', as it has been termed,[12] is to underline the absolute control the author exercises over the speakers. Bernard Palissy's 'Demande' and 'Response', however vividly their voices are realized, can never achieve the solidity of the most blandly characterized speakers in a 'historical' dialogue – say, the Ercole Strozzi of Bembo's *Prose della volgar lingua*.[13] 'Theire names I have geven unto them in greeke and Englishe, callinge the preacher, μισοτόκος, which I doe englishe Ockerfoe, as enemye to usurie. The merchant I do name, κακέμπορος, whom I do tearme Gromelgayner, and for shortnes write him sometimes Gromel . . .'[14] By the time Thomas Wilson has finished his laborious explanation of the rationale of the speakers' names in his *Discourse upon Usury* (1572), his 'Christian reader' is likely to have a fair suspicion of the positions these figures will adopt.

The reader of a dialogue like Wilson's will also be justified in presuming that, whatever the upshot of the discussion, it will represent the author's own views on the subject under discussion. In many such dialogues, indeed, the fictional exchange is acknowledged to be a mere embellishment: it is no accident that Wilson entitles his work a 'treatise' on usury, adding that it has been written 'by way of dialogues and orations' for the 'better variety and delight' of his readers. This is not to say, of course, that all 'fictional' dialogues are dogmatic in character: they can be as dialogical, or as monological, as their 'documentary' counterparts. My point is simply that, in a fictional dialogue, however complex and nuanced their relations, the author's exchange with the reader is never further complicated – as it must be in 'documentary' forms of the dialogue – by the autonomous life of the dialogic fiction as a 'portrait' of an actual social group.[15]

The other two great classical writers of dialogue, Plato and Cicero, both use the dialogue form to represent conversations between historically identifiable interlocutors in realistic settings. Beyond this superficial resemblance, however, the use which Plato and Cicero make of their interlocutors and the importance which they give to the criterion of verisimilitude in the dialogue differ considerably. Plato chooses as his speakers prominent men from his own and the previous generation, and he provides a certain amount of circumstantial detail about the time when the dialogues are set.[16] The historical identity of the speakers is by no means an incidental or decorative feature: indeed, as critics are increasingly recognizing, not only the early Socratic *colloquia* but even the later, less obviously dramatic dialogues only yield their full meaning when due attention is paid to the intricate interplay of *ethos*.[17]

That said, however, it is obvious to any reader of Plato's dialogues that his primary intent in depicting the Athens of his day is not historical or commemorative, but philosophical. The form of the Socratic dialogues is determined by the need to portray Socrates' thought in a manner which does not betray its dialectical quality by enclosing it in a monological form. A dramatic context is necessary for the unfolding of the dialogues' arguments, but – except, of course, in the case of the dialogues associated with Socrates' trial and judgment – it is relatively unimportant exactly what that context *is*. The burden of history hangs far more lightly over Plato's dialogues than it does over Cicero's, and it is telling that, where Cicero's dialogues are generally narrated, and prefaced by scrupulously researched historical accounts of their settings, Plato's take a dramatic form which throws us airily *in medias res*, with, at most, a brief introductory scene.

By contrast with the Greek, the distinctive characteristic of the Roman dialogue is a preoccupation with the individual, the concrete, the historically verifiable. This change of emphasis has been well described by Pierre Grimal, who points out, in Cicero, that 'l'opposition des doctrines' – the lifeblood of Plato's dialogues – 'est certainement moins importante [in Cicero] que l'opposition des hommes, de leurs humeurs, de leurs tempéraments, de leurs préjugés'. The interlocutors of Cicero's dialogues, far more tangibly than Plato's, 'paraissent accompagnés du cortège invisible, mais sensible, des actions qu'ils ont réellement accomplies':[18] an impression deliberately and painstakingly created, as Michel Ruch has shown in his account of Cicero's research on the historical background of his dialogues.[19]

The new prominence of the documentary element in Roman dialogues demanded a corresponding adjustment in the way that these dialogues were read. Cicero's interlocutors play a vital role as guarantors to the 'authority' of his arguments and, for the first time, the reader's presumed acquaintance with the interlocutors' reputations becomes an essential and calculated element in the effect of the work as a whole.[20] Plato's dialogues would obviously be impoverished if their speakers, instead of Socrates or Gorgias, were simply named 'Philosopher' or 'Sophist'. But they would not be impoverished in anything like the same way as a dialogue like Cicero's *De oratore*, where the speakers, more than midwives, act as *godfathers* to the truth.

For this reason, verisimilitude and the pretence of fidelity to history play a different and much more significant role in Cicero's art of dialogue than they did in Plato's. The reader of Cicero's dialogues may not believe they are faithful transcriptions of great men's conversations, any more than the modern television viewer believes that the celebrities who feature in advertisements really swear by the products they endorse. But, if the vital persuasive mechanism of *auctoritas* is to work, it is necessary for the reader at least to suspend disbelief in the documentary character of the dialogue. Plato had already given some attention to the problem of how to anchor the dialogue in history and it is with Plato that the device originates of having the circumstances of a dialogue narrated in a short prefatory sketch by someone who had been present at the scene.[21] It is only in Cicero, however, that the pretence that the dialogue is a transcription begins to perform a vital role in the economy of the work as a whole.

The importance accorded to the 'authority' of the speakers in the Roman dialogue testifies to the authoritarian character of the society which produced it. Pierre Grimal has argued persuasively that the form of dialogue which came to perfection with Cicero reflects the assumptions of a society far more hierarchical than the Greek *polis*: a society which conceived of culture as the prerogative of the ruling oligarchy. This difference is most strikingly reflected in the different settings of Greek and Roman dialogues, and the very different qualities stressed in the presentation of the speakers. Where the Greek dialogue most typically takes the form of a casual conversation, struck up on a street-corner between strangers or passing acquaintances, the Roman dialogue is a far more exclusive affair, frequently set in a patrician villa: the gathering of a chosen few.[22] And where Plato characterizes his speakers by their 'life' and 'learning' – to use the revealing distinction of a sixteenth-century Italian critic – Cicero is far more likely to do so by their 'breeding' and 'career'.[23]

The difference in character and emphasis between Greek and Roman dialogues is well illustrated by a passage at the beginning of Book II of the

De oratore, where Crassus refers dismissively to the Greek habit of launching into abstruse philosophical debate without regard to the occasion or the company.[24] As Grimal points out, understood in its historical context, Crassus' outburst is not the philistine carping it might seem; rather, his remark is one which reveals the gulf between the conceptions of the social function of culture which prevailed in Socrates' Athens and in Cicero's Rome. Crassus' peers were more than willing to explore Greek thought themselves, but the thought of a philosopher, a modern Socrates, bearding passers-by in the forum and inciting them to virtue was one that this closed class of senators found indecorous, even dangerous. In a society like that of Rome, where power and knowledge were confined to the few, it was felt to be as well to keep high culture in the villas and out of the streets.[25]

The attitude of the élite to the circulation of culture in Cinquecento Italy was, of course, far closer to that which informs the dialogues of Cicero than those of Plato. The development of printing, which had 'opened' written culture to an extent hitherto inconceivable, only increased the protectionist tendencies of the cultural production of the courts. Especially as the Counter-Reformation gained momentum, in the second half of the century, it was increasingly felt that the spread of learning below a certain stratum of the social hierarchy was something which could only lead to imbalance and dissent. Tasso was not the only late-sixteenth-century courtier who would have found the thought of philosophy being manhandled by the common herd as distasteful as that of a princess being married to a serf.[26]

It is unsurprising, then, to find that Cinquecento dialogues which employed historical figures as interlocutors tend to share the characteristics of the Ciceronian dialogue: the choice of speakers of a relatively high social status, a close attention to historical accuracy and an overwhelming concern with decorum. As in the Roman dialogue, verisimilitude in representation was essential to guarantee the authority which prestigious interlocutors conferred on the arguments of the dialogue. It was reassuring for the aristocratic reader to know that the knowledge imparted in the dialogue emanated from one of his own class, and it was flattering for the would-be aristocrat to be admitted vicariously, through his reading of the dialogue, to the aristocratic circles it portrayed.[27] This double effect, a crucial factor in the appeal of the genre in the Renaissance, was only possible if the reader could be induced to suspend his disbelief in what were, of course, essentially, fictional works.

The passage in the preface of Castiglione's *Cortegiano* from which the epigraph to this chapter was chosen has an emblematic value in the history of the Italian allegiance to Cicero.[28] The enduring influence on

Italian and European thought of this 'arch-text' of Renaissance court culture is well known, but what has been less explored is its importance, at least in Italy, as a formal model for the dialogue.[29] It is of the greatest significance for the history of the genre in Italy that Castiglione should have chosen to cast his discussion of the perfect courtier not as a treatise, but rather as a dialogue and, specifically, a Ciceronian dialogue, on the model of the *De oratore*. His choice was portentous: the supreme elegance of the *Cortegiano*'s style and the unmatchable glamour of its subject-matter ensured that Castiglione's imitation of Cicero would find imitators in turn. The structure of the *De oratore*, mediated through the *Cortegiano*, established itself as the basic grammar of the vernacular dialogue for much of the sixteenth century.

Questions of humanistic *pietas* and philosophical allegiance aside, Castiglione's choice of the *De oratore* as his model for the *Cortegiano* was by no means casual. The form of documentary dialogue Castiglione adapts from Cicero is perfectly calculated for the task which the text sets out to perform. His definition of the perfect courtier, like Cicero's of the perfect orator, gains an incomparable persuasive force from the fact that it is elaborated by speakers who are themselves living exemplars of the *ethos* which the book is defining and guarantors of the efficacy of its recipe for social success. The parallel is enthusiastically underlined by Castiglione's first English translator, Sir Thomas Hoby, who alerts his readers that:

Cicero bringeth in to dispute of an Oratour Crassus, Scevola, Antonius, Cotta, Sulpitius, Catulus and Cesar his brother, the noblest and chiefest Oratours in those dayes: Castilio to reason of a Courtier, the Lorde Octavian Fregoso, Syr Fridericke his brother, the Lord Julian de Medicis, the L. Cesar Gonzaga, the L. Francescomaria della Rovere, Count Lewis of Canossa, the L. Gaspar Pallavicino, Bembo, Bibiena and other most excellent Courtiers, and of the noblest families in these dayes in Italy, which all afterwards became Princes, Cardinalles, Bishoppes and greate Lordes.[30]

Of course, it would be as misleading to represent the form of the *Cortegiano* as a strict and unmediated imitation of Cicero as it would be to suggest that Castiglione's courtier is simply a modern-dress replicant of Cicero's orator.[31] The imitation of Cicero, in Castiglione and his followers, was overlaid by post-classical influences: pre-eminently that of the *cornice* of Boccaccio's *Decameron*, with its *brigata* of exquisitely idealized speakers, masked by poetic names. This 'semi-fictional' model of dialogue proved popular throughout the century, especially for dialogues on the quintessentially Boccaccian themes of women and love.[32] But, even in more strictly 'Ciceronian' dialogues, a Boccaccian influence is often detectible, revealing itself in structural features, like the appointment of a 'king' or 'queen', but also, more subtly, lending a distinctly unCiceronian inflection of playful gallantry, especially in their presentation of women speakers, for whom antiquity offered no precedents.[33]

With this caveat, however, it seems safe to assert that the principal model for the polite Italian dialogue was Cicero, rather than Plato, and that the reasons for this preference are sociological, rather than purely philosophical or literary. The main evidence for this is to be found in dialogue practice, which will be examined in more depth in the following chapters, but there are interesting hints of a consciousness of the different sociological connotations of Platonic and Ciceronian dialogue in the theoretical writings on the genre which began to emerge, after about 1560. In Carlo Sigonio's *De dialogo liber* (1562), Plato is proposed, along with Cicero and Xenophon, as a trinity of exemplary and unsurpassable figures, on whose art modern practice should be based.[34] But, when he comes to his detailed prescriptions for the 'time', the 'place' and the *personae* of the dialogue, it begins to become clear that Sigonio has certain reservations about Plato as a model. It is assumed that the speakers will be statesmen and dignitaries, with little leisure at their disposal, and the time and place of the conversation must be consonant with their *ethos*.[35] Sigonio manages to justify Plato's disregard for such matters by recalling the exceptional character of his protagonist, Socrates, to whom 'omnia tempora omnesque loci inscitiae juvenum depellendaeque et sophistarum arrogantiae contundendae viderentur aptissimi'.[36] But Plato's casualness in this respect clearly causes him unease and he concludes that the modern writer would do better to adhere instead to the less eccentric practice of Cicero.[37]

The value-system underlying Sigonio's somewhat equivocal attitude to Plato is particularly clearly revealed in his discussion of the opening of the *Phaedrus*. The 'mirabilis suavitas' of Plato's description of the dialogue's natural setting is not denied, but the *Phaedrus* is presented as a model to be wondered at rather than imitated. It is scarcely decorous for a philosopher – still less a statesman – to be seen wandering aimlessly up riverbanks, discoursing of love with a beardless youth. Far more respectable, and more reliable as a model for imitation, is Cicero's version of the *locus amoenus* topos, at the opening of the *De oratore*, carefully adjusted to fit the senatorial decorum of his speakers.[38] Sigonio's contemporaries were happy to follow his advice and it is interesting to note that, in the closest imitation of the *Phaedrus* that the century produced, Tasso's *Nifo, overo del piacere onesto* (1585), Sigonio's one-time pupil, is careful to offset the nonchalant charm he found in his model with a very un-Platonic attention to the social credentials of his speakers.[39]

For reasons which will be examined in a later chapter, as the Cinquecento wore on, Italian writers became increasingly attracted to Platonic structural and argumentational models.[40] But, where matters of decorum were concerned, even the most dedicated admirers of Plato tended to remain closer to Ciceronian practice. The vogue for Plato may have shifted the balance from narrative to dramatic forms, but dialogues did not spill out from the court to the *piazza*, or extend their castlist to include the modern equivalents of Meno's slave.[41] And, while Socratic questioning was seized on as a means of enlivening the teaching process, it was recognized as a model to be handled with kid gloves: as Tasso rather disarmingly comments in his *Malpiglio, overo della corte*, for a modern courtier to behave like Socrates would be a 'cosa odiosetta, anzi che no'.[42] The Socratic method, in Plato, is inseparable from Socrates' bluff, teasing, faintly patronizing *ethos* and it was only with some adjustment – or distortion – that it could be adapted to fit the manners and values of the late sixteenth-century Italian court.[43]

The problem of the relations between Platonic and Ciceronian influences in the dialogues of this period is a delicate one, and one it would be impossible to deal with here in the detail it deserves. For the moment, what is important to stress is the general point that the different forms of the dialogue are not interchangeable structural variants, but stylizations of quite different forms of social interaction. The ideological charge is obvious when we look at features of the dialogue like the social etiquette of the speakers: clearly, hierarchical and ceremonious societies will favour deferential and ceremonious forms of speech. But what is less obvious is that seemingly neutral, structural features may also bear a sociological message, if a rather more heavily encoded one. A writer's – or a whole society's – choice between 'fictional' and 'documentary' forms of dialogue may be a clue to a great deal more than simply their aesthetic tastes.

The exceptions to the Ciceronian norm of Italian dialogue production go far to confirm the sociohistorical interpretation I have suggested to explain it. The neo-Ciceronian model proposed by Castiglione and modified, but not substantially altered by later writers, dominated the dialogue production of the Italian courts and their ever-widening circles of influence.[44] It is only among those increasingly rare *ambienti* which were resistant to court culture, that we can find a dialogue production which consistently infringes Ciceronian statutes of verisimilitude and decorum, whether it tends towards purely fictional models or uses real interlocutors, but treats them in a 'comic', or at least a non-celebratory manner.

The most prominent protagonists of this 'irregular' dialogue production were the so-called *poligrafi*: the literary odd-job-men who swarmed hopefully around the Venetian printshops in the middle decades of the sixteenth century.[45] Of the writers generally considered to form part of this group, almost all produced one or more works in dialogue form and, in several cases, dialogues formed a significant portion of their literary output. The best-known, and the most original of these dialogues – apart from the *Ragionamento* and *Dialogo* of Pietro Aretino, who may, for convenience, be grouped with these writers – were Nicolò Franco's *Dialoghi piacevoli* (1539) and Anton Francesco Doni's *I Marmi* and *I Mondi* (1552–3).[46] More representative, however, is the more workaday output of a writer like Lodovico Dolce, who, between 1539 and 1565, produced a *Dialogo piacevole* on the tribulations of marriage and five didactic dialogues on subjects ranging from mnemonics and painting to the education of women.[47] Originality was, in any case, scarcely an issue with these hard-pressed opportunists of the pen: Lodovico Domenichi cheerfully raided Henricus Cornelius Agrippa for his *Nobiltà delle donne* (1549) and Ulrich von Hutten for his *Dialogo della corte* (1562),[48] while Giuseppe Betussi, Francesco Sansovino and Bartolomeo Gottifredi recycled the commonplaces of the enduringly fashionable casuistry of love.[49]

Generalization over such a range of dialogues cannot fail to be misleading and a distinction must be made between the Lucianic fantasies of a Franco or a Doni and the soberer works of more orthodox writers like Dolce and Domenichi.[50] Where the historical consistency of their speakers is concerned, the creations of the *poligrafi* vary from Franco's gods and demons and Doni's talking statues, to the quotidian but fictional 'Fabritios' 'Doroteas' and 'Hortensios' of Dolce's erudite dialogues, to the identified, but 'comically' dramatized figures of Aretino's *Ragionamento delle corti*. For all their differences, however, the works of the *poligrafi* do share certain characteristics. They tend, almost without exception, to take the dramatic format characteristic of the Lucianic tradition, rather than the more 'respectable' narrative, Ciceronian form.[51] Their scene-setting is generally minimal, their language colloquial – even slangy, at times – and their speakers, even if identified contemporary figures, unceremoniously drawn. When contrasted, say, with the dialogue production of native Venetian patricians of the period, the challenge they offer to the norms of the neo-Ciceronian tradition is striking.[52]

To speak of a 'challenge' in this context may seem exaggerated, but is evidence that, at least in some cases, a conscious challenge to the norms of polite dialogue is included. This is perhaps clearest in the case of Aretino's 'dialogo puttanesco',[53] but Franco and Doni as well, in their practice as in their rare theoretical pronouncements, seem deliberately to flout the established conventions of the courtly Ciceronian dialogue. When Franco announces, in the seventh of his *Dialoghi piacevoli* (1539), that he will not follow contemporary practice and 'pigliare a usura i nomi da gli huomini famosi, e grandi' as interlocutors;[54] or when Doni, in *I Marmi* (1552–3), explodes conventions of 'time' and 'place' and renounces any pretence to verisimilitude,[55] they are taking a stand against a prestigious and well-established tradition in the dialogue: one which reigned, more or less unchallenged, outside the political no-man's land of the Venetian type-shops and one which would long survive the feverish experimentation of their peers.[56]

Writers like Domenichi and Franco were quite as aware as theorists like Sigonio of the different social connotations of the different forms of the dialogue. It is no accident that the only work in Domenichi's collected *Dialoghi* (1562) which takes a 'decorous' narrative form and which is referred to, in a term which echoes Castiglione, as a 'portrait' of a given society, is the only one whose speakers are drawn from the higher echelons of society.[57] Nor is it fortuitous that the only dialogue of Franco's which insists on its 'documentary' status, as a faithful record and celebration of the conversations of named interlocutors, was the *Dialogo delle Bellezze* (1542), composed while he was under the protection of the local aristocracy of Casale da Monteferrato, where Guazzo would later write his *Civil conversazione*.[58]

The Cinquecento witnessed few other significant deviations from Ciceronian standards of decorum and verisimilitude in the dialogue, and certainly none which can match that of the *poligrafi* in self-consciousness, consistency and scale. One other exception to the Ciceronian hegemony is, however, worth mentioning here: the dialogue production of Florence before about 1550. In this case, of course, it would be utterly inappropriate to speak of a group of writers, or to attempt to identify a 'Florentine' manner of dialogue with its own conventions and norms. To compare a Boccaccian *divertissement* like Agnolo Firenzuola's *Ragionamenti d'amore* (1525) with a technical treatise like Machiavelli's *Arte della guerra* (1521) would clearly be absurd, as it would be to compare the dialogues produced in the political ferment of the twenties with those written two decades later, in the period of the definitive consolidation of Medici rule.[59] Even within narrower divides than this, generalization risks being misleading: the difference in tone and structure between two works as close in time and theme as Francesco Guicciardini's *Dialogo del reggimento di Firenze* (1521–5) and Antonio Brucioli's first *Dialoghi* (1526–9) is as wide as the difference between the backgrounds, careers and political ideals of their authors.[60]

In the case of the Florentine dialogue, therefore, it would seem prudent to proceed by exclusion and to concentrate on defining what this dialogue was *not*. With the exception of Guicciardini's *Dialogo* and Machiavelli's

Arte della guerra, it was not until 1564, with Lionardo Salviati's *Dialoghi dell'amicizia*, that a work was produced which met in full Ciceronian criteria of verisimilitude and decorum. Of course, besides Lucianic fantasies, dialogues set in contemporary circles did exist before this date, but the documentary element in such dialogues tended to be of secondary importance. In some cases, we are not given enough information to identify the interlocutors firmly,[61] and there are instances of dialogues being converted from a historical to a fictional form.[62] More significantly, even where a dialogue is presented as an historical event, the commemorative and celebratory intention which generally distinguishes the neo-Ciceronian dialogue is often lacking. No other Florentine writer went as far to the other extreme as Luigi Guicciardini, who has the dubious honour of being the only sixteenth-century Italian author I have encountered to choose as the speaker of a dialogue a man he had recently had killed.[63] But the existence of a dialogue as frankly critical of its interlocutors as Guicciardini's *Del Savonarola* (*c.* 1531) does alert us to a significant feature of Florentine dialogue production: the comparative rarity, at least in the first half of the Cinquecento, of dialogues which use prestigious speakers, in Ciceronian style, to lend authority to their argument.

Even an obviously commemorative dialogue like Machiavelli's *Arte della guerra* (1521) is very far from being a 'portrait', in Castiglione's sense of the word. The *Arte della guerra* would seem to fall naturally into my category of Ciceronian dialogues. It has a serious subject; it is set in an identified *locus amoenus* – the Orti Orcellari – and it has a cast-list of dignitaries, introduced to us in a reverential narrative preface.[64] In fact, however, from the first words of the dialogue, Machiavelli takes his distance from the Ciceronian tradition. Cosimo Rucellai's first remark – that the trees in his garden were chosen by an ancestor in homage to classical custom – is greeted by a rather truculent observation of Fabrizio Colonna's, that, rather than limiting their imitation of the ancients to trivial matters like gardening, the Italian ruling classes would do better to turn their attention to more serious affairs. What interests him is not what the Romans got up to in the shade of their plane trees, but what they were capable of in battle, in the glare of the noon-day sun.[65]

One of the things which the ancients did in the shade was, of course, to conduct their dialogues; and Machiavelli's protest against the hollow imitation of classical social refinements applies, we soon learn, to the form as well as the content of his essay in the genre. The passage I have described is a clear allusion to the *incipit* of Cicero's *De oratore*, and Machiavelli uses it to distinguish his manner of dialogue from that of his illustrious predecessor, in much the same way as Cicero had used the parallel passage to mark his distance from Plato's *Phaedrus*.[66] Of the Ciceronian dialogue, in the *Arte della guerra*, little more than the sparsest of structural frameworks remains. After the first page, narration devolves into a dramatic format and, soon afterwards, discussion is abandoned in favour of a series of interminable technical speeches on the part of the main speaker, Colonna. Perhaps unfortunately, given the historical interest of its setting, there is no attempt in Machiavelli's dialogue to capture the flavour of a real conversation among a particular circle of people, as there is, for all its stylization, in a work like the *Cortegiano*. Indeed, Castiglione's modest description of his 'portrait' as a mere sketch, barren of the charms of perspective and colour, could be applied with far greater justice to the *Arte della guerra*.[67]

The exceptions I have been examining tend to confirm the rule that the great majority of dialogues of the Italian Cinquecento conform, in certain key respects, to Ciceronian models. The point of this chapter has been to suggest that the reason for this preference is sociological, rather than purely literary: that, as much as anything else, it was the elitist stamp of the Ciceronian dialogue which guaranteed the form's success in the cultural economy of the Italian courts. This may well be so, but this factor alone cannot answer the crucial question of why it should only be in Italy, and not elsewhere, in the equally elitist courts of, say, Spain or England, that a tradition of Ciceronian dialogue should have established itself. It is this problem, undoubtedly complex, but fundamental to my task here, that the next chapter will address.

3   The uses of the dialogue in sixteenth-century Italy: celebration and control

Et vengo fra me medesimo considerando che i piaceri della musica, delle feste, delle giostre, delle comedie e tutti gli altri giuochi, e spettacoli siano nulla, rispetto alla gioia che si sente nella conversazione de' gentili spiriti

Stefano Guazzo, *La civil conversazione* (1574)[1]

Questa non è passe da venire a disputare della luna, né da volere, nel secolo che corre, sostenere né portarci dottrine nuove

Piero Guicciardini (1615)[2]

The discrepancy between the norms of dialogue practice in Italy and elsewhere, in the sixteenth century, is so striking that it seems quite unaccountable that it has never been remarked upon.[3] It is only, in fact, in Italy, that the use of identifiable historical figures as the interlocutors in dialogues was anything other than an exceptional occurrence. In France, in Spain, in Germany, in England, even in dialogues on the most serious of subjects, the Lucianic convention of using fictional interlocutors prevailed almost unchallenged. What, in Italy, was a styleme of a circumscribed comic mode was, in the rest of Europe, an unmarked element in the grammar of the literary dialogue.

Examples can be found, of course, of dialogues written outside Italy which conform, more or less, to 'documentary', neo-Ciceronian models. Guy de Brués's *Dialogues contre les nouveaux Academiciens* (1557) represent a conversation between the poets Baïf and Ronsard and the lawyers Guillaume Aubert and Jean Nicot, in which not only the use of named contemporary figures, but also the setting, the structure and the overall tone of the discussion testify to a sustained imitation of Platonic and Ciceronian models.[4] Of other French writers, Louis Le Caron uses prominent literary figures like Ronsard and Rabelais in his dialogues,[5] and Jacques Peletier du Mans, in the introduction to his *Dialogue de l'Ortografe et Prononçiation Françoese* [sic] (1550), explicitly states his intention to draw on his interlocutors' reputation, in Ciceronian style, to lend authority to his argument.[6] In England, Thomas Starkey staged the religious controversy of his day in a *Dialogue between Reginald Pole and*

Thomas Lupset (*c*. 1533–5),[7] while, in Spain, Cristóbal de Villalón chose distinguished contemporary academics as the interlocutors of his *Scholástico* (1535–9).[8] But these non-Italian documentary dialogues are isolated exceptions. The documentary dialogue was, essentially, an Italian form and, significantly, Villalón, at least, had to defend himself against accusations of having plagiarized Castiglione.[9] If we except a few works produced by foreign writers in Italy or under some proven Italian influence,[10] the great majority of non-Italian dialogues of this period follow the policy proudly stated by an English writer of dialogues in the following century: 'Here are no particular Characters attempted, nor is there any intention to provoke or expose any Person living.'[11]

Faced with this discrepancy between Italian and non-Italian practice, the immediate question which arises is *why*: why it should have been that dialogues which use identified contemporary figures as interlocutors were so widespread in Italy as to be almost the norm, and so rare elsewhere to be numbered among a mere handful of exceptions. It is a question to which it would be rash to attempt to provide a definite answer, given our current, rather patchy knowledge of the various national traditions. All I propose to do here – in a speculative spirit and with no pretence at exhaustiveness – is to identify some of the factors which may have contributed to the initially perplexing situation described above.

The first of these is undoubtedly the existence of a precedent for the vernacular documentary dialogues of the Cinquecento, in the distinguished tradition of neo-Latin dialogues produced by Italian humanists in the preceding century, which followed in the wake of Leonardo Bruni's *Dialogi ad Petrum Paulum Histrum* of 1401. Of course, by no means all fifteenth-century humanist dialogues were documentary in form. The Quattrocento also saw much experimentation with Lucianic forms – we have only to think of Leon Battista Alberti's *Intercenales* or *Momus*. But a solid tradition of neo-Ciceronian documentary dialogue did establish itself, and dialogues like Poggio Bracciolini's *De avaritia* (1428) or Cristoforo Landino's *Disputationes Camaldulenses* (1475) clearly aspire to portray and commemorate Roman or Florentine humanist circles, at the same time as conveying an argument.[12] The neo-Latin documentary tradition continued to flourish well into the Cinquecento, with some writers – most notably, Pietro Bembo – producing dialogues in both Latin and the vernacular.[13] This is clearly a factor which cannot be ignored, when attempting to account for the prevalence of documentary modes in the vernacular dialogue. Even if the latter rapidly developed conventions of its own, the influence of the more established humanist tradition on the fledgling genre should not be underestimated, in this respect, as in others.[14]

We should be careful, however, in attributing too much weight to this question of precedent: after all, the literary production of the Quattrocento humanists rapidly became part of the European cultural heritage, and their formal and philosophical innovations were as influential abroad as at home. At most, then, the consideration of humanist precedent can lead to a reformulation of our original question. Why did this form of the dialogue not pass, with the other species of classical dialogue revived by the humanists, into the mainstream of European culture? Or, to put it another way, what were the peculiarities of Cinquecento Italian culture which encouraged the seeds of the neo-Latin Ciceronian dialogue to blossom, there and only there, into a distinctively modern form of documentary dialogue, adapted to the mood and manners of the courts?

To answer this question, it will be necessary to consider more closely what functions the documentary dialogue performed in Italian society at this time, and how those functions differ from those performed by the fictional dialogue, in Italy and elsewhere. I have suggested that one respect in which the dialogue differs from other genres of exposition is that it is uniquely equipped to provide a 'portrait' of communication in a given society. The documentary dialogue, as a plausible depiction of a contemporary conversation, clearly has an advantage over fictional forms in this respect. One important problem to confront, then, in accounting for the success of the documentary dialogue in Italy is why it should be that this capacity for 'portraiture' was more important there than elsewhere.

One reason for Renaissance Italy's insatiable appetite for self-images may well be the precocity with which Italian society developed. The princely courts of the Italian fifteenth and sixteenth centuries were the breeding-grounds of a distinctive social style which was destined to become the common currency of the great national monarchies of the *ancien régime*.[15] Books like Castiglione's *Cortegiano* and Stefano Guazzo's *Civil conversazione* became such influential textbooks of European manners because they answered a social need, a need felt earlier and more keenly in Italy than elsewhere. As Christoph Strosetzki has observed, the art of 'civil conversation' codified in such books was not simply a 'jeu de l'ésprit': 'la théorie de la conversation represésente le savoir professionel d'une classe noble qui . . . a perdu son pouvoir politique et dès lors . . . n'a plus qu'une fonction purement représentative'.[16] In Italy, where the humiliations of foreign occupation had forced the reality of its impotence home, the problem of formulating a new self-definition for this disenfranchised elite was an urgent one.[17] Updating feudal *cortesia* with a well-calculated infusion of Ciceronian *urbanitas*, deftly juggling political realism with a seductive aesthetic of human potential, the Italian Cinquecento provided a compelling – and enduring – solution to this problem.

It is not only through its textbooks of courtesy that Italy taught the world how to behave. The Ciceronian dialogue – like that other quintessentially Italian genre, the volume of letters – is a representation and a celebration of the art of *civil conversazione* as practised in the Italian courts.[18] This commemorative function of the dialogue is at its most obvious, and its most self-conscious, in those dialogues, like the *Cortegiano* and the *Civil conversazione*, where the subject-matter under discussion is 'conversation' itself. Castiglione alludes on a number of occasions to the exemplary role of his speakers, whose urbanity and wit are living illustrations of the graces the dialogue is teaching.[19] One of Guazzo's earliest readers describes his concluding symposium as a 'gentil essempio' which puts into practice the rules laid out in the preceding discussion.[20] In a sense, however, whatever their subject-matter, all dialogues which represent a contemporary dispute may be seen as 'esempi' for an unwritten subtext on the art of conversation; 'covertly expressing' – in the words of an English translator of one such dialogue – 'an excellent form of Court-like exercise'.[21]

In some degree, then, the Italian vogue for the Ciceronian dialogue may be explained as one aspect of a much larger phenomenon. Like the courtesy textbooks which codified it, and the letters which enacted it, the dialogues which illustrated the art of *civil conversazione* were fragments in the composition of a new human and social ideal. One reason why the task of self-definition fulfilled by these genres was such a crucial one in Cinquecento Italy was, I have suggested, that the new political realities of the age had so cruelly exposed the bankruptcy of previous self-images. Another reason for this exasperated need for self-portraiture, a more concrete one, was the political disunity of Italy. To put it simply, the Italian cultural elite felt an urgent need to remind the world of its existence precisely because it was the national elite of a nation which did not exist.

In a nation like Tudor England, where the court constituted a central, uncontested nucleus of power, there existed a compact and highly visible ruling class, delineated by the force-field of patronage, and consecrated as the creator and custodian of social and cultural values.[22] In Italy, where no such real political nucleus existed, this same cultural role was performed by a far more fluid and intangible ideal 'court' or 'academy', united across political boundaries by a shared language and literary heritage, rather like the ideal *curia* Dante imagines in the *De vulgari eloquentia*. This was an entity which existed, of course, only as a generous figment of the collective imagination, and it is hardly surprising under the circumstances that the Italian cultural elite showed such an anxiety for self-definition. In a nation so politically divided, this elite could only maintain its identity and guarantee its function by constantly reminding itself of its members, proclaiming its existence to itself and the rest of the world.

The processes by which it does this are too familiar to merit much comment. Reading the courtly literature of the Cinquecento is a curiously sociable experience: it is scarcely possible to turn a page without encountering the familiar names of poets, princes and *donne di palazzo*, whom we have met in the last poem or dialogue, and the one before that. Any genre – even the most improbable ones – offers opportunities for this kind of literary socializing. The last canto of Ariosto's *Orlando Furioso* begins with a panorama of Italian court and literary society broad enough to justify Machiavelli's pique at being left out, 'come un cazzo'.[23] The dedications of Matteo Bandello's *novelle* open the secret gardens of the *Decameron* model to the public world of the courts.[24] And even the most ostensibly private of literary forms, the *canzoniere*, went public in this period: where Petrarch had addressed his love-lyrics exclusively to the mysterious Laura, Bembo wrote his for a whole series of women, the brightest lights of Italian court society, transferring the ideal *locus* of lyric composition from the lonely 'cameretta' to the salon.[25]

However, even if with ingenuity it was possible to 'name names' in any genre, certain forms, like the volume of letters or the Ciceronian dialogue, were particularly suited to the task. This is a factor which cannot be ignored in accounting for the popularity of these forms in Renaissance Italy. It is not fortuitous that the vernacular documentary dialogue, born with the *Cortegiano*, was nurtured in the polemical works of the *questione della lingua* – texts in which the provenance of the interlocutors is of central importance to the argument and issues of unity and *italianità* are constantly to the fore.[26] The *cornice* of a Ciceronian dialogue is a sort of window-display of Italian elite society; a freeze-frame of the national cultural identity *in fieri*.

Up to this point, I have been considering the positive factors which encouraged the development of a tradition of documentary dialogue in Italy. It would also be possible to turn the question around and investigate the *negative* reasons why this type of dialogue should have prevailed in the peninsula to the near-exclusion of other forms. One such reason may be the growing unacceptability, in Italy, of its chief rival. The species of dialogue which enjoyed the greatest success outside Italy, in this period, was the fictional, satirical model originated by Lucian, and popularized by the immensely influential *Colloquia* of Erasmus (1518–33).[27] As is the case with any genre in a literary culture based on the practice of imitation, this model of dialogue bore the stamp of its makers, and, like any designer product, its credit rose and fell with the reputation of its label. One explanation for the relative unpopularity of Lucianic–Erasmian forms of dialogue in Cinquecento Italy may simply be the suspicion with which the founding fathers of the genre were regarded: a suspicion which intensified to open condemnation as the century wore on.

The reputation of Lucian in sixteenth-century Italy is a subject which has not been sufficiently studied, but, from what can be gathered from a sampling of contemporary testimonies, it appears to have followed a similar course to that described by Christopher Robinson in France, in the same period.[28] In both countries – and throughout Europe – in the fifteenth and the early sixteenth centuries, Lucian was regarded as a reputable model for moralistic satire. His work was commended as a 'perfect example of how to blend humour and instruction': its irreverence and corrosive wit serving an ultimately serious purpose.[29] After the Reformation, however, and particularly after about 1550, his reputation declined, and he began to be presented as a subversive, bent on undermining respect for philosophical, political and – most crucially – religious authority: a prototype of the 'heretics' sapping the strength of the modern Church. In the Milanese and Venetian Indexes of 1554, Lucian was placed on the *Catalogo degli eretici* and, in the first papal Index, of 1559, two of his most controversial works were banned. Finally, in 1590, at the order of Sixtus V, Lucian's entire *œuvre* followed the *Mors peregrini* and the apochryphal *Philopatris* onto the Index.[30]

The reputation of Erasmus in sixteenth-century Italy followed much the same parabola as that of the writer who had inspired his colloquies and who, it was alleged by Catholics and Lutherans alike, had also influenced him in profounder and more pernicious ways.[31] Erasmus' criticisms of the Church provoked fierce controversy in Italy from the 1520s onwards, but his scholarship continued to command respect, and his religious thought exercised a profound influence in Italian Reformist circles.[32] By the 1540s, however, even as Pietro Lauro was publishing the first vernacular translation of the *Colloquii famigliari*,[33] pressures for censorship were already beginning to mount. Niccolo Franco notes in the eighth of his *Dialoghi piacevoli* (1542) that, at the time of writing, the College of Cardinals was doing all it could to prevent the distribution of Erasmus' works in Rome,[34] and, although Franco attributes this to rancour over the *Ciceronianus* dispute and not to any founded 'scrupolo di eresia',[35] this attempted censorship represents the shape of things to come. In 1559, Erasmus was placed on Paul IV's Index among the *eretici di prima classe* and, even if the rigours of this ban were subsequently somewhat mollified, the story of his Italian reputation remains one of an irrevocable fall from grace.[36] In Giambattista Marino's *Galeria* (1619), Erasmus appears as an 'Anticristo', his 'candido inchiostro' indelibly stained by the impurity of his faith.[37]

The form of dialogue practised by Lucian and Erasmus seems to have suffered from the eclipse of their reputations, just as, in the following century, the nascent genre of the scientific dialogue would find itself compromised by the notoriety of Galileo's *Dialogo sui massimi sistemi*.[38] In the first decades of the sixteenth century, the Lucianic–Erasmian dialogue was enthusiastically embraced by Italian writers of Reformist sympathies, and it seemed set to become a standard vehicle for theological and social debate.[39] With the Counter-Reformation, however, of course, the development of the genre was choked off, its recent history as an ally of 'heresy' overlaying its respectable fifteenth-century past.

The aura of heresy which surrounded the form may have been one factor which militated against any widespread use of the Lucianic dialogue in Italy, but it should be noted that the abandonment of the form may have been motivated at least as much by scruples of decency as of orthodoxy. Around the third and fourth decades of the century, particularly in Venice and Siena, dialogues with fictional interlocutors of a low social standing were frequently used as vehicles for social satire and erotic fantasy of a type which would have been inconceivable in the stricter atmosphere of post-Tridentine Italy.[40] This cannot have been without its effects on the subsequent fortunes of the genre, and it is perhaps scarcely surprising that, during the Counter-Reformation, the form of dialogue 'contaminated' by writers like Pietro Aretino should have followed their scandalous subject-matter into a common disrepute.

This hypothesis is confirmed by the treatment that Lucian and the Lucianic dialogue receive in Carlo Sigonio's *De dialogo liber* (1562). The *De dialogo* is by no means the dispassionate descriptive analysis of the genre it may at first appear. I have already commented on the way in which, in his treatment of Plato and Cicero, Sigonio makes his preferences for certain forms of the dialogue clear,[41] and, where Lucian is concerned, his normative pretensions are even more obvious. Lucian is pointedly excluded from the canon of classical *auctores* to be imitated and condemned in strong language for contaminating a once serious tradition with louche and indecorous themes.[42] Sigonio's fury against Lucian's 'corruption' of the dialogue seems to centre in particular on the sub-genre of the *Hetairikoi dialogoi* (*Dialogues of the Courtesans*), and it is not difficult to identify the contemporary abuses which are the real objects of his wrath. The formal ideal he proposes – the decorous and high-minded Ciceronian dialogue – is clearly intended as a corrective, not only structural but ideological, to what he regarded as pernicious in the dialogue production of his time.[43]

The ethical case against the Lucianic dialogue, presented rather shrilly by Sigonio, is brought out more clearly in Sperone Speroni's more reasoned attack on the genre in the third part of his *Apologia dei dialoghi* (1584). In a critique of his own youthful dialogues, which he earlier defended as satires on love, Speroni confesses that, whatever his satirical intent, an author who imitates with due exactitude the ramblings of 'ignorant' lovers inevitably implicates himself in the levity of his fiction.[44] From this perspective, the Quattrocento humanists' view of a moral Lucian, a Silenus hiding wise teachings under a veneer of apparent flippancy, seems merely the result of a dangerous sophistry. The comic dialogue is terminally compromised, and the only 'safe' solution for the dialogue is for the writer to renounce comic distance, and to portray interlocutors as reputable and as authoritative as himself.[45] Speroni's stress in his passage – inevitably, in view of the character of the dialogues of his own, which he is attacking here – falls on the dangers the Lucianic dialogue tradition presents to sexual morality, rather than on the more serious threat it may present to religious orthodoxy. The dubious record of the Lucianic dialogue on this score is not forgotten, however, and Speroni states the unspoken dread which underlies much Italian prejudice against the form when he recalls the fate of the historical Lucian, a 'cristiano battezzato' who, through playing with the fire of comic imitation, finished as a 'diabolico Epicureo', as damned as the heretics he portrayed.[46]

Of course, there is no real reason why the speakers of Speroni's proposed corrective dialogue, as long as they possess the requisite *gravitas*, should be historically identifiable figures rather than creatures of his fantasy. Works like Ascham's *Toxophilus*, or Pontus de Tyard's *Discours philosophiques* are sufficient proof that the use of fictional speakers in a dialogue need not signal a lack of serious purpose. Although unease with the indecorous connotations of certain forms of Lucianic dialogue may go some way towards explaining the peculiarities of Italian dialogue in the Cinquecento, they cannot explain why Italian writers ran straight from the arms of Lucian into those of Cicero; why – with the significant exception of a few Italian writers like Giordano Bruno, working in exile, outside Italy – Italian dialogues on serious subjects almost invariably took a documentary form.[47]

To explain this, it is necessary to turn from political and prudential to more properly literary factors and, in particular, to the importance that the *regulation* of literature, by classical precedent and formal poetics, assumed in Italy in this period. The middle decades of the sixteenth

century marked a turning-point in Italian literary culture. The great
upsurge of interest in Aristotelian literary theory, signalled by the appearance of the first commentaries on the *Poetics* in the late 1540s, ushered in
what has been aptly termed an 'Age of Criticism', in which theory gained
an ever more imperious grip – not to say stranglehold – on literary
production.[48] To understand the dialogue production of this period in
Italy, it is necessary to view the vicissitudes of the genre against the
backdrop of this more general upheaval. As is the case with other genres,
the history of the dialogue in the later Cinquecento is, increasingly, the
history of the impact of literary theory. In the later part of the century, the
Aristotelian criteria of verisimilitude and unity of time, place and argument would shape dialogue production in a way which would have been
unimaginable in the first half of the Cinquecento, and which would
remain inconceivable outside the boundaries of Italy.

A parallel may fruitfully be drawn here with the far better-known
phenomenon of the Cinquecento 'reform' of the epic. The vernacular
dialogue established by Castiglione and Bembo was, like the Ariostan
romance, a genre whose poetics had developed spontaneously, through
an inspired mixture of classical imitation and a sensitive response to the
demands of an audience.[49] That the mixture worked was indisputable, in
both cases, but, in both cases, by the 1560s, it had begun to be felt that
these flourishing but undisciplined genres should be submitted, in the
interests of their own dignity, to the pruning-hook of Aristotelian theory.
The aim of Sigonio's *De dialogo liber* is analogous to that of contemporary reformers of the epic: the promotion of a new, strictly classical and,
above all, morally serious form of the dialogue, which would be able to
equal and perhaps surpass the productions of the ancients.[50]

The new critical orthodoxy, enthusiastically espoused, affected dialogue production at every level. Specifically, it favoured the development
of a Ciceronian tradition in dialogue, in two distinct, though associated
ways. Firstly, the imperative of a strict imitation of the classics meant that
writers of serious dialogue turned to the great precedents of Plato,
Xenophon and Cicero, all of whom had employed documentary forms of
the dialogue. Secondly, the stress on a *reasoned* imitation, based on the
universal criteria for literary production discovered by Aristotle, produced a tendency to sift through classical dialogue production for those
works which responded best to Aristotelian analysis. One of the most
important criteria, for the Aristotelian theorist, was verisimilitude, and
here Cicero, with his scrupulously researched and documented fictions,
was at a distinct advantage over his Greek predecessors.

Critical documents from the formative years of Aristotelian genre
criticism testify to the presence of an exacting audience, whose scruples

about verisimilitude could only be satisfied by a Ciceronian historical rigour. Lodovico Castelvetro, in his *Giunte alle 'Prose' del Bembo* (1572),[51] probes mercilessly into the historical circumstances of the supposedly real conversation recorded in Pietro Bembo's *Prose della volgar lingua* and concludes that it is highly unlikely that such a discussion could have taken place.[52] Girolamo Muzio, in his *Varchina* (1573–4) speaks in scandalized tones of Benedetto Varchi's attempt to pass off a dialogue half as long as Boccaccio's *Decameron* as an after-dinner chat.[53] These are extreme cases: Muzio himself admits that it would be pedantic to 'dar la misura a' Dialoghi coll'oriuolo', and Tasso proposes that the writer of dialogues should have a poet's, rather than a historian's, relation to factual circumstance.[54] But, even if not all practitioners of the dialogue adhered to strict standards of verisimilitude, this criterion was one which even the most fanciful writers found it difficult to ignore.[55] Certainly, it is difficult to imagine an Italian dialogue, written after 1560, which could throw together real and fictional characters with the abandon of, say, Cristoforo Landino's *De vera nobiltate* (*c.* 1487), or which could ignore the constraints of history in quite such a cavalier way.[56]

The new values ushered in by the triumph of prescriptive literary theory can go a long way towards explaining the Italian preference for documentary forms of the dialogue. One final consideration must be added, however, before we can hope to understand this preference in full. The rule-bound academic classicism of the 'Age of Criticism' in literature is one manifestation of a more general trend in Counter-Reformation Italian culture. The culture of late sixteenth-century Italy was ideologically a timid one, shackled into nervous orthodoxy by political and religious repression. The prevailing atmosphere of conformism affected the matter as well as the form of dialogues. A concerted attempt by the spiritual and secular authorities to tighten their grip on the circulation of ideas, complemented by an understandable tendency to self-censorship in writers, resulted in a situation in which – although much discussion took place, in constant and heated, though often petty controversies – one cannot help forming the impression that there was little of weight to be discussed. In an era in which even a dialogue as respectful of the *status quo* as the *Cortegiano* had to be rigorously pruned of its mild excursions into social criticism,[57] it is scarcely surprising that few writers were prepared to risk using the dialogue to dramatize truly controversial moral or philosophical issues.

By no means the least among the reasons for the success of the Ciceronian dialogue in Italy is that it is a form uniquely well suited to the cultivation of consensus. The ballast of the interlocutors' 'authority' in such dialogues weighs heavily on their argument, and the clash of ideas and personalities tends to be deadened by the dictates of decorum. It is a point made by Sperone Speroni, the shrewdest of the Cinquecento theorists of the dialogue, when he characterizes the Ciceronian narrated dialogue as more 'onesto' than the Platonic or Lucianic dramatic form. In the dramatic dialogue, anything goes: the author has no commitment to the speakers, but simply places them on stage, like a comic dramatist, and leaves them to the mercy of the public. In the narrated dialogue, on the other hand, having introduced the speakers 'courteously, in the manner of a host', it is only natural that the author should continue to operate a form of benign censorship on their behalf, recording 'only those statements which it could bring them honour to record' ('quei soli detti delle persone da lui condotte . . . che gli sia onore il parlarne').[58]

Clearly, for an author who wished to use the dialogue to dramatize a real conflict of opinions, the muting effect of decorum would be an intolerable constraint. Eva Kushner cites, as an example of the free and frank exchange of ideas which characterizes the French sixteenth-century dialogue, a passage from Jacques Tahureau's *Second dialogue* (1565) in which one interlocutor lambasts another for his crude and self-defeating arguments: 'ie ne vi jamais un homme qui alleguast plus cruement les saintes Escritures, ne qui plus bravement se coupast la gorge de son couteau mesme que toi'.[59] Clearly, what is permitted here to a fictional 'Democritic' would be unimaginable in, say, Castiglione's Bembo or Machiavelli's Fabrizio Colonna. Erasmus could scarcely have written his *Ciceronianus* as he did if he had been concerned for the 'onore' of a flesh-and-blood Nosoponus, and it is noteworthy that, of the most original philosophers of the late Cinquecento, Francesco Patrizi uses real interlocutors, but treats them in an uncelebratory manner, far closer to the spirit of Plato than of Cicero,[60] while Giordano Bruno – writing, of course, outside Italy and arguably outside the Italian tradition of dialogue – renounces the documentary mode of dialogue almost entirely.[61] Galileo's *Dialogo dei massimi sistemi* (1632), indisputably the greatest Italian dialogue of ideas, chooses a prudent compromise where the identity of the speakers is concerned, balancing a real Salviati and Sagredo against a fictional Simplicio. We have only to imagine the impossibility of the 'villain' of Galileo's *dialogue à clef* being named Cremonini or Delle Colombe to understand the extent of the restraints imposed by the adoption of a fully documentary form of the dialogue.[62]

The neo-Ciceronian dialogue of late-Cinquecento Italy was ideally suited to its age and its birthplace in being rather a vehicle of conventional wisdom than a forum for the discovery of new truths. It developed in part to answer a localized sociological need for self-definition and self-portraiture; in part, as a result of an equally localized literary trend towards a strict reconstruction of the classical genres. It differs from the dialogue as practised elsewhere in Europe by being, precisely, a *genre* and a self-conscious one, rather than simply an infinitely flexible method for the informal presentation of ideas. Unique in the ends it set itself and the means by which it achieved them, it demands to be read in a quite different way than any form of purely fictional dialogue.

I have argued in this chapter that the Ciceronian dialogue of Cinquecento Italy is the product of a particular social reality and that it is only by considering it within this historical context that we can reach an adequate understanding of its formal peculiarities. The distinguishing characteristic of this species of dialogue, its capacity for 'portraiture', is one which had a special relevance for the aristocratic and exasperatedly self-conscious society of the Italian courts. By virtue of this capacity, the Ciceronian dialogue was able to perform a range of important social functions and these, as much as any argumentational merits of the genre, account for its phenomenal and durable success.

My aim, in this chapter, has been to explain the differences between Italian dialogue production and that of other European nations. This comparative perspective has entailed a focus on the macroscopic, social factors which affect dialogue use. This approach may be helpful in tackling the question of why an entire culture, in a given period, should favour one form of dialogue over another, but, clearly, it is of little use in establishing why an individual writer might choose the Ciceronian dialogue as a vehicle for his ideas. Besides those considered here, there are other, more concrete and immediate advantages to be gained from using a documentary form of the dialogue, rather than a fictional dialogue or a straight didactic treatise. To reach a real understanding of the place of the Ciceronian dialogue in the cultural economy of Cinquecento Italy, these other factors in dialogue use must be taken into account.

4   The uses of the dialogue in sixteenth-century Italy: commerce and courtesy

Oggi dì . . . quasi tutti siamo rivolti col pensiero a contrattare
Stefano Guazzo, *La civil conversazione* (1574)[1]

One of the principal discrepancies between modern and pre-modern perceptions of literary discourse is that literature is no longer conceived of today, as it was within the classical, rhetorical tradition, as something 'continuous with reality', as 'action in the world'.[2] Like a classical oration, a Renaissance literary work was often addressed to a specific, closely studied audience and intended to persuade its listeners to a particular line of action. Indeed, in the Renaissance, when the writer's intentional audience was less likely to be a crowd than a small group of acquaintances and patrons, the art of 'accommodating' discourse to the expectations of its listeners became still more important than it had been in classical times.[3]

The close and sociable nature of the relationship between writers and readers in the Renaissance courts affected the character of literary production in every conceivable way. In an age in which few writers were able to earn a living by their art alone, authorship constituted one element, among others, in a courtier's career. This meant that, besides its stated aims of instructing and delighting, literature was called on to perform a variety of 'public relations' functions for its author, ranging from flattery and self-advertisement to sniping and self-defence.[4] Genres like the occasional poem or the commemorative dialogue represent only the tip of an iceberg of a literature gauged for its perlocutionary effects.[5]

This chapter will be concerned with the practical considerations of literary 'public relations' which may have induced Renaissance courtiers to favour the dialogue form. As might be expected, the pragmatic advantages of the documentary dialogue are generally passed over in silence by theorists of the genre. Sforza Pallavicino, it is true, in his *Trattato del dialogo*, mentions as one of the principal 'advantages of writing in dialogue', the potential the dialogue offers to 'honour the memory' of its speakers.[6] But, as he soon makes clear, Pallavicino is referring to dead and therefore disinterested speakers and the implied motives of the writer are the unimpeachable ones of showing *pietas* to the dead and offering the reader 'a stimulus to Virtue'.[7] In practice, not all writers of dialogue were so scrupulous and those who drew their speakers from the land of the living were often less concerned with what might be of benefit to the world at large than with what might prove to be directly profitable to them.[8] Giovanni Fratta, in his *Della dedicatione dei libri* (1590), is more realistic than Pallavicino when he identifies the Ciceronian dialogue as a form of 'dedication': a convenient and time-honoured way to 'ampliar la riputatione a gli amici'.[9]

Fratta's is a useful parallel. The tacit exchange which takes place in the dialogue is analogous to that involved in a dedication, but with the added advantage for the writer that – between speakers, background figures and friends mentioned in passing – the dialogue provides a far greater scope than any but perhaps Bandello's idiosyncratic dedications to cast the net of flattery and ingratiation wide.[10] For the interlocutor, a mention in a dialogue brought publicity and honour. For the writer, besides the acknowledged benefits of goodwill and protection, a 'dedication' in a dialogue might, on occasion, bring more tangible rewards.

The stakes were high. An appearance in one of Sperone Speroni's dialogues was, in the words of Aretino, 'un tesoro che per sempre spenderlo mai non iscemerà'.[11] On an immediate level, it gave the interlocutor a flattering and widely circulated portrait. But beyond this, even more tempting, lay the prospect of literary immortality, celebrated by Marco Mantova Benavides, in a particularly purple passage of his *Discorsi sopra i dialoghi di M. Sperone Speroni* (1561):

Quanto si deono rallegrare l'anime di quelli che già passarono di questa vita all'altra, e maggiormente quei che vivono . . . da un tant'huomo, anzi non huomo, ma semideo e sopra naturale, essere state immortalate . . . Che più bella statua, che più bei trofei, o trionfi della lor virtù . . . poteano desiderare?[12]

Speroni's celebrity as a writer may have pushed up the market value of an appearance in his dialogues to the point of apotheosis,[13] but this lofty transaction is not unrepresentative of the sort of dealing which went on in all documentary dialogues.[14]

The author's side of the bargain was no less lucrative than the speakers'. Few writers were as crude in their dealings as the unnamed hypocrite mentioned by Fratta, who attempted to charge his interlocutors for the privilege of appearing in a dialogue,[15] or as Benedetto Varchi who – if we are to believe the uncharitable Castelvetro – used the honour of a role in his *Ercolano* as an instrument of seduction.[16] But more decorous deals are constantly being struck in the documentary dialogues of the period, and a glance through the prefaces of a few such works is enough to reveal the range of 'public relations' functions the form could be put to. A mention in dialogue was a valuable token in the flourishing contemporary commerce in honour: valid currency for settling debts of gratitude or creating new ones, for fostering speculative acquaintances or rewarding the friendships of years.

Castiglione was well aware of the potential the dialogue offered for managing his public relations and recent studies have exposed the care with which he adjusted the cast-list of the *Cortegiano* in accordance with the differing social and political priorities of different stages of his career.[17] But the most revealing testimony to the dialogue's place in the commerce of honour is provided by Tasso's letters of his prison years, the time when he was composing the first of his *Dialoghi*. These letters constitute a sort of fossilized record of the public relations strategy of a late-Renaissance courtier, preserving many of the delicate and banal transactions which a writer at liberty might not have committed to paper. In them, Tasso shows himself acutely conscious of the value of his dialogues as an instrument of public relations, whether on the humiliatingly direct level of bartering 'honourable mention' for clean linen,[18] or on the loftier but by no means disinterested level of returning a duke's testimonial.[19] The dialogue has a well-defined place in Tasso's league of occasional genres and, in one interesting letter, we find him protesting that, while he is prepared to reward a minor patron by mentioning his son in a dialogue, he draws the line at prostituting his talents to celebrate the family in verse.[20] Easier to write than occasional poetry and more apparently disinterested, the dialogue was in many ways the ideal encomiastic genre. Although it is not always so easy as in Tasso's case to identify the element of social commerce involved in a writer's use of the dialogue, it is a factor in the success of the genre which we cannot afford to ignore.

Of course, the transaction between the writer and the interlocutors of a dialogue was not always as straightforward as these examples may imply. Like the dedication to which Giovanni Fratta compares it, the Renaissance court dialogue was addressed to a double audience: first, to the inner circle of patrons and friends actually named as speakers or dedicatees and, secondly, beyond this charmed circle, the wider, anonymous public of the printed word. Correspondingly, the choice of prestigious interlocutors for a dialogue has two distinct, though associated functions: the first, already dealt with, to oil the wheels of the writer's real or hoped-for social relations, and the second, to establish the social and intellectual credentials of the work.

Clearly, it would be artificial to draw too firm a line between these two motives: they can be, and almost always *are*, inextricably linked. But we should be aware, when considering why a given writer has elected to use the dialogue form, that the reasons may lie with the desire to lend authority to an argument, more than any direct commerce in honour. In such cases, the balance of power in the exchange is skewed towards the interlocutor rather than the writer, and the *topos* whereby a writer delegates the authorship of the work to its protagonists may be seen, on occasion, as more than a mere gesture of modesty.[21] Giovanni Fratta gives an amusing example of an abuse of this trade in authority: the case of a writer who, 'having taken on a subject too heavy to carry on his own shoulders', decided to write his work as a dialogue and chose as his main speaker a learned and dignified cleric. The victim, alarmed at this appropriation of his name, and concerned for his good reputation, went post-haste to Padua, stormed into the print-shop and insisted on his removal from the dialogue.[22]

Such extreme remedies were rarely called for, but there are instances of writers rather awkwardly clearing themselves in their hyperdialogic of the possible charge of having misrepresented figures obviously chosen for their authority. Giuseppe Malatesta, in his *Della nuova poesia overo delle difese del Furioso* (1589), rather ingeniously bluffs out the discrepancies between the views attributed to Sperone Speroni in his dialogue, and those expressed by the Paduan critic *in propria persona*, by having his Speroni undertake the defence of Ariosto purely as a rhetorical exercise.[23] More bluntly, Bartolomeo Meduna has the Alessandro Piccolomini of his *Lo scolare* (1588) announce at the beginning of the dialogue: 'non intendo obligarmi in tutto a quello, che altre volte ho scritto'.[24] Such infelicities are a clear indication of the high value placed on authority in the dialogue. Rather than choosing an unknown speaker, more adaptable to their purposes, some writers, at least, went to considerable pains to endorse their views with a 'name'.

The choice of individual interlocutors of great intellectual or social prestige is only the most obvious way in which the dialogue can be used to reinforce the authority of an argument. More subtly, the choice of the format of civil conversation can in itself be used to confer a certain social authority on the argument, by establishing the author's right to a hearing in polite society. This function of the dialogue was obviously of particular interest to those whose birth and rank did not automatically entitle them to such a hearing. As Frank Whigham has observed, 'sheer residence within courtly discourse can itself be read as a sign of "arrival"',[25] and there could be few more blatant advertisements of an author's right to residence than his imitation of the preferred medium of court discourse, a private 'ragionamento'.

This strategy is at its most useful when the subject of the dialogue is one whose right of residence in polite discourse is problematic. In Orazio Toscanella's rather perfunctory classification of dialogues by their subjects in his *Alcune avvertenze del tesser dialoghi* (1567), the third and lowest category is represented by dialogues on 'tutte le parti, che hanno odor di humiltà':[26] agriculture, architecture and the other 'mechanical' arts. Toscanella's division is distinctly eccentric, and is of little help in relating the matter of his contemporaries' dialogues in any meaningful way to the level of their style. But it does reveal very clearly the current prejudice against any art which was tainted with 'practice'; and it helps us to define a sub-group of dialogues, concerned with the mechanical arts, which use the dialogue form self-consciously, to dignify their subject-matter. Those I intend to consider here are two: one on horsemanship, Claudio Corte's *Il Cavallarizzo* (1562), and one on military architecture, Giacomo Lanteri's *Due dialoghi del modo di disegnare le piante delle fortezze* (1557).[27]

Both Corte's dialogue and Lanteri's have two quite different ends, each requiring a quite separate strategy of presentation. The first, in each case, is simply that of conveying a body of technical information of the authors' respective arts, and here the conventions of literary dialogue are otiose, even obstructive. The second end of these works is, however, that of defending the social status of the arts in question, and it is here that the hidden persuaders of dialogue come into play. Corte in particular marks this division in his argument quite explicitly. His first two, purely technical, books are written in the form of a treatise and it is only in the final book – an apology for his art – that the dialogue first makes its appearance.[28] It is interesting to note that Corte's English translator omits this last book, along with Corte's elaborate dedications and his lavish apparatus of classical allusions: all the 'manifold digressions' which do so much, in the original, to press his subliminal message.[29]

Corte was well aware of the pragmatic advantages of the dialogue form, and he states explicitly that one of his reasons for using it was 'to name some of [his] patrons and friends'.[30] There are clues, though, as well, that his choice of the dialogue has a subtler rhetorical function. The conversation takes place, in the best tradition, in a *locus amoenus*: 'luogo bellissimo e molto atto a sì fatti ragionamenti'.[31] The argument of Book III, on the perfect equerry, is clearly patterned on the *Cortegiano*, but Corte shows some signs, too, of having meditated on the *form* of Castiglione's dialogue.[32] The social rituals of court society are used to calculated effect,[33] and the interlocutors of Corte's dialogue – most of whom are, incidentally, quite superfluous to the discussion – are characterized as both accomplished horsemen and practised courtiers.[34] The sight of these courtierly stablemen mixing with prominent members of the Roman nobility is undoubtedly part of the dialogue's apologetic strategy. When Corte, as author and protagonist, flaunts his own classical learning, he is providing evidence for his assertion that the perfect equerry must be schooled in the humanist disciplines.[35] Similarly, his point that the perfect *cavallarizzo* must be noble, handsome and accomplished – a 'fratello del Cortegiano'[36] – is given persuasive support by his depiction of a group of these paragons in the flesh, going faultlessly through the *dressage* of a civil conversation.

Like his colleague, Sidney's John Pietro Pugliano, Corte is induced by his 'strong affection and weak arguments' to champion his art with blithe confidence as the highest of all human callings.[37] Giacomo Lanteri, less naive than Corte, is more equivocal in his attitude to the status of his profession, and his use of the dialogue form is more obviously manipulative.[38] The subject-matter of his *Del modo di disegnare le piante delle fortezze* is hardly suited to conversation and the dialogues are, unsurprisingly, resoundingly 'monological'.[39] Lanteri's use of the dialogue can only be ascribed to his desire to show that, in an age in which 'meccanico' was a 'voce d'ingiuria',[40] the theory at least of his mechanical art was a subject worthy of civilized men.[41] Certainly this is the only possible explanation – apart from that of blatant ingratiation – which can account for the narrated dialogue with which Girolamo Cattaneo opens his discourse on geometry in the first dialogue. His account of a conversation on the subject between himself and his patrons is, as argument, spectacularly otiose, being mainly occupied with the expressions of his 'riverenze' and the 'cortesie' of his listeners. But its subliminal message is clear enough: that the theory of military architecture is a subject of the greatest interest to the 'nobilissimi' Conti d' Arco, and that, therefore, if it is frequently 'insulted' and 'despised' as a mechanical art, that is only because of the false snobbery of the 'ignorante vulgo'.[42]

For writers like Corte and Lanteri, the trappings of Ciceronian dialogue become the means by which a subject-matter of socially dubious status can assert a sort of squatters' right to residence in courtly discourse. This is by no means the least of motives why a writer might choose to cast a didactic treatise in the form of a dialogue: indeed, it is no doubt among the reasons which prompted another, more renowned 'mechanic', Galileo, to favour the dialogue form in his writings. But a study of writers with an axe to grind is obviously not the best way to understand the complexity of the task of social mediation which the sixteenth-century dialogue might be called on to perform. Apart from the rather strident public relations work examined in the last section, there were subtler and more radical ways in which writers of Ciceronian dialogue could exploit the form's capacity to reproduce a polite conversation.

Before setting out to explore these byways of literary etiquette, it may be useful to return, for a moment, to the question of the social and performative dimension of Renaissance literature, touched on at the beginning of this chapter. The picture sketched out there requires some refinement: by the sixteenth century, the invention of print had transformed literary activity far more than is sometimes acknowledged, and an intimate, closed-circuit model for cultural production and consumption would hardly apply to a phenomenon like the dissemination of Calvinist tracts. Even within the courts, where it has far greater application, the view of literature as an extension of personal interaction is perhaps best seen as reflecting an ideal or convention as much as a reality. Courtiers who wrote would very often, for reasons of social decorum, present their works as written for a circumscribed manuscript audience. But this was a convention, as much as anything else, and many must have shared the ambition confessed with engaging frankness by Stefano Guazzo, in his *Dialoghi piacevoli* (1586) to see 'l'opere da loro . . . composte . . . passare per le mani di cento mila Lettori, e renderli al mondo gloriosi, e immortali'.[43]

With these reservations, however, the concept of Renaissance court literature as an *intimate* literature is a useful one. It is easy for the modern critic, accustomed to our own far more impersonal literary economy, to underestimate the degree to which, in the early modern period, polite literature was conceived of as a personal exchange between an author and an audience. Recent speech-act theories of literature have sought to remind us that literary discourse is a form of utterance, differing in detail, but not in kind, from utterance in everyday speech.[44] Renaissance readers and writers would have needed no such reminder. Literature, like speech, like dress, like dancing, was felt as a sort of *performance* and it was subject to the same social etiquette which governed these other pursuits.[45]

Like any activity designed to put one's talents on display, writing brought great rewards but, with them, considerable dangers.[46] To produce a manuscript inevitably requires a notable investment of labour. To publish it implies a certain conviction of its worth. Both industry and ambition are involved in the production of a literary work and both were qualities calculated to induce unease in the self-respecting courtier. To publish was to put one's reputation for *sprezzatura* on the line: a danger pointed up by George Pettie – with a nice air of contempt for such Italianate refinements – when he identifies 'those which mislike that a Gentleman should publish the fruits of his learning' with 'some curious Gentlemen who think it most commendable in a Gentleman, to cloake his art and skill in everie thing, and to seeme to doe all things of his own mother wit'.[47]

We can gain an idea of quite how indecorous the act of publication might be by comparing it with parallel acts in civil conversation. 'Literary speech' is analogous to extended speech-acts in oral exchange, in that one speaker – the writer – dominates and the others – the readers – are silent.[48] The problems of etiquette raised by this imbalance of power are similar in both cases. We have no record, of course, of how, in actual conversations, speakers in the Renaissance courts confronted these problems of etiquette. But we do possess valuable evidence of the way it was felt that they *should* be confronted; both directly, in the explicit prescriptions of contemporary manuals of courtesy, and, at one remove, in the stylized depiction of conversation in dialogues.

Renaissance courtesy textbooks show an acute awareness of the potential for indecorum in situations in which one speaker dominates an exchange. Giovanni Della Casa, in the *Galateo* (1558), observes that the balance of power in any conversation is always skewed towards the speaker and concludes that, in the interests of social harmony, no one in the company should seek to appropriate more than their fair share of this 'maggioranza'.[49] The same point is made by Stefano Guazzo, in his *Civil conversazione* (1574), where conversation is compared to tennis – 'il giuoco di palla' – in that the distribution of turns between the players is governed by 'corrispondenza'. For Guazzo, to hog the conversation at a feast is as uncouth as it would be to monopolize the wine. 'Il voler dire ogni cosa e non ascoltar niente' is not less than a form of social despotism – 'una specie di tirannia'.[50]

The first duty of speakers who find themselves in a dominant position is to ensure that their *maggioranza* will be free from any taint of 'tyranny'. The impression to be aimed at, to quote Guazzo again, is that one's tongue has been stirred into action by necessity, rather than will.[51] The means by which this end can be achieved have been sensitively explored by Wayne Rebhorn in his sociological analysis of the *cornice* of the *Cortegiano*. Castiglione's speakers – and the speakers of any sixteenth-century Ciceronian dialogue – 'frame' their speeches with elaborate protestations which Rebhorn terms 'deference rituals'.[52] The aim of these rituals is to present taking the floor as a 'fatica', rather than an 'onore': a task for which the speaker feels patently unqualified and which he is only undertaking out of politeness and duty.[53] By respecting this convention, deprecating their abilities and extolling the judgment of their audience, Castiglione's speakers succeed to perfection in reconciling their effective dominance of the conversation with contemporary etiquette manuals' prescriptions for a 'modest manner of speech'.[54]

Pomposity and self-importance are not the only spectres to be exorcized from court discourse. In speaking, as in writing, as in any activity, *sprezzatura* is of the essence and the speaker who is called on to give an impromptu dissertation must be careful to avoid the appearance of having thought too hard in advance. As the principal speaker of Scipione Bargagli's *Turamino* (1602) observes, it is one thing to start speaking spontaneously on a subject, carried along on the flow of the conversation, but quite another to set oneself up as an expert and deliver a speech.[55] When Castiglione's Lodovico da Canossa lightly rejects an offer of time to prepare himself and improvises forty chapters of effortless good sense,[56] he is setting a standard of accomplished but exquisitely amateur discourse which would remain an ideal as long as the behavioural *ethos* he describes.

It was an ideal which applied, as I have suggested, in literature as in speech and the 'frames' with which Renaissance writers surrounded their literary utterances are directly comparable with those employed by speakers like Turamino or Canossa. J.W. Saunders, trawling the prefaces of Tudor court literature, has identified a whole series of such gestures, designed, like their equivalents in speech, to display writers' modesty and *sprezzatura*. The most common of these are an insistence on the writer's reluctance to publish until forced by importunate friends, a corresponding stress on the delay between composition and publication and a modest denigration of the value of the work, which is presented, more often than not, as merely the product of an idle half-hour.[57] Devices like this will be familiar to any reader of Italian court literature – they are elegantly exploited, to look no further, by Castiglione himself.[58] But they are only the most obvious of a highly sophisticated repertoire of gestures which writers used to avoid the air of demagoguery and ambition which might otherwise accompany the act of expounding their views in print. The most radical of these gestures – not a 'frame' but an integrated element in the structure of a work – is the use of dialogue rather than direct exposition as a means of presenting one's views. Writers of dialogues, and, specifically, of documentary dialogues, present themselves in a quite different way than the writer of a treatise. By maintaining the pretence that the dialogue is a transcription of a conversation which really took place, they are voluntarily reducing their status from that of the original thinker, the *author*, to that of a simple 'manual copiatore degli altriu detti'.[59]

Clearly, this is only a fiction, but it is one which can be turned to effect. In the first place, it assists in establishing the author's *sprezzatura*: rather than a scholar, burning the midnight oil to construct a laborious treatise, the writer of a dialogue emerges from the book as a careless and sociable creature, who has simply recorded the fruits of a pleasant afternoon's listening. And, secondly, the convention of transcription helps to absolve writers from the slur of 'ambizione', by revealing the work they were publishing as scarcely their own work at all. This feature of the genre would alone, one suspects, have been enough to guarantee its popularity in a culture in which modesty – to appropriate a metaphor of Castiglione's – was the condiment of every act.[60] Certainly, it was seized on eagerly by writers and exploited for all it was worth. Battista Guarini, in a letter to Jacopo Contarini, the protagonist of his *Segretario* (1594), insists that the honour of the dialogue's authorship is Contarini's alone; that, if his own name were to be removed from the work, it would be a matter of indifference, while the removal of Contarini's name would ruin the entire work.[61] Claudio Tolomei, in his *Cesano* (1525), in an echo of Socrates' obstetric imagery, describes his interlocutors as the true progenitors of a work which the 'sterile' author could never have written himself.[62] And Bernardo Trotto, in his *Dialoghi del matrimonio* (1578), takes the same line of imagery a stage further, and portrays himself as a wet-nurse, bashfully returning his charges to their mother, fully conscious of how much his rustic ministrations have coarsened her eloquent thoughts.[63]

A keen awareness of the social capital to be made out of this convention is apparent in Speroni's *Apologia de' dialoghi* (1574–5), in a passage which exploits to the full the potential for self-reference offered by the device of a dialogue-within-a-dialogue. The third part of the *Apologia* contains a narrated dialogue, set in Rome, in which one of the speakers, Silvio Antoniano, is called on by his companions, at a certain point, to summarize Plato's *Sophist*. He accepts the task with some reluctance, aware that 'l'ascoltare più che 'l parlare è da me' and that, in such august company ''l tacere mi tocarebbe'.[64] There is, however, one possibility for reconciling modesty and obedience: he will recount to his companions a dialogue which took place in the Accademia delle Notti Vaticane, and which he had witnessed in the capacity of a humble 'auditore'. Antoniano insists in the 'proemio' to his speech on his role as a vessel for the genius of others. In recounting a dialogue he can scarcely, in fact, be said to be speaking at all: 'nel riferirvi le cose udite, quasi parlandomi la memoria, non che io ragioni, come volete, mi parerà; ma che, siccome io sono uso, io oda ancora e ascolti'. As a vessel for others' speeches, at the same time 'parlando vi ubbidirò; e secondo il mio privilegio tacerò ragionando'.[65]

Antoniano's use of the dialogue form to minimize his authority as a speaker is an elegant reproduction of Speroni's strategy in adopting the genre in his writing.[66] In choosing the dialogue form, the writer is renouncing an authorial role, and becoming, like the reader, an admiring eavesdropper on the conversation of others. It is this levelling effect which makes the dialogue, in Tasso's judgment, the 'pleasantest and least irksome' of didactic genres.[67] A treatise casts its writer and reader in the role of master and pupil. In the dialogue, on the other hand, their relationship is more like that of a pair of hunting-companions, sharing equally in the excitement, the fatigue and the glory of the chase.[68]

Tasso's dashing image of the dialogue as a kind of intellectual outward-bound course calls our attention to a further, significant factor in the genre's appeal. It has already been noted, in chapter 1, that the dialogue assigns a different and far more active role to the reader than other philosophical genres. Where a treatise simply presents the reader with a barrage of argumentation, to be accepted or rejected wholesale, a dialogue projects the reader's reactions into the argument itself. One consequence of this is that, as recent commentators on Plato have emphasized, the dialogue offers the closest approximation possible within a written text to the responsiveness of the spoken word.[69] Of course, the obdurate muteness of writing, of which Socrates complains in the *Phaedrus*, cannot be entirely overcome in what remains a written form. But, by mimicking the form of a conversation, by anticipating the reader's objections and giving them a resonance within the text, the dialogue goes some way, at least, towards remedying this deficiency.

This interactive quality in the dialogue form would have particular value, of course, to a reading public with particular reason to be sensitive to the 'tyranny' of monological written discourse. When considering the appeal of the dialogue form in the sixteenth century, it is as well to consider that the vernacular dialogue was addressed, for the most part, to a newly literate public: a public of 'idioti', who, had they been born a century, even half a century earlier, would have been effectively excluded from the world of learning. Obviously, the experience of these readers is not directly comparable with that of the members of a primary oral culture, on its first encounter with writing. But it seems safe to assume, even so, that the reading public created, or empowered, by print, must have been aware, with an intensity that it is difficult for a late twentieth-century reader to imagine, of the 'deadness' of the letters lying before them on the page.

The dialogue permitted writers to temper the abruptness of their address to this audience by filtering it through the more familiar and responsive medium of speech. The closest parallels to a didactic treatise in the world of oral exchange are a lecture, a sermon or a harangue: speech-acts whose unacceptability in the world of the courts are only too apparent. The dialogue form allows an argument to be structured not as a lecture but a *conversation*: an exchange in which – to use Guazzo's analogy – just as in the 'giuoco della palla', every statement is followed by an equal and opposite reaction. At least vicariously, the dialogue returns to readers the right of reply we normally relinquish in a 'literary speech situation'.[70] Many readers of neo-Platonic treatises on love may have felt a desire, at the end, to pull their writers back down to earth. In the *Cortegiano*, through the offices of a mischievous Emilia Pio, they are finally given the opportunity to see this desire fulfilled.[71]

The scope which the dialogue offered for a diplomatic management of the relations between readers and writers must have constituted a very significant part of its appeal in the Renaissance court. A writer whose primary audience was the newly literate public of the courts faced an unprecedented problem of etiquette: how to address an audience composed of educational inferiors but social equals, in a society in which good manners had been elevated to the status of an art. The problem was particularly pressing in the case of didactic works, where the dangers of stepping on one's readers' toes were particularly acute. To teach such an audience, accessibly, suavely, above all without condescension, was a task which tested a writer's resources of diplomacy to the full.

The ambassadorial role which dialogue played in these delicate circumstances is well illustrated by an episode in the third book of the *Cortegiano*. At the beginning of the discussion on the status of women, prompted by the exigencies of his subject matter, Castiglione indulges in an uncharacteristic bout of technical disputation, on questions such as the different admixtures of the humours in women and men and whether the relation between the sexes may be equated with that between matter and form.[72] The passage is a necessary concession to the tone of contemporary debate on the subject and is pointedly directed at the more learned in the dialogue's audience.[73] But Castiglione is well aware that, in catering for the erudite section of his public, he may alienate those readers unacquainted with the sectoral language of science. A change of direction is clearly required, and he duly diverts the discussion back to its usual, more accessible level.

The fiction of dialogue permits this transition to be realized with tact. The instigator of the change is Emilia Pio, who brusquely intervenes to demand that the disputants abandon their incomprehensible jargon and conduct their argument in a language more consonant with experience. Emilia's point is a reasonable one and she is an eminently flattering model for the readers whose rights she defends: intelligent, articulate, well able to hold her own and – most significantly of all – invested with the regulation of the dispute. What might have been a patronizing gesture by the writer is presented as a victory for the reader, who is portrayed as – rightly and reasonably – holding the reins of the argument.

Female interlocutors, guaranteed by their sex the right to be decorously ignorant, were much exploited in the vernacular dialogue as stand-ins for an unschooled audience. But men, as well, could serve, if supplied with a suitable pretext for their lack of acquaintance with the particular subject-matter of the dialogue. From the Ercole Strozzi of Bembo's *Prose della volgar lingua* (1525) – a Latinist whose expertise in his field more than compensates for his ignorance of vernacular grammar[74] – to Tasso's young courtiers, who have neglected their studies for a life of action, Cinquecento dialogues are filled with speakers whom even the touchiest reader could have no scruples about accepting as companions in their ignorance.

Certain of Tasso's dialogues give a particularly flattering twist to the depiction of the relations between author and reader by choosing 'pupils' of a higher social status than their 'masters'.[75] Another instance of this stratagem is Galeazzo Florimonte's *Ragionamenti* (1554), which show the philosopher Agostino Nifo, in conversation with his patron, Ferrante Sanseverino, the Prince of Salerno. One function of the unusual choice of a prince as interlocutor is doubtless to assure the 'active' reader that the subject in question – moral philosophy – is of more than 'contemplative' interest. Another, I suggest, is to compensate the reader, in what is a markedly didactic and one-sided dialogue, for the unseemly *maggioranza* which the writer is forced to assume.

Florimonte's strategy of deference in his construction of the dialogue is carried through, at a localized level, in his tactics of argumentation. At the beginning of the dialogue, he has Sanseverino express his apprehension about tackling the intricacies of moral philosophy without a sufficient grounding in the arts of grammar and logic. This is a fear which was likely to be shared by many of Florimonte's readers, and one he is concerned to assuage. But he is equally aware of the danger of appearing to patronize his audience; and it is here that the mediation of the dialogue comes into its own. Nifo is made to reply with the flattering suggestion that Sanseverino has asked this question out of courtesy, rather than necessity: the prince is himself, as is well known, an expert in both of the disciplines in question, and his question can only have been motivated by a concern for the other listeners present.[76]

The needs of the ignorant reader are met when, respecting his patron's delicacy, Nifo resolves to teach Sanseverino as though he were addressing 'quei che non hanno né grammatica né logica'. But these needs are met, by an author who was not for nothing the dedicatee of the *Galateo*, with the flattering insinuation that they are not his needs at all. The suggestion that a speaker is feigning ignorance is the high-point of a consistent strategy, on the part of writers of dialogue, to shield their readers from the indignity of an overtly didactic address.[77] If the dialogue functions by speaking without speaking – Speroni's 'tacere ragionando' – it is because it is an attempt to solve the courtly writer's most pressing problem, of how to teach an audience without appearing to teach.

5 Castiglione's *Cortegiano*: the dialogue as a drama of doubt

E grande errore parlare delle cose del mondo indistintamente e assolutamente e, per dire cosi, per regola.

Francesco Guicciardini, Ricordi (1530)[1]

. . . non solamente a voi po parer una cosa ed a me un'altra, ma a me
stesso poria parer or una cosa ed ora un'altra.

Baldassare Castiglione, Il libro del Cortegiano (1528)[2]

Up to this point, in attempting to account for the popularity of the
dialogue in the Italian Renaissance, I have been stressing the social and
diplomatic aspects of writers' use of the form. This emphasis has been
intended as a corrective, since these powerful factors in the dialogue's
appeal have been very largely ignored in the past, by historians and critics
intent on the philosophical significance of the genre. This is not to say,
however, that other, methodological or epistemological concerns may not
also have a role in individual writers' decision to adopt a dialogue form in
their works. It would be as misleading to interpret a writer's choice of the
dialogue form simply as an exercise in literary etiquette as it would be to
ignore the weight that questions of etiquette may have had in this choice.[3]

The phrase from the *Cortegiano* quoted above, as an epigraph to this
chapter, comes from a passage at the beginning of the dialogue, in which
Lodovico da Canossa is expressing his misgivings about his suitability for
the task which he has been given, of 'forming the perfect courtier in
words'. Canossa is only too aware of his own inadequacies and the
difficulty of the enterprise; and, when Emilia Pio teases him that she has
chosen him precisely *because* of his wrong-headedness, to guarantee a
lively debate, he wryly responds that there may be more truth in her jibe
than she knows. He will accept the commission only on condition that his
companions do not look to him for an authorized version. All he can give
is his own opinion, which they may take or leave, as they choose: 'né io già
contrasterò che 'l mio [giudicio] sia migliore del vostro; ché non solamente
a voi po parer una cosa ed a me un'altra, ma a me stesso poria parer or
una cosa ed ora un'altra'.[4]

I suggested in the last chapter that this kind of ritual disclaimer of authority may be interpreted as a social manoeuvre, intended to display the speaker's courtierly ethos. This is certainly true, and Canossa's proem – something of a masterpiece of the genre – is as fluent an expression of hesitancy and inadequacy as one could hope for. But this interpretation does not exhaust the significance of Canossa's disclaimer, any more than it does that of Castiglione's parallel gesture, when, reluctantly accepting Alfonso Ariosto's commission to define the perfect courtier, he renounces that 'certo ordine e regula di precetti distinti, che 'l piu delle volte nell'insegnare qualsivoglia cosa usar si sole', and announces that he will instead present his arguments as a dialogue.[5] Like Canossa, Castiglione is reluctant to be seen to be taking a didactic role incompatible with the behavioural aesthetic he is preparing to unfold. But, in both cases, beyond the courtier's obligatory bashfulness, lurks a profound unease with the epistemological assumptions which inform conventional didactic modes.

The motives for Castiglione's mistrust of 'the usual methods of teaching' may be reliably reconstructed if we integrate his dedicatory letter to Ariosto with his other reflections on problems of knowledge scattered elsewhere in the book. In the treacherous realm of social *mores* – the unmapped territory into which his quest for the perfect courtier is leading him – truth is a commodity extremely difficult to come by. For one thing, the nature of the subject-matter itself militates against certainty: it is almost impossible to reach a reliable judgment on phenomena which vary erratically across time and space and whose variations are governed not by reason but simply by custom and whim. What is more, the difficulties of measurement are compounded by the unreliability of the instruments we dispose of. How can we make an objective judgment when we are ourselves trapped in the folds of history, when changing fashions and the vagaries of our own tastes can make us applaud today what we will despise in the future and reject those habits and values which our forefathers espoused?[6]

Error emerges, in the *Cortegiano*, almost as a defining characteristic of the human condition. Even the apparently incontrovertible evidence of the senses is liable to distortion. The body plays tricks on the mind and the mind enthusiastically reciprocates: to the ruined palate, all wines, however 'precious and delicate', will taste bitter; while perfectly healthy palates may register the same wine as tasting quite different on different occasions, depending on which vineyard it is thought to come from.[7] Countless factors can affect our judgments – nostalgia, malice, satiety and, above all, the *amour propre* whose machinations Castiglione exposes with the finesse of a La Rochefoucauld.[8] There can be little hope, in this morass of misjudgment, of reaching a considered opinion, still less anything which approaches a universal and absolute truth. Confronted with conflicting views on some issue – say, on what constitutes the perfect courtier – what half-way reliable means do we have for distinguishing the false from the true?

Faced with this problem, Castiglione does not fall back on the bewildered relativism which might seem the only solution. He remains convinced that truth does exist; that each thing has its 'vera perfezione' and that this perfection is something which can be discovered through the agency of reason.[9] What is unlikely is that we will be able to reach it alone, as individuals: short-sighted, stumbling and blind to our own errors and prejudices as we are. A governing image of the *Cortegiano* – the spectre the book has been written to banish – is the man convinced he is sane when all around him can see he is mad.[10] One strong reason for Castiglione's rejection of conventional didactic practice is that it fails to account for the fact that it is when we are most stubbornly convinced that we are in the right that we are most liable to be in the wrong.

In life, a counterbalance to our own errors can be sought in a dialogue with our fellows: that dialogue which Canossa elicits at the beginning of the *Cortegiano* by freely admitting the limited and partial nature of his own views.[11] In a written work, such a dialogue is, of course, technically impossible, but, within obvious limitations, a book can transcend its inevitably monological nature, by a strenuous effort of the writer's dialogical imagination. By choosing to cast the *Cortegiano* in the form of a fictional conversation, Castiglione asserts his allegiance to the practice of cultural dialogue. In his letter to De Silva, Castiglione hints that the only sure way to orientate ourselves in the dark wood of conflicting opinions is to follow the nose of 'la commune opinione' which – 'ancor che perfettamente non conosca' – 'sente però per instinto di natura un certo odore del bene e del male'.[12] The dialogue of the *Cortegiano* finds its profoundest justification as an instrument for sounding out this elusive consensus; for pursuing opinion in its natural habitat, the 'dispersive' sphere of oral exchange, in which tastes and ideas are born and die without hardening into 'precepts'.[13]

The remainder of this chapter will be taken up with a reading of the *Cortegiano* – or part of it – which will attempt to show how Castiglione uses the resource of dialogue to deal with a particularly delicate matter of opinion: the question of how the courtier should conduct his relations with his prince. This will, inevitably, entail something of a slowing-up in the rhythm of my argument: to unravel even a few of the *Cortegiano*'s 'molte fila' will require a considerable investment of time and patience.[14] It is hoped, however, that this investment will be felt to be justified by its results. For it is only by observing it in action, and by patiently tracking its meandering *via*, that we can appreciate the dialogue's potential for conveying dialectical thought.

It is frustrating that, writing, as he did, twenty years before the 'redis-covery' of Aristotle's *Poetics*, Castiglione never felt called on to justify or discuss his poetics of dialogue. An intriguing clue to the self-conscious-ness with which he used the form is offered, however, by his one impor-tant statement on this problem, in a letter of 1527 to Alfonso de Valdés, attacking Valdés for his defence, in a dialogue, of the calamitous sacking of Rome. Foreseeing that Valdés might defend his work on the grounds that it is written as a dialogue, Castiglione reminds him, with a lordly understatement, that 'a noi altri ancora è nota la maniera academica dello scrivere in dialogo' and acknowledges that the genre allows the writer the luxury of not committing himself to any one view.[15] But Valdés has forfeited any privilege he might claim to an objective presentation by identifying himself too closely with one figure in his dialogue. 'Voi non siete', Castiglione accuses him, 'tanto cauto nello scrivere, che non si conosca qual è la persona del dialogo la cui sentenzia voi approvate, e quella a cui fate dire mille semplicità acciò che più facilmente sia redar-guita. E vedesi che le opinioni di Lattanzio sono le vostre, e voi siete Lattanzio; e perciò non sarà inconveniente da qui indietro (sic) mutarvi nome e chiamarvi Lattanzio'.[16]

It would be rash, of course, to attempt to extrapolate a complete poetics of the dialogue from an offhand comment, written in a bitterly polemical context. With this caveat, however, it may be possible to make some – appropriately cautious – use of the concept of 'caution', which Casti-glione adduces here as a guiding principle of the writer of dialogues. 'Caution' is a quality particularly crucial to the writer of a polemical dialogue, who, without some attempt at detachment, will forfeit all the credibility to be gained by his choosing an 'objective' mode of argument. But, in any dialogue – even a dialogue like the *Cortegiano*, which includes substantial passages of uncontroversial exposition – a poised and deliber-ate detachment from the interlocutors and arguments being dramatized is a crucial element in the writer's art.

The *Cortegiano* is a long and heterogeneous work, effortlessly enfol-ding in its loose remit of 'forming the perfect courtier' a series of digress-ive discussions on the prime talking-points of the day. It is difficult to generalize about the manner in which Castiglione uses the dialogue or the level of real dialectic present in the work, as this varies considerably according to the nature of the subject under discussion. While Castiglione never stoops to the crude partisanship of which he accuses Valdés, certain episodes are notably 'incautious', in the sense defined above. The issue of language, in the first book, provokes a heated dispute between two interlocutors, one of whom – Canossa – is unmistakably identifiable as a spokesman for the author.[17] The discussion of women's status, in the third book, is similarly 'incautious': although here the distribution of the feminist thesis between two main speakers complicates the issue and demands a more nuanced reading.[18]

These two disputes are, however, in some ways, exceptional cases: both are set-piece discussions between speakers representing fiercely polarized positions, within battle-lines already well established in the polemics of the day. More typical of Castiglione's art of dialogue are those long passages in the first two books and the first half, at least, of the fourth, in which a principal speaker who carries the burden of exposition – and whom we might be tempted, lazily, to equate with the author – is harried by a questioner, or a number of questioners and forced to defend his views. It is here, where Castiglione's orchestration of the dialogue is at its most 'cautious', that the potential of the form for dramatizing an 'unfinished' thought is most clearly revealed. And it is here – to be precise, in the first half of the second book of the dialogue – when Federico Fregoso rashly broaches the delicate subject of the courtier's relations with his prince.

The discussion starts with the seemingly uncontroversial statement from Fregoso that the courtier should devote himself, heart and soul, to the duty of pleasing his prince. This may appear innocent enough – after all, the courtier's profession is service – but it is immediately met with an accusation, from a minor speaker, Pietro da Napoli, that the courtier, in that case, will be little more than 'un nobile adulatore'.[19] Pietro's objection is swiftly dealt with, and his voice carries little authority, but the mention of flattery leaves an awkward resonance in the discussion. Fregoso's reply shows an awareness of having stumbled onto difficult terrain, when he specifies that, even if it is the courtier's duty to sway in the winds of his master's desires, he should never bend further than the bounds of morality permit.[20] However glancingly, the question of the courtier's moral autonomy from the prince has been raised, and, once raised, the issue proves notably reluctant to lie down.

Not long afterwards, indeed, Vincenzo Calmeta interrupts Fregoso with a point which, if conceded, would call into question the premises on which his whole argument, and the whole dialogue is founded. Fregoso, cautioning the courtier against the appearance of grasping for favours, has just stated that 'per aver . . . favor dai signori, non è miglior via che meritargli',[21] Calmeta counters that this is simply not the case; that 'l'esperienza ci [fa] molto ben chiari del contrario' and that 'oggidí pochissimi sono favoriti da' signori, eccetto i prosontuosi'.[22] Taken to its logical conclusion, Calmeta's argument would imply that the courtier should measure his actions not by principle, but by expedience; not by what he knows to be right in the comfortable world of absolutes, but by what he suspects will function best in the imperfect courts of the day.

The implications of Calmeta's line of argument are immediately apparent to Fregoso, even if he attempts to steer the conversation onto less dangerous ground. After a brief, comparative detour into the manners of the French and Spanish courts, he firmly restates his essential point, that the courtier should always '[tendere] al bene . . . né mai s'induca a cercar grazia o favor per via viciosa, né per mezzo di mala sorte'.[23] But Calmeta will not relinquish his point, and, perhaps mindful of his own time in the service of Cesare Borgia, he insists that a man of such high moral scrupulousness would cut little ice with the princes of the day.[24]

Fregoso responds with a concession, acknowledging, for the first time, that unprincipled princes *do* exist, and that the exigencies of service may not always be easily squared with the dictates of conscience. He continues to insist, however, that a prince's vice does not exculpate his henchmen. If a courtier discovers his prince to be 'vicioso e maligno', he should instantly leave his service, rather than compromising an inch.[25] Fregoso's attempt at compromise does not release him from the hook, as Calmeta immediately reminds him of something which Castiglione himself had good reason to know from experience, that leaving one's lord is a risky and difficult business. In Calmeta's grim vision, the courtiers of a prince who turns out to be evil 'sono alla condizion di que' malavventurati uccelli, che nascono in trista valle'.[26]

Fregoso replies doggedly that a man's moral duty should outweigh all other considerations.[27] But he is quickly under attack again, this time from Lodovico Pio, who steps up the tempo of the assault and confronts him with his most difficult question so far. Is the courtier obliged to obey his prince 'in tutte le cose che gli comanda, ancor che fossero disoneste e vituperose'? And if not – if, as the flagging Fregoso claims, 'in cose disoneste non siamo obligati ad ubedire a persona alcuna' – then is the alternative simply to refuse, to his master's face?[28] Is a courtier, realistically, in a position to refuse *anything* to his prince? If the prince whose trust and affection he has laboriously gained should ask him, say, to commit murder, can he be expected to sacrifice the labour of a lifetime by questioning his orders?[29]

Hard-pressed, and with the discussion drifting into dangerously concrete and particularized territory, Fregoso is forced into a position of moral equivocation which skews the *Cortegiano* disconcertingly close to the mood of Machiavelli's *Prince*:

Voi dovete ... ubidire al signor vostro in tutte le cose che a lui sono utili ed onorevoli, non in quelle che gli sono di danno e di vergogna ... *Vero è che molte cose paiono al primo aspetto bone, che sono male, e molte paiono male e pur son bone.* Però è licito talor per servizio de' suoi signori ammazzare non un omo ma dieci milia, e far molte altre cose, le quali, a chi non le considerasse come si dee, pareriano male, e pur non sono.[30]

The distance Fregoso has travelled from conventional discussions of morality may be gauged by comparing a treatment of the same problem by Castiglione's most significant predecessor in the field of court ethics, the Quattrocento Neapolitan statesman, Diomede Carafa, author of the treatise *Dello optimo cortesano* (1479). Carafa is quite clear that, where there is a conflict of duty and conscience a courtier's first duty is not to the prince, but rather to himself and to God. There is no grey area between good and evil; the best of ends can never justify foul means, since God will never allow good to come from morally dubious actions. Carafa's intransigence on this issue is backed by an optimism about the limits of human evil, which calls to mind Castiglione's comments, in the preface to Book II, on the innocence of fifteenth-century court culture: the prelapsarian naïveté of an era less 'copious in vice' than his own.[31] Carafa concludes that, if the courtier is requested to do something which he finds morally repugnant, he should simply refuse, safe in the knowledge that, even if his prince is momentarily offended by his refusal, he will come round, in the long run, to recognizing and respecting his virtue.[32]

In contrast with Carafa's calm moral certainties – and his own, earlier intransigence – Fregoso's lapse into relativism has the character of a *volte-face*. But his unexpected concession does not win him the truce that he must have been counting on. He is immediately in trouble once more, this time from Gaspare Pallavicino, the *enfant terrible* of the dialogue, who asks whether he would care to explain how one can tell what is right from what merely appears so. Pallavicino's deceptively ingenuous question points up the depth of the water in which Fregoso is floundering. With no room left for manoeuvre, he is compelled to retreat, and blankly refuses to continue, claiming – quite accurately – that, on this subject, 'troppo saria che dire'.[33]

Fregoso's admission of defeat crowns a long and brilliantly orchestrated sequence of dialogue which has brought theory into awkward juxtaposition with practice, and the comfortably ideal with what Machiavelli would call 'la verità effettuale della cosa'.[34] The sequence concludes when, unable to draw him on the definition of virtue, Pallavicino asks Fregoso the less awkward question of the degree to which the courtier charged with performing some commission on behalf of his prince should feel himself free to disobey the letter, if not the spirit of his master's instructions, if circumstances demand such a change.[35] Fregoso replies that it is best to be cautious, and concludes with a chilling example of what disobedience to one's prince can result in: an anecdote about the Roman consul Publius Crassus Mucianus punishing a subordinate's trivial and fully justified modification of his orders by having him savagely beaten to death.[36]

On this note of sour warning, with a relief which transpires from the page, Fregoso is finally free to 'lassar da canto ... questa pratica de' signori'.[37] The conclusion of his argument is deliberately ambiguous. If Mucianus' behaviour is typical of the arrogance and brutality of princes, as Fregoso suggests it is,[38] then where does that leave his earlier, optimistic assertion that the courtier will be able to reconcile the imperatives of morality and obedience to his lord? Are we to conclude that Calmeta's jaded vision of courtiership was, after all, the correct one; that the only way to survive in the courts is by relinquishing one's own moral standards?

The text, at this point, can offer no answers, only painful and difficult questions. While we are in no way encouraged to question that Fregoso's initial, 'Carafan' position is the correct one, we are forced to recognize that, in the less than ideal world in which the courtier must operate, to attempt to adhere to such high moral standards may bring about his downfall. The kind of morality which can be conveyed in neat sound-bites of 'precept' will be of little use, it is suggested, in a world in which practice corresponds so woefully little to theory.[39] Where there are no easy answers, an honest moralist should not aim to feed readers with comforting – or even Machiavellianly chilling – 'precetti distinti', but simply to unfold before them a dialogue between conflicting perspectives, to sharpen their sense of the issues involved and open a space for the exercise of their own moral judgment.

The localized tensions which dog Fregoso during his brief dominance of the discussion in Book II call attention to the structurally similar, but far larger-scale tension between his arguments and those expounded by Count Lodovico da Canossa on the previous day. It is a point worth stressing, as it has been insufficiently recognized by critics, that the perspective of the second book of the treatise is subtly but significantly different from that of the first. Canossa's 'formation' of the courtier, in Book I, rests on the reassuring premise that the means to success in the courts is through virtue: that 'grace' is the surest path into the graces of the prince. The effect of Fregoso's contribution, on the other hand, is to insinuate that all is not as it should be in the courts; that rewards are allocated less according to merit than to luck or the whim of the prince, and that the surest means to success may not be so much through 'virtù' as 'ingegno' and 'arte'. If Fregoso finds it so hard to contain the cynical Calmeta, in the passage discussed above, this may be, in part, because his antagonist is doing little more than drawing out to the full the implications of certain tendencies present in his own, far more decorous argument.

Fregoso's brief, in the second book, is to discuss how the courtier should put into action all the numerous qualities and talents Canossa has endowed him with in the first.[40] There is no obvious reason why Fregoso's contribution should do anything but smoothly complement his predecessor's and, indeed, he does all he can, at the start of his speech, to represent what he has to say as no more than an appendix to Canossa's dissertation of the previous night.[41] We should not be fooled by this modesty, however, especially when Fregoso's own analysis of courtly behaviour offers a clue for its deconstruction. When disguising himself at Carnival, Fregoso advises, the courtier should not aim at a strictly accurate imitation, but should leave enough clue to enable his audience to guess at his true identity and to revel in the flatteringly paradoxical relationship between the reality and the mask. Thus, a young man may disguise himself as an old man, a noble as a shepherd in rags. But they should be careful to include some detail calculated to give the game away – the latter, perhaps, by riding a horse which would cost a shepherd his life-savings, the former by letting his youthful physique and bearing give the lie to his grey beard.[42]

Fregoso's 'masking' of his speech as a footnote to Canossa's is similarly disingenuous and it does not take long for the muscle of this thesis to emerge.[43] The point around which his arguments revolve is the need for the courtier to respect the norm of decorum: to calculate his behaviour to accord with the time and the place. This may seem incontestable, even banal, when applied to social accomplishments: as one of Fregoso's listeners contemptuously points out, no one needs to be told not to tell jokes at funerals, or go around dancing the *moresca* in the middle of the street.[44] But the far-reaching, perhaps subversive implications of Fregoso's point becomes clear when – in a splendidly sly exposure of the distance between his perspective and Canossa's – he extends this principle from social skills to the virtues of the soul.

Canossa had identified warfare as the 'principal profession' of the courtier and courage in battle as the virtue most crucial for him to possess.[45] Fregoso concurs with this verdict, referring back explicitly to Canossa's statements, and agrees that, on one level, there is nothing more to be said.[46] However, he adds, in a telling postscript, attention to the rule of decorum could teach the courtier that it would be wise for him to calculate the time and place appropriate to his displays of courage, in order to ensure the maximum return from his investment of virtue.

Pur sotto la nostra regula si potrà ancor intendere, che ritrovandosi il cortegiano nella scaramuzza o fatto d'arme o battaglia di terra o in altre cose tali, dee discretamente procurar di appartarsi dalla moltitudine, e quelle cose segnalate ed ardite che ha da fare, farle con minor compagnia che po, ed al cospetto di tutti i piu nobili ed estimati omini che siano nell'esercito, e massimamente alla presenzia e, se possibil è, inanzi agli occhi proprii del suo re o di quel signore a cui serve; perché in vero è ben conveniente valersi delle cose ben fatte. Ed io estimo, che sì come è male cercar gloria falsa e di quello che non si merita, così sia ancor male defraudar se stesso del debito onore, e non cercarne quella laude, che sola è vero premio delle virtuose fatiche.[47]

The discrepancy between this and Canossa's opinion, in Book I, is so marked that it cannot be anything other than intentional. Fregoso's predecessor had insisted on the need for the courtier to manifest his courage regardless of circumstance: indeed, he had specified that the only men who show the quality of spirit required of the perfect courtier are those who perform acts of courage 'ancor quando pensano di *non esser d'alcuno né veduti, né mirati, né conosciuti*'.[48] What Fregoso is presenting as a gloss on Canossa's teaching on virtue is in fact a full-scale revision. Discretion – in Canossa's sterner judgment, a token of pusillanimity – has become, for Fregoso, something dangerously close to the better part of valour.

The implications of this shift of values is, unsurprisingly, not spelled out in the *Cortegiano*. Fregoso's treatment of the need for flexibility in ethics is as sinuous as the subject demands, and he is quick to backtrack when an interlocutor like Calmeta, in the passage above, incautiously stretches his arguments to their logical conclusions. But, by the end of his contribution, the tendency of his arguments is clear. What, for Canossa, had been intrinsic qualities, rooted in the soul of the courtier, Fregoso, in the course of Book II, gradually but inexorably uproots.

The premise of Canossa's argument, in Book I, had been that virtue brings its due reward, that – as he asserts with a neat etymological legerdemain Fregoso later takes pleasure in exposing – 'chi ha grazia quello è grato'. Fregoso is less optimistic. Social success depends crucially on the perceptions of those around us and human perceptions are notoriously fickle and subject to distortion. It by no means follows that, just because a courtier possesses the qualities Canossa has allotted to him, he will necessarily win the applause and promotion he deserves. Indeed, the contrary may occur:

Ma perché par che la fortuna, come in molte altre cose, così ancor abbia grandissima forza nelle opinioni degli omini, vedesi talor che un gentilomo, per ben condizionato che egli sia e *dotato di molte grazie, sarà poco grato* ad un signore e, come si dice, non gli arà sangue, e questo senza causa alcuna che si possa compreendere [. . .] e da questo nascerà che gli altri sùbito s'accommodaranno alla volontà del signore [. . .] di sorta che, se fosse il più valoroso uomo del mondo, sarà forza che resti impedito e burlato. E per contrario se 'l principe si mostrarà inclinato ad un ignorantissimo, che non sappia né dir né far, saranno spesso i costumi e modi di quello, per sciocchi ed inetti che siano, laudati con le esclamazioni e stupore da ognuno, e parerà che tutta la corte lo ammiri ed osservi . . .'[49]

The implications of this admission are far-reaching. Once it is accepted that there is no automatic link between virtue and its reward, then it becomes possible – and perhaps necessary – to construct an alternative, parallel art of behaviour, addressed specifically to the problem of how to please an audience. 'Oltre al valore', as Fregoso concludes the passage cited above 'voglio che 'l nostro cortegiano . . . s'aiuti ancora con ingegno ed arte'.[50] The way to achieve social success becomes not to improve the intrinsic quality of the product – the self – but rather to learn to package and market it more effectively.

Perhaps the best way of defining what takes place in Book II of the *Cortegiano* is as a *rhetoricization* of ethics. An essential element in classical rhetoric – one increasingly stressed in the Renaissance – was the skill of 'accommodating' one's language and *ethos* to appeal to a particular audience.[51] What Fregoso does, in Book II of the *Cortegiano*, is to apply this rhetorical paradigm beyond speech to realms of human behaviour traditionally governed by ethics. When the courtier is advised to accommodate his discourse to the different audiences he may find himself speaking to, we are still safely within the bounds of classical rhetorical theory. But when he is told to adjust his *behaviour* to his audience – say, to hold back in battle when no-one is watching – this introduces a kind of slippage, a destabilization of ethics which, as is plain from the dispute discussed above, between Fregoso and Calmeta, could have dangerous results.

An accusation frequently levelled at rhetoric, from Plato onwards, has been that of providing equally powerful support for the false and the true. If rhetoric – at least in its sophistic and Aristotelian guise – is a morally neutral art of discourse,[52] so Fregoso's 'rhetoricized ethics' comes dangerously close to providing a morally neutral science of human behaviour, in which virtue is effectively replaced by the ability to simulate virtue. It never quite comes to this, of course: Fregoso continues to insist, like his predecessor, that the courtier should actually *be* virtuous, as well as appearing so. But his emphasis on techniques of manipulating appearances is such that, without compromising himself, he provides all the necessary hints for one less scrupulous than himself – a Machiavelli, or a Iago – to develop into a fully-fledged art of simulation.[53]

It would be impossible, in the present context, to follow Fregoso's argument in Book II through all its intricately dramatized sequence of feelers and feints and retractions. The point it is essential to stress here is that Fregoso's contribution, replying at a discreet distance to Canossa's, fulfils precisely the same function within the macrostructure of the *Cortegiano*, as the more telling and least manageable interjections of the minor speakers have in the microstructure of individual discussions. Fregoso's implicit critique of Canossa casts a veil of doubt over his predecessor's arguments, without definitively invalidating or superseding them. The two perspectives on behaviour embodied by Canossa and Fregoso are juxtaposed, unreconciled: in dialogue. It is only outside the text, in the mind of the reader, that a possible synthesis can be found.

On the most crucial issue raised in Book II – the courtier's moral status and his relations with the prince – the internal jury of the *Cortegiano* remains out. The dialectic between Canossa's 'ethical' and Federico Fregoso's 'rhetorical' standpoint is further complicated later, in Book IV of the dialogue, when Ottaviano Fregoso intervenes with an ambitious and uncompromising bid to elevate the courtier from the primarily ornamental function he is given in the first three books to a far more exalted status as moral and political adviser to his prince.[54] And Ottaviano's is by no means the last word on the subject: quite apart from the enduring corrosive influence which the arguments of Book II continue to exert, even here, Ottaviano's speech is continually pin-pricked, at a local level, by his own scepticism and that of his listeners. His glorious vision of wise courtiers navigating virtuous princes on a course of prosperity and peace is shadowed by what Lauro Martines has called the 'organizing image' of Book IV: the realistic picture of vain princes and toadying courtiers with which Ottaviano's speech starts.[55] It is an image which all his subsequent eloquence cannot entirely exorcize and, however much Ottaviano's stirring vision may appeal to our idealism, we are never quite allowed to forget the gap between reality and the ideal.

The only means of concluding what could otherwise be an endless, inconclusive see-sawing between the ideal and reality is to strip the courtier, Marsyas-like, from his political shell and project him into the safe, hermetic capsule of Neoplatonic ascent. But, for all the eloquence of Bembo's closing hymn of spiritual love, the dynamics of the *Cortegiano* are not an unfailing crescendo. The supremely subtle episode, at the end of Bembo's speech, when Emilia Pio plucks gently at his robe to return him to earth reminds us that neither his sublime vision of man's spiritual potential, nor Ottaviano Fregoso's celebration of good government can definitely erase the earlier and more earth-bound discussions of the realities of court life. At the end of the *Cortegiano*, we are deliberately left in suspense, as the perpetually simmering dispute on women rekindles and the courtiers retire with the promise of further discussions to come.

Nothing is resolved. The moment of sublime, irreducible harmony which descends on the company with the discovery of the dawn outside is destined to be as momentary and irrecoverable as the inspiration which prompts the speech of Bembo's which precedes it, as any intuition of wholeness or resolution within the human sphere.

In a brilliant discussion of the *fortuna* of Castiglione's image of the courtier in the Renaissance, Sydney Anglo calls attention to the paradoxical nature of the *Cortegiano*'s reception. How is it possible that a book which could win the approval of moralists like Roger Ascham, usually so quick to condemn the 'cunning, new and diverse shifts' of Italian manners, could also have inspired an increasingly cynical literature of manipulation and deceit, in which morality is reduced to a matter of pure expedience?[56] The *Cortegiano* has provoked, and continues to provoke, bewilderingly different reactions in its readers: a tribute to that 'caution' the lack of which its author derided in Valdés. Are we to identify Castiglione's true voice in his main speakers' earnest syntheses of classical and humanist thought, or in the cynical one-liners which occasionally interrupt them?

The problem is more apparent than real, caused by deficiencies in reading rather than ambiguities of the text. Castiglione's discussion of moral issues is not wavering, or dishonest, or disingenuous: he is as much himself when he is breathing new life into the ideals of classical antiquity as when he is puncturing the same ideals with a weary allusion to their lack of correspondence to practice. Distilled out of their matrix in dialogue, neither side of the argument does justice to the complexities of his thought. The solution is to stop waiting for the 'real Castiglione' to stand up, and to concentrate instead on developing a reading as flexible as the thought unfolded in the text.

When we return, after reading the *Cortegiano*, to the 'poco di escusazione' which prefaces it, Castiglione's motives for choosing the dialogue form for his argument become clear. The distinction between the 'certo ordine di precetti' he rejects and the dialogue form he embraces is that identified by Francis Bacon, between a 'magistral' mode of transmission, which presents a set of conclusions in a form which demands a simple consensus, and an 'initiative' mode which, by laying bare the stages by which those conclusions were reached, offers the reader a 'thread' on which to spin an original network of knowledge.[57]

Instances of this kind of genuinely dialogical use of the dialogue were, however, comparatively rare in the Cinquecento in Italy. Among Castiglione's numerous imitators, few showed any consciousness of or sympathy for the complexities of his heroic attempt to translate conversation into print. In many later dialogues, while the shell of a conversational structure remains, what it conveys is an unashamedly monological discourse. It is fair to say that, if the dialogue remained in currency, it owed its survival less to its argumentational merits than to its skills in public relations: less to the deep than the surface lessons of Castiglione's practice.

The differences in the use of the dialogue in Castiglione and, say, Galeazzo Florimonte or Battista Guarini can obviously be explained, to a great extent, by differences in temperament and talent. But this is not the whole story: these writers' very different practice of the genre betrays differences in their conception of its function which are not purely idiosyncratic. A reading of dialogue produced in the first and second halves of the Cinquecento reveals a marked progression from 'dialogical' to monological, magisterial forms. This gradual descent of the dialogue into monologue – its chronology, its symptoms, its causes – forms the subject of the second part of this study of the genre.

6   The changing form of the Italian Renaissance dialogue

> ... qui princeps est sermonis ... is nostram de rebus putatur aperire sententiam
>
> Carlo Sigonio, *De dialogo liber* (1562)[1]

'It will be assumed that whoever is the main speaker in the dialogue will be expressing the views of the author.' This statement of Sigonio's, with its calm assumption that every dialogue will be ruled by a *princeps*, is a good indication of how far the dialogue of the later sixteenth century had travelled since the relatively 'democratic' model of Castiglione's day. The chapters which follow will be an attempt to account for this change, in the light of contemporary developments in cultural politics and intellectual practice.

Before embarking on this more specific task, however, it may be useful first to trace a brief history of the dialogue form in the Italian Cinquecento. That such a history is needed cannot be in doubt. Despite a recent revival of critical interest in the theory and practice of the Cinquecento dialogue, there has been no very convincing attempt, to date, to trace the history of the genre throughout the century. Trajectories have been tentatively proposed, changes and turning-points identified; but no single study so far has taken account of a sufficiently broad and representative range of examples of the genre to produce much more than summary and partial conclusions.[2]

What follows is by no means intended as an attempt at a comprehensive survey of Italian Cinquecento dialogue production. What concerns me here is a specific question – the level of authorial detachment in the dialogue – and other characteristics of the dialogue will be mentioned only in passing. It is hoped, however, that, the present chapter will at least help to lay the foundations for a future and more exhaustive study of the way in which the dialogue evolved.

Any attempt to trace the development of the Cinquecento dialogue must start in the previous century, with the humanist revival of the classical genre. The Italian Quattrocento dialogue has been better served by critics than the dialogue of the following century and the paragraphs which follow will do no more than to touch on those aspects of fifteenth-century dialogue production which may help to illuminate, by contrast, later developments in the genre.[3] No attempt will be made at completeness: in a period characterized by its formal exuberant experimentation, the comments here refer uniquely to the Ciceronian, documentary variant of the genre.[4]

The driving force behind the Quattrocento dialogue is the humanist faith in discussion as a means of access to the truth. For all their considerable differences, dialogues like Leonardo Bruni's *Dialogi ad Petrum Paulum Histrum* (1401–6), Poggio Bracciolini's *De avaritia* (1428) and Lorenzo Valla's *De vero falsoque bono* (1431–41) all express this shared faith in the possibility of reaching truth – a human and collective truth – by means of disputation.[5] Within the fictional exchange of the dialogue, rhetorical discussion is used as an instrument in the search for truth on moral issues and, outside this fiction, the dialogue itself is conceived of as a *provocatio*, spurring the learned reader on to join the continuing quest.[6]

The characteristic form of the humanist dialogue, especially that of the first half of the century, is the Ciceronian one of a debate between two or more sharply opposed positions.[7] This is not to say that all Quattrocento dialogues are truly 'dialogical' in character or that they limit themselves to 'provoking' their readers, without attempting to guide them. As David Marsh has observed, the humanist dialogue, unlike its Ciceronian models, often concludes with a scene of reconciliation: 'a concensus confirmed by the opinions of great men who agree concerning the truth'.[8] Though they tend to portray dissent, often in a lively and polemical form, humanist dialogues often betray the stamp of their author's own moral stance and, to this extent, the ethos of the interlocutors, however vividly realized, is in some sense subsidiary to the argument.[9]

For all its dialectical structure, there is, then, a tendency towards closure and 'monologue' in the humanist dialogue. There is even evidence that some writers conceived of the dialogue as having a principally expository function, dismissing its more grandiose claim to be a means of discovering new truths.[10] It is important to note, however, that, even where it does not evince a 'dialogical conception of truth', the humanist dialogue *does* express a 'dialogical conception of the cognitive process'.[11] This sense of the acquisition of knowledge as a collective enterprise is the life-blood of the Quattrocento dialogue, and the feature which most clearly differentiates even the most 'monological' productions of the age from the far more uncompromisingly monological forms which would succeed them in the following century.

Another distinguishing feature of the Quattrocento dialogue is, of course, its erudite character. Written in Latin, humanist dialogues are addressed to a learned audience: a factor which clearly differentiates them from the subsequent vernacular tradition of moral dialogue and which should be taken into account when considering many of their characteristics, from the adventurousness of their arguments,[12] to the sophistication of their tone and the exalted nature of their themes. The Ciceronian dialogue is used in this period, indeed, almost exclusively for the discussion of broad moral issues, suited to a treatment by argument *in utramque partem*, and not, as it would later be, for the exegesis of a particular art.[13] It is only in the Cinquecento, when the dialogue began to address an audience of 'idioti', that the Cicero of the *Partitiones oratoriae* would become a model on a par with the Cicero of the *De natura deorum*.

The most significant changes in the use of the dialogue between the fifteenth and sixteenth centuries result, it may be suggested, from the vast extension of the reading public with the advent of print. The new audience for vernacular literature, eager to take possession of the fruits of classical learning, but impatient of erudition, tended to demand, on the one hand, more supple and colloquial, more self-consciously *contemporary* forms of dialogue and, on the other, a dialogue slanted towards information, rather than philosophical enquiry. As the century wore on, with the absorption of vernacular, and particularly Boccaccian, elements into the genre, the Italian dialogue began to lose its classical profile, and to gain a new and distinctive physiognomy of its own.[14] At the same time, the form which the humanists had reserved, more or less, for debate on controversial moral issues came to be used increasingly, in the course of the Cinquecento, simply as a means of presenting factual information in an easy and palatable way.

This is not to suggest, that *all* vernacular dialogues were simple didactic compendia. A conflicting trend, apparent especially in the formative years of the genre, was towards dialogues which went to the other extreme, relinquishing all centripetal tendencies towards synthesis and resolution, in favour of a disinterested representation of opposing points of view. If the movement of the Quattrocento humanist dialogue is, most characteristically, towards consensus, the dialogue of the first half of the sixteenth century is as likely to end with the participants as convinced as they were at the outset that they are in the right and their opponents in the wrong. This practice of dialogue for dialogue's sake may perhaps be seen as reflecting the 'hedonistic' and anti-humanistic tendencies which have been identified in the literary and rhetorical culture of the period. As the humanist ideal of a union of philosophy and eloquence crumbled,

rhetoric was freed to choreograph its own irresponsible dramas of persuasion, without being tied to the tiresome duty of pursuing the truth.[15]

The two contrasting tendencies identified here may be conveniently
illustrated by a swift review of the dialogues of the *questione della lingua*:
the polemic in which the vernacular dialogue won its spurs as a tool of
debate. Of the dialogues of the 1520s, Pietro Bembo's *Prose* (1525) and
Giangiorgio Trissino's *Castellano* (1529) best represent the didactic and
monological trend. Both dialogues make some pretence, at the outset, of
representing a genuine conflict of opinion: the *Prose* in the decorous form
of a Ciceronian debate; the *Castellano* in a more openly combative
two-man dispute. But it does not take long, in either case, for the reader to
identify the *princeps sermonis*, and much of both dialogues is occupied
with uncontested exposition. The *Prose*, in fact, after the first book,
devolve into a lightly dialogized grammar textbook. The *Castellano*
prolongs its unconvincing agonistic structure until the end, when a prestigious and 'disinterested' witness is wheeled on – the poet Iacopo Sannazaro – to give an enthusiastic endorsement to the arguments of the
princeps.[16]

Trissino's overt glee in victory is unusual for the period. Far more
typical is Claudio Tolomei's more guarded *Cesano, de la toscana lingua* (*c.*
1525–9), which, again, however, is no more than a polemical tract in
disguise. The *Cesano* takes the symposium form, of a series of uninterrupted speeches by prominent spokesmen for all the main sides in the
language debate. This structure gives the speakers a run for their money,
and the dialogue ends with no 'victor'. But the sympathies of the author
are never genuinely in question. The champion of Tuscan, Gabriele
Cesano, is given the last word in the dialogue, and a good fifty pages more
in which to express his views than the most privileged of the previous
speakers. We are left in little doubt that Cesano's speech – to quote an
early reader of the dialogue – is intended as a 'diffinitiva sentenza': as the
author's final word.[17]

For all their stylistic and structural differences, Bembo's, Tolomei's and
Trissino's dialogues represent a more or less unashamedly monological
use of the dialogue form. Two other dialogues, however – one, like these,
from the 1520s, one from rather later – use the dialogue in a far more
'dialogical' and a far more sophisticated way. If the dialogues mentioned
in the previous paragraph are, at least in part, polemical works, Pierio
Valeriano's *Dialogo della volgar lingua* (*c.* 1524–7) and Sperone Speroni's
later *Dialogo delle lingue* (1542) are better characterized as metapolemic.
Both works employ the device of interlocking dialogues-within-dialogues
to contextualize the views of the various participants in the debate on
language and to examine the sectoral interests which underlie their theo-

retical stances. Neither work attempts to promote a univocal solution to
the problem at hand: indeed, Valeriano's *Dialogo* ends on a note of
calculated irresolution.[18] Rather, by showing the range of uses to which
language is put, they insinuate the suggestion that different languages will
be needed for different purposes, and that the criterion which should
prevail in deciding on which version of Italian should be used in a given
circumstance should be functionalism, rather than some dubiously absolute hierarchy of merit.[19]

Speroni's *Dialogo delle lingue* forms part of an extraordinary volume of
dialogues, which combine a poetics of 'comic' representation, which we
would normally associate with the Lucianic–Erasmian tradition in dialogue, with a cast of characters and a choice of themes typical of the more
sober, Ciceronian dialogue.[20] Speroni's dialogues are in many ways as
difficult to place as the writer who produced them, and it would certainly
be misleading to cite them as typical of any phase of dialogue production.[21] It may not be too rash to suggest, however, that the *Dialoghi*
can be seen as the high point of an important, if not universal, trend
towards authorial 'self-annihilation', in the *dialogistica* of the first four
decades or so of the sixteenth century. Obviously, it can be dangerous to
generalize in this way, and it would be unwise to underestimate the very
considerable differences of culture, background, convictions and intellectual practice which separate Speroni from, say, Castiglione. But,
beneath these differences, there is something in common: some shared
fund of epistemological wariness, which distinguishes their work from
that of both the humanist thinkers who preceded them, and – more
obviously – from the less speculative, more dogmatic writers who followed. It does not come entirely as a surprise to discover that Speroni was
an attentive reader of the *Cortegiano*, or that what interested him in
particular were, apparently, those passages of metadialogic which most
clearly reveal Castiglione's commitment to a dialectical and probabilistic
conception of the truth.[22]

A natural dividing-line in the history of the dialogue – as in that of most
sixteenth-century literary genres – falls around the sixth decade of the
century, in the period of the Council of Trent. The reasons for this have
already been examined, in part, in chapter 3, and the chapters which
follow will offer a more detailed analysis of the factors affecting dialogue
production in this period. The present chapter seeks to do no more than
to register the changes which took place in this period, without attempting
to account for them in more than a summary way.

It has already been noted that, besides the 'dialogical' tendency of
which Speroni is the most self-conscious representative, the early years of

the Cinquecento in Italy also saw the development of strictly didactic and 'monological' forms of the genre. Dialogues like Trissino's *Castellano*, or the second and third books of Bembo's *Prose*, mark the beginning of a development which would prove more enduring than the early Cinquecento's flamboyant, but short-lived, flirtation with 'comic' and dramatic forms. Few writers were as forthright in their rejection of the dialogue's dialectical vocation as Alessandro Citolini, who announces flatly in the preface to his *La tipocosmia* (1561), that 'per lever . . . ogni impedimento del dialogo, io do ad un solo tutto il carico de 'l ragionamento'.[23] But what Citolini states bluntly as a principle, many writers, rather more discreetly, adopted in their practice. By the time Lodovico Castelvetro wrote his disparaging account of the genre in his *Poetico* (1570), a substantial body of works had been produced which correspond to his scathing description of dialogues which have one interlocutor 'domandare, senza fare opposizione o contradire, accioché il rispondente scopra simplicemente l'opinione sua, o doni alcuni insegnamenti di scienza o d'arte'.[24]

Castelvetro's criticism of such dialogues as showing 'vanità' on the part of their authors alerts us to the fact that this radical change in the use of the dialogue did not occur without opposition. Especially where the form of a dialogue was used to give an air of spurious objectivity to a transparently slanted discussion of some controversial issue, the docility of the subordinate speakers was frequently the subject of criticism. Francesco Visdomini remarks on the 'inaudita pazienza' of a speaker in Scipione Bargagli's *Turamino* (1602), who, indeed, scarcely ventures a word in the dialogue, apart from the odd sally of applause.[25] Benedetto Varchi – himself one of the worst offenders in this practice – ironizes in his *Ercolano* (1570) on a contemporary's description, in a dialogue, of an interlocutor who 'da prima molto scredente . . . era poi più dolce, che la sapa, e non solo credeva, ma approvava alle due parole tutto quello, che gli era detto'.[26] When Tasso, in his *Dell'arte del dialogo* (1585), denounces the laziness of modern writers who allow their dialogues to lapse into effective monologue,[27] he is voicing a concern that he was not alone to feel.

It is noteworthy, however, that Tasso's proposed corrective to this abuse is not a more truly open and 'dialogical' dialogue, but simply a more artful and challenging variant of the didactic manner, in which, as in Plato, it is the teacher – 'quel ch'insegna' – who asks the questions and his pupil – 'colui ch'impara' – who provides the much-prompted responses.[28] Tasso's phraseology here is suggestive. Perhaps the principal difference between the dialogues of the first half of the Cinquecento and the second is this: the expectation that a dialogue will contain a speaker who teaches and a speaker who accepts to be taught. Criticisms of authorial 'vanità', like those cited above, do not constitute a serious challenge to this new definition of roles within the dialogue. Though it may still be criticized by those with a vested interest in the *questione* of a dialogue, the practice of having a 'Lattanzio' – or even oneself in person – to put one's views across is no longer a flaw which may be reproached on formal grounds.[29]

The dialogue theory which began to emerge in the second half of the Cinquecento provides evidence of this newly didactic conception of the genre. As we have seen, for a critic like Carlo Sigonio, it is legitimate and even necessary that one interlocutor should be accredited as spokesman for the author.[30] Orazio Toscanella asserts, still more baldly, that 'la persona, che sostiene la materia principale del Dialogo, deve esser più grave, più dotta, e più perita delle altre persone introdotte',[31] while Alessandro Piccolomini speaks approvingly of dialogues in which one or more speakers dominate the conversation 'come principali et quasi maestri degli altri'.[32]

The most systematic development of the 'Sigonian' poetics of the dialogue is to be found in Giambattista Manso's *Trattato del dialogo* (1628). Manso's basic division between the various 'favellatori' of a dialogue is between the *princeps* – 'colui ch'insegna' – and the others – 'coloro che apprendono'.[33] The 'offices' of these speakers are understood as fixed and absolute: indeed, Manso explicitly states that 'colui ch'una volta s'è della persona di maestro investito non dee nello stesso Dialogo discepolo divenire'.[34] So fundamental are these 'uffici' that they are assumed into the statutes of 'decorum', and Manso specifies that besides a conventional *ethopoiìa* – the representation of the speakers' characters – an author must also strive always to respect 'il decoro [delle persone] verso gli offici assegnati loro nella disputatione'.[35]

In practice, the 'uffici' in a late Cinquecento dialogue tend to be allotted, more and more strictly, according to the criterion of age. One of Castiglione's chief innovations to the Ciceronian model of dialogue had been his elimination of any firm divide between older and younger speakers.[36] In later dialogues, however, this division reappeared and the most common pattern for the *cornice* of dialogues from the 1560s onwards became one where hushed young 'discepoli' sit at the feet of venerable 'maestri'.[37] Angry young men like Castiglione's Gaspare Pallavicino are nowhere to be found, except, ironically enough, – though, it must be admitted, in a somewhat muted guise – in the pages of the last dialogues of the octogenarian Sperone Speroni.[38]

It is in the context of this shift towards more authoritative and monological forms of dialogue that we should seek to understand a further, significant development in the genre: the growing interest, in the course of the century, in Platonic models of dialogue. The first signs of a new interest in Platonic dialogue are apparent from around the mid-century: most notably, in the works of the Venetian neo-Platonist, Francesco Patrizi,[39] but also in lesser writers, like Scipione Ammirato, who describes himself in a dialogue of 1562, as 'con la lezzion platonica . . . tutto dato ne' dialoghi'.[40] Despite the evangelism of its enthusiasts, Platonic structural models never came to oust the more established dialogue forms: there is some truth – as well as a good dose of self-congratulation – in Tasso's assertion, in 1585, that the majority of writers of dialogues in the vernacular refused to rise to the formal challenge of Socratic questioning and persisted in preferring lazier and 'less artful' Ciceronian models.[41] Nevertheless, even if the influence of the Platonic dialogue never filtered much beyond the most sophisticated fringe of dialogue production, it did provide a necessary injection of new energies into the flagging tradition of the post-humanistic vernacular dialogue, and, in the hands of Tasso and Patrizi, in particular, it produced some impressive results.

In a culture which was turning, increasingly, towards 'monological' modes of argumentation, Plato supplied a stylishly oblique but still markedly hierarchical model for the dialogue, more in keeping with the spirit of the times than a Ciceronian debate between equals.[42] Of course, in fact, Plato's dialogues are anything but straightforwardly 'monological', and sixteenth-century commentators could not but acknowledge this fact. For the most part, however, the tendency was to minimize their dialogical qualities: for Patrizi, for example, the apparent failure of many Platonic dialogues to reach a univocal conclusion is simply a device intended to restrict his teaching to a chosen few.[43] It is interesting to note that, with the significant exception of Sperone Speroni, all late-sixteenth- and seventeenth-century commentators who consider the role of Socrates in Plato's dialogue tend to interpret him, unproblematically, as a spokesman for the author.[44]

The assumption which underlies the theory and practice of the dialogue from the *De dialogo* onwards is that the dialogue is essentially a magisterial, not an initiative genre.[45] With the collapse of humanist ideals, discussion is no longer conceived of as a means for exploring the truth, and written dialogue has relinquished its corresponding role as a *provocatio*. Truth now appears as an absolute, hallowed by authority and defined by political interest: a commodity to be meted out by an omniscient *princeps sermonis*. Little remains, in the dialogues of the late Cinquecento, of the ideals which had inspired the revival of the genre in the previous century – as little as remains of the spirit of Ciceronian argument *in utramque partem* in the Jesuits' *Ratio studiorum*, where it is advised that students practising the 'utile essercizio del disputare' should be supervised by 'qualcuno, il quale diriga gli argomentanti, e dalla disputa rileva e dichiari la dottrina che deve tenersi'.[46]

With the loss of its argumentational *raison d'être*, the Ciceronian dialogue was doomed. Although didactic forms of the genre survived well into the seventeenth century, their place in the hierarchy of expository genres was an increasingly marginal one.[47] When the dialogue *did* reappear, in the Settecento, as a genuine tool of speculation and enquiry, it sprang from the newly grafted French Lucianic tradition, rather than from the dead wood of the native Ciceronian stock.[48]

It would be misleading to write off the post-Tridentine dialogue entirely: Tasso's dialogues and, even later, Galileo's *Dialogo sui massimi sistemi* are enough to prove that there was life in the genre yet. Nevertheless, scanning many of the dialogues written in this period, the reader is forced to concur with seventeenth-century critics who viewed the form as otiose, productive only of tiresome *longueurs*.[49] Where there is no epistemological justification for the use of the dialogue, the charms of its fiction soon fade and, where the wild card of the characters' *ethos* is replaced by the loaded dice of 'official' roles, the element of suspense so essential to the genre is irrevocably lost. What is surprising, in these circumstances, is not that the dialogue fell out of favour, but rather that it succeeded in surviving as long as it did. Its persistence is a testimony to the importance of the role it played in literary 'public relations', which clearly outweighed the disadvantages of its argumentational redundancy.

I have spoken of a 'survival' of the humanist dialogue into post-humanist culture. In fact, however, in order to survive, the dialogue was forced to adapt to such a degree that it would almost make sense to describe it as a wholly new genre. While preserving the outward forms of a civil conversation, the dialogue of the late Cinquecento assimilated itself as far as possible to the patterns of monological discourse. Some manifestations of this tendency have already been alluded to – the ever stricter allocation of 'uffici' in a dialogue, for example, or the ever more frequent presence of a pseudo-authorial *princeps sermonis*. Others will require a more detailed exposition, most notably the move towards 'ordered' structures and 'methodical' forms of argument.

In the final two chapters of this study, I shall examine more systematically the process by which the dialogue was gradually transformed from within. First, however, it will be necessary to establish in rather more detail the reasons why this metamorphosis took place. The most obvious factor, already dealt with in part, is the radical reorientation of Italian culture which took place with the Counter-Reformation. The implications of this change for the practice of dialogue were massive and far-reaching, and they merit closer examination than I have been able to give them here.

7   The theory and practice of the dialogue in Counter-Reformation Italy

> ... infinita sendo la turba delle bugie, le quali adombrano le scienzie, sempre da esse con ogni cura, come da peste contagiosa, si dee guardar lo 'ntelletto
>
> Sperone Speroni, *Apologia dei dialoghi, parte terza* (1571)[1]

Among the works on the poetics of dialogue which began to emerge after 1560, the only one which departs from purely formal considerations, and makes a serious attempt to deal with the cultural politics of the genre, is Sperone Speroni's *Apologia dei dialoghi* (1574–5). The political focus of the *Apologia* was partly determined by the circumstances which led to its composition: the traumatic and ludicrous fact of Speroni's dialogues being denounced to the Inquisition, and the author's subsequent, justly indignant, endeavours to clear his name.[2] Even the most superficial reading of the resulting work, however, should be enough to convince us that its apologetic format is little more than a pretext for a work which aspires to synthesize the reflections of a lifetime. At the same time one of the century's most distinguished writers of dialogue and one of its most incisive and original thinkers on the arts of discourse, Speroni was uniquely qualified to analyse the complex phenomenon of communication by dialogue. In the *Apologia*, combining a practitioner's sensitivity to poetics with a cultural historian's broad diachronic perspective, he provides the best guide we have to the religious and political factors which determined the trajectory of the dialogue in late-Cinquecento Italy.

The originality and importance of Speroni's contribution to dialogue theory have not always been recognized. In the past, the *Apologia* has tended to be neglected or undervalued by critics, who have concentrated instead on the more orthodox theories of Sigonio and Tasso. More recently, Mario Pozzi's excellent 1978 edition of the *Prima parte* of the *Apologia* has done much to stimulate interest in what is now recognized as 'the most compellingly modern' of all Renaissance writings on dialogue.[3] In some respects, however, this edition has finished up by doing Speroni a disservice, since, by privileging a single strand – and, precisely, the most 'modern' – in a complex and sinuous argument, it has led to a tendency to misrepresent the significance of the whole.[4]

The structural complexities of the *Apologia* may go some way to explain why this work was long neglected by critics. Letters written at the time of its composition and first discreet circulation suggest that Speroni regarded his treatise as a rhetorical *tour de force* and that the effect of the work – to leave the reader somewhat dizzied and unsure of his intent – is a calculated factor in the construction of his argument.[5] In the first and second parts, Speroni defends his dialogues from the standpoint of a literary critic, referring to the traditional privilege of rhetoric to hold truth conditions in abeyance and outlining a poetics of the dialogue as 'gioco'. At the beginning of the *Terza parte*, assailed by conscience, he renounces this self-deludingly neutral line of reasoning and embarks on a palinode clearly inspired by contemporary political literary theory. From this perspective, the writer of dialogue is accountable not merely to art but to his duties as a citizen, and political interest replaces poetics as the ultimate arbiter of his practice. The *Quarta parte* opens with a further retraction, this time addressed not to the writer's conscience but to God, in which Speroni confesses his error in defining his 'guilt' in purely secular terms. In an ingenious refutation of his arguments in the *Terza parte*, Speroni argues here that no civil regime has the moral competence to censor any literary work and that the right of judgment must ultimately rest with God and his ministers on earth.[6] What starts as a bold defence of artistic freedom ends, in effect, as a paean to the repressive cultural policy which the Church, at the time of his writing, was beginning to put into effect.[7]

The question of the sincerity of this volte-face goes beyond the scope of my argument and, in any case, it is one which would be near impossible to resolve.[8] What is important for my purpose here is that, in the first and second halves of the *Apologia*, Speroni provides us with two contrasting conceptions of the function of the literary dialogue, which, translated into practice, result in two quite distinct species of the genre. The first, based on Speroni's analysis of his own dialogues of the 1530s and 40s, corresponds to what I have been calling the 'dialogical' or 'open' dialogue. The second, sketched in more speculatively, though illustrated by an example, is far closer to the model of 'monological', 'closed' dialogue which, at the time when Speroni was writing the *Apologia*, was asserting itself with such vigour.

One reason why a reader might be tempted to doubt the sincerity of Speroni's final retraction in the *Quarta parte* is the sheer verve with which his original defence of his dialogues is conducted, in the *Parte prima*. The starting-point for Speroni's exploration of the poetics of dialogue is provided by his 'trial' by the Inquisition, which brings into focus some of the most crucial questions facing writers in his age. Was the function of the writer or orator to 'instruct' or to 'delight'? How far could the author of a literary work be held accountable for his message? Where, exactly, should the bounds of artistic freedom be drawn? The 'open' dialogue, with its ostented 'annihilation' of the author, is perfectly calculated as a test-case for these issues.[9] At the same time, however, it is a genre which interests Speroni a great deal in its own right, and he is at pains to assert that his celebration of the dialogue transcends its immediate apologetic function.[10]

Speroni's central premise in the *Prima parte* – the 'punto onde deriva la [sua] difesa come da centro circunferenzia' – is the 'privilege' of exemption from normal truth conditions shared by the parent arts of dialogue: poetry, rhetoric and dialectic.[11] Working from a characteristically anti-humanistic hierarchy of modes of cognition, Speroni asserts that true 'scienzia' is the preserve of demonstrative logic, accessible only by the 'strada utile aristotelica' followed in the schools. The alternative *via* of dialogue is less arduous, but also less profitable, leading to the vineyards and gardens of 'gioco', rather than the sober farmlands of truth.[12] A dialogue may *sound* as though it is saying something, but this appearance of substance is illusory. In fact, the dialogue can provide no more than a beguiling simulacrum of knowledge, as persuasive and as deceptive as a parrot's imitation of speech.[13]

Speroni's identification of dialogue as a 'ritratto di scienza' has important implications for the status of the genre. His immediate point, of course, is that the author is not responsible for the ideas expressed in a dialogue: indeed, he may himself be 'ignorant' of the truth.[14] His duty is merely to dramatize the alternative positions which may be held on a given issue, refraining from any simplistic pre-emptive solution. The sole criterion for judging a dialogue is the degree to which the writer has respected the speakers' decorum: whether their views are true or false is entirely beside the point. 'Messa in silenzio la sola e propria sua voce', the writer of a dialogue leaves the scene empty for the play of its 'varii nomi e costumi' and 'novi e varii ragionamenti'.[15] It is for the reader to judge between them or, better, to transcend them in a new synthesis: the 'contrasto' of the protagonists merely acts as a tinder-box, sending out sparks of truth to be nourished by the 'kindling' of the reader's receiving mind.[16]

Speroni's treatment of the open dialogue contains moments of great insight, as when he hints at the ways in which the verbal and structural tricks of the comic dramatist of action may be translated into the dialogue's drama of argumentation.[17] There are also moments of considerable dignity, as when, in defiance of the Inquisition and the spirit of the age, he argues that the reading public should be accorded the opportunity to exercise its own moral judgment and that 'mai la ignoranzia, che non sa eleggere e rifiutare, non fu bontà'.[18] The brilliance with which he argues the case for the open dialogue should not, however, blind us to the fact that, even in this first part of the *Apologia*, Speroni does allow for the possibility of more 'authoritative' species of dialogue and a more direct, magisterial relationship between the author and his readers.

In a passage which ranks the arts of discourse according to their level of 'certitude', Speroni hints that somewhere between the 'scienzia' generated by logic and the airy 'persuasions' of rhetoric lies the problematic field of dialectical 'opinione', and that this may be tapped by a form of dialogue which is 'non formato a giuoco'.[19] It seems probable that, in defining this 'serious' dialogue, Speroni is thinking of certain of the dialogues of Plato, who is placed in this passage, with Socrates and Xenophon, between Aristotle, on the one hand – the master of all science – and Cicero, on the other – the sophistical trickster *par excellence*.[20] This hypothesis is confirmed by a fragment, *Della imitazione*, written outside the exigencies of an apologetic context, where Speroni goes still further in acknowledging the truth-value of Platonic dialogue. Here, while he continues to class Plato as, for the most part, 'oratore, o al più dialettico', Speroni gives him credit for occasionally transcending his self-imposed limitations, in those passages of his dialogues which use definition and division.[21]

The possibility and precedent do exist, then, for a dialogue which is more than an artful tissue of lies. Besides the obvious question of the type of argumentation employed, Speroni is alive to the subtler means by which a writer can vary the level of his presence in his dialogues, and one of the most perceptive passages in the *Apologia* concerns the different degrees of authorial control in the various different species of dialogue. A familiar, if controversial, division in contemporary dialogue theory was that between dramatic, narrated and 'mixed' dialogues.[22] But, where other theorists were united in speaking of this division as a purely formal one, Speroni is alive to the fact that it signals a real difference in tone; that the level of social decorum thought appropriate in a 'comic' dramatic dialogue is quite different from that which obtains in the more reverent, narrative form. In the dramatic dialogue, the author takes as clear a distance from the characters as the comic dramatist and, Speroni implies, depicts them in a scarcely more flattering light. In the narrated dialogue, on the other hand, the writer is expected to exert a far greater degree of control: having led one's speakers onto the scene 'cortesemente, quasi lor oste', one should report 'quei soli detti ... che gli sia onore il parlarne', censoring out all those which do not live up to this ideal.[23]

Speroni's point here shows great insight into the practice of his contemporaries.[24] But it is also not devoid of theoretical implications, and in this respect his statement that, in the narrated dialogue, imitation of 'le persone' is combined with imitation of 'lo scrittore' is of more than formal interest. The intrusion of the *persona* of the writer into the dialogue disrupts its controlled play of rhetoric more than is immediately apparent. Speroni's glance here at the mechanics of supervision in the dialogue, his allusion to a dialogue in which the writer retains some control, prepare us for the far more drastic forms of control and self-censorship which he will go on to deal with in the third part of the treatise.

Despite a degree of preparation, however, in the first part of the treatise, the *volte-face* of the *Parte terza* still strikes us as complete.[25] Speroni's principal contention here is that art should be subject to political control, whether this takes the form of the discreet self-censorship recommended at the outset or the full-blown state surveillance envisaged by the end. In the *Parte prima*, the norm which governed the construction of the dialogue had been the purely artistic criterion of 'il decoro delle persone'. In the *Parte terza*, this trade decorum, the province of 'l'arte privata',[26] is subordinated to the higher consideration of 'il decoro dello scrittore'. The writer's duty, as a 'costumata e civil persona', is to write nothing which might compromise the interests of public morality. When he betrays this duty in his pursuit of the chimeric demands of his 'arte privata', then the resulting works, for all their technical sheen, will have lost their *raison d'être*. The implications of this argument for the case in question are clear. The writer of the comic dialogue described in the *Parte prima*, annihilating himself in order to mimic the follies of others, is guilty of a form of dilettante cultural anarchy which would be intolerable to any self-respecting regime.[27]

Speroni's arguments here are drawn from the stock of current Aristotelian political literary theory. They reflect a belief which was becoming widespread in the later Cinquecento, that politics, as the 'architectonic' art, was within its rights in controlling the production of all other manual and liberal arts.[28] Whether Speroni held with this belief is a matter of some doubt, though the demolition of these arguments in the *Parte quarta* would seem to suggest his dissent.[29] In any case, what is important for the present argument is not Speroni's own convictions on the matter, but the value of his arguments on the 'decoro dello scrittore' in explaining the developments that the dialogue form had undergone in his age.

Speroni gives few concrete indications, in this part of the *Apologia*, of the form which a dialogue written in accord with citizenly decorum might take. The possibility of a comic dialogue is, of course, eliminated from the outset: indeed, Lucian, the founding father of this disreputable genre, is one of the examples Speroni cites to show the moral degradation which results from a writer's disregarding his duties as a citizen.[30] The responsible writer should write 'tale . . . quale egli è': that is, as Speroni has specified, as a 'civil e costumata persona'.[31] Where the dialogue is concerned, this implies a far closer and more responsible relationship between the writer and his interlocutors than that which had been envisaged in the first part of the *Apologia*. There, the limits of authorial surveillance, even in the narrated dialogue, had extended only to a sifting of 'honourable' and 'dishonourable' utterances. Here, as Speroni acknowledges in a critique of his juvenile practice, self-censorship should start at an earlier stage, in the choice of the *dramatis personae*. 'Doveva io in scrivendo', he admits, 'non torcer gli occhi e la lingua dalle mie proprie condizioni, ma formare anzi alla mia sembianza l'altrui persona ne' miei dialogi, cioè correggerle ed ammonirle.'[32]

The cast of the future dialogue will be 'civili e costumati', appropriate spokesmen for their author and role models for the reader. We are close here to the sort of relations between writer, audience and interlocutors which we find in the monological dialogue and we may presume that this was the form of the genre which Speroni is condoning here. A letter of the time, which hints at the character of the projected expurgated version of the *Dialoghi* gives some indication of the limited place that he envisaged in the new 'decorous' dialogue for argument *in utramque partem*. Criticising the *Dialogo dell'usura* – with the *Della discordia* the most 'paradoxical' of his dialogues – Speroni notes in his letter that he erred in not refuting the 'sophistries' of his eponymous heroine. This might have been done in two ways: either by giving Ruzante's silent friend a more active, corrective role or by 'closing' the dialectic of the dialogue down by having its hero elect, at the end, on natural, 'civil' and 'Christian' grounds, rather to die in poverty than to become rich by culpable means.[33]

One means, then, Speroni suggests, by which a writer may preserve his own decorum while retaining at least the semblance of dissent within his dialogues is by concluding a lively discussion between opposing parties with a final, unequivocal, quasi-authorial intervention. This is a solution which would prove increasingly common as the Cinquecento wore on, especially in dialogues on controversial subjects.[34] It is also, interestingly, the model of the narrated dialogue on sophism with which Speroni concludes the *Parte terza*, which we are surely justified in seeing as an example – if, perhaps, a rather ironic one – of the model of dialogue he is recommending in this section of the treatise.

The content of this dialogue – a characteristically subtle and ambivalent work – is, unfortunately, outside the scope of the present argument.[35] What is of interest here is that the narrated dialogue of the *Terza parte* is formally unimpeachable as an example of the new dialogue Speroni has been recommending. Where characters and setting are concerned, it is incomparably graver, more 'civile' and 'costumata' than those of early dialogues like the rather bohemian *Dialogo d'amore*.[36] Taking literally his own advice that the writer of dialogues should form his speakers in his own image, Speroni has placed himself in the dialogue, along with a group of distinguished scholars and churchmen, headed by a cardinal and dominated by an intimate of St Carlo Borromeo. The discussion on sophism is permitted in this context as a carnival diversion – 'anche i sofisti son tutti maschere'[37] – but we are made aware that for these speakers this is a brief respite from more elevated pursuits. The conversation is terminated by Cardinal Marcantonio da Mula, who points out that, since they are now near the end of the period of Carnival, having passed the evening in decorously indecorous 'comic' discourse, 'ragion vuole che noi in guisa la terminiamo, che senta alquanto della quaresima'.[38] This statement, which cues in a speech on the 'sophistry' of all secular science, is a fitting epitaph for the open dialogue which Speroni had defended with such vigour. The carnival of dialogue, he perceived, was over, its mask of sophism put into storage and the careless idol of 'gioco', under whose aegis it had held its revels, had been ousted by the lenten face of 'utile' and truth.[39]

How intentionally we cannot be sure, the third and fourth parts of the *Apologia dei dialoghi* give us a shrewd indication of the path that the dialogue was to travel. Further, in his distinction here between artistic and political decorum, Speroni supplies us with a useful instrument for charting its progress on this path. The tradition of the open dialogue, he suggests, was set on a collision course with secular and religious authority. Some form of censorship was inevitable, whether voluntary or imposed, and, if writers wished to avoid the institutionalized surveillance of the Inquisition, they would do well to observe the rules of self-censorship laid down in his *Terza parte*.

The issues raised by Speroni were not developed with equal lucidity by other Cinquecento writers on the dialogue, though they do find some echo in Tasso's defence of his *Nifo overo del piacere onesto*. The position expressed here on authorial accountability in the dialogue is something of a compromise, one characteristic both of Tasso's own thought and the spirit of his age. As far as the 'occasione' of the dialogue – its setting and characters – is concerned, Tasso is keen to assert the writer's freedom

from the constraints of precise historical accuracy.[40] Where the 'ragioni',
the message of the dialogue are involved, however, he is prepared to admit
a far higher degree of accountability than the Speroni of the first part of
the *Apologia*. Tasso shows himself aware of the possibility of defending
his dialogue, as Speroni did his, as pure 'gioco'. But he rejects it at once,
defining the *Nifo* as a 'ragionamento di cose gravi': a serious work which
pretends to making a serious statement on the world.[41] Tasso's dialogues,
far from being mere 'ritratti', simulacra of 'scienzia', can lay claim to
providing a dose of the real thing: indeed, in a formula closer in spirit to
Speroni's third than his first part, Tasso flatters himself that 'ne' miei
Dialoghi la verità ci abbia tanta parte, quanto basta per non escludere
ogni convenevolezza de' ragionatori'.[42] This attitude is reflected
throughout the argument of the *Risposta*, much of which is taken up with
a defence of the principal speakers' 'ragioni', which is plainly intended to
bring out – beneath surface adjustments of *ethos* – the underlying coinci-
dence of these imitated 'ragioni' with Tasso's views on the subject and
with what is 'true in absolute terms'.[43]

The *Risposta*, however, merely sketches out Tasso's position on
authorial accountability, without pursuing its epistemological and formal
implications. It was only in the Seicento, after the trial of Galileo had
brought the issue of accountability dramatically into focus, that the Jesuit
critic and historian, Sforza Pallavicino – like Speroni and Tasso, himself a
writer of dialogues – would give the problems raised half a century earlier
the attention they deserved.[44] Though Galileo is never mentioned by
name, his presence haunts Pallavicino's whole discussion of the genre,
and perhaps the best way to interpret the section on dialogue in the
latter's *Trattato dello stile e del dialogo* (1662) is as an attempt to lay the
scandalous spectre of the *Dialogo sui massimi sistemi* to rest.[45]

This hidden curriculum entails a focus on the *function* of the dialogue,
which makes the *Trattato* particularly valuable for the purposes of the
present argument. More systematic than Speroni, Pallavicino provides us
with a far clearer and more exhaustive typology of the ways in which the
dialogue may be used to convey or conceal its author's views. The crucial
passage for this distinction is chapter XXXV of the treatise, in which
Pallavicino confronts the claim that the dialogue is fatally flawed as a
teaching instrument by its wilful 'oscurità' and, in particular, by its
avoidance of conclusions.[46] Anxious that all dialogues should not be
tarred by the same brush, Pallavicino answers this criticism by identifying
as a sub-species of the genre those dialogues which 'lasciano dubbioso chi
legge, a qual parere l'Autore inclini'.[47]

There are various reasons, he suggests, apart from technical ineptitude,
which might prompt a writer to adopt this oblique form of the dialogue.

Like Cicero in the *De natura deorum*, he may genuinely want to explore, without conclusion, 'quanto negli Atti della natura e dell'intelletto si registra in favore d'amendue l'opinioni'.[48] On the other hand, like Plato in some of his earlier dialogues, he may be using the dialogue to jolt complacent readers out of slack habits and facile assumptions and to arouse in them 'l'avidità di speculare con sottigliezza'.[49] In the first case, the dialogue dramatizes the impossibility of conclusion. In the second, a substantive conclusion is of no concern to author or reader: what matters is the lesson in method enshrined in his eristic.

Pallavicino acknowledges that, measured by the strict criterion of didactic efficiency, both these 'manners' of dialogue are in some way 'diffettuose'.[50] He is sensitive enough to recognize that, as Speroni had argued in the first part of the *Apologia*, the type of active reading demanded by the open dialogue is itself an intellectually formative experience. But the scope and epistemological resonance of this observation in Speroni is severely reduced in the more clear-cut, less speculative atmosphere of the *Trattato*. The choice between, in Bacon's terms, magistral and initiative forms of argumentation has nothing to do with any theoretical stance on the limitations of human knowledge. It is presented, quite simply, as a problem of taste: of whether the reader prefers to take on the active role of an 'Arbitro' or to remain in the more comfortable and less demanding position of a 'Scolare'.

While he shows a certain sympathy with readers who seek the challenge of arbitration,[51] Pallavicino's main concern at this point is to show that the dialogue can satisfy the humbler needs of the 'scolare'. Cicero's *De oratore*, the late Platonic dialogues and Augustine's *Contra academicos* and, of the moderns, Bembo's *Prose*, Bargagli's *Imprese* and Tasso's *Forno* are all cited as examples of the 'maniera insegnativa perfetta' in dialogue. A model emerges of a dialogue which is no more than a show-case for the writer's opinion: a dialogue whose notional dialectic serves only to expose more clearly the 'fondamento' of the author's thought.[52]

Slightly different is the case of those dialogues on controversial subjects which employ the techniques of the open dialogue to 'closed' didactic ends. Where a writer wishes to convey opinions opposed to the views of the multitude, Pallavicino discourages him from adopting a straightforward didactic manner. By forcing his views importunately on an audience heavily fortified with false opinion, he risks seeing even 'i borghi dell'udito' closed in his path. The only practicable way to liberate his readers' intellects from the 'tirannia' of ensconced 'falsità' is to introduce his views surreptitiously, 'modestamente e come private', in the hope that, finally, 'conosciuto il lor merito, l'intelletto spontaneamente le chiami alla signoria'.[53]

This third potential motive for using an open – or pseudo-open – dialogue is radically different in character from those I have mentioned above, in that it does not imply a probabilistic or a problematic attitude to truth. Reading Pallavicino's lively description of a siege of received opinion, it is tempting to relate it to the example of Galileo,[54] though it is more likely that he is thinking of his own recently published *Del Bene*. In any case, the important point is that, neither in Galileo's case nor in Pallavicino's, is there any hint that the dialogue is a formal translation of the author's own 'ignorance', or that he, like Castiglione's Canossa and his creator, is capable of thinking, on the subject in hand, 'or una cosa ed ora un'altra'.[55] What Pallavicino is describing here, in completion of his typology, is a closed dialectical dialogue, more insinuating than the 'maniera insegnativa pefetta', but accomplishing, though more obliquely, the same didactic role.[56] It is important to recognize that when Pallavicino finally comes to talk explicitly of authorial accountability, his implicit point of reference is this closed dialectical dialogue. This is especially significant because the section of the *Trattato* which deals with this subject is presented as a supplement – though in reality it is a corrective – to Speroni's poetics of the open dialogue in the first part of the *Apologia*.[57]

The 'comic' Speroni is in fact an unnamed antagonist throughout the whole second half of the *Trattato*: unsurprisingly, since the vision Speroni offers of the dialogue as pure 'gioco' presents such a radical challenge to Pallavicino's views on the didactic capacities of the genre. At the beginning of his section on dialogue, Pallavicino makes the important point that – 'che che in contrario ne sentisse lo Speroni' – the dialogue is not an imitative genre in the same sense as, say, comic drama.[58] The first reason he adduces is 'material'. The principal task of the writer of a dialogue (*l'industria più operosa*) is 'il ritrovamento della verità e delle ragioni'.[59] The mimetic element in dialogue – 'il distender ciò [la verità e le ragioni] con parole proporzionate a parlatori familiari e specolativi' – is in reality no more difficult (*malagevole*) and no more important in the writer's art than the less obvious imitation which takes place in any other 'scrittura di prosa'.[60] Pallavicino's second, 'formal', reason for denying the dialogue its status as an imitative genre involves an even clearer statement of his dissent from Speroni's position. Poetry and dialogue have quite different principal objects and the aim of the writer of dialogues is primarily 'l'insegnamento'. Pleasure, which Speroni had placed at the centre of his poetics, has a purely instrumental role in Pallavicino's view of the dialogue. For the author of the *Trattato*, the dialogue aims at pleasure as a strictly secondary end, and only because, as a means of maintaining the attention of the reader, it is 'profittevole . . . all'acquisto e all'aumento della scienza'.[61]

By striking at the premise which underlies Speroni's argument, Pallavicino implicitly attacks the controversial conclusion Speroni had drawn from it: that the dialogue, as 'gioco', lies in a sort of ethical no-man's-land, and that the writer is therefore free to attribute to his interlocutors any opinion he chooses, however extravagant it may be. Pallavicino is keenly aware of the dangers inherent in this freedom. There remains a place, within his closed dialogue, for the expression of 'paradoxical' opinions, but the language with which he describes the structure of its 'contrasto' reveals very clearly just how limited and secondary that place is.

The protagonists of Pallavicino's dialogue are allotted quite distinct roles, one within and one without the sphere of rhetorical 'gioco'. At the beginning of the dialogue, a 'sostenitore della falsa opinione' is introduced, who seduces the reader, like Ariosto's Alcina, with the siren-song of his eloquence. Then, just as the hapless reader is succumbing to his sophistries, the Logistilla of the piece is brought in – the 'insegnatore del vero' – to reveal his antagonist's proofs as vile and fallacious 'incanti'. The purpose of 'paradox' in this form of dialogue is not, as it was for Speroni, to throw the readers of the dialogue back on their own judgment, but rather to propel them into the waiting arms of the truth. Pallavicino's theory of the dialogue assumes an active reading, in the sense that readers, seduced by rhetoric and then disabused by logic, acquire a 'shield' against any false persuasion they may fall victim to in future.[62] But the reader's sphere of action is strictly patrolled and demarcated, and certainly Pallavicino's 'mal accorto lettor' is never accorded the vital creative role envisaged by Speroni when he describes the dialogue as the tinder-box of truth.[63]

Just how sheltered Pallavicino in fact feels that the reader should be is revealed when he turns to the issue of the scope permitted to paradox. Speroni, at a pious moment, discussing the reform of his dialogues, had suggested that 'dangerous' opinions like those in the *Dialogo dell'Usura* should not be allowed to escape without an unequivocal refutation.[64] Pallavicino goes one step further. Mild paradox may be permitted, within the limits already prescribed, but no expression of 'empia credenza' or 'viziosa cupidità' may be permitted under any circumstances within the dialogue. The point is made with an emphasis best explained in the proximity of the Galileo affair, which had illustrated with tragic clarity the dangers of any such dalliance.[65] 'E disdetto all'Autore,' Pallavicino insists, 'eziandio sotto qualunque pretesto, ed in persona di qualunque Disputante il far mai comparir queste serpi con onorata sembianza di verità o di virtu'.[66] Good intent is no safeguard, and the sternest of palinodes inadequate protection: 'la carità e la prudenza richiede che niuno coll'arte sua presti a questi angui leggiadro ammanto per travestirsi; benché il facessi a fine di spogliarneli poi tosto con ignominia'.[67]

Although, doubtless, the harsh lesson of Galileo's condemnation lends an edge of shrillness to his protestations, Pallavicino's stance here may be regarded as no more than the logical conclusion of the line of reasoning sketched out by Speroni in the third part of the *Apologia*. The exigencies of 'decorum', of 'charity' and 'prudence' had brought about, by Pallavicino's day, the development of a dialogue which is in fact no more than a pious monologue in disguise. The dialogues of the past, even the relatively recent past, were inevitably regarded in this climate with a certain degree of mistrust. In his introduction to Marcantonio Foppa's edition of Tasso's unpublished dialogues (1666), nervous about his author's occasional forays into 'dangerous' speculation, Giovanni Pietro Bellori earnestly reminds the reader that the dialogue is 'un semplice racconto', in which all opinion is proposed, at best, 'dubitativamente'.[68] Bellori's arguments are those of the 'comic' Speroni, but his tone is entirely different. If such a defence is necessary for an author who, as Bellori is careful to remind us, demonstrated his piety convincingly elsewhere, we are left to assume that any writer less secure in his credentials would do well to avoid the dangers involved in following in Tasso's path.

In a dialogue of 1574, by a little-known Luccan writer, Niccolò Granucci, one interlocutor interrupts another in full flight, during a defence of the equality of women, to warn him of the danger of 'qualche censura', since 'il nostro Padre Inquisitore non vuole si disputi, né che si scriva di questa materia'.[69] It is a striking incident; a rare rendering of the threat of institutional censorship hanging over the dialogue, and one which it would be tempting to identify as a perfect *exemplum* of the conditions which led to what might be termed the closure of the dialogue.

In fact, however, a concentration on actual incidents of ecclesiastical censorship would produce a simplistic account of what was a far more complex phenomenon. In the present chapter and my discussion of the fate of the Lucianic dialogue, in chapter 3, I have attempted to do justice to the less direct, more capillary means by which the cultural policies of the Counter-Reformation contributed to the closure of the dialogue. This development should not be mapped so much by grand gestures of institutional censorship, like Galileo's trial or the expurgation of the *Cortegiano* – though obviously, they had their impact – as by the constant, subterranean erosion of the dialogue's dialectical structure recorded on the pages of apparently objective works of poetic theory. From Sigonio's condemnation of the comic dialogue to Pallavicino's fully fledged theory of the didactic vocation of the genre, dialogue theory charts the progressive reduction to decorous, 'responsible' monologue of a form of argumentation which had originally, in its very structure, proclaimed its autonomy from authorial control.

The implications of this process for the form of the literary dialogue are clearly visible in Valerio Marcellino's *Il Diamerone* (1564). Published by Giolito, at a moment when the Venetian publishing houses were turning from a predominantly humanistic to a primarily devotional output,[70] the *Diamerone* is clearly – painfully clearly – the product of a period of transition. Marcellino's choice of a dialogue form for what is, in effect, a homily on the vanity of earthly existence, in itself signals his keenness to capture a market accustomed to lighter fare;[71] and, from its initial introduction of a sickly host, the poet Domenico Venier, to its final scene of Sperone Speroni rapt in contemplative transports, the *Diamerone* does all it can to shadow Castiglione's *Cortegiano*.[72] But the closeness of Marcellino's imitation – a closeness of detail, rather than spirit – ultimately only serves to reveal the distance which separates him from his model.

The *Diamerone* is structured as a dispute between two opposing factions, one of which expresses a materialist, the other a religious viewpoint. Gestures are made, as in the *Cortegiano*, to ensure the right to dissent and the author goes to some pains to create an illusion of lively debate. For all this, however, it is apparent from the beginning of the dialogue that the odds are overwhelmingly stacked in favour of one party. The leader of the materialist faction is the impeccably orthodox Dionisio Atanagi[73] – an unlikely devil's advocate who, even as the two sides prepare to do battle, acknowledges that his opposition has a purely instrumental role, as a foil to the 'verità' of Speroni and Venier.[74] It comes as no surprise when, at the end of the dialogue, the 'parte giusta' wins out and the listeners remain 'del tutto cambiati dell'animo loro primiero'.[75]

In this highly artificial confrontation, the complex apparatus of open dialogue which Marcellino borrows from Castiglione has a notably impoverished role. All the delicate social mechanisms identified by Wayne Rebhorn in his study of the 'interaction rituals' of the *Cortegiano* are scrupulously imitated in the *cornice* of the *Diamerone*. The main speakers preface their contributions with protestations of reluctance to speak; moments of conflict in the discussion are smoothed over by healing laughter; the danger of real aggression is exorcised by an extravagant fiction of combat.[76] But where, in a truly open, conflictual dialogue, these devices have a structural function, in the *Diamerone*, they have no more than a decorative role. Speroni's reluctance to take the floor does not, unlike Canossa's in the *Cortegiano*, signal any real doubt about the authority of his views.[77] Laughter is not used to remind us of the duty of detachment, but simply to mark off more firmly the wrong and trivial from the right.[78] Finally, the bellic imagery which, in the *Cortegiano*, serves both to highlight and to defuse the protagonists' dissent, in Marcellino's dialogue merely underlines their fundamental unanimity. The 'materialist' Atanagi's initial, swashbuckling description of the dialogue as a 'duel'[79] becomes absurd when we see him pitched against an eminent cleric, whose 'arme di sacrestia', like Orlando's Duridana, are so obviously of a quite different temper from his own puny rationalist sword.[80]

The *Diamerone* illustrates very clearly the problem identified by Speroni in the *Apologia dei dialoghi*. The laws of poetic decorum demand that both positions in a dialectical dialogue should be realized as plausibly and persuasively as possible. On the other hand, the higher demands of the writer's decorum as a Christian and a citizen require that the victory of the 'parte giusta' should never be seriously at issue. These conflicting demands are difficult to bring into harmony at the best of times, but, as the *Diamerone* demonstrates, they become still more difficult to reconcile when the dialogue's argument touches on articles of faith.

Of course, the *Diamerone* is something of an exception. Marcellino's attempt at a Ciceronian religious dialogue was one which found few imitators[81] and it is rare to find a work which betrays the marks of self-censorship in quite such an obvious way. A glance at the expurgated *Cortegiano* of 1584, however, or the second part of the *Apologia*, where Speroni counters, point by point, the objections of his accuser, is enough to reveal quite how broad the range of issues was which might be felt to require some vigilance on the part of the 'decorous' writer. References to 'fortuna', slurs on princes, risqué *badinage* were all susceptible to a scrupulous, self-imposed control which, inevitably, operated to the detriment of 'comic' poetic decorum.[82] One solution to the problem was, like Marcellino, to surround any 'dangerous' utterance by a cumbersome apparatus of disclaimers. But the solution which prevailed was, unsurprisingly, the far easier one of simply leaving what was indecorous to say unsaid.

The history of the unsaid is, by nature, an impossible one to write. We may gain some idea of the impact of self-censorship on the dialogue by looking at the rare instances of overt discretion like Granucci's, cited above, or by tracing the filigree of calculated reticences in Tasso's supremely sly dialogue works.[83] For the most part, however, a study of this subject is limited to the notation of an absence: the almost total absence, in dialogues produced in the last third of the century, of any thesis which offered a substantial challenge – however hedged with caveats and disclaimers – to the political or religious orthodoxies of the day.

8 From the 'girevole strada' to the straight and narrow path

Richiedon leggitore introdotto bene, attento, assentito e valoroso, che ne sappia cavar que' tesori che vi son quasimente affogati nel dialogo, ed in una maniera di trattarli anzi stravagante, che no.

Orazio Lombardelli, *I fonti toscani* (1581)[1]

This observation of Orazio Lombardelli's on Pietro Bembo's *Prose della volgar lingua* (1525), can tell us a great deal about the reasons for the decline of dialogue in late-Cinquecento Italy. In particular, stemming as it does from formal and methodological considerations, it provides a useful corrective to any temptation to interpret this phenomenon simply as a result of the cultural policies of the Counter-Reformation. The glamour of the explanation considered in the previous chapter – the cultural reverberations of censorship – should not blind us to the many less dramatic factors in the culture of the age which may have an equal weight in determining developments in the dialogue. After all, whatever Lombardelli is objecting to in Bembo's *Prose*, it is certainly not their capacity to act as a covert channel for the expression of what Sforza Pallavicino might term 'empia credenza' or 'viziosa cupidità'.[2]

It is important to stress that Lombardelli's critique of the dialogue is not referred to a work like Castiglione's *Cortegiano*, which makes a genuine attempt to represent a plurality of voices. The *Prose della volgar lingua* are – especially after the first book – indisputably monological in character: indeed, they would be cited by Pallavicino as one of the supreme examples of the 'maniera insegnativa perfetta' in dialogue, precisely because of the clarity with which they reveal 'l'opinione dello Scrittore'.[3] It is not, then, the ambiguity of the dialogue form that Lombardelli is protesting against but rather the unsystematic way in which it presents its arguments. In his impatience with the dialogue's 'girevole strada', Lombardelli was not alone.[4] This methodological scruple, as much as any ideological factor, would lead to the decline and the eventual demise of the genre.

In 1528, in the early years of the vernacular dialogue tradition, Castiglione had presented the dialogue as an alternative to that 'certo ordine o regula di precetti distinti' which 'l più delle volte nell'insegnare qualsivoglia cosa usar si sole'.[5] Half a century later, Stefano Guazzo feels himself constrained to excuse himself for having failed to 'seguire interamente l'ordine d'Aristotele',[6] and the greatest compliment the admirers of his *Civil conversazione* can pay it is that it manages to retain the 'ordine della dottrina Aristotelica' while dallying with the 'vaghezza del Dialogo Platonico'.[7] Between these two ideals of the dialogue, as 'disordered' narrative and ornamented order, lies a gulf between two quite different views on what Bacon would call the 'wisdom of tradition': the method employed in didactic works and the 'architecture' of their 'frame'.[8] My task in the concluding chapters of this study will be to examine those developments in Cinquecento thinking on 'tradition', 'order' and 'method' which would most significantly influence the practice of the dialogue.

The *Cortegiano*'s most explicit comments on the problem of pedagogical method occur in Book IV of the dialogue, where Ottaviano Fregoso makes his bid to promote the courtier from the essentially decorative function ascribed to him in the first three books to a more exalted role as moral and political counsellor to his prince.[9] At first appearance, Ottaviano admits, the courtier may not appear the man most suited to this task, and the rulers of the ancient world had, more predictably, turned to philosophers for advice. But this is no longer an option: the princes of the present day, spoilt by adulation and swelled with self-love, would never tolerate the preaching of the 'severe philosophers' of old. It is the courtier, now, armed with the graces he has been taught in the first two books of the dialogue, who holds out the only hope of exerting a beneficial influence on the prince. He will not do so, naturally, by the distinctly unsubtle means favoured by moral philosophers: by thrusting before the prince's eyes the 'orrida faccia della vera virtù'.[10] His will be an oblique and edulcorated style, a waving of carrots, rather than a flourishing of sticks: a calculated camouflage of the 'hard path' of government with the 'flowers' and 'fronds' of delight.[11]

Castiglione's own matter, in his dialogue, is not as grave as that allocated to the courtier in Book IV, but his projected audience of 'nobili cavalieri' and 'valorose donne' may be presumed to be as resistant as their prince to the advances of those philosophers who attempt to administer their teachings neat, without the 'dolce liquore' of eloquence.[12] His problem, in presenting a digest of classical teaching to a vernacular audience, is essentially the same as his courtier's, or that of Philip Sidney's poet in the *Apology for Poetry*: to provide 'food for the tenderest stomachs', coddled by less demanding pastimes and intolerant of the 'studious painfulness' demanded by conventional philosophical discourse.[13]

The solution which Castiglione opts for is, of course, to renounce the form of the academic treatise altogether and to cast his arguments in the more digestible form of a 'civil conversation'. The resulting dialogue is, in Lombardelli's terms, 'extravagant' in the extreme. Though stylized, inevitably, the *Cortegiano* makes a serious and consistent attempt to respect the rhythms of oral exchange, and is willing to sacrifice linearity and system to this end. Frequently, the discussion of a subject will start from an offhand comment on the part of a speaker and only under the pressure of his listeners' objections and questions will the speaker gradually work his way back to the principles on which his argument is based.[14] Definitions, when they are provided at all, are not supplied at the outset of an argument, but delayed until a point where they seem to arise spontaneously from the flow of the debate.[15] Digressions weave busily in and out of the carrying thread of the dialogue; heated disputes are abandoned without a conclusion being reached; entire lines of argument are punctured by a single shaft of wit. The impatient readers of Lombardelli's day, chafing at the inefficiency of the *Prose*, must have found the work of Bembo's great contemporary more dawdling yet.

Castiglione's *sprezzatura* is such that we are scarcely conscious, when reading the *Cortegiano*, of the scaffolding of order on which his deceptively structureless structure is hung. But, as is fitting in the product of the 'formator del cortigiano', the apparent 'artlessness' of the *Cortegiano* conceals a meticulous 'art'; and, on a few, strictly circumscribed occasions, Castiglione lets his mask slip to reveal the 'disorder' of his dialogue as deliberate, as a choice. Two passages in the dialogue, in particular, merit our close attention, for what they reveal of the methodological decisions which underlie his argumentational practice. Both, significantly, occur during discussions of subjects which had aroused considerable controversy, in which Castiglione was intensely conscious of participating in a public *querelle*. The first is the thwarted attempt at Socratic questioning which concludes the discussion on language, in Book I of the dialogue; the second, the slightly more successful bout of scientific disputation which opens the debate on women, in Book III.

The first episode occurs in a long-simmering debate over the correct form for the literary vernacular, between Lodovico da Canossa, who argues that the language of literature should mirror contemporary court usage, and Federico Fregoso, who champions the use of archaic literary Tuscan.[16] After much inconclusive wrangling on the symptoms of their difference, the two men seem on the point of addressing its deeper cause, as Canossa, with a series of cruelly well-judged questions on imitation, begins forcing Fregoso to clarify his views on the nature of literature. If claims to literary distinction rest, as Fregoso maintains, on the quality of the *words* a writer uses, then, since Silius Italicus uses more or less the same vocabulary as Virgil, it must be concluded that his *Punica* is the equal of the *Aeneid*.[17] Fregoso's defeat seems assured, but, at this crucial point, Canossa's initiative is cut short by the intervention of Emilia Pio, who condemns the dispute on language as 'troppo lunga e fastidiosa' and forbids the participants to continue.[18]

It is Emilia, too, who, curtails the debate in Book III between Giuliano de' Medici and Gaspare Pallavicino, on the biological arguments against the equality of women. Here the problem is not so much one of technique as of terminology: the nature of the subject-matter necessitates an excursion into scholastic language, which sits awkwardly with the preponderantly non-technical register of the dialogue. Both participants have already expressed some doubts on the wisdom of leading the discussion into such 'subtleties',[19] and their fears are confirmed when they are instructed by Emilia, in a tone of some impatience, to 'usci[re] una volta di queste vostre "materie" e "forme" e maschi e femine e parla[re] di modo che siate intesti'.[20]

It is clear that, on both occasions, Emilia Pio is acting in her official capacity as lieutenant to the Duchess, and that her interventions are necessary to keep harmony in the group. In the first instance, by reducing an urbane general discussion to a heated, two-man dispute, Canossa is breaking all the most cherished norms of civil conversation, especially the modesty and detachment which forbids excessive attachment to one's own ideas and the courtesy which guarantees equal access to all the participants in a discussion.[21] The second episode is, likewise, a breach of conversational etiquette, since, by introducing technical language accessible only to those who have had at least a basic grounding in natural philosophy, the men of the party are, in effect, excluding their female companions.

Within the fiction of the dialogue, then, these vignettes of frustrated argumentation have an important role to play in mapping out the boundaries of civil conversation. Outside that fiction, however, they also play a significant part in spelling out the term of Castiglione's 'conversation' with his readers and defining the level of argument appropriate in his dialogue. The harmonious and accessible blend of 'soft', rhetorical forms of argumentation employed in the *Cortegiano* is not, as the incidents discussed above demonstrate, the only register of which the author would have been capable. Nor is it – as he hints in these incidents – always the most efficient and conclusive means of handling a given topic. It is, however, the sole form of argumentation accessible to the audience Castiglione was trying to reach, of readers who, like the women who represent them in the dialogue, were unfamiliar with, perhaps hostile to, the culture of the schools. It is also, on a deeper level, the only form of argumentation which can do justice to Castiglione's conviction that, at least in the sphere of human *mores*, no firm 'scienza' is possible, and that the nearest we can come to the truth is a sensitive sounding of consensus.

By experimenting with and rejecting more technical modes of argumentation, Castiglione signals to the learned among his audience, in a gesture of supreme *sprezzatura*, that he is eminently capable of navigating the 'gran pelago' of contemporary controversy, and that, were it not for the constraints of the genre he has chosen, he would be able to say more than he does.[22] At the same time, by hinting at the way in which the fiction of the dialogue cramps his style, Castiglione invites us to consider the principles underlying his choice of the form. Other means of argument might be more rigorous or more conclusive than civil conversation, but they would, he suggests, inevitably involve a sacrifice of *corrispondenza*. The use of the traditional language of scholastic disputation would reduce that section of his audience unfamiliar with *materie* and *forme* from the status of *arbitri* to that of mere *scolari*. The use of a heavily slanted, pseudo-dialogical form like Socratic questioning would similarly deprive his audience of a genuine right to reply. The first principle of his dialogue in the *Cortegiano* is to preserve an equal, dynamic, open relationship with his reader. If strict order and argumentational rigour have to be forfeited, on occasion, it is a sacrifice he and his readers must be prepared to make.

The forms of argumentation used in the *Cortegiano* reflect, on the one hand, a humanistic equation of *sapienza* with rhetoric and, on the other, a close accommodation to the demands of a certain audience. Technical forms of argument are purged from the dialogue, on the first count, because they appear idle pedantries, inelegant and remote from experience and, on the second, because they demand a training its audience did not possess. In their place, Castiglione offers a form of argument made to measure for the court; as modest, as unaffected, as 'amateurish' as the courtier himself.

The half-century which followed the publication of the *Cortegiano* saw a profound change in the 'wisdom of tradition', which challenged at its very roots the humanist ideal of eloquence and transformed the horizon of expectations of the new audience of the vernacular. The most acute theorists and tireless propagandists of the new post-humanist – even anti-humanist – culture were the group of critics and *volgarizzatori* who made up the Accademia degli Infiammati in Padua in the 1540s and 1550s and whose influence filtered out rapidly, if in a rather diluted form, to Florence and the northern courts in the following decades.[23]

Recent critics have identified this change as one aspect of a more general, politically and economically determined 're-feudalization' of culture, which resulted in a far more rigid segregation and stratification of the various intellectual disciplines.[24] In a political climate in which the ideals of civic humanism seemed impossibly remote, in which intellectuals were constrained to renounce their last dreams of political influence and to resign themselves to a role as academics or simple functionaries of the courts, the idea of a redefinition of the sciences as closed professional disciplines had an undoubted protectionist appeal. The rapidly hegemonic neo-Aristotelianism of the mid-century re-established the dignity of school philosophy, challenged by the claims of the humanists, and facilitated the emergence of new disciplines like literary criticism. Most significantly for my present argument, this age also witnessed a change in the public perception of learning, which – in crude terms – ceased to be perceived as a sublime 'sapienza', to be digested by the individual through his experience of the world, and began to be felt, far more technically, as 'scienza', a commodity like any other and the province of professionals.

A shift as vast and capillary as this is perhaps best seized in its effects and nowhere are those effects more apparent than in the changes which took place in the dialogue. After half a century of tireless *volgarizzazione*, not only the 'materie' and 'forme' which Emilia Pio had so objected to, but far more technical scholastic terminology had become acceptable in the dialogue. Philosophers – not as 'severe', perhaps, as Castiglione's bogeyman, but unmistakably professional – had begun to become a popular choice as the principal speakers of dialogues, dealing out lightly popularized doctrine to their willing *auditores*.

More fundamentally, the argumentation of the dialogue had begun to tend, in most cases, towards a dialectical, rather than a rhetorical paradigm.[25] This change is reflected in the theory of the dialogue, as well as in its practice: by 1585, when Tasso wrote his *Discorso dell'arte del dialogo*, it is scarcely surprising to encounter a criticism of Cicero for handling disputation in a manner more suited to an orator than a dialectician.[26] Already by the mid-century, readers were beginning to demand from the dialogue the sort of self-consciously methodical reasoning to which they were becoming accustomed in the vernacular philosophical *trattato*. Instead of an unresolved discussion *in utramque partem*, the dialogues of the later part of the century tend increasingly to portray a dialectical argument, which proceeds systematically through the stages of definition and division to an unequivocal conclusion.

Of course, I am not suggesting that Paduan post-humanism had any explicit brief for the dialogue. As we have seen, Speroni, the most prominent member of the Infiammati and its most successful writer of dialogues, proposed that the genre should frankly acknowledge its incapacity to transmit *scienza*, and revel instead in the dazzling play of a newly disenfranchised rhetoric. Later, however, as the 'rigorismo aristote-lico' of 1540s Padua began to dissolve into what Francesco Bruni has termed a 'frammentarismo erudito',[27] its legacy in the dialogue was revealed as a sort of loose aesthetic of rigour. The late-Cinquecento dialectical dialogue is characteristically the product of a compromise. Its arguments are conducted in a register best described by Chaim Perelman and Lucie Obrecht-Tyteca's term 'quasi-logical discourse'[28] – in Speroni's terms, neither a fully-fledged, purely ludic rhetoric nor the strict demon-strative logic which it sometimes masquarades as.

I shall reserve for my next chapter a detailed examination of the argumentation of this new form of 'quasi-logical' dialogue. For the moment, I propose to illustrate my brief overview of these 'anti-humanist' developments in the dialogue by looking at a particularly eloquent group of examples of the genre: the dialogues produced by Tasso and his contemporaries at Ferrara in the last two decades of the century. The virtue of this choice lies in the sharp contrast between the argumentation of these dialogues and that of my previous example, the *Cortegiano*; a contrast all the more striking because the Ferrarese dialogues in question are, like Castiglione's, addressed to a court audience and, like his, impli-citly proposed as models of communication at court.

In the Ferrara of the late sixteenth century, economically and morally decadent, heirless and doomed to devolve to the papacy, the court dialogue and the independent court culture of which it was an expression had a final flowering in the works of writers like Annibale Romei and Torquato Tasso.[29] It is poignant to note that both Romei and Tasso had passed a portion of their adolescence at the court of Guidobaldo II at Urbino;[30] and it is perhaps not too fanciful to read their dialogues as a more or less conscious attempt to write a new *Cortegiano* for the markedly colder climate of their age. Romei's *Discorsi* (1585), indeed, are structu-rally and thematically very close to Castiglione's model: a series of lengthy discussions between a mixed group, on a ceremonial occasion, covering the entire curriculum of 'le cose . . . in che per l'ordinario si trattengono ragionando nelle corti le ben create dame e i cavalieri'.[31] Tasso, too, at one time, seems to have planned such a work, perhaps set in Urbino and featuring Castiglione's son Camillo as a principal speaker.[32] This work was never realized, however, and apart from a wistful allusion in the *Gonzaga secondo overo del giuoco*, Tasso seems to have jettisoned this rather anachronistic form. His *Dialoghi*, viewed as a volume, share the *Cortegiano*'s ambition to codify discourse at court.[33] But Tasso shows himself keenly aware that the form of communication he is proposing to map has changed almost beyond recognition since the time of Castiglione, and that any dialogue which aspires, like his, to epitomize court discourse, must take a form more consonant with the spirit of his age.[34]

Before turning to Tasso's formal innovations, though, it will be illuminating to look for a moment at Romei's more traditional – perhaps even deliberately anachronistic – dialogue.[35] It is here, paradoxically, where the formal debt to the *Cortegiano* is greatest, that the gulf which separates the culture of Alfonso II's Ferrara from the distant glories of Guidobaldo I's Urbino most clearly appears.

The *Discorsi* open, like the *Cortegiano*, with a glittering description of the court.[36] We are told of its ruler, watching benign and God-like over his subjects' business and pleasure; of the splendid palaces he has scattered like jewels over his whole territory; of his courtiers, measuring out the seasons with their 'sollazzi', as in some latterday Salone dei Mesi. The speakers of the dialogue – the cream of the court – start their conversation with elaborate exchange of compliments, which appear to be preparing the ground for a *giornata* of light social banter. When the discussion begins to get underway, though, it rapidly becomes apparent that Romei's ethereal *brigata* is less featherweight than it seems; that, in the words of his contemporary English translator, 'this excellent form of Court-like exercise' is 'grounded on the firm foundation of Aristotelian and Platonical doctrine'.[37]

The distance which separates Romei's *Discorsi* from the model of the *Cortegiano* is perhaps most immediately apparent in the make-up of the group. The most prominent role a professional philosopher can hope for in the *Cortegiano* is a cameo appearance, and it is inconceivable to imagine a Pomponazzi or a Nifo bantering with the ladies in the dialogue itself.[38] In Romei's *Discorsi*, in contrast, one of the most authoritative speakers is the philosopher, Francesco Patrizi, at the time employed in the Studio of Ferrara, who blends his urbane but still distinctly 'professional' voice with those of more conventional courtly figures like Ercole Tassoni and Camillo Gualengo.[39]

Another indication, in the *Discorsi*, of the narrowing of the gulf between the culture of the court and the Studio is the markedly didactic form the *giornate* of the dialogue take. The *Cortegiano* is, of course, hardly a free-for-all; as in the *Discorsi*, for each new topic of discussion, the burden of exposition is allotted to a single speaker. In the *Cortegiano*, however, the hierarchy between principal and secondary interlocutors is deliberately blurred: it is recognized in the statutes of the debate that anyone can interrupt at any time.[40] The *giornate* of the *Discorsi*, in contrast, are structured more like a public debate or a conference than a natural conversation. In each case, the main speaker starts by delivering an uninterrupted lecture, and it is only at a second moment that the audience intervenes with its 'doubts'.

A final indication of the difference in the character between the *Cortegiano* and the *Discorsi* is the unquestioning acceptance afforded in the later dialogue to the kind of technical argumentation we have seen being scrupulously edited out of its model. A good index of this change is the degree of familiarity with philosophical terminology displayed by the female speakers in the dialogue. As we have seen, Castiglione uses his women interlocutors to delineate a section of his audience which is unfamiliar with, and resistant to, scholastic exposition.[41] Romei, on the other hand, has his duchess, Margherita Gonzaga, deal effortlessly with 'elements' and 'compounds', while the 'dottissima' Tarquinia Molza can bandy quotations from the Philosopher as well as any of the men.[42] At one point, it is true, Gualengo finds himself explaining the difference of 'contrari positivi' and 'privativi' for his 'Queen', Camilla Costabile.[43] But it is presumed that she, and the other ladies, will be eager to correct their ignorance, and the hegemony of philosophical discourse receives no serious challenge. There is none of that breezy contempt for 'authority' which enlivens the *Cortegiano*. Epithets like 'dotto' and 'sottile', anathema in the *Cortegiano*, are here intended as compliments, and Patrizi meets no contradiction when he defines the *letterato*'s battery of argumentational techniques as 'i sillogismi, le induzioni, gli entimemi' and, only lastly, 'gli esempi'.[44] Rather than genuine 'idioti', the work seems to be addressed to what Romei engagingly refers to elsewhere as 'semidotti': a 'half-learned' audience, with a grounding, at least, in the language and methods of the schools.[45]

The respectful and well-informed attitude to philosophical language displayed by the speakers of the *Discorsi* is symptomatic of the status of philosophy in the court of Ferrara. The Ferrarese Studio had always operated in close alignment with the courts and, by Romei and Tasso's day, relations were particularly close. As the careers of figures like Giambattista Giraldi Cinzio and Antonio Montecatini demonstrate, academic success was a recognized route to the highest honours of the Ferrarese court;[46] and philosophy enjoyed a particularly brilliant public profile, after Montecatini's virtuoso defence of over a thousand Aristotelian *conclusioni* revealed the subject's unexpected potential as a spectator sport.[47]

It should not be thought, however, that the academic tone of Romei's *Discorsi* can be dismissed as a quirk of custom. The greater social acceptability of school philosophy testified by the *Discorsi* is, I have suggested, the symptom of a much vaster change taking place in this period, in public perceptions of the role of learning in society. As the wavering demarcation line between rhetoric and philosophy was stiffened into an iron curtain, as formal schooling began to be stressed at the expense of experience and eloquence, as 'scienza' became the province of a new caste of professional secular intellectuals, so 'tradition' began to be conceived of less as an exchange of opinion, as it is in the *Cortegiano*, and more as a contract, an exchange of commodities: 'dottrina' for 'onore'.[48]

For all their differences, Romei's *Discorsi* still share with Castiglione's *Cortegiano* a structure based on the ideal of a conversation between equals. Some speakers, of course, are more authoritative than others, and it has already been commented that the division of roles within each individual *giornata* is more institutionalized than it was in Castiglione. But this institutionalization is relative: the *princeps* of one day is the challenger of the next, and the character of the discussion as, precisely, a *discussion* between equals is respected.

Tasso's *Dialoghi*, on the contrary, represent a marked departure from this pattern. Most typically, his dialogues consist of a conversation between, at most, two or three speakers, locked into airtight 'offices' which will remain constant through the dialogue. The *princeps sermonis* is generally a philosopher, while the others are usually courtiers – much younger than the *princeps* for the most part and mindful of their companion's superior wisdom, contented with their role as pupils and gratifyingly willing to learn.

The only occasion on which one of Tasso's courtiers attempts a challenge on his companion's monopoly on knowledge is, significantly enough, in his earliest dialogue, *Il Forno overo de la nobiltà* (1580), in which the eponymous hero, Antonio Forni, shows something of the spirit and irreverence of the *idioti* of Sperone Speroni's dialogues, as he teases the philosopher Agostino Bucci about the near-religious allegiance he and his 'sect' owe to Aristotle, jibes at definitions of familiar concepts which depart from everyday usage, and tempestuously demands that his companion speak to him as 'one courtier to another'.[49] In a revised version of this dialogue, however, dating from 1585-7, the character of Forni is reduced to little more than a cipher.[50] His earlier rebelliousness entirely quelled, he admits from the start of the dialogue that tasks like defining nobility, which some – including, perhaps, his former self – have thought to belong to the courtier, should in fact be recognized as exclusively the province of the philosopher. The only exception he allows, in what sounds very much like a pointed allusion to Castiglione, is the unlikely event that the courtier is 'tale . . . quale da alcuni è formato'.[51]

It is difficult not to read this passage as a manifesto for a more rigorous and didactic philosophical dialogue, and an explicit rejection of the genteel amateurism of the previous courtly tradition. Forni's rebellion of 1579 is not repeated, except perhaps parodistically in the *Minturno overo de la bellezza* (1592–3), written in Naples, where the role of courtier is taken by the irredeemably vapid Girolama Ruscelli.[52] Elsewhere in the *Dialoghi*, even where, as in the *Gonzaga secondo overo del giuoco* (1581–2), a self-taught courtier is seen to upstage a professional philosopher, he does so not by calling into doubt the hegemony of the other's sectoral discourse, but quite simply by beating him at his own dialectical game.[53]

The philosophers who feature in the *Dialoghi* are, of course, very different from the unregenerate pedants of courtly demonology: the 'graceless bookworms' whom Giambattista Pigna, himself a glowing example of a philosopher made good, had warned would never succeed in winning the good graces of their prince.[54] As his inaugural oration to the Accademia Ferrarese of 1570 bears witness, Tasso was acutely aware of the problems of accommodating academic discourse to an audience to whom 'già il nome solo di scuole e di dottori suona in non so che modo spiacevole'.[55] The philosophers he features in his dialogues are all men who had shown themselves capable of adapting their skills to this choosy market: Marsilio Ficino, Agostino Nifo, Simone Porzio, Agostino Bucci and – with a zeal for self-promotion which is touching, considering the circumstances in which the dialogues were written – the writer himself, in the transparent Platonic guise of a 'Neapolitan Stranger'.[56] All show themselves skilled in accommodating their arguments to a 'courtly and chivalric register', fine-tuning their ethos, their arguments and examples to meet individual prejudices and tastes.[57]

The *Dialoghi* may, in fact, be seen as a kind of laboratory for the elaboration of a pedagogical ethos adapted to the modern court. Once it is accepted that the learning process does not consist of a collective process of discovery, but rather as the transfer of knowledge from a greater vessel to a lesser, problems of pedagogical etiquette become pressing. The *ex cathedra* tones of the stereotyped school philosopher are, of course, utterly out of bounds in the court; the first requirement for the court philosopher is modesty. The ironic Socratic *persona* is more promising, but, even here, some adjustment is necessary: the arrogance lurking beneath Socrates' professions of ignorance would not have escaped a courtier's practised eye and, as Tasso wryly comments, in *Il Malpiglio overo della corte*, 'potrebbe parer a' cortigiani cosa odiosetta anzi che no, se alcun dicesse di non saper nulla e, riprovando sempre quel che'è detto da gli altri, volesse rimaner al disopra in tutte le questioni'.[58] This is a question of nuance, however. Diplomatically handled, Tasso was quick to see that a watered-down form of Socratic questioning could provide the basis for an oblique and artful, entirely modern and eminently courtly *psicogagia*, which blurs the crudity of the power relations between pupil and teacher and converts the learning process into a sophisticated game.[59]

Like the *Cortegiano*, Tasso's *Dialoghi* aspire to provide a sort of grammar of communication at court, though with a 'professional' slant quite alien from the spirit of the *Cortegiano*. They do not aim at producing a universal formula for conversation at court, but rather to depict localized solutions for the various tasks a court philosopher might be called on to perform. In the *Gonzaga secondo*, the *Cavaletta* and the *Molza*, the situation is akin to that in the *Cortegiano*: a courtier is called on to improvise a philosophical dissertation to entertain a female audience. In the *Forno* and the *Porzio*, the problem is less one of 'diletto' than of 'utile': the young courtiers Antonio Forni and Muzio Pignatello, impatient with the esoteric irrelevancies of the schools, seek a form of 'dottrina' already packaged for application to active life. The *Cataneo* and the *Malpiglio secondo*, discussions between fellow-scholars, define situation in which more technical forms of argument are called for. Some dialogues deal with subjects like love and beauty, consecrated by the courtly dialogue tradition, while others, notably those on problems of poetics, are a self-consciously innovative attempt to introduce new subjects into the matrix of civil conversation. Each new situation, each new subject and audience, requires a series of slight, sometimes microscopic adjustments in tone: the argumentation may be more or less dialectical, the terminology more or less technical, the proportion of example to enthymeme or argument to digression minutely but tangibly altered.

For all this variety, however, the argumentation of the *Dialoghi* remains consistently 'technical', as is immediately apparent if we contrast it with that of a dialogue like the *Cortegiano*. Even the resolutely anti-academic Antonio Forni, in the first version of the *Forno*, is revealed to possess unexpected reserves of 'armi filosofiche' beneath the deceptive veneer of his 'isprezzatura cortegiana'[60] and, although Tasso goes to considerable pains to maintain an air of spontaneity in his conversations, they tend to be firmly structured on Platonic dialectical models and academic in both their terminology and their techniques of argumentation. The iron hand of logic is always present beneath the velvet glove of 'accommodation'. In the exquisitely courtly *Gonzaga secondo*, without explicitly stating the principle that any account of a subject must start from a definition, Giulio Cesare Gonzaga gently persuades his interlocutrix, Margherita Bentivoglio that, before discussing such practical issues as how to win at cards, she must first address the fundamental question of 'quel che sia il giuoco'.[61] In *La Molza overo de l'amore*, which takes the form of an analysis of various classical and modern definitions of love, Tasso casts a veil of courtesy over his procedure by comparing his initial review of ancient authorities on the subject to the dowagers at a ball, who are ready for action while the 'giovanette' are still busy with their dress.[62] But this cannot altogether disguise the fact that the dialogue is essentially an academic exercise; that the dowagers in question are Empedocles, Lucretius, Plotinus, Aristotle, Plato and Aquinas, and that they – and their audience – can take in their stride terms like 'la parte concupiscibile' or 'l'oggetto amabile', which would have been inconceivable in the far lighter rhythms of a dialogue like the *Cortegiano*.

In some respects, like their neo-Platonic structure and their use of scholastic terminology, Tasso's *Dialoghi* are undoubtedly characteristic of their age. However, the deftness with which Tasso treads the dividing-line between Court and Academy and the sheer variety of his experiments with the dialogue genre make it difficult to use the *Dialoghi* as an index to the practice of his time. Moreover, as Guido Baldassari has astutely observed, many of Tasso's dialogues, more than inquests into the truth, are imitations of possible inquests, which use the dialectical stylemes of a methodical 'investigation', rather in the spirit of Speroni, purely to mock up a convincing *ritratto* of the truth.[63] More reliable as an index to the dialogue production of the age, because more pedestrian, more 'closed' and more decided in its academic bias, is a work by Tasso's protégé, Annibale Pocaterra, *Due dialoghi della vergogna* (1592).[64]

Pocaterra's *Dialoghi* are dedicated to Alfonso d'Este, and set in the sphere of his court: indeed, in a narrative twist unusual in a 'dramatic' dialogue, we are given a degree of local colour in the speakers' rapturous description of the Montagnuola, a favoured site for the pastorals and pageants of the court.[65] Standing on this eminently courtly promontory, however, Pocaterra's interlocutors, all Ferrarese and faithful servants of the Duke, look with a certain nostalgia towards the Monti Euganei, near Padua, where we learn that two of them had studied in their youth.[66] This glance from the court to the Studio is, we soon learn, prophetic of the academic tone of the 'sottile questionare' which follows.[67] Despite their courtly setting, the *Dialoghi* keep one eye on the hills above Padua, and a firm framework of 'order' underlies the polished rhetoric of their discourse.

The role-division in the *Dialoghi* is fairly strictly defined. The acknowledged 'insegnatore del vero' is Orazio Ariosto; the 'adversary' and occasional devil's advocate, Alessandro Guarini; and the eager 'auditore', the young Ercole Castello.[68] Under Ariosto's guidance, the argument of the dialogue takes the form of a quasi-Platonic dialectical 'investigazione': shame is first defined – a process which takes, all in all, almost a hundred

pages – and then the various types, causes and occasions of shame are
duly 'divided'. 'Order' is stressed throughout, and Pocaterra concludes
with the modest suggestion that he has outdone the 'padre dell'ordine e
della metode [sic]', Aristotle himself.[69]

The *Dialoghi* end with a formal summary of the divisions of shame – a
device, incidentally, in open breach of the fiction of orality.[70] Well before
this final gesture of closure, however, Pocaterra has made quite clear his
lack of sympathy with the relativistic assumptions which inform the
structure of dialogues *in utramque partem*. The dialectical matrix of
argumentation adopted by Pocaterra allows no scope for those arguments
from experience which had opened the *Cortegiano* to the vagaries of
'opinion'. Ariosto's definition of shame as 'timor d'infamia' originates in
Aristotle, and Guarini's objections to the formula are equally text-bound,
stemming from formal quibbles about the acceptability of the definition
qua definition rather than from any substantive doubts about its correspondence to the facts.[71] Throughout the dialogue, the hegemony of
dialectic goes unchallenged, while rhetoric is formally banished to an
ornamental role[72] and impressionistic forms of argument are invariably
ruled out of court. In a significant passage early in the first dialogue, the
authority of poets is found to be illegitimate, since poets deal in 'tutte l'
opinioni cosi vere, come verisimili o credute', while the business of the
present discussion is to 'determinar la verità delle cose'.[73] Pocaterra and
his speakers have none of Castiglione's, or Canossa's, scruples about the
difficulty of reaching the truth, in the face of a bewildering 'varieta de'
giudici'.[74] The assumption which lies behind Pocaterra's tranquil and
linear argumentation is that, if the right information is fed into the
dialectical conveyer-belt in the right order, a precise, accurate and
unequivocal truth must inevitably result.

In this brief description of the dialogues produced in late sixteenth-
century Ferrara, I have stressed the way in which the cultural changes
sketched in at the beginning of this section were registered on the sensitive
gauge of dialogical argumentation. In general terms, it seems that a
far-reaching revision of the hierarchy of arts and sciences and a reassessment of their place in society had, by the end of the century, resulted in
the development of a form of dialogue which did not present itself simply
as a transcription of opinion, but advertised its status as a vehicle of the
truth.

The advantage of looking at a group of dialogues as diverse as those of
Romei, Tasso and Pocaterra has been to show that this development was
by no means uniform or linear. These writers' solutions to the problem of
teaching in conversation differ, and the use of language and forms of

argumentation devised for the pursuit of certainty does not always result in a dialogue which propounds an unequivocal conclusion. Several of Romei's *giornate* end without resolution,[75] and Tasso's dialogic *œuvre* contains, besides unashamedly closed dialogues like the second *Forno*, others far closer to Speroni's paradigm of a dialogue of pure 'gioco'. Scholastic language and ordered discussion do not always go hand in hand with argumentational closure. Nevertheless, I have suggested that the growing prestige of academic philosophy at the court and the court audience's increasing acceptance of its sectoral language is indicative of a newly professionalized conception of 'tradition', which is not least among the factors which led to the closure of the dialogue. The paradigm of argumentation, for late sixteenth-century writers of dialogue, is not discussion but teaching and the very language they use – the language of Aristotelian science – implies a magisterial conception of knowledge, as a body of doctrine to be communicated, rather than a fund of wisdom to be enriched by creative exchange.

9   From the open dialogue to the closed book

David Hume, *Dialogues concerning Natural Religion* (1779)

One of the formal developments in the dialogue mentioned in the previous chapter deserves a more thorough examination than it was practicable to give it there. In contrast with the programmatically 'disordered' dialogue of Castiglione's era, the dialogue of the late sixteenth century shows an increasing preoccupation with system, method and order. Word like 'ordine' and 'metodo' recur frequently and anxiously in authors' prefaces and interlocutors' compliments: dim reflections of the mighty controversy which, as Francis Bacon rather discreetly puts it, had been 'moved' concerning the 'method of tradition' in his time.[1] The present chapter will chart this intrusion of method into the dialogue, and, in doing so, will seek to bring to light the underlying reasons for the genre's decline.

The search for the philosopher's stone of 'method' had occupied Renaissance scientists and dialecticians since Agricola and, in the absence of any universally acknowledged directive from the ancients, it had spawned a vast and bewildering series of solutions.[2] In the dialogues I am considering, however, it would be vain to look for reflections of the more sophisticated developments in the field, and one suspects that the methodology of most writers owed as much to imitation of Plato's practice as to reference to his precepts or those of contemporary writers on logic. In concrete terms, the upshot of the late-Cinquecento dialogue's aspiration to order tended to be the adoption of a quasi-Platonic method of definition and division, like that of Pocaterra's *Due dialoghi*, examined in the previous chapter.[3] First apparent in the 1560s, in the work of neo-Platonists like Scipione Ammirato, the method of definition and division rapidly became almost *de rigueur* in the dialogue.[4] In 1567, in his – admittedly rather eccentric – *Avvertenze* on the use of the dialogue, Orazio Toscanella can take it for granted that 'prima s'ha da difinire la materia di cui si disputa . . . Dapoi s'ha da dividere, overo da distribuir nelle sue parti; e da disputarla secondo l'opinione delle varie sette . . . o de i dotti huomini'.[5] The process of definition, in particular, was regarded with almost fetishistic reverence, since, in Romei's words, 'dalla buona diffinizione nasc[e] la soluzione di tutti i dubbi che occorrano nella scienza'.[6] The treatment of definition in dialogues from the mid-century onwards is one of the clearest illustrations of the Cinquecento dialogue's gradual march towards order – it is as natural for Tasso, in 1585, to start his dialogue on the court with a definition as it was for Castiglione, in 1528, to omit this vital preliminary.[7] At first, this flagship of dialectical method appears to have been felt as something of an intrusion: the protagonist of Lodovico Domenichi's courtly *Dialogo dell'amore* (1562) is apologetic about interrupting the flow of the conversation to define the concept of love, and excuses himself on the grounds that, if the dialogue should be recorded, he and his fellow-speakers would be the laughing-stock of 'filosofi selvatichi', who would tax them with having ignored the 'Methodo d'Aristotile'.[8] In more academic dialogues, with no female interlocutors, less circumspection is needed, but we still find Scipione Ammirato, in his *Il Rota overo dell'imprese* (1562) treating the process of definition with some caution, and insisting that the sort of definition required in a civil conversation need not be as precise, as 'appuntata', as that demanded by the philosophers.[9]

To remain within the same subject area, for a moment – the developing science of emblems – we may note that Ammirato's methodology is an advance on the first dialogue on the subject, a decade earlier, Paolo Giovio's *Dialogo delle imprese* (1555).[10] Later dialogues on the same theme, however, make his approach look distinctly amateurish. The need to start by defining the subject is increasingly something which goes without saying and, instead of a brief and apparently optional starting-point for discussion, definition expands to become virtually the ordering principle of the argument. The definition of an emblem given by the main speaker of Scipione Bargagli's *La prima parte dell'imprese* (1578) is far more technical and articulated than that of Ammirato's *princeps* and, in response to a listener's earnest request for further elucidation, he goes on to give a detailed and learned account of its 'genere' and 'differenze' which comprises, more or less, the entirety of the theoretical part of the dialogue.[11] Tasso, in his *Il Conte overo de l'imprese* (1594) goes still further, though with a characteristic elegance which makes his 'ordering' less intrusive. Not only does the Forestiere Napoletano here furnish his own extensively justified definition of the *impresa*, but, in a critical review of the definitions of previous writers, he even gives us a sort of miniature treatise on definition itself, based chiefly on Aristotle's treatment of the subject in the sixth book of the *Topics*.[12]

As the Cinquecento wore on, the argumentation of works in dialogue form came increasingly to respect a pre-established notion of dialectical order, so that by the time that Stefano Guazzo was writing his *Civil conversazione* (1574), it was already beginning to be accepted that the duty of the writer of dialogue was to combine stylistic 'vaghezza' with a certain attention to method.[13] This growing adherence to an extrinsic norm, quite alien from the humanistic matrix within which it had developed, was a significant factor in the literary dialogue's 'closure' and decline. As contemporary observers were well aware, 'ordered' argument is intimately incompatible with a plausible representation of informal speech. The preface to Lodovico Dolce's *Dialogo de' colori* (1565) excuses the lack of 'ordine' in the dialogue by pointing out that the author has deliberately limited himself to recording only 'what might come to mind in the course of a real conversation'.[14] Paolo Giovio smuggles a similar excuse into the fiction of his *Dialogo dell'imprese* (1555), when he has one speaker reassure the other that 'qui non bisogna governarsi con ordine' and that he may list examples in the order in which they naturally fall into his mind.[15] Alessandro Piccolomini, in his commentary on the *Poetica* (1575), goes to considerable lengths to minimize this conflict, insisting that there really do exist speakers who are sufficiently learned and articulate to pull streams of systematic argumentation out of their hats on demand.[16] The fact that he needs to explain this, however – and that he does so in a notably unconvinced manner – is evidence of a continuing unease about the appropriateness of introducing method into the madness of oral debate.

The clearest statement of the *reasons* for the incompatibility between conversation and order occurs in Scipione Bargagli's *Turamino* (1602), when an interlocutor expresses the fear that, by asking a question, he will 'disrupt the order' established by the *princeps sermonis*, Virginio Turamino. Turamino replies, on behalf of this creator, with a definitive statement of the predicament of the late-sixteenth-century writers of dialogues, suspended like Guazzo between the 'vaghezza' of conversation and the exigencies of order. 'In simili nostri ragionamenti', he remarks, 'non si può già tenere l'ordine si che tutti o ciascun d' essi passino per il filo della sinopia . . . talché ne riesca quello che chiaman metodo nelle buone scritture'. The reason is simple: 'queste [le buone scritture] dipendon da un solo intelletto e da una sola penna', while 'quelli' – their 'ragionamenti', and by implication the dialogue which records them – 'nascono da diverse lingue e da vari intelletti, a' quali non sovviene in un'ora e in un ponto [sic] medesimo di tutti i concetti ad un proposito'.[17]

An ordered argument, Bargagli clearly sees, implies the presence of an ordering intellect: an intellect, moreover which, at the moment of writing, is in full possession of all its stages and assured of its conclusion. The impression of simultaneity essential to the workings of the open dialogue is utterly negated by a structure which refers the reader to that frozen moment – that 'ora', that 'punto' – when the writer puts pen to paper. A truly open dialogue, like that described by Speroni in the first part of his *Apologia dei dialoghi* is the product of 'diverse lingue' and 'vari intelletti', including, crucially, that of the reader, the new occupant of the vacuum created by the author's self-annihilation.[18] In the ordered dialogue, on the other hand, the presence of a pre-ordained and immutable structure, which announces its autonomy from the contingencies of its fiction, has the effect of closing the dialogue to any intervention by its readers, and reducing their role to the passive one of the reader of a treatise.

This discrepancy between a dialogical structure and an implicitly monological argument is one reason why, in Hume's words, cited as an epigraph to this chapter, 'to deliver a system in conversation scarcely appears natural'.[19] Another, and more profound reason, associated with this, may be the inherently *written* character of systematic argument. Bargagli's description of the dialogue as the product of 'una sola penna' is significant. Systematic thought of the type represented in Aristotelian dialectic is inconceivable in an oral culture: as Bargagli intuits, it depends upon the invention of the pen. This is, indeed, as Walter J. Ong has observed, the central paradox of Plato's dialogues: that a form devised as a means of escaping the limitations of writing becomes the vehicle of a form of argument which would be unthinkable if writing did not exist.[20]

The culture within which the Renaissance dialogue developed was, of course, a highly literate one and its products cannot be likened to those of primarily oral societies. It is true, nonetheless, that this culture retained a high dose of residual orality, which affected at the profoundest levels its habits of discourse and thought.[21] It is true, also, that the humanist strand in this culture – the strand which produced the dialogue – represented a turning away from the markedly *written* forms of scholastic argumentation to rhetorical models which were felt to reflect more closely the rhythms of speech.[22] The distinction was one of which Renaissance thinkers may be presumed to be more conscious than we are. It is telling that, despite the existence of oral disputations and printed poetry, when Philip Sidney compares scholastic and poetic argumentation in the *Apology for Poetry*, he still figures the poet's discourse as oral, 'a tale which holdeth children from play', while the philosopher's 'obscure definitions' possess 'margents' – material or otherwise – to be 'blurred with interpretations'.[23]

The forms of argument most characteristic of the humanist dialogue are those rhetorical techniques, like *exemplum* and analogy, which most clearly betray their roots in an oral culture. The oral element in dialogic argumentation was accentuated in the early years of the vernacular dialogue, when, aware of addressing an audience relatively unused to written argument, writers consciously strove to adhere to the 'disordered' patterns of everyday speech. Castiglione's Emilia Pio, protesting against the dryness of her companions' syllogistic reasons and demanding a more accessible and concrete, if less conclusive argument by example, represents an element in his audience which he could not afford to ignore.[24]

In the later dialectical dialogue, as 'written' techniques like definition began to insinuate their ghostly 'margents' into ever more bookish conversations, 'oral' techniques like *exemplum* were firmly, if gradually, suppressed. They were not entirely eliminated, of course: their ornamental value was acknowledged, and the most skilful writers, like Tasso, while acknowledging their weakness as arguments, made considerable dramatic capital out of their intrinsic ambiguity.[25] In general, however, they were regarded with suspicion and a degree of contempt, precisely because of their looseness, their susceptibility to various readings. Scipione Ammirato, in his *Maremonte* (c. 1560) has an interlocutor declare, somewhat sniffily, that since 'esempi' are always 'prontissimi a provar due cose contrarie', they can hardly be taken seriously as instruments for discovering the truth.[26] Still more derisively, in his *Ercolano* (1570) – one of the most self-consciously 'ordered' of dialogues – Benedetto Varchi pronounces that 'tutti gli argomenti del *sicut*, ovvero del *come*, zoppic[ano]' and that *exemplum* is 'il più frivolo argomento che si possa fare'.[27]

This rejection of a constitutionally 'open' and rhetorical form of argument is a further proof of the 'professionalization' of the dialogue identified in chapter 8. It can be accounted for superficially by the shift in pedagogical ideals outlined in that chapter: a change which privileged didactic exposition at the expense of debate. But this shift itself cannot be fully explained outside the context of a broader historical process: the gradual change which took place, with the invention and diffusion of print, from an oral to a visual paradigm of communication.

The increasing obsession with method which I have charted in the dialogue of this period may be seen as one symptom of the vast shift in patterns of thought occasioned by the diffusion of print.[28] The early print culture of which the humanist dialogue is an expression retained a conception of intellectual activity as essentially *discursive*. Its instruments of inquiry, rhetoric and dialectic, were arts of discourse, not pure arts of thinking: vehicles of a thought which, even in its most 'written' forms, still shaped itself as a dialogue with other voices and other minds.[29]

In the course of the sixteenth century, however, as the solipsistic mental habits of print culture became more and more deeply internalized, thought began to be – gradually, painfully – extricated from the world of discourse. The new concept of a formal logic autonomous from disputation and teaching would not find a clear formulation before Descartes and the Port-Royalists but, long before then, Ramist logic, while still eminently 'communicative', bore unmistakable traces of the rift which was to come.[30] It is perhaps scarcely surprising that the dialogue of Ramus' age should have tended away from true dialogue towards an elaborate monologue, turning its speakers from active protagonists into the custodians of a method elaborated, far from the clamour of their voices, by the writer's solitary pen.

Gradually, almost imperceptibly, in the course of the Cinquecento, the dialogue ceased to be 'listened to' as a sort of conversation and began to be perceived, quite simply, as a literary fancy dress. Like any of the subliminal changes brought about by the advent of print, this is a difficult process to chart. Some evidence is, however, forthcoming and there is a particularly striking manifestation of this change in the increasing incidence in dialogues of visual modes of presenting information.

More and more frequently, in the second half of the Cinquecento, especially in dialogues on technical matters, the typographical presentation of the work defies any attempt at an aural reconstruction of the conversation it purports to represent. A good example is Benedetto Varchi's *Ercolano* (1570): a dialogue clearly designed to appeal to the eye, rather than to the ear. The 'dubitazioni' and 'quesiti' which Cesare Ercolani poses to his interlocutor – the author himself – are numbered and set out in a fashion which at once destroys any illusion that we are listening to a conversation:

[Ercolani] '. . . per non perdere tempo . . ., vi propongo primieramente queste sei dubitazioni:

> LA PRIMA, Che cosa sia favellare
> LA SECONDA, Se il favellare è solamente dell'huomo
> [LA] TERZA, Se il favellare è naturale all'huomo . . .[31]

Varchi's reply – 'IL PARLARE, O VERO FAVELLARE HUMANO ESTER- IORE NON E ALTRO, CHE MANIFESTARE AD ALCUNO I CONCETTI DELL'ANIMO MEDIANTE LE PAROLE' – is capitalized in a way which could only make sense to the ear if we imagined him, most incongruously, speaking this part louder than the rest.[32] In his subsequent 'dichiarazione' of this formal definition, each of its constituent words continues to be capitalized and the *incipit* of each of his answers to Ercolani's doubts is indented and capitalized like a chapter heading.[33] For all his care to evoke a lively and conversational register, Varchi's dialogue, as a dialogue, simply does not make sense. At times, it verges on the ridiculous – it is implausible enough that the speakers should quote passages from previous treatises from memory, but when they start to give page references and publication details for their citations, we are made painfully aware of the degree to which typographical innovations like footnotes are incompatible with the fiction of civil conversation.[34]

Where our efforts to suspend disbelief are perhaps most sorely tested are those passages in the *Ercolano* in which dialogue yields to diagrammatic exposition: in its 'divisions', reminiscent of those found in Ramist textbooks, and in the seven-page section of pronouns, presented in tabular form.[35] Similarly, Ercole Bottrigari's dialogue on music, *Il Desiderio* (1594), contains illustrations of keyboard harmonies, while Giacomo Lanteri's *Del modo di disegnare le piante delle fortezze* (1557) and, of course, Galileo's *Dialogo dei massimi sistemi* (1638) are illustrated fairly lavishly with diagrams and figures.[36] The degree to which verisimilitude is respected in these cases varies from one dialogue to another: Bottrigari makes hasty mention of the presence of a 'Clavicembolo' to justify his inclusion of diagrams, and Galileo is notably scrupulous in his handling of props.[37] Despite these niceties, however, the effect of the inclusion of such devices in dialogue is to undermine the reader's faith in the fiction of the conversation portrayed and to make him aware of the book before him as a physical object, rather than an utterance.

It could be argued, of course, that such dialogues constitute a special case and that, if authors like Bottrigari and Varchi had recourse to diagrammatic presentation, it was simply because of the exigencies of their highly technical subject-matter. It is certainly true that, because of the nature of their argument, the *Desiderio* and the *Ercolano* need the resources of typography in a way that the *Cortegiano* does not. But it must be recognized that the fact that the dialogue was increasingly used in textbooks on geometry and grammar may be a symptom of the desiccation of its oral element rather than a cause. The intrusion of diagrams and tables into dialogues on technical subjects is only the most obvious manifestation of a deeper cultural change, which struck at the very roots of the dialogue and the communicational ideal it expressed.

It has been argued convincingly, by Ong and others, that the advent of print and the new sense of the book as an 'object' brought with it new tendencies to an impersonal, authoritative discourse.[38] By virtue of its physical 'completeness', its illusion of finality, the printed book 'can convey the impression, subtly, but tangibly, that the material the text deals with is similarly complete or self-consistent'.[39] In this way, typography encourages the convention of a fixed authorial viewpoint, which readers may accept or refuse, but whose remoteness and self-sufficiency they cannot realistically challenge.[40]

These developments favoured the growth of genres like the textbook, the 'art', the manual,[41] but, at the same time, they stifled the fragile genre of dialogue at its roots. The 'openness' of the open dialogue depends in an intangible but crucial fashion on its fiction of orality. In a crude formula: the more we, the audience, believe in the work as a dialogue, the less remote and self-sufficient we will feel the text to be; the less impenetrable, the less static, the less closed to our intervention. On the other hand, anything which destroys our illusion and make us aware of the book as an object, the product of a single author – in Bargagli's words, 'una sola penna' – will tend to make us less actively involved in the production of its meaning. The open dialogue rests on a fragile pact between author and reader, held together by mutual fictions, which cannot survive the more rigid role-divisions enforced by the advent of print.

The complex links between order, closure and the effects of print are well illustrated by the editorial fate of humanist dialogues in the later part of the century. At the beginning of chapter 8, I cited Orazio Lombardelli's methodological critique of Bembo's *Prose* as evidence of late-sixteenth-century unease with the disorder of the dialogues of the first decades of the century. Bembo's argument, according to Lombardelli, is so 'drowned' in the flow of his dialogue that it is difficult, if not impossible, to use the *Prose* as a work of reference.

Lombardelli's remarks betray the prejudices of a typographical culture, which perceives books as objects to be handled rather than speeches to be listened to. His particular criticism of the *Prose* – that 'all'improviso non vi si può ritrovar cosa, che altri voglia' – is really a reaction against the fact that, unlike the textbooks being produced in his own age, Bembo's dialogue is structured to resemble a fragment of oral discourse rather than a spatially negotiable repository of accessible, labelled doctrine. The remedy he proposes is that quintessential product of a visual culture: a 'tavola', a table of contents, appended to the work by its editors, 'perché [le *Prose*] venissero lette più volentieri'.[42]

The effects of this sort of editorial intervention are clearly illustrated in the Cinquecento publishing history of the *Cortegiano*. The first annotated edition of Castiglione's dialogue was issued by Giolito in 1541. From 1552, the task of editing the work was consigned to the Venetian *poligrafo* Lodovico Dolce, and the next two decades saw a series of ever more elaborate editions, decked out with a lavish apparatus of *argomenti* and *postille* and meticulously mapped by an ever-expanding *Tavola delle cose notevoli*.[43] These additions must certainly have been of assistance to impatient readers like Lombardelli. Where the Aldine first edition is a book which 'can only be assimilated by being read through', these later editions allow the dialogue to be 'skimmed through', in search of the facts.[44] But in addition to guiding readers to find what they were looking for, the notes and indexes of editors like Dolce also, more tendentiously, suggest to them *what* they should look for, insinuating the possibility of a 'correct' reading of a dialogue which had originally been carefully structured to permit any number of readings.

In attempting to establish the reasons for the closure of dialogue into monologue, we should be wary of attributing too much weight to any single factor. The emphases of Dolce's commentary bear the unmistakable imprint of post-Tridentine political and religious piety[45] and, to this extent, his intervention may be interpreted as one of the series of phenomena of censorship examined in chapter 7. But the effects of the *Index librorum prohibitorum* must be balanced against those of the *index locorum*. As Carlo Ossola has pointed out, regardless of the context of its prescriptions, the very act of reducing an argument like that of the *Cortegiano* into the rigid categories of a *tavola* structured as a series of rules in itself does a certain violence to the nature of the dialogue. Instead of following through the subtleties of an artful 'paradosso', we are encouraged to use the *Cortegiano* as a straightforward work of reference, a textbook, a 'catalogo'.[46] Dolce's index, in effect, confers on the dialogue that fixed authorial viewpoint which Castiglione had tried so hard to avoid. In Dolce's edition, the *Cortegiano* becomes precisely what its author says the dialogue is *not*: a series of 'precetti distinti' on which, by a diligent use of the index, the prospective reader may impose the 'ordine' he desires.[47]

The changes in reading habits brought about by the medium of print militated at a very fundamental level against the sort of reading demanded by the humanist dialogue. In particular, by sundering literary discourse from its roots in spoken utterance, print destroyed the fragile parallelism which had so suggestively bound together the dialogue's fictional conversation and its real 'conversation' with the reader.

This development had serious consequences for the unity of the dialogue. As written and spoken discourse diverged ever more widely, it was inevitable that the strain would begin to show in a genre which had, traditionally, attempted to weld them together. In the final section of this chapter, I intend to look at a dialogue which, better than any other, illustrates the tensions of a genre which was falling apart at the seams. A dialogue which started life as a treatise, written by an author who is patently ill at ease with the dialogue form, Battista Guarini's *Il Segretario* (1594) is a fitting end to a study which has set out to chart the decline of the genre.

Il Segretario appears to have started life as a treatise on epistolary style, doubtless intended as a showplace for the professional skills of its

temporarily unemployed author.[48] Guarini's decision to convert his original *Lettera sulle lettere* into a dialogue was probably motivated, in great
part, by considerations of 'public relations': the dialogue format permits
him to give honourable mention to a group of Venetian patrons and
friends, primarily Iacopo Contarini, the host and *princeps* of the dialogue
and a man of considerable standing in the Republic.[49] More subtly, by his
deft use of a Venetian political perspective, the dialogue allows Guarini to
voice his frustration with the 'servitude' of court employment without
risking a potentially damaging statement *in propria persona*.[50]

Another reason why Guarini was attracted to the dialogue form may be
surmised from a particularly self-referential passage in the dialogue itself.
The *Segretario* opens with a scene in which one interlocutor, Sebastiano
Venier, or Veniero, is called on to narrate to the others a discussion on the
status of the secretary which he had witnessed the previous day. As he
struggles with the task, one of his companions suggests a radical alternative: that, instead of simply recounting the dialogue 'da riferente', he
might re-enact it, 'da disputante', along with the rest of the group.[51] This
method, all agree, will have the inestimable advantage that, by turning
Veniero's passive listeners into active, involved participants, it will re-
kindle the 'caldo' and 'libertà' of the original debate.[52]

This scene's application to problems of literary exposition will be
instantly apparent. Like Montaigne, Guarini is aware that 'the study of
books' is 'a languishing and weak kind of motion', lacking the heat and
vigour generated by 'jelousie' in conversation.[53] To correct this failing,
Guarini, like Plato, turns to the remedy of dialogue – a written form
which, by mirroring the structure of an oral exchange, seeks to conduct
the heat of conversation onto the pages of a book.[54]

Even without this dramatized declaration of intent, it would be obvious
to the reader that one of Guarini's prime concerns in his dialogue is that
of reproducing the creative rivalry of live conversation. In the first part of
the *Segretario*, at least – the first 'arringo', as it is significantly termed –
every point is hotly contested and metaphors of combat abound.[55] The
complex rituals of free and equal discussion are scrupulously observed
and Contarini, the dominant speaker, makes a great play of modesty,
eliciting his companions' views at every stage and deflecting their compliments back to them.[56]

For all this, however, the *Segretario* is very far from an open dispute.
Every clash of opinion, however fierce, punctually terminates in victory
for a *princeps sermonis* whose authority as 'padre' and 'maestro' is never
really in question.[57] The 'caldo' of the *Segretario*'s conversational format
is in reality exploited only for the most superficial of ends. Rather than a
Speronian spark, igniting the fire of truth in the reader's responsive

ingegno, the dialogue has become a sort of microwave oven, dutifully re-heating a 'dottrina' which has already been pre-cooked.[58]

Of course, there is nothing surprising about this. In its methodical format and monological function, the *Segretario* is typical of its age. What gives this dialogue its particular interest, especially for my present purpose, is that Guarini does not limit himself to improvising an 'orderly' variant of dialogue by adapting outdated models to fit the needs of the moment. Instead, in the episode already alluded to, of Veniero's failed attempt at narration, Guarini sets out to provide a theoretical grounding for this practice.

In a telling scene at the beginning of this episode, the reluctant 'riferente' is given conflicting advice by his companions on how to narrate a dialogue. The options which emerge are two. Contarini's suggestion is that Veniero reconstruct the dispute according to 'la regola de' filosofi', using the 'order' of its argument to revive his memory of its 'circostanze', 'cose' and 'concetti'.[59] The alternative, proposed by Zeno, is to abandon this 'ordine di natura' in favour of an 'ordine del caso'. What this means in practical terms is that 'starting from the beginning', Venier should first narrate the 'circumstances of the discussion' and then, 'just as they come along', the sequence of assertions and replies.[60]

These contrasting narrative formulae neatly encapsulate two quite different approaches to argumentation in the dialogue. In Zeno's scheme, it is the 'occasione' of the dialogue which becomes the ordering principle for its subsequent argumentation. The 'ordine' of the argument – such as it is – its 'concetti' and its 'cose', are all determined by its 'circostanze' of place, person and time.[61] In Contarini's formula, on the other hand, the dialogue is orchestrated principally by the structure of its argument, which is conceived of as existing apart from the contingencies of the debate. In practice, the form of dialogue Zeno is describing is that practised by Castiglione or Speroni, in which the initial dramatic datum fundamentally conditions the progress of the argument. The dialogue outlined by Contarini, in contrast, is that which developed in the later Cinquecento: the 'quasi-logical', ordered dialogue, prepared to bend to breaking-point the fiction of its 'ritratto' in order to clear a path for the stately progress of method.

Needless to say, Guarini makes his preference for the latter option clear.[62] Zeno's proposal is only offered as a poor second to Contarini's and when Venier pursues this soft option, his 'dialogue' predictably descends into chaos. His narration gets off to a good start when Agostino Michele, the most authoritative of its interlocutors, produces a clearly formulated 'proposizione contenziosa' which, if pursued systematically, would lay the grounds for an orderly discussion.[63] But Michele's proposal

is soon drowned out, and Veniero concludes, in what reads like a carica-
ture of the humanist dialogue, that 'poi disse ognuno confusamente
quello che ne sentiva . . . finché . . . quand' era la contesa e più calda e più
dilettevole . . . senza decisione alcuna si terminò'.[64] Contarini asks in
vain for a more detailed account of each speaker's methods and arguments, their 'mezzi' and 'ragioni'. The 'substance' of the speakers' reasoning, we learn, was so bound up with irrelevancies (*parti inutili*) that an
ordered synopsis would be impossible.

The episode as a whole reveals Guarini's highly equivocal attitude to
the dialogue's project of reproducing the conditions of oral exchange. He
is keenly aware that any serious attempt to translate conversation into
print will inevitably bring with it something of the inconclusiveness, the
false starts, the dead ends, the sheer *messiness* which characterize conversation in its natural sphere. For a writer who is seeking to use the form as
a matrix of invention or for the reader frustrated with the smug closure
and self-sufficiency of written discourse, this creative, quasi-oral disorder
is one of the principal attractions of dialogue. For a writer like Guarini,
on the other hand, who views the dialogue simply as a means of 'disposition' or for a reader like Orazio Lombardelli, intent on learning and
impatient with redundancy, those elements in the dialogue which most
clearly betray its radical or oral discourse are, at best, otiose and, at
worse, seriously obstructive.

The disorderly elements in a dialogue cannot be entirely eliminated if it is
to retain the rhetorical merit of a spurious 'caldo' and 'libertà'. What
Guarini is proposing in theory and what he demonstrates in his practice, is
that these 'parti inutili', the detritus of a superannuated cult of orality,
should be kept, as far as possible, from disrupting the dialogue's 'substance'. The implications of this become plain if we look at the argumentation of *Il Segretario*. Guarini's dialogue takes to extremes that
process of sifting out rhetorical techniques which I identified in the first
section of this chapter as characteristic of the dialogues of the later Cinquecento. Devices like metaphor and example are used sparingly and,
though they may be praised as 'delightful', Guarini makes clear that they
are intended as, at most, a 'suggello' to arguments already signed and
delivered.[65] Metaphor is acceptable only in an illustrative, not its generalizing function[66] and, on those rare occasions when an interlocutor does
attempt to use *esempio* as a means of furthering his argument, his hapless
image is analysed, dissected and boiled down into its naked 'ragione', in a
way which utterly deprives it of any imaginative resonance.[67] What
Guarini objects to in metaphor is precisely what had appealed to earlier
writers of dialogue: its 'diversità' – the gap between the literal and figurative
planes, which opens the way for idiosyncratic interpretation and dissent.[68]

The same sort of censorship which Guarini applies to rhetorical argumentation is apparent in other areas. Prime victims are those social rituals of deference and *modestia* which had played such a delicate structural role in dialogues like the *Cortegiano*, reminding the reader that no speaker holds a monopoly on the truth.[69] These 'ceremonie' had remained useful in establishing a polite social tone and Guarini continues to use them liberally to orchestrate his discussion. But he is always careful to label them as 'superfluous' and 'fruitless' (*soverchie e infruttuose*), and one speaker, Girolamo Zeno, is half-jokingly awarded the role of 'Censore' to ensure that these 'intingoli e saporetti di perditempo e di modeste parole' are not allowed to interfere with the serious business of debate.[70]

The profoundly inorganic conception of dialogue which informs the *Segretario* is characteristic of the age in which Guarini was writing. One of the chief advantages cited by champions of the dialogue was its capacity, modelled as it was on the non-linear patterns of oral discussion, to absorb any number of 'essempi', 'discorsi' and 'digressioni'.[71] Conversely, for its detractors, like those cited by Sforza Pallavicino, the dialogue's 'episodii che vannosi perpetuamente intralacciando' were the main culprits in its lamentable incursion on the audience's time.[72] In any case, in this age of Aristotelian orthodoxy, a firm division was made between the necessary and contingent elements in dialogue. The essential part of the dialogue was a unified questione, which played the same organizing role as the *favola* of a poem.[73] Any digressions from this *questione*, like the *episodi* of a poem, are conceived of as inessential and must be clearly labelled as such.

A traditional metaphor for the dialogue, since classical times, had been the banquet or symposium: as rich and various in its material provisions as the dialogue was in its arguments. In the *Segretario*, Guarini updates this image in accordance with the spirit of his age, when he has Venier recommend that, for 'noi amatori della frugalità filosofica', it will be advisable to 'ferma[re] il gusto in una sola vivanda'.[74] In this strict diet, as we have seen, social *ceremonie* and inconclusive arguments become a self-indulgence to be frowned on.[75] Substantive digressions fare little better: while they may be tolerated for the 'belle considerazioni' they introduce into the argument, we are never allowed to forget that they are, precisely, digressions, 'di niuna efficacia per quella pruova che si vorrebbe'.[76]

It is, paradoxically, in the name of unity – unity of argument – that Guarini undertakes his task of restructuring the literary dialogue. In the course of this process, however, the deeper unity between mimesis and argumentation which had characterized the humanist dialogue is irrevocably lost. The effect of Guarini's censorship is to isolate and marginalize those 'mimetic' elements in the dialogue which do not contribute directly to the substance of its argument. The finished product is a dialogue which can be read as a monological treatise, whose conversational form is no more than an awkward and cumbersome decorative veneer.

On one level, the *Segretario* is a painfuly clear example of the radical disunity of argument and form which afflicted the late-Cinquecento dialogue. Ironically, however, on another level, its argument and form are in harmony, as both are expressions and symptoms of a single historical process.

I have suggested that the formal disunity of dialogues like the *Segretario* is a sign of the profound shift in consciousness provoked by the new medium of print. The effect of Guarini's radical restructuring of the dialogue is to pare off the lingering accretions of oral patterns of communication and thought. The humanist dialogue he is seeking to reform had owed what he saw as its lamentable disorder to its pursuit of an elusive union between the spoken and the written word. By Guarini's time, the spheres of the oral and the written had diverged to such an extent that this end was not only no longer realistic but no longer even desirable.

That portion of the argument of the *Segretario* which concerns the status of rhetoric reflects a similar lack of sympathy with the ideals of an oral culture. Guarini's dialogue is a particularly relentless expression of the general post-humanist tendency to reduce rhetoric to the purely technical skills of disposition and elocution. A strict distinction is observed between 'parole' and 'concetti', rhetoric and science, elocution and thought.[77] The Secretary's art, in Guarini, is as far from the classical and humanist ideal of eloquence as its timid, servile, politically neutral practitioner is from his classical and humanist forebears.[78]

One reason for this impoverishment in the status of rhetoric was, of course, local and political. The humanist vision of a union of eloquence and wisdom rested, as Guarini was well aware, on republican ideals of a collective exercise of power which, by his day, had long ceased – outside Venice, at least – to have any base in reality.[79] But another, far deeper and more intangible process which contributed to the downgrading of rhetoric was the gradual desiccation of the residual orality in Western culture, which followed on the invention and 'internalization' of print.

In his characterization of Ramist rhetoric as the product of a 'visual' mentality, Ong describes the new status of the art with exemplary clarity:

Like all rhetoric, Ramist rhetoric is concerned with expression, with communication, with speaking, with not only a subject-matter but an auditor. But it is a rhetoric which has renounced any possibility of invention within this speaker-auditor framework; it protests in principle if not in actuality, that invention is limited to a dialectical world where there is no voice, but only a kind of vision.[80]

It is a description which might be applied not only to Guarini's theory of rhetoric, but also to his theory and practice of the dialogue. Like Ramus' rhetoric, Guarini's dialogue is not a matrix of invention, but simply a means of 'disposing' a pre-established argument. It is the product of a 'voiceless' culture; a culture which formulates its truths in a space abstracted from the clamorous hustle of 'casi' and 'occasioni'. Such a culture could have no real use for a form like the Ciceronian dialogue, which mounts its cognitive constructs on the shifting ground of a congress of voices.

I am not implying, of course, that the monological tendencies of typographical culture reduced all discourse to unequivocal didactic exposition. The sort of probabilistic thought for which the dialogue had long served as vehicle did not, of course, disappear: indeed, it gained new refinements from the new sense of self ushered in by the culture of print. But it was no longer a collective enquiry, an activity which took place in the forum or the villa or the court. The new *locus* for the sifting of opinion was the lonely tower of Montaigne; its new vehicle the eminently 'typographical' genre of the essay.[81]

For a while, resting on the laurels of a prestigious tradition, the dialogue survived and even, paradoxically, in Galileo's *Dialogo sui massimi sistemi* served as a vehicle for one of the first great products of a recognizably modern scientific mentality. But it survived only in an etiolated form, severed from its roots in orality; desiccated into a simple instrument of disposition. Sforza Pallavicino, Galileo's contemporary, justifies the dialogue's quasi-oral structure using an analogy as far removed as possible from conversation – the teaching situation, in which an unchallenged 'Maestro' hammers home an unchallenged doctrine though the power of his eloquence.[82]

Sigonio, in his *De dialogo liber*, had described the dialogue as one of two potential *vie* of human knowledge: a sociable complement to the lonely path of demonstrative reasoning, pursued *tacita quadam animi agitatione*.[83] Already, in 1562, to present these two ways as parallel and equal was something of an anachronism.[84] A century later, when Pallavicino was writing, the last murmurings of classical rhetorical culture were being definitively drowned out by the clamorous silence of Cartesian logic. The last remaining function of the dialogue – now simply the literary equivalent of a lecture – was to convey the truths elaborated in the silent reaches of the mind.

Notes

1 PROBLEMS OF METHOD

1 In *The Works of Lucian. Translated from the Greek by Several Eminent Hands* (London, 1711), pp. 45–6.

2 On the lack of any systematic theoretical discussion of dialogue in antiquity, see Michel Ruch, *Le préambule dans les œuvres philosophiques de Cicéron: essai sur la genèse et l'art du dialogue* (Paris, 1958), pp. 7–8 and Jon R. Snyder, *Writing the Scene of Speaking: Theories of Dialogue in the Late Italian Renaissance* (Stanford, 1989), p. 21. For Aristotle's brief and ambiguous comments on dialogue, see *Poetics*, 1447a28; also Snyder, pp. 30–3 and K. J. Wilson *Incomplete fictions: the Formation of the English Renaissance Dialogue* (Washington D.C., 1985), pp. 4–9.

3 Northrop Frye, *Anatomy of Criticism: Four Essays* (Princeton, 1957), p. 13. Frye's point in this passage is that 'the critical theory of genre is stuck precisely where Aristotle left it'.

4 On the attempts to formulate a theory of the dialogue in Italy in this period, see Snyder, *Writing the Scene of Speaking*; Luisa Mulas, 'La scrittura del dialogo', in Giovanna Cerina, Cristina Lavinio and Luisa Mulas (eds.), *Oralità e scrittura nel sistema letterario* (Rome, 1982), pp. 245–63 and Raffaele Girardi, *La società del dialogo. Retorica e ideologia nella letteratura conviviale del Cinquecento* (Bari, 1989), pp. 27–63 and pp. 81–103. On individual theorists, see Girardi, '"Elegans imitatio et erudita": Sigonio e la teoria del dialogo', *Giornale storico della letteratura italiana*, vol. 163, fasc. 523 (1986), pp. 328–31; Guido Baldassari, 'L'arte del dialogo in Torquato Tasso', *Studi Tassiani*, vol. 20 (1970), pp. 5–46 and Jean-Louis Fournel, *Les dialogues de Sperone Speroni: libertés de la parole et règles de l'écriture* (Marburg, 1990), pp. 187–223.

5 Benedetto Croce, 'L'arte del dialogo secondo il Tasso', in *Poeti e scrittori del pieno e tardo Rinascimento* (Bari, 1945), vol. I, p. 121. The context of Croce's observation is a critique of Rudolf Hirzel's massive history of the dialogue, *Der Dialog, ein literaturhistorischer Versuch* (Leipzig, 1895).

6 Mark Jordan, 'A Preface to the Study of Philosophical Genres', *Philosophy and Rhetoric*, vol. 14, no. 4 (1981), pp. 202 and 206; see also Alan G. Gross, *The Rhetoric of Science* (Cambridge, Mass., and London, 1990), pp. 3–20, esp. p. 16. The question of genre in philosophy has been addressed by Julián Marias, *Philosophy as Dramatic Theory*, trans. J. Parsons (University Park, Pa., and London, 1971), pp. 1–35; Albert W. Levi, 'Philosophy as Literature:

the Dialogue', *Philosophy and Rhetoric*, vol. 9, no. 1 (1976), pp. 1–20; Berel Lang, 'Towards a Poetics of Philosophical Discourse', *The Monist*, vol. 63, no. 4 (1980), pp. 449–53 and Charles L. Griswold, 'Style and Philosophy: the Case of Plato's Dialogues', in the same volume of *The Monist*, pp. 530–46. On genre in scientific writing, see Maria Luisa Altieri Biagi, 'Forme della communicazione scientifica', in Alberto Asor Rosa (ed.), *Letteratura italiana. III. Le forme del testo. II. La prosa* (Turin, 1984), pp. 891–947.

7 For a useful distinction between 'dramatic' and 'ontological' perspectives in the interpretation of Plato, see Stanley Rosen, *Plato's 'Sophist'. The Drama of Original and Image* (New Haven and London, 1983), pp. 1–7. For bibliographical surveys of the 'dramatic' trend within Plato criticism, see Michael C. Stokes, *Plato's Socratic Conversations. Drama and Dialectic in Three Dialogues* (London, 1986), pp. 1–3 and R. Desjardins, 'Why Dialogues? Plato's Serious Play', in Charles L. Griswold (ed.), *Platonic Writings, Platonic Readings* (London and New York, 1988), n. 21 to p. 119. The volume in which this latter essay appears gives a good indication of the vitality of the debate on Plato's use of the dialogue: apart from Desjardins's contribution, see also the essays by K. M. Sayre, Jürgen Mittelstrass and Charles L. Griswold, as well as the concluding 'dialogue' between Nicholas P. White and Hans-Georg Gadamer. Studies of philosophers other than Plato which show a sensitivity to the poetics of the dialogue form include M. Morrisoe, Jr, 'Hume's Rhetorical Strategy: a Solution to the Riddle of the *Dialogues concerning Natural Religion*', *Texas Studies in Literature and Language*, vol. 11, no. 2 (1969), pp. 963–74 and (also on Hume) 'Characterization as Rhetorical Device', *Enlightenment Essays*, vol. 1 (1970), pp. 95–107 and K. J. Wheeler, 'Berkeley's Ironic Method in the *Three Dialogues*', *Philosophy and Literature*, vol. 4, no. 1 (1980), pp. 18–32.

8 See, for example, Riccardo Scrivano, 'Nelle pieghe del dialogare bembesco', in Giulio Ferroni (ed.), *Il dialogo. Scambi e passaggi della parola* (Palermo, 1985), esp. p. 102. Scrivano proposes a definition of the dialogue as a 'discussione o dibattito', whose components are 'la situazione', 'gli interessati' and 'l'arbitro della situazione'. He is forced to conclude by admitting, however, that, in practice, the dialogue may not consist of a real discussion but simply the refutation of one antagonist by another and that, of the three component parts in dialogue, one or more is frequently lacking.

9 See, for example, on the field covered by the present study, Giovanna Wyss Morigi, *Contributo allo studio del dialogo nell'epoca dell'umanesimo e del Rinascimento* (Monza, 1950).

10 Jordan, 'A Preface to the Study of Philosophical Genres', p. 205.

11 David Simpson, 'Hume's Intimate Voices and the Method of Dialogue', *Texas Studies in Literature and Language*, vol. 21, no. 1 (1979), pp. 68–71. Statements of the same distinction can also be found in, for example, Lang, 'Towards a Poetics of Philosophical Discourse', p. 451 and Griswold, 'Style and Philosophy', p. 544.

12 Sforza Pallavicino, *Trattato dello stile e del dialogo* (Rome, 1662), p. 344; see below, chapter 7, pp. 77–9. The image of the reader as judge is, perhaps, ultimately Ciceronian: see C. J. R. Armstrong, 'The Dialectical Road to Truth: the Dialogue', in Peter Sharratt (ed.), *French Renaissance Studies*

1540–1570: Humanism and the Encyclopedia (Edinburgh, 1976), p. 43 and n. 42.

13 Levi, 'Philosophy as Literature', p. 11.

14 James Tyrrell, introduction to *Biblioteca Politica* (1718), cited in E. R. Purpus, 'The Plain, Easy and Familiar Way: the Dialogue in English Literature, 1660–1725', *English Literary History*, vol. 17 (1950), p. 50, n. 18.

15 Anthony Ashley Cooper, 3rd Earl of Shaftesbury, *Characteristics of Men, Manners, Opinions, Times, etc.*, ed. J. M. Robertson (London, 1900), vol. II, p. 338.

16 Shaftesbury, *Characteristics*, vol. I, p. 132; see also vol. II, pp. 339–41, on the necessity to provide both sides in a dialogue with strong arguments.

17 'L'arte del dialogo in Torquato Tasso', p. 37. The dialogues in question are *Il Forno overo della nobiltà* and its sequel, *De la dignità*, both written in 1580 and revised in 1585–7.

18 ('the Writer's opinion and its foundations are so clearly reflected in them') *Trattato dello stile e del dialogo*, p. 346.

19 For a useful discussion of the different configurations of what he terms the 'communication fictive' of the dialogue, see Michel Le Guern, 'Sur le genre du dialogue', in J. Lafond and André Stegmann (eds.), *L'Automne de la Renaissance, 1580–1630* (Paris, 1981), pp. 143–4.

20 The distinction between dramatized and narrated dialogues, and that between fictional and 'historical' dialogues are discussed in chapter 2 of this study.

21 The terms are taken from Roman Jakobsen 'Linguistics and Poetry', in T. Sebeok (ed.), *Style and Language* (Cambridge, 1960), p. 353.

22 The classical *locus* for the comparison is the Greek commentator Artemon, cited in Pseudo-Demetrius, *De elocutione*, 223. The passage was frequently cited by critics of both genres in the Renaissance: see, for example, Angelo Poliziano, *Commento inedito alle selve di Stazio*, ed. Lucia Cesarini Martinelli (Florence, 1978), p. 18; Carlo Sigonio, *De dialogo liber* (1562), in *Opera omnia*, ed. Filippo Argelati (Milan, 1732–7), vol. VI, c. 447D; Torquato Tasso, *Discorso dell'arte del dialogo* (1585), ed. Guido Baldassari, *La rassegna della letteratura italiana*, vol. 75, series 7, nos. 1–2 (1971), p. 130. For a more extensive and original comparison between the letter and the dialogue, see also the dedicatory letter of Luca Contile's *Lettere* (1564), discussed in Amedeo Quondam, 'Dal "formulario" al "formulario": cento anni di "libri di lettere"', in *Le carte messaggiere. Retorica e modelli di comunicazione epistolare: per un'indice dei libri di lettere del Cinquecento* (Rome, 1981), p. 21.

23 For a classic statement of the influential notion that the philosophical dialogue has surfaced during 'the revolutionary periods of world history' (fifth-century Athens, Renaissance Italy, eighteenth-century France) 'both as a sign and as a mode of expression of their spiritual strife,' see Hirzel, *Der Dialog*, vol. II, pp. 443–4. Little work has been done to date on the more specific social and cultural factors which may condition the emergence of the dialogue, in various periods of history, but see, for example, Armstrong, 'The Dialectical Road to Truth', for an interpretation of the Renaissance dialogue as the formal expression of the radical epistemology of humanist dialecticians like Agricola and Sturm; also Steven Rendall, 'Fontanelle's Art of Dialogue and His Public', *Modern Language Notes*, vol. 84, no. 4 (1971), pp. 496–508, which interprets

Fontanelle's adoption of the dialogue form as a reaction to changes within the constitution of the reading public in his age.

24 In this respect, the dialogue might profitably be compared with forms of argument like the aphorism and the essay, which may not dramatize the relations of addresser and addressee in quite the same way as the dialogue, but which nevertheless, by virtue of their form, call this relation into question. On the relation between Montaigne's essay and the dialogue form, see Hugo Friedrich, *Montaigne*, trans. R. Rovini (Paris, 1968), pp. 373–5; R. A. Sayce, *The Essays of Montaigne. A Critical Exploration* (London, 1972), pp. 38–40 and Margaret M. MacGowan, *Montaigne's Deceits: the Art of Persuasion in the 'Essais'* (London, 1974), esp. pp. 54–5.

25 See Antonfrancesco Doni, *La libraria* (1550), ed. Vanni Bramanti (Milan, 1972), pp. 127–8: 'la molta comodità de' libri e gran quantità . . . ci hanno oggi mai fatta una selva inestricabile sugli occhi dell'intelletto' ('books are so easily available now, and in such great quantities, that they form an impenetrable forest around the eyes of the mind'). For a discussion of this and other contemporary testimonies to the impact of print, see Amedeo Quondam's valuable study, *La letteratura in tipografia*, in Alberto Asor Rosa (ed.), *Letteratura italiana. II. Produzione e consumo* (Turin, 1983), pp. 566–72 and 613–31.

26 Sforza Pallavicino, *Storia del Concilio di Trento* (1656), in *Storia del Concilio di Trento ed altri scritti*, ed. Mario Scotti (Turin, 1962), p. 444: 'si sono tanto diffuse le lettere da un secolo e mezzo in qua, che forse è ora maggior la copia di chi sa scriver libri, che per addietro di chi gli sapesse intendere'. Pallavicino also notes that 'tutte l'opere insieme dal primo sorger della Chiesa fuor delle grotte fin all'anno mille e cinquecento constituiscono picciola porzione rispetto di quelle che da indi in qua sono uscite' ('all the works written from the dawn of Christianity until the year 1500, put together, amount to only a tiny fraction of those which have appeared since that date').

27 The bibliography on the cultural impact of printing is immense. An important study is Elizabeth L. Eisenstein, *The Printing Press as an Agent of Change: Communications and Cultural Transformations in Early-Modern Europe* (Cambridge, 1979); a useful, brief introduction, Walter J. Ong, *Orality and Literacy; the Technologizing of the Word* (New York and London, 1982), pp. 117–38. On the impact of printing in Cinquecento Italy in particular, see also Amedeo Quondam, *La letteratura in tipografia* and, by the same author, '"Mercanzia d'onore" / "mercanzia d'utile": produzione libraria e lavoro intellettuale a Venezia nel Cinquecento', in Armando Petrucci (ed.), *Libri, editori e pubblico nell'Europa moderna. Guida storica e critica* (Bari, 1977), pp. 51–104; also, most recently, Claudia Di Filippo Bareggi, *Il mestiere di scrivere: lavoro intellettuale e mercato libraio a Venezia nel Cinquecento* (Rome, 1988).

2 HISTORY AND INVENTION IN THE DIALOGUE

1 ('I shall recount a series of discussions on this subject which once took place between some very remarkable men . . .') *Il Libro del Cortegiano, con una scelta delle Opere minori*, ed. Bruno Maier (Turin, 1964), p. 81.

2 On the importance of this ethical irony in the *Malpiglio*, see Dain A. Trafton,

'Tasso's Dialogue on the Court', *English Literary Renaissance Supplements*, no. 2 (1973), pp. 3–10.

3 *Les Morales de Torquato Tasso* (Paris, 1612), vol. I, p. 1. Badouin's policy of replacing Tasso's historical interlocutors by fictional names is consistent throughout the volume.

4 It may, however, be relevant to note that, a year after the publication of *Les Morales de Torquato Tasso*, Badouin produced a translation of Lucian's dialogues, in *Les œuvres de Lucien* (Paris, 1613). On Lucian as the originator of the 'fictional' dialogue, see below.

5 See below, chapter 3.

6 See below, chapter 4.

7 In *Utopia*, More depicts himself in conversation with the Utopian Raphael Hythloday, Stephen Greenblatt, *Renaissance Self-Fashioning* (Chicago, 1980), pp. 36–7, argues convincingly that the two figures represent, respectively, More's 'public self' and 'all within him that is excluded from this carefully-crafted identity'. Heywood's *Il Moro* (1556) is given a realistic setting, in Chelsea, and it is clearly intended as a celebratory portrait of More (see Heywood's dedicatory letter to Cardinal Pole, at p. 2 of the edition by Roger L. Deakins (Cambridge, Mass., 1972)), but its historical consistency is under-mined by the fact that his interlocutors are identified only by their Christian names, and clearly represent types rather than individuals. A different case again is Etienne Dolet's *Dialogus de imitatione Ciceroniana* (1535), which presents More in conversation with Simon de Neufville in Padua: a scene presented as historical but in fact highly implausible, since More had never been to Italy and was, at the time of the dialogue, imprisoned in the Tower (see E. V. Telle, *'L'"Erasmianus sive Ciceronianus" d'Etienne Dolet* (Geneva, 1974), p. 42).

8 Clearly, what follows is intended as no more than the barest outline of a subject which would require an entire book to cover it in the detail it deserves. A more comprehensive survey of classical influence on Renaissance dialogue production would have to take into account a far broader range of classical and post-classical influences, including Xenophon, Plutarch, Macrobius and Boethius.

9 For Lucian's claims to have invented a wholly new species of dialogue, see his *The Double Indictment* and *To One Who Said 'You're a Prometheus in Words'*, in *Works*, trans. A. M. Harman, K. Kilburn and M. D. MacLeod (Cambridge, Mass., 1960–5), at, respectively, vol. III, pp. 145–51 and vol. VI, pp. 425–7. On the justice of these claims, see J. Hall, *Lucian's Satire* (New York, 1981), pp. 64–71 and Pierre Grimal, 'Caractères généraux du dialogue romain, de Lucilius à Cicéron', *L'information littéraire*, vol. 7, no. 5 (1955), p. 194. On Lucian's influence in the Renaissance, see Emilio Mattioli, *Luciano e l'umane-simo* (Naples, 1980), C. A. Mayer, *Lucien de Samose et la Renaissance française* (Geneva, 1984) and Christopher Robinson, *Lucian and his Influence in Europe* (London, 1979), pp. 81–144.

10 The phrase is from *Lucian's Defence against one who calls him Prometheus*, trans. T. Ferne, in *The Works of Lucian*, vol. I, p. 13.

11 Mustapha Kemal Bénouis, *Le dialogue dans la littérature française du seizième siècle* (The Hague and Paris, 1976), p. 51.

12 For the term, and an exemplifcation of the practice in the sixteenth-century French dialogue, see Kemal Bénouis, *Le dialogue*, pp. 186–7.

13 On the surprisingly lively characterization of the unpromisingly named 'Demande' and 'Response', the protagonists of Bernard Palissy's *Recepte véritable* (1563), see E. Kushner, 'Le dialogue en France de 1550 à 1560', in M. T. Jones-Davies (ed.), *Le dialogue au temps de la Renaissance* (Paris, 1984), p. 150. On the flatness of Bembo's depiction of Ercole Strozzi, and his reliance on the stereotypes of classical tradition, see Scrivano, 'Nelle pieghe del dialogare bembesco', pp. 105–6.

14 *Prologue to the Christian Reader*, in Thomas Wilson, *A Discourse on Usury by way of dialogue and orations, for the better variety and more delight of all those that shall read this treatise* (1572), ed. R. H. Tawney (London, 1925), p. 192.

15 My reference here is to Castiglione's famous description of his *Libro del Cortegiano* (1528) as a 'ritratto di pittura' of the court of Urbino (*Cortegiano*, p. 71; the passage is cited below, n. 67). The analogy between portraiture in the visual arts and the verbal portraiture of the documentary dialogue is an illuminating one, even though I share some of the reservations expressed by Eduardo Saccone, in 'The Portrait of the Courtier in Castiglione', *Italica*, vol. 61, no. 1 (1987), pp. 2–4, about the weight of meaning which has been attached to it in some recent criticism.

16 On the level of verisimilitude in Plato's dialogues, see Ruch, *Le préambule dans les œuvres philosophiques de Cicéron*, pp. 31–2.

17 See especially the two studies by Stanley Rosen, *Plato's 'Symposium'* (New Haven and London, 1968) and *Plato's 'Sophist'* (New Haven and London, 1983); also Stokes, *Plato's Socratic Conversations* p. 446.

18 ('the conflict between doctrines is certainly less important than the conflict between individuals: their characters, their temperaments, their prejudices . . . seem to be accompanied by the invisible, but tangible entourage of the actions they have performed in real life') Grimal, *Caractères généraux*, p. 195; see also Wilson, *Incomplete Fictions*, pp. 23–45.

19 Ruch, *Le préambule*, esp. pp. 47–8, 112–14 and 379–408.

20 See Grimal, *Caractères généraux*, p. 197; also M. Levine, 'Cicero and the Literary Dialogue', *The Classical Journal*, vol. 53, no. 4 (1958), p. 147.

21 See, for example, *Symposium* 172a–174a and *Phaedo* 57a–59d. Ruch, *Le préambule*, p. 32, relates Plato's use of eye-witness narrators to current forensic practice.

22 Grimal, *Caractères généraux*, p. 196. The most striking, and self-conscious, instance of this difference is the opening of Cicero's *De oratore*, where Scaevola's allusion to the *Phaedrus* only serves to signal the difference in tone between the two dialogues (*De oratore*, I vii, 28–9; see also Woldemar Görler, 'From Athens to Tusculum: Gleaning the Background of Cicero's *De Oratore*', *Rhetorica*, vol. 6, no. 3 (1988), p. 216, n. 4). The exception to the rule stated here, in Greek dialogue, is the symposium form: more exclusive than the Socratic colloquium, but, needless to say, quite alien in tone and mood from the decorous gatherings portrayed by Cicero. Ruch, *Le préambule*, p. 45, n. 3, notes a precedent for the 'dialogue de villa' in the Greek writer Praxiphanes, but the exception here serves, more than anything, to prove the rule.

23 Carlo Sigonio, *De dialogo liber*, c. 466:B: 'Haec ego non nego, quin mirifica

quadam sint suavititate condita omnia, sed ratio personarum fecit, quae non generis, sed vitae, non rerum gestarum, sed doctrinae nobilitate sunt commendatae, ut quanto plus habet jucunditatis, tanto magnificentiae minus.' ('I do not deny that [Plato's dialogues] have remarkable charm. But the speakers are chosen on the criterion of their lifestyle, rather than their breeding, and their learning, rather than their deeds, so that the dialogues lose in magnificence what they gain in charm.') It is interesting to note that the one significant exception to Cicero's rule of using patrician speakers in his dialogues – the slave of the *Tusculan Disputations* – is punctually identified as an exception by Torquato Tasso, in his *Discorso dell'arte del dialogo*, p. 128. For further discussion of the passage, see my 'Rhetoric and Politics in Tasso's *Nifo*', *Studi secenteschi*, vol. 30 (1989), p. 24.

24 *De oratore*, II iv 18: 'omnium autem ineptiarum [of the Greeks], quae sunt innumerabiles, haud scio, an nulla sit maior, quam, ut illi solent, quocumque in loco, quoscumque inter homines visum est, de rebus aut difficillimus, aut non necessariis, argutissime disputare' ('of all the innumerable manifestations of the Greeks' lack of a sense of decorum, the worst is their habit of launching into the most subtle disputes, on extremely complex and abstruse subjects, without regard for the place or the company').

25 Grimal, *Caractères généraux*, p. 196; Levine, 'Cicero and the Literary Dialogue', p. 146.

26 *Lettera del Signor Torquato Tasso nel quale paragona l'Italia alla Francia* (1571), in *Tre scritti politici*, ed. Luigi Firpo (Turin, 1980), p. 124: 'Il terzo costume che io non lodo, [in France] è che le lettere, e particolarmente le scienze, abandonate da' nobili, caggiono in mano della plebe: perché la filosofia (quasi donna regale maritata ad un villano), trattata da gli ingegni di plebei, perde molto del suo decoro naturale . . .' ('The third custom I deplore in France is that culture, and particularly the sciences, abandoned by the nobility, have fallen into the hands of plebians. For philosophy, when it is manhandled by plebian minds, loses much of its natural dignity, like a woman of regal stock, married to a peasant.') See also, more generally, on Cinquecento theorists' assumptions about the social composition of the audience for literary dialogue, Baldassari, 'L'arte del dialogo in Torquato Tasso', pp. 13–16.

27 On this sort of socially differentiated reception, see Frank Whigham, 'Interpretation at Court: Courtesy and the Performer–Audience Dialectic', *New Literary History*, vol. 14, no. 3 (1983), pp. 6234-4. For further discussion of the importance of 'authority' in sixteenth-century Italian dialogues, see below, chapter 4, pp. 36–7.

28 Prefatory letter to De Silva, in *Cortegiano*, p. 81: 'recitaremo alcuni ragionamenti, i quali già passarono tra omini singularissimi a tale proposito: e benché io non v'intervenissi presenzialmente, per ritrovarmi, allor che furon detti, in Inghilterra, avendogli poco apresso il mio ritorno intesi da persona che fedelmente me gli narrò, sforzerommi a punto, per quanto la memoria mi comporterà, ricordarli, acciò che noto vi sia quello che abbiano giudicato e creduto di questa materia omini degni di somma laude, ed al cui giudizio in ogni cosa prestar si potea indubitata fede' ('I shall recount a series of discussions on this subject which once took place between some very remarkable men.

I did not take part in them myself, since I was in England when they took place, but I did have an account of them, shortly after my return, from a person who narrated them faithfully to me. And, as far as my memory permits, I shall attempt to reproduce them precisely, in order that you may know what was thought and believed on this issue by a group of men worthy of the highest praise and whose judgment on all matters may be utterly relied on'). For a discussion of Castiglione's presentation of the dialogue, see Eduardo Saccone, 'Trattato e ritratto: l'introduzione del "Cortegiano"' in *Modern Language Notes*, vol. 93, no. 1 (1978), pp. 1–21, esp. p. 4, n. 10, where Saccone compares this passage to its source in *De oratore*, I vi 22–3.

29 On the *Cortegiano* as 'architesto', see Girardi, *La società del dialogo*, p. 66. On its Italian and European *fortuna*, see José Guidi, 'Reformulations de l'idéologie aristocratique au XVIe siècle: les différentes rédactions et la fortune du *Courtisan*', in Centre Interuniversitaire de Recherche sur la Renaissance Italienne, *Réécritures. Commentaires, parodies, variations dans la littérature italienne de la Renaissance* (Paris, 1983–4), vol. I, pp. 137–40; Adriano Prosperi (ed.), *La corte e il Cortegiano. II. Un modello europea* (Rome, 1980); C. Ossola, *Dal 'Cortegiano' all''Uomo di mondo'. Storia di un libro e di un modello sociale* (Turin, 1987), esp. pp. 43–98 and Sydney Anglo, 'The Courtier. The Renaissance and Changing Ideals', in A. G. Dickens (ed.), *The Courts of Europe. Politics, Patronage and Royalty, 1400–1800* (London, 1977), pp. 32–53. The formal influence of the *Cortegiano* on Italian dialogue has not been the subject of systematic research; on borrowings by individual writers, see chapter 4, p. 38 and n. 33; chapter 7, p. 82 and n. 72 and chapter 8, p. 90 and n. 31. On the imitation by later writers of one particular feature of the *Cortegiano* – the flight of eloquence which gives the published version of the dialogue its distinctive ascensional structure – Ezio Raimondi, 'Il problema filologico e letterario dei *Dialoghi* di T. Tasso', in *Rinascimento inquieto* (Palermo, 1966), pp. 256–7; also Baldassari, 'L'arte del dialogo in Torquato Tasso', pp. 32–4 and, by the same critic, 'Interpretazioni del Tasso. Tre momenti della dialogistica di primo Seicento', *Studi Tassiani*, vol. 37 (1989), p. 80 and n. 70.

30 Dedicatory letter to Lord Henry Hastings, in *The Book of the Courtier*, trans. Sir Thomas Hoby, ed. W. Raleigh (London, 1900), p. 7. Castiglione's most explicit allusion to the exemplary role of the speakers occurs at *Cortegiano*, I xii, pp. 99–100, where, proposing as the entertainment for the evening the 'game' of defining the perfect courtier, Federico Fregoso points out that 'chi volesse laudar la corte nostra . . . ben poria senza suspetto d'adulazion dir che in tutta la Italia forse con fatica si ritrovariano altrettanti cavalieri cosi singulari, ed oltre alla principal profession della cavalleria cosi eccellenti in diverse cose, come or qui si ritrovano; però, se in loco alcuno son omini che meritino esser chiamati bon cortegiani e che sappiano giudicar quello che alla perfezion della cortegiania s'appartiene, ragionevolmente si ha da creder che qui siano' ('anyone who wanted to praise this court could say without any suspicion of flattery that, in the whole of Italy, it would perhaps be difficult to find so many distinguished knights gathered together in one place as there are here: men who excel not only in their principal profession of warfare, but also in many other activities. So that, if there are good courtiers anywhere, and men qualified to judge what perfection in courtiership consists in, it may be

reasonably assumed that they are to be found here'). See also the prefaces to books III and IV (pp. 335–6 and 445–8). On Castiglione's criteria in choosing his speakers, see Piero Floriani, *I gentiluomini letterati. Studi sul dibattito culturale nel primo Cinquecento* (Naples, 1981), pp. 50–67; also, for a rather harsher judgment on Castiglione's distortion of the facts, in his assemblage of an ideal court at Urbino, Cecil H. Clough, 'La "famiglia" del Duca Guido-baldo da Montefeltro ed il *Cortegiano*', in Cesare Mozzarelli (ed.), *'Famiglia' del Principe e famiglia aristocratica* (Rome, 1988), esp. p. 341. For details of the careers of those chosen, the *Dizionarietto biografico* appended to Vittorio Cian's edition of the dialogue (Florence, 1916) and Cecil H. Clough, 'Francis I and the Courtiers of Castiglione's *Courtier*', in *The Duchy of Urbino in the Renaissance* (London, 1981). See also chapter 4, n. 17, below.

31 On Castiglione's modifications to the Ciceronian figure of the orator, see Daniel Javitch, *Poetry and Courtliness in Renaissance England* (Princeton, 1978), chapter 1.

32 For Boccaccio's statement of his reasons for disguising the names of his (in fact, almost certainly, fictional) interlocutors, see *Decameron*, ed. Vittorio Branca (Turin, 1980), pp. 29–30. For examples of Boccaccian influence in the dialogues of the Italian Renaissance, see Pietro Bembo, *Gli Asolani* (1505), in *Prose e rime di Pietro Bembo*, ed. Carlo Dionisotti (Turin, 1966), esp. p. 317, where Bembo echoes Boccaccio's reasons for choosing to disguise his interlo-cutors 'con infinta voce'; also Agnolo Firenzuola, *Ragionamenti d'amore* (1525) and *Dialogo delle bellezze delle donne* (1541), in *Opere*, ed. Delmo Maestri (Turin, 1977), esp. p. 717, where Firenzuola describes the female speakers of the dialogue as real women hidden 'sotto un sottil velo' and pp. 719–20, where he rather coyly acknowledges his identification with the protagonist, Celso. Other examples of dialogues with 'disguised' speakers include Lodovico Dolce's *Dialogo del modo di tor moglie* (Venice, 1538); Girolamo Zabata's *Ragionamento di sei nobili fanciulle genovesi, le quali con assai bella maniera de dire discorrono di molte cose allo stato loro appartenenti* (Pavia 1585) and Moderata Fonte's fascinating *Il merito delle donne* (Venice, 1600). The influence of Boccaccian models on the dialogue was counter-balanced by the intrusion of classical elements into the *cornici* of Boccaccian novella-collections: see, for example, Girolamo Parabosco's *I Diporti* (1550), where a series of *novelle* is narrated by a *brigata* of prominent contemporary figures, all male, who would seem more at home in a philosophical dialogue, and who, indeed, discuss the possibility of engaging in a dialogue on love or moral philosophy, before deciding to opt for story-telling: see *I Diporti*, in *Novellieri minori del Cinquecento. G. Parabosco – S. Erizzo*, ed. Giuseppe Gigli and Fausto Nicolini (Bari, 1912), p. 15.

33 The inclusion of women speakers is one of the great innovations of the vernacular humanist dialogue of the sixteenth century. A proud consciousness of the novelty represented by women interlocutors is apparent in the intro-duction to Book III of Pietro Bembo's self-consciously Boccaccian *Asolani* (1505) (*Prose e rime di Pietro Bembo*, p. 458): 'io stimo che saranno molti, che mi biasimeranno in ciò, che io alla parte di queste investigazioni le donne chiami, alle quali più s'acconvenga negli uffici delle donne dimorarsi, che andare di queste cose cercando. De' quali tuttavia non mi cale.' ('I imagine

that there will be many people who will criticize me for having called in women to participate in these investigations [into the nature of love], on the grounds that it is more fitting for women to devote themselves to their womanly tasks, than to interest themselves in these things. But I care nothing for these critics.') Despite the precedent of *Gli Asolani*, the introduction of women in learned dialogues remained controversial, especially when they were given leading roles. For two interesting justifications of the practice, on the grounds of women's intellectual equality with men, see the dedicatory letters of Niccolò Vito di Gozze's *Dialogo della bellezza, detto Antos* (Venice, 1581) and Marcantonio Piccolomini's unpublished dialogue on women of 1538, cited in Marie-Françoise Piéjus, 'Venus bifrons: le double idéal féminin dans *La Raffaella* d'Alessandro Piccolomini', in *Images de la femme dans la littérature italienne de la renaissance. Préjugés misogynes et aspirations nouvelles* (Paris, 1980), p. 94.

34 On the life and works of Carlo Sigonio (*c.* 1520–84), philologist, historian and professor at Padua and Bologna, see William McCuaig, *Carlo Sigonio. The Changing World of the Late Renaissance* (Princeton, 1988), pp. 3–95; also, more briefly, Snyder, *Writing the Scene of Speaking*, pp. 39–40. On the *De dialogo liber* – Sigonio's only excursion into literary theory – see Snyder, pp. 41–86, McCuaig, pp. 50–3 and Girardi, '"Elegans imitatio ed erudita"'. On the motives behind Sigonio's exclusion of Lucian from his canon of classical authorities, see below, chapter 3, p. 28.

35 *De dialogo, c.* 459B–C: 'Est autem magnopere providendum, ne dies, locusque congressus ab ipsa eorum, quos in colloquium adducimus, discrepit dignitate; neque enim satis decorum, aut consonum foret, principes reipub. viros, et in maximis eius curis, et negociis occupatos, aut quocunque die, aut quencunque in locum ventitare, ut de iis subtilius rebus disputando exquirerent, quae in arte, et scientia aliqua versarentur.' ('One should be particularly careful to ensure that neither the time nor the place is unfitted to the dignity of those whom we have introduced in the dialogue. For it would hardly be decorous or fitting to have the leading citizens of a republic, men involved in the highest and weightiest affairs of state, showing up at just any time and place to discuss the most recondite aspects of some art or science.')

36 *De dialogo, c.* 461C: 'all times and places seemed perfectly appropriate for banishing the ignorance of youth and combatting the arrogance of the sophists'. The passage is a defence of Plato against the criticism of Greek dialogue in Cicero's *De oratore*, II iv 18, cited above, n. 24.

37 *De dialogo, c.* 461D: 'Nobis, tamen, quibus Socrates non est exprimendus, dandam esse putaverim operam diligenter, ut quam maxime possimus, hanc ex loco, et tempore verisimilitudinis et decori laudem assequamur; quod Ciceronem inprimis fecisse animadvertimus, cum homines in maximis potius reipublicae rebus, quam in studiis litterarum exercitatos induceret.' ('But we, who are not trying to describe a Socrates, should, I think, give ourselves up to the task of ensuring, as far as possible, that we achieve a reputable standard of verisimilitude and decorum in our choice of time and place – something which we consider Cicero was the first to do, when he introduced speakers versed in the highest affairs of state, rather than in literary studies.')

38 *De dialogo, c.* 466B and *c.* 458E–460A; also, on the differences in detail and

tone between the opening scene of the *Phaedrus* and Cicero's imitation of this scene, Görler, 'From Athens to Tusculum', p. 216, n. 4. Another good example of Sigonio's concern with the social standing of the speakers in dialogue is his comment on Xenophon's *Oeconomicus*, at *De dialogo liber*, *c.* 455B–C.

39 See below, chapter 4, n. 75; also, more generally, on Tasso's sensitivity to the difficulties of social decorum posed by the imitation of Plato, see my article, 'Rhetoric and Politics in Tasso's *Nifo*', pp. 21–5. On Tasso's imitation of the *Phaedrus* in the *Nifo*, see pp. 71–2 and p. 86 of the same article; also, on the opening scene in particular, Carnes Lord, 'The Argument of Tasso's *Nifo*', *Italica*, vol. 56, no. 1 (1979), pp. 25–6.

40 See below, chapter 6, pp. 67–8.

41 On the distinction in sixteenth-century dialogue theory between narrative and dramatic dialogues, see below, chapter 7, p. 73. The shift from narrative to dramatic forms, in the course of the Cinquecento, is the subject of some acute observations in Piero Floriani's *I gentiluomini letterati*, pp. 42–9; see also Nuccio Ordine, 'Il dialogo cinquecentesco italiano tra diegesi e mimesi', *Studi e problemi di critica testuale*, vol. 37 (1988), pp. 155–79. There is a danger of misrepresentation, however, in presenting this shift as absolute: see Franco Pignatti, 'Il *Dialoghi* di Torquato Tasso e la morfologia del dialogo cortigiano rinascimentale', *Studi Tassiani*, vol. 35, no. 36 (1988), pp. 39–41, on the continuing vitality of the 'Castiglionesque manner' in late-Cinquecento dialogue.

42 ('a mite irritating'); for the context of Tasso's comment, see below, chapter 8, p. 94 and n. 58.

43 The principal sources for the conversational etiquette of this period are Giovanni Della Casa's *Galateo* (1558) and Stefano Guazzo's *Civil conversazione* (1574). For a recent reading of the *Civil conversazione*, which highlights its importance as a key to the rhetoric of contemporary dialogues, see Girardi, *La società del dialogo*, pp. 65–79. For a good example of the process of 'gentrification' undergone by the Platonic dialogue in its transfer to the Italian courts, see Scipione Ammirato's two dialogues with contemporary settings, *Il Maremonte overo de l'ingiurie* (*c.* 1560) and *Il Rota overo de l'imprese* (1562); also, as a control, the same author's *Il Dedalione overo del poeta* (1560), where the speakers are a fictional 'Tiresia' and 'Dedalione' and Ammirato's enthusiastic imitation of Plato is freed from the constraints of decorum and verisimilitude.

44 On the virtual hegemony enjoyed by court culture after the consolidation of Medici rule in Florence, see Giancarlo Mazzacurati, *Il Rinascimento dei moderni; la crisi culturale del Cinquecento e la negazione delle origini* (Bologna, 1985), pp. 35–7 and pp. 209–11.

45 On this group of writers, and the novelty they represented within the Italian and European cultural economy, see Quondam, '"Mercanzia d'onore"', pp. 93–104, P. F. Grendler, *Critics of the Italian World 1530–1560. Anton Francesco Doni. Nicolò Franco. Ortensio Lando* (Milwaukee, 1969) and, most recently, Di Filippo Bareggi, *Il mestiere di scrivere*.

46 Aretino, though not, of course, strictly a *poligrafo* himself, has been included here because of his close association with this group of writers and because his dialogue production shares – and, indeed, helped establish – some of the

characteristics of the 'Venetian' dialogue practice identified here. Apart from his most famous works, the *Ragionamento della Nanna e della Antonia* (1534) and the *Dialogo nel quale la Nanna insegna alla Pippa* (1536), Aretino also wrote two other dialogues, the *Ragionamento delle corti* (1538) and *Le carte parlanti* (1543). On Franco and Doni, see, in general, Grendler, *Critics of the Italian   orld*, pp. 38–49 and 49–65 and Di Filippo Bareggi, *Il mestiere di scrivere*, pp. 15–16, 63–4 and 245 (on Franco) and pp. 25–31 and 73–5 (on Doni); also, on these two writers' art of dialogue, Girardi, *La società del dialogo*, pp. 107–28 and pp. 161–86. Doni, in addition to *I Marmi* and *I Mondi*, also wrote a *Dialogo della musica* (1544), while Franco wrote two dialogues besides the *Dialoghi piacevoli: Il Petrarchista* (1539) and a *Dialogo delle Bellezze* (1542). Another writer of dialogues it seems appropriate to consider here, because of his connections with Franco, is Giovanni Iacopo Bottazzo, a fellow member of the short-lived Accademia degli Argonauti (see Di Filippo Bareggi, *Il mestiere di scrivere*, pp. 124 and 132–3), who published a volume of *Dialoghi maritimi* (Mantua, 1547). A projected second volume, with dialogues by Bottazzo, Franco and Giovanni Francesco Arrivabene (see *Dialoghi maritimi*, p. 127v) was, it appears, never published.

47 On Dolce's life and works, see Di Filippo Bareggi, *Il mestiere di scrivere*, pp. 38–40, 58–60, 248 and 286–91. His dialogues are a *Dialogo del modo di tor moglie* (1539); a *Dialogo piacevole in difesa de' mal avventurati mariti* (1542); a *Dialogo della institution delle donne* (1545); the *Dialogo della pittura* (1557) – his best-known work, featuring Pietro Aretino as the main speaker – a *Dialogo del modo di accrescere la memoria* (1562) and a *Dialogo de i colori* (1565).

48 On Domenichi's career, in Venice and Florence, see Di Filippo Bareggi, *Il mestiere di scrivere*, pp. 22–6, 70–3 and 246, esp. pp. 71–2, on his plagiarism of Agrippa's *De nobilitate et praecellentia foeminei sexus* (1529), which had been published anonymously in an Italian translation in Venice in 1545. On Domenichi's reworking of von Hutten's *Misaulus* (1518) in his *Dialogo della corte*, see Pauline M. Smith, 'The Anti-Courtier Trend in Sixteenth-Century French Literature' (Geneva, 1966), p. 25, n. 1. Domenichi published the *Dialogo della corte* in 1562, in a collection with six other dialogues.

49 The dialogues referred to here are Betussi's *Dialogo amoroso* (1543), *Il Raverta* (1544) and *La Leonora* (1557), Sansovino's *Ragionamento nel quale brevemente s'insegna a' giovani la bella arte d'amore* (1545) and Gottifredi's *Specchio d'amore* (1547). On the sixteenth-century debate on love, and especially on the phase represented by these dialogues, see Mario Pozzi's introduction to his reprint of Giuseppe Zonta's 1912 anthology, *Trattati d'amore del Cinquecento* (Bari, 1975), which contains all the dialogues cited above, with the exception of Betussi's *Dialogo*, along with a *Dialogo dell'infinità di amore* (1547) by the Roman courtesan Tullia d'Aragona. On the *poligrafi* mentioned here, see, besides the bibliography cited by Pozzi, Di Filippo Bareggi, *Il mestiere di scrivere*, pp. 21–2 and 69–70 (on Betussi) and pp. 16–20 and 64–9, on Francesco Sansovino. Sansovino was also author of another work in dialogue form: the tourist guide, *Delle cose notabili che sono in Venetia* (1561).

50 It should be noted that, in considering the different character of the output of the *poligrafi*, sociological factors may be relevant: figures like Dolce,

Domenichi and Betussi, members of respectable and moneyed, though non-noble, families had considerably greater access to aristocratic patronage than writers like Franco and Doni: see Grendler, *Critics of the Italian World*, pp. 68–9 and, for more detail on these writers' backgrounds, Di Filippo Bareggi, *Il mestiere di scrivere*, p. 21 (on Betussi), p. 23 (on Domenichi), p. 26 (on Doni) and p. 39 (on Dolce). The dangers involved in generalizing about a group of writers as heterogenous as the *poligrafi*, or drawing too fast a distinction between the *poligrafi* and other writers is illustrated by the fact that Dolce – the only native Venetian among the *poligrafi* – was a friend of both Cristoforo da Canal and Antonio Pellegrini, cited in n. 52, and appears in Pellegrini's *Segni della natura*.

51 On the place of this distinction in Cinquecento dialogue theory and, in particular, on Sperone Speroni's characterization of the narrative dialogue as more respectable ('onesto') than the dramatic, see below, chapter 3, p. 32 and chapter 7, p. 73. On Cicero as the originator of the narrated dialogue, see Sigonio, *De dialogo liber*, c. 450C–E.

52 See, for example, Cristoforo Da Canal's *Della Milizia marittima* (c. 1553) (on which see Alberto Tenenti, *Cristoforo Da Canal. La marine Vénitienne avant Lépante* (Paris, 1962)) and Antonio Pellegrini's *I segni della natura ne l'huomo* (1545). Both dialogues are narrative in format, and both employ high-born interlocutors. For later and better-known examples of this Venetian neo-Ciceronian tradition in dialogue, see Giovanni Maria Memmo's *Dialogo nel quale . . . si forma un perfetto Prencipe, e una perfetta Republica, e parimente un Senatore, un Cittadino, un Soldato, e un Mercatante* (Venice, 1563) and Paolo Paruta's *Della perfettione della vita politica* (Venice, 1579).

53 The element of formal parody in the *Ragionamento* and *Dialogo* has been noted recently by critics: see, for example, G. Innamorati's entry in the *Dizionario biografico degli italiani* (Rome, 1960–   ), vol. IV, p. 97; Ordine, 'Il dialogo cinquecentesco italiano tra diegesi e mimesi', pp.163–4 and, more particularly, on Aretino's treatment of the *topos* of the *locus amoenus*, see Renzo Bragantini, 'La novella del Cinquecento: rassegna di studi, 1960–1980', *Letere italiane*, vol. 33, no. 1 (1981), pp. 113–14.

54 ('To beg or borrow the names of the famous and the great'): *Dialoghi piacevoli*, pp. cviv–cviir. Another dialogue of Franco's, *Il Petrarchista* (1539), contains a witty deconstruction of the convention of presenting the dialogue as a tran-scription of a real conversation: see pp. 36–7 of Roberto L. Bruni's edition of the text (Exeter, 1979), where the speaker Sannio [Franco himself] is forced to admit that his account of a French innkeeper's long and eloquent discourse, in Tuscan, on Petrarch's life was, in fact, a reconstruction, by him, of an original in which 'molte de le . . . parole non fussero intelligibili, perché il più che se ne potea intendere chiaramente, era quando proferiva il Petrarca, e madonna Laura, e Valchiusa . . . et altre simili parole più atte a proferire, che intra-vengono nel narrare de la sua vita' ('many of the words were unintelligible, and the only thing which could be heard clearly was when he mentioned Petrarch, or Laura, or Vaucluse or other such easily pronounced words, which crop up in the story of Petrarch's life'). The comic effect is enhanced by the fact that the substance of Messer Roberto's speech is in fact drawn, often verbatim, from the contemporary commentaries Franco is satirizing.

55 See *I Marmi*, ed. Ezio Chiorboli (Bari, 1928), vol. I, pp. 23–4, where Doni dismisses verisimilitude as a criterion for judging the dialogue and admits that 'questo [i.e. the dialogue form] è un trovato per poter favellare di varie materie' ('a convention, which allows one to deal with a whole range of subjects') (though he later reassures readers still anxious about the historical exactitude of his representation that the Chancellor of the (fictional) Academia Peregrina, who was present at the discussions, 'ci fa fede che la cosa tiene i due terzi del verisimile' ('assures us that the thing is about two-thirds true to life')). The setting of the *Marmi* is the antithesis of the exclusive villas and courts of the Ciceronian tradition: the steps of the Florentine Duomo, where passing speakers are free to drop in at will.

56 The dramatic and colloquial style of the Venetian *poligrafi* died with them, around 1560: see Grendler, *Critics of the Italian World*, pp. 17–18, who identifies the period from 1556 to 1564 as 'the end of the era of the *poligrafi*'; also Quondam, '"Mercanzia d'onore"', pp. 73 and 103.

57 For Domenichi's description of the *Dialogo d'amore* as a 'ritratto d'uno honorato e piacevol ragionamento', see his *Dialoghi*, p. 2. The dialogue is set in the court of Modena, and the speakers are, with one exception, members of the local nobility. Note that Domenichi justifies his choice of the dialogue form in this work by referring explicitly to the criterion of authority which underlies the practice of the Ciceronian dialogue: he has chosen such illustrious interlocutors, he says, 'percioché molte volte le cose sogliono più e meno havere d'auttorità et di riputatione, quanto più e meno stimati sono coloro, i quali pigliano a favellare d'esse' (p. 1) ('because, often, the degree of authority and respect we accord to what is said depends on the reputation of the people who are saying it').

58 The dialogue is distinguished from Franco's other works in dialogue form not only by its historical format, but also by its self-conscious elevation of tone and subject-matter. On Franco's stay at Casale, see Grendler, *Critics of the Italian World* p. 43. A similar distinction might be made between Giuseppe Betussi's dramatic Venetian dialogues – the *Raverta* (1543) and the *Dialogo amoroso* (1544) – and his narrative *Leonora* (1557), written in 1552, during his stay in Melazzo, near Savona. On Betussi's circumstances at the time of the composition of his dialogues, see Giuseppe Zonta, 'Note betussiane', *Giornale storico della letteratura italiana*, vol. 52 (1908), pp. 332 and 341. More generally, on the attempts made by almost all the *poligrafi* to gain a secure post at court – attempts which bely their often virulent anti-court rhetoric – see Di Filippo Bareggi, *Il mestiere di scrivere*, pp. 242–81, esp. p. 244.

59 On the difference in subject-matter between Florentine dialogues of the 1520s and those of the following decades, see Felix Gilbert, 'Machiavelli in an Unknown Contemporary Dialogue', *Journal of the Warburg Institute*, vol. 1 (1937), pp. 165–6. For a detailed account of Cosimo I's cultural policy and its effects, see Michel Plaisance's two articles in André Rochon (ed.), *Les écrivains et le pouvoir en Italie à l'époque de la Renaissance* (Paris, 1973–4): 'Une première affirmation de la politique culturelle de Côme 1er: la transformation de l'Académie des "Humidi" en Académie Florentine (1540–1542)', in vol. I, pp. 361–438, and 'Culture et politique à Florence de 1542 à 1551', in vol. II, pp. 149–242.

60 On the *Dialogo* and its place in the development of Guicciardini's political thought, see Mark Phillips, *Francesco Guicciardini. The Historian's Craft* (Toronto, 1977), pp. 31–8. On Brucioli's dialogues, see Carlo Dionisotti, *Machiavellerie* (Turin, 1980), pp. 193–226.

61 The interlocutors of Francesco Berni's dramatic *Dialogo contra i poeti* (Rome, 1526) include, besides the author himself, Giovanni Sanga and Giovanni da Modena, a character identified only by his forename, 'Marco'. Similarly, Bartolomeo Cerretani's unpublished *Storia in dialogo della mutazione di Firenze* (1520), set in Modena, in Francesco Guicciardini's house, includes, besides Guicciardini himself and Giovanni Rucellai, two Savonarolan exiles, 'Lorenzo' and 'Hieronimo', whose identity has not been established (see Silvano Seidel Menchi, 'Alcuni atteggiamenti della cultura italiana di fronte ad Erasmo', in Luigi Firpo and Giorgio Spini (eds.), *Eresia e riforma nell'Italia del Cinquecento* (Florence, 1974), p. 85, n. 57). Even when the cast-list is in order, there may be other departures from documentary accuracy: Donato Giannotti's narrative dialogue *Della repubblica de' Vinziani* (1525–6), set in Pietro Bembo's house in Padua, with a cast of eminent Venetian interlocutors, contains a striking number of anachronisms and chronological discrepancies (see Giannotti, *Opere politiche*, ed. Furio Diaz (Milan, 1974), p. 471, n. 1).

62 On the changes in the identities of the speakers in the three editions of Antonio Brucioli's *Dialoghi* (1526–9, 1537–8 and 1544–5), see Dionisotti, *Machiavellerie*, pp. 199, 202–5, 220 and 224–5.

63 On the circumstances surrounding the composition of Guicciardini's *Del Savonarola, ovvero dialogo tra Francesco Zati e Pieradovardo Giachinotti il giorno dopo la battaglia di Gavinana* (c. 1531), see Bono Simonetta's introduction to his edition of the dialogue (Florence, 1959), esp. pp. 17–29. The work, unpublished during its author's lifetime, is clearly intended as a justification of Guicciardini's actions when he took over from Giachinotti as governor of Pisa in 1530 and had him executed. Note that, although this dialogue is exceptional in its virulently critical attitude to its interlocutors, Guicciardini's treatment of the speakers in another dialogue, the *De libero arbitrio*, was scarcely celebratory: a letter to his brother, of 30 May 1533, speaks of his proposal to replace the names of his interlocutors with Greek names 'per offendere meno' (see Gilbert, 'Machiavelli in an Unknown Contemporary Dialogue', p. 163).

64 See *Arte della guerra*, in *Opere*, ed. Sergio Bertelli and Franco Gaeta (Milan, 1960–5), vol. II, pp. 330–1. Machiavelli announces in the preceding dedicatory letter, addressed to Lorenzo di Filippo Strozzi, that his intention in the dialogue was to honour the memory of Cosimo Rucellai.

65 *Arte della guerra*, pp. 330–1. For a more articulated attack on the dilettantism of Italian humanism, in *propria persona*, see also the *proemio* to the first book of Machiavelli's *Discorsi sopra la prima deca di Tito Livio*, in *Opere*, ed. Mario Bonfantini (Milan and Naples, 1954), pp. 89–90.

66 See *De oratore*, I 28 and the observations of Francesco Tateo, *Tradizione e realtà nell'Umanesimo italiano*, (Bari, 1967), pp. 235–6 and Görler, 'From Athens to Tusculum', pp. 216–28.

67 In Castiglione's dedicatory letter to Miguel De Silva, the dialogue is compared to 'un ritratto di pittura della corte d'Urbino, non di mano di Raffaello o

Michel Angelo, ma di pittor ignobile e che solamente sappia tirare le linee principali, senza adornar la verità di vaghi colori, o far parer per arte di prospettiva quello che non è' ('a painted portrait of the court of Urbino; not from the hand of a Raphael or a Michelangelo, but by an inferior painter, who is only capable of sketching in an outline, and not of adorning the truth with beautiful colours or deceiving the eye with perspective') (*Cortegiano*, p. 71).

3 THE USES OF THE DIALOGUE IN SIXTEENTH-CENTURY ITALY: CELEBRATION AND CONTROL

1 ('And I have been thinking to myself that the pleasures of music, feasting, jousting, comedies and all other pastimes and spectacles are as nothing, compared with the joys one can find in refined conversation') Stefano Guazzo, *La civil conversazione*, 6th edition (Venice, 1579). p. 168. The speaker is the author's brother, Guglielmo.

2 ('This is not the place to come to if you want to dispute about the moon: the times are wrong for trying to express new doctrines') Letter from Piero Guicciardini, Medici resident in Rome, to Curzio Picchena, commenting on the Galileo trial of 1615 (cited in Antonio Rotondò, 'La censura ecclesiastica e la cultura', in *Storia d'Italia. Vol. V. I documenti. 2* (Turin, 1973), p. 1467).

3 As far as I am aware, there has been no attempt at a comparative study of the dialogue production of different European cultures in the Renaissance, though several valid studies of individual national traditions have appeared in recent years. On the dialogue in France, in this period, see Kemal Bénouis, *Le dialogue dans la littérature française*; Le Guern, 'Sur le genre du dialogue', Armstrong, 'The Dialectical Road to Truth' and the various articles by Eva Kushner: 'Reflexions sur le dialogue en France au XVIe siècle', *Revue des sciences humaines*, fasc. 148 (1972), pp. 486–90, 'Le dialogue de 1580 à 1630; articulations et fonctions', in J. Lafond and André Stegmann (eds.), *L'Automne de la Renaissance 1580–1630* (Paris, 1981), pp. 149–62, and 'Le dialogue en France', pp. 151–67. On the dialogue in Spain, see Jacqueline Ferreras, *Les dialogues espagnols du XVIème siècle, ou l'expression littéraire d'une nouvelle conscience* (Paris, 1985). On the English Renaissance dialogue, see E. Merrill, 'The Dialogue in English Literature', *Yale Studies in English Literature*, vol. 42 (1911) (reprinted New Haven, 1969) and, more recently, Roger L. Deakins, 'The Tudor Prose Dialogue: Genre and Anti-Genre', *Studies in English Literature 1500–1900*, vol. 20, no. 1 (1980), pp. 5–24, and Wilson, *Incomplete Fictions*. Where Italian dialogue is concerned, there has been no attempt at a comprehensive overview of Cinquecento dialogue production comparable with David Marsh's *The Quattrocento Dialogue; Classical Tradition and Humanist Innovation* (Cambridge, Mass., and London, 1980), at least since Giovanna Wyss Morigi's unsatisfactory *Contributo allo studio del dialogo nell'epoca dell'umanesimo e del Rinascimento* (Monza, 1950). Recent studies on aspects of Italian dialogue production in this period include Girardi, *La società del dialogo*, Floriani, 'Il dialogo e la corte' and Ordine, 'Il dialogo cinquecentesco italiano tra diegesi e mimesi'.

4 On de Brués's imitation of Plato and Cicero in the *Dialogues*, see P. P. Morphos, *The Dialogues of Guy de Brués: A Critical Edition with a Study in*

Renaissance Scepticism and Relativism (Baltimore, 1953), p. 29; also Thomas Greenwood, 'L'apologie rationelle de Guy de Brués', *Revue d'histoire et de philosophie religieuses*, vol. 36 (1956), pp. 42–4.

5 See *Les dialogues de Louis Le Caron Parisien* (Paris, 1555). Of Le Caron's dialogues some, like *Le Valton, de la tranquilité de l'esprit* and *Le Ronsard, ou de la poesie* have real interlocutors; some, like the two *Courtisans*, use purely fictional speakers and others, like *La Claire, ou de la Prudence du Droit* use real figures, disguised by literary pseudonyms – a device also employed by Guillaume du Vair, in his *Traité de la Constance et Consolation ès calamitéz publiques* (1594) and perhaps by Pontus de Tyard in some of his apparently fictional dialogues (see Kemal Bénouis, *Le dialogue dans la littérature française*, p. 184).

6 *Dialogue de l'Ortografe et Prononçiation Françoese*, p. 42: 'je n'introdui point personnages feins ni obscurs, mes qui sont tous de conoessence chacun au son androet, pour le plus suffisant, et pour homme de grand esprit' ('I shall not introduce fictional or unknown speakers, but figures who are well-known in their respective areas, for their expertise and brilliance').

7 On the probable date of Starkey's dialogue, see Kathleen M. Burton's edition (London, 1948), pp. 193–6. Roger Deakins has calculated that, of the two hundred and thirty-odd Tudor dialogues extant, only five come close to fulfilling the stipulations on verisimilitude and decorum laid down by Carlo Sigonio in his *De Dialogo liber* (see 'The Tudor Prose Dialogue', p. 16.) It should be noted, however, that, of these five, two – More's *Utopia* and Ellis Heywood's *Il Moro* (on which see above, chapter 2, p. 10) – use a mixture between real and invented characters, while Thomas Elyot's *Of the Knowledge that Maketh a Wise Man* (1532) is a conversation between Plato and Aristippus. The only two dialogues from the British Isles in this period to employ exclusively real figures in a realistic contemporary setting are Starkey's *Dialogue* (though this was written in Italy: see n. 10, below) and George Buchanan's *De Jure Regus Apud Scotos* (Edinburgh, 1579), a dialogue between the author and Thomas Maitland.

8 See R. J. A. Kerr, 'Prolegomena to an edition of Villalón's *Scholástico*', *Bulletin of Hispanic Studies*, vol. 32 (1955), pp. 132–9 on the date of composition of the *Scholástico* and pp. 206–7 on its setting and interlocutors. Of the Spanish dialogues surveyed by Ferreras, the *Scholástico* is the only one which may be considered genuinely 'documentary', though there are instances of dialogues in which real figures are alluded to under fictional names (see *Les dialogues espagnols*, vol. II, pp. 1039–40).

9 See Villalón's *Prohemio*, in *El Scholástico*, ed. M. Menéndez y Pelayo (Madrid, 1911), p. 7, where the author recounts his opponents' accusation that 'quis[e] tanto seguir al conde Baltasar Castellon en el *Cortesano*, que quasi le treslad[e]' ('that I imitated the model of Castiglione's *Cortegiano* so closely that my work is almost a translation of his'). His subsequent remarks make it clear that the accusation referred to the 'estilo del dialogar' as well as to the substance of the dialogue. Note that this passage is omitted in the later manuscript of the dialogue (*c.* 1538–9), which was used by R. J. A. Kerr in his more recent edition of the dialogue (Madrid, 1967). On the fortunes of Castiglione's dialogue in Spain, see Guidi, 'Reformulations de l'idéologie aristocratique', p. 139 and n. 64.

10 The best-known examples of documentary dialogues written by foreign authors in Italy are Francisco de Holanda's so-called *Dialoghi di Roma* (1536) and Juan de Valdés's *Diálogo de la lengua* (1535), to which one might add Thomas Starkey's *Dialogue between Reginald Pole and Thomas Lupset* (*c.* 1533–6), written when the author was in Padua (see K. M. Burton's edition of the dialogue (London, 1948), p. 198). An analogous case is that of documentary dialogues presented as original, but which are in fact translations or adaptations of Italian works. Diego de Salazar's *Tratado de Re Militari* (Logrono, 1536) is a translation of Machiavelli's *Arte della guerra.* Lodowick Bryskett's *A Discourse of Civill Life* (London, 1606) is an unacknowledged adaptation of Giraldi Cinzio's *Dialoghi della vita civile* (1565) (see J. H. P. Pafford's introduction to Bryskett's *Literary Works* (Farnborough, Hants., 1972), pp. xii–xiii). It is interesting to note that an Italian connection can also be established in the case of one of the very few examples of documentary dialogues produced in seventeenth-century France, Jean Chapelain's *La lecture des vieux romans* (1647): see Chapelain, *Lettere inedite a corrispondenti italiani*, ed. P. Ciureanu (Genoa, 1964), pp. 92–4.

11 Jeremy Collier, address *To the reader*, in *Of Pride*, one of the four dialogues contained in his *Miscellanies in Five Essays* (London, 1694), cited in Purpus, 'The Plain, Easy and Familiar Way', p. 49, n. 14.

12 Bracciolini's *De avaritia* is set in Rome, in curial circles, and his interlocutors include Antonio Loschi and Bartolomeo da Montepulciano. The interlocutors of Landino's dialogue constitute a virtual *Who's Who* of Florentine humanist and political circles: they include, besides Landino himself, Leon Battista Alberti, Marsilio Ficino, Alamanno Rinuccini and Lorenzo and Giuliano de' Medici.

13 Bembo wrote three Latin dialogues: *De Aetna* (1495–6) – his first published work; *De Virgilii Culice et Terenti Fabulis* (1503) and *De Guidubaldo Feretrio deque Elizabetha Gonzagia Urbini ducibus* (*c.* 1509–10). The *De Guidubaldo* is of particular interest in the present context, as an Italian translation by the author exists: see M. Lutz's recent edition of the Italian version (Geneva, 1980) and Floriani, *I gentiluomini letterati*, pp. 34–9; also, more generally, on the continuities between Bembo's Latin and vernacular dialogues, *Prose e rime di Pietro Bembo*, pp. 12–13.

14 It seems at least probable that the first sixteenth-century theorist of the dialogue form, Carlo Sigonio, had the neo-Latin dialogue tradition, rather than the vernacular, in mind, in his recommendations in the *De dialogo liber.* In any case, it is interesting to note that the only modern work in dialogue form referred to in Sigonio's *œuvre* (in a commentary on Cicero's lost *Hortensius*, of 1559) is a neo-Latin work, Iacopo Sadoleto's *De laudibus philosophiae* (Lyons, 1538): an attempted reconstruction of the *Hortensius*, and a work which ideally meets Sigonio's prescriptions in the *De dialogo.* On Sadoleto's dialogue, and Sigonio's approving reference, see McCuaig, *Carlo Sigonio*, pp. 293–5 and 298–9.

15 On the genealogy and diffusion of the ideal of courtesy in Europe, see Ossola, *Dal 'Cortegiano' all'Uomo di mondo'*, esp. pp. 131–51. On the European influence of Italian courtesy books, besides the bibliography on the *fortuna* of the *Cortegiano* given above, chapter 2, n. 29, see also John L. Lievsay, *Stefano*

Guazzo and the English Renaissance (1575–1675) (Chapel Hill, 1961); E. Bonfatti, *La 'Civil conversatione' in Germania* (Udine, 1979); Daniel Javitch, 'Rival Arts of Conduct in Elizabethan England: Guazzo's *Civile conversation* and Castiglione's *Courtier'*, *Yearbook of Italian Studies* (1971), pp. 178–98 and, most recently, Giorgio Patrizi, 'La "Civil Conversatione", libro europeo', in Giorgio Patrizi (ed.), *Stefano Guazzo e la 'Civil Conversazione'* (Rome, 1990). Still invaluable for its extensive bibliography of primary works on courtesy and related subjects is Ruth Kelso, *The Doctrine of the English Gentleman in the Sixteenth Century, with a Bibliographical List of Treatises on the Gentleman and Related Subjects Published in Europe to 1625* (Urbana, 1929).

16 ('the theory of conversation represents the professional expertise of a nobility which has lost its political power and now only has a purely representative function') Christoph Strosetzki, *Rhétorique de la conversation: sa dimension littéraire et linguistique dans la société française du XVIIème siècle*, trans. Sabine Seubert (Paris, Seattle and Tübingen, 1984), p. vii. Strosetzki is referring to the situation of the French nobility after the Fronde, but his point is equally applicable to sixteenth-century Italy.

17 On the crisis in confidence suffered by the Italian ruling classes in the first decades of the Cinquecento, see Lauro Martines, *Power and Imagination. City-States in Renaissance Italy* (New York, 1979), pp. 416–65, and, for an interpretation of Castiglione's *Cortegiano* as a product of this crisis, Guidi, 'Reformulations de l'idéologie aristocratique', esp. pp. 123–32. See also, on the changing status of the courtier in this period, Walter Barberis, 'Uomini di corte nel Cinquecento', in *Storia d'Italia. Annali. 4. Intellettuali e potere*, ed. Corrado Vivanti (Turin, 1981), pp. 857–75 and Franco Gaeta, 'Dal comune alla corte rinascimentale', Alberto Asor Rosa (ed.), *Letteratura italiana. I. Il letterato e le istituzioni* (Turin, 1982), esp. pp. 241–55.

18 On the peculiar character of the genre of vernacular letter-collections as they developed in Cinquecento Italy, see Quondam, 'Dal "formulario" al "formularo"', pp. 13–17. On contemporary perceptions of the relation between the letter and the dialogue, see above, chapter 1, n. 22. On the complex social role played by these two genres in the different, though related, system of cultural relations in Quattrocento Italy, see Vincenzo De Caprio, 'I cenacoli umanistici', in Alberto Asor Rosa (ed.), *Letteratura italiana. I. Il letterato e le istituzioni* (Turin, 1982), esp. pp. 800–3.

19 See, for example, *Cortegiano*, II xliii, p. 257, where Federico Fregoso illustrates his definition of 'detti pronti ed acuti' ('sharp, quick-fire banter') by referring to the witty ripostes that 'spesso tra noi se n'odono' ('are often heard here among us'). On the 'essemplarità' of the speakers in the *Cortegiano*, see above, chapter 2, p. 15; also Floriani, *Il gentiluomini letterati*, p. 46; Ossola, *Dal 'Cortegiano' all' 'Uomo di mondo'*, esp. pp. 32–3 and 51–2.

20 Gabriello Frascati, prefatory letter to Guazzo, *La civil conversazione*, see also p. 135r and p. 168r of the dialogue, where the symposium of the last book is identified as a representation of 'la vera forma della conversazione'.

21 See the dedicatory letter of J[ohn] K[epers]'s translation of Annibale Romei's *Discorsi* (1585), *The Courtier's Academy* (London, 1598): 'The first Author supposeth these discussions to have fallen out in the Court of Ferrara, in the

noble assemblies of divers Ladies and knightes, covertly expressing an excellent form of Court-like exercise.'

22 On the social organization of the Tudor court and the constitution and functioning of the English cultural elite of the time, see Frank Whigham, *Ambition and Privilege; the Social Tropes of Elizabethan Courtesy Theory* (Berkeley and London, 1984), pp. 6–18.

23 See *Orlando Furioso*, XLVI, 1–19; also Alberto Casadei's illuminating study of Ariosto's revisions of the passage, 'L'esordio del canto XLVI del *Furioso*: stategia compositiva e varianti storico-culturali', *Italianistica*, vol. 15, no. 1 (January–April 1986), pp. 53–93. For Machiavelli's annoyance at his omission from the list of poets, in the 1516 edition, see his letter of 17 December 1517, to Lodovico Alamanni, in *Lettere*, ed. Franco Gaeta (Milan, 1961), p. 383; also Casadei, pp. 89–90, on the reasons for Ariosto's almost total exclusion of representatives of Florentine culture, both here and, more tellingly, in the broader and more genuinely 'Italian' panorama in the 1532 edition.

24 On Bandello's dedications, see Adelin-Charles Fiorato, 'Bandello et le règne du père', in Rochon (ed.), *Les écrivains et le pouvoir*, vol. II, pp. 98–102.

25 On this 'socializzazione' of the *canzoniere* in Cinquecento Italy, see Guglielmo Gorni, 'Veronica e le altre: emblemi e cifre onomastiche nelle rime di Bembo', in Cesare Bozzetti, Pietro Gibellini and Ennio Sandal (eds.), *Veronica Gambara e la poesia del suo tempo nell'Italia settentrionale* (Florence, 1989), esp. pp. 39–40.

26 For readings of the *Cortegiano* and of Pierio Valeriano's *Dialogo della volgar lingua* (c. 1524) which show particular sensitivity to the role played by the dialogue form in expressing and fostering a sense of Italian cultural unity, see Floriani, *I gentiluomini letterati*, pp. 50–67 and 68–91; also, on the *Cortegiano*, José Guidi, 'Baldassare Castiglione et le pouvoir politique: du gentilhomme de cour au nonce pontificiel', in Rochon (ed.), *Les écrivains et le pouvoir en Italie*, esp. p. 259. Other contributions to this early stage of the *questione della lingua* which take the form of documentary dialogues are Bembo's *Prose della volgar lingua* (1525), Claudio Tolomei's *Il Cesano* (1525) and *Il Polito* (1524), and Giangiorgio Trissino's *Il Castellano* (1529). For a useful introduction to the debate, with further bibliography, see Mario Pozzi's introduction to his recent anthology, *Discussioni linguistiche del Cinquecento* (Turin, 1988).

27 On the complex publishing history of the *Colloquia*, see Craig R. Thompson's preface to *The Colloquies of Erasmus* (Chicago and London, 1965), pp. xxi–xxv. The historical consistency of the speakers in Erasmus' *colloquia* varies, in much the same way as that of Lucian's speakers: most are purely fictional, but some are historical figures, represented either under their own names, or under more or less transparent pseudonyms.

28 See Christopher Robinson, 'The Reputation of Lucian in Sixteenth-Century France', *French Studies*, vol. 29, no. 4 (1975), pp. 385–95.

29 See Robinson, *Lucian and his Influence in Europe*, pp. 81–95, esp. p. 94; also Mattioli, *Luciano e l'umanesimo*.

30 On the ecclesiastical censorship of Lucian, see Robinson, 'The Reputation of Lucian', p. 394; also Paul F. Grendler, *The Roman Inquisition and the Venetian Press, 1540–1605* (Princeton, 1977), pp. 96, 99 and 117. More generally, on censorship and its effects on Italian culture in this period, see Rotondò, 'La

censura ecclesiastica e la cultura', esp. pp. 1401–2, 1424–42 and 1449–71 and Nicola Longo, 'La letteratura proibita', in Alberto Asor Rosa (ed.), *Letteratura italiana. Vol. V. Le questioni* (Turin, 1986), pp. 978–88; also chapter 7, below.

31 On the Lucianic influence in the *Colloquia*, see Robinson, *Lucian and his Influence in Europe*, pp. 165–91. It should not be forgotten, of course, that Erasmus was also a translator of Lucian: see Craig Thompson, *The Translation of Lucian by Erasmus and St. Thomas More* (New York, 1940) and Erika Rummel, *Erasmus as a Translator of the Classics* (Toronto and London, 1985), pp. 49–52. For the Catholic Church's attack on Erasmus, see below, n. 36. For accusations from the Reformist camp that Erasmus was 'a follower of Lucian and an atheist', see Albano Biondi, 'La giustificazione della simulazione nel Cinquecento', in Luigi Firpo and Giorgio Spini (eds.), *Eresia e riforma nell'Italia del Cinquecento. Miscellanea I* (Florence and Chicago, 1974), pp. 31–2.

32 On the reception of Erasmus in Italy, especially in the 1520s–30s, Silvana Seidel Menchi, 'Alcuni atteggiamenti della culturà italiana di fronte ad Erasmo (1520–1536)', in Luigi Firpo and Giorio Spini (eds.), *Eresia e riforma nell'Italia del Cinquecento. Miscellanea I* (Florence and Chicago, 1974), pp. 69–133, 'La circolazione clandestina di Erasmo in Italia. I casi di Antonio Brucioli e di Marsilio Andreasi', *Annali della Scuola Normale Superiore di Pisa (Lettere e Filosofia)*, series 3, vol. 9, no. 2 (1979), pp. 573–601 and 'La discussione su Erasmo nell'Italia del Rinascimento', in *Società, politica e cultura a Carpi ai tempi di Alberto III Pio. Atti del Convegno Internazionale, Carpi, 19–21 maggio, 1978* (Padua, 1981), pp. 291–382; also Myron P. Gilmore, 'Anti-Erasmianism in Italy; the Dialogue of Ortensio Lando on Erasmus' Funeral', *Journal of Medieval and Renaissance Studies*, vol. 4, no. 1 (1974), pp. 1–14 and 'Italian Reactions to Erasmian Humanism', in H. A. Oberman and T. A. Brady Jr (eds.), *Itinerarium Italicum. The Profile of the Italian Renaissance in its European Transformations* (Leiden, 1975), pp. 61–115.

33 Lauro's translation *Colloquii famigliari di Erasmo Roterodamo* was published twice, in Venice, in 1545 and 1549; see Benedetto Croce, 'Sulle traduzioni e imitazioni dell'*Elogio* e dei *Colloqui* di Erasmo', in *Aneddoti di varia letteratura*, 2nd edition (Bari, 1953–4), vol. 1, pp. 414–16.

34 Franco, *Dialoghi piacevoli*, pp. cxv–cxir. Franco adds, however, that 'non resta per questo ch'egli non si stampi e ristampi, non si venda e rivenda, e non si legga e rilegga per ogni luogo . . .' ('this has not stopped [Erasmus'] works from being printed and reprinted, sold and resold, read and reread throughout Italy'). Franco's *Dialoghi* themselves were not to escape censorship and, as is scarcely surprising, this and other references to Erasmus are omitted in the expurgated edition of 1606 (see Girardi, *La società del dialogo*, pp. 124–5 and notes 22–3.) On Franco's continuing loyalty to Erasmus, even during his trial of 1569, see Grendler, *Critics of the Italian World*, pp. 112–13.

35 Seidel Menchi, 'Alcuni atteggiamenti', p. 105 and Gilmore, 'Anti-Erasmianism', p. 11, identify three distinct motives behind Italian hostility to Erasmus in the 1520s and 1530s: Erasmus' anti-Ciceronianism, his suspected heresy and his 'barbarian' dismissal of Italian culture.

36 A useful overview of Erasmus' *fortuna* in Counter-Reformation Italy is Paul

F. Grendler, with Marcia G. Grendler, 'The Survival of Erasmus in Italy', *Erasmus in English*, vol. 8 (1976), pp. 1–42.

37 *La Galeria*, ed. Marzio Pieri (Padua, 1979), vol. I, p. 133.

38 See below, chapter 7, n. 45.

39 For Erasmus' influence on individual Italian writers of dialogue, see Grendler, *Critics of the Italian World*, pp. 112–13 and Girardi, *La società del dialogo*, pp. 107–28, on Niccolò Franco; Seidel Menchi, 'Alcuni atteggiamenti', pp. 79–83, on Bartolomeo Cerretani and the same critic's 'La circolazione clandestina', pp. 576–84, on Antonio Brucoli. On Erasmus' influence in the two 'anomalous' areas of dialogue production identified in chapter 2, see, on Florence, see Dionisotti, *Macchiavellerie*, pp. 211–15 and p. 223 and, on Venice, Christopher Cairns, *Pietro Aretino and the Republic of Venice: Researches on Aretino and his Circle in Venice 1527–1556* (Florence, 1985), esp. pp. 82–3.

40 On the 'dialogo osceno', see Nino Borsellino, 'Morfologie del dialogo osceno: La *Cazzaria* dell'Arsiccio Intronato', in Giulio Ferroni (ed.), *Il dialogo. Scambi e passaggi della parola* (Palermo, 1985), esp. pp. 113–14 and, on the demise of the genre, pp. 120–3. The best-known examples are, of course, Pietro Aretino's *Ragionamento della Nanna e della Antonia* (1534) and *Dialogo nel quale la Nanna insegna alla Pippa* (1536), which were placed on the Index in 1559, along with Aretino's other works. Another influential erotic dialogue of the period – more decorous than Aretino, but still decidedly risqué, at least by the standards of the later sixteenth century – was Alessandro Piccolomini's *La Raffaella, dialogo della bella creanza delle donne* (1539), on which see Borsellino, pp. 119–20 and Piéjus, 'Venus bifrons'.

41 See above, chapter 2, p. 16.

42 See *De dialogo*, c. 447A–C, where, echoing Diogenes Laertius' *Life of Plato*, Sigonio defines the original province of the dialogue as philosophy and politics. The serious Platonic tradition was respected until Lucian corrupted it with an injection of comic and indecent subject-matter: 'hanc . . . consuetudinem ab omnibus ante sancte custoditam, primus etiam . . . Lucianus depravavit atque corrupuit, cum de rebus ridicuis, de amoribus ac fallaciis meretriciis loqui coegerit' ('this convention was respected by all writers until Lucian corrupted and ruined it, introducing talk of absurdities, of love and the wiles of whores'). Sigonio goes on to cite Lucian's proud announcement of his invention of the genre of comic dialogue, in *A Double Indictment* (see above, chapter 2, p. 10), and remarks bitterly on the loss of dignity this innovation signalled for the genre: 'quo consilio quantum de vetere illa dialogi dignitate detraxerit, cum flagitiosissimum ac turpissimum quenque sermonem in dialogum introduxerit, nemo non videt' ('no one can fail to see how much this change detracted from the previous dignity of the genre, by introducing the most shameful and obscene talk into the dialogue'). For the views of other critics of the period, see Girardi, *La società del dialogo*, pp. 28 and 36.

43 The prescriptive element in the *De dialogo* has been justly stressed by recent critics: see Girardi, 'Elegans imitatio et erudita', p. 325 and *La società del dialogo*, pp. 38–9; Deakins, 'The Tudor Prose Dialogue', pp. 11–12 and Snyder, *Writing the Scene of Speaking*, pp. 83–6.

44 *Apologia dei dialoghi*, in *Opere*, ed. Marco Forcellini and Natal dalle Laste

(Padua, 1740), vol. I, pp. 333–46, esp. p. 334: 'lo introdur ne' dialogi li adulatori, le cortegiane e li innamorati . . . ed imitarli per dilettare, è ben decoro di tutti loro, ma fa vergogna allo autore' ('writers who introduce flatterers, courtesans and lovers into their dialogues, and imitate their speech for the delight of the public, may be respecting the decorum of their characters, but are putting themselves to shame'). For the context of this argument, and, in particular, for the distinction between artistic and social decorum on which it rests, see below, chapter 7, p. 74. It should be noted that the dialogues Speroni is defending in the *Apologia* – his works of the 1530s, published in 1542 – are not 'Lucianic' in the sense I have been using it here, in that they do not use fictional characters but real historical figures. Especially in the dialogues on love, however, these interlocutors are treated in a detached, even satirical fashion, which differentiates them from the contemporary neo-Ciceronian tradition.

45 *Apologia dei dialoghi*, p. 335: 'doveva io in scrivendo [. . .] non torcer gli occhi e la lingua dalle mie proprie condizioni, ma formare anzi alla mia sembianza l'altrui persone ne' miei dialogi' ('when writing, I should never have turned my attention away from my own qualities; rather, I should have fashioned the characters in my dialogues in my own likeness'). At p. 334, Speroni stipulates that the author of dialogues should be a 'costumata e civil persona' ('a well-mannered and decent human being'). For a contemptuous characterization of the *persone* of his early dialogues, see *Apologia dei dialoghi*, pp. 334–5.

46 *Apologia dei dialoghi*, p. 345: 'Luciano sofista, uso a trattare in quei suoi dialogi . . . nove menzogne di tutti i Dei de' gentili . . ., alla perfine perduto il senno e la fede, di cristian battezzato . . . in un diabolico Epicureo si tramutò veramente.' ('The sophist Lucian, who got into the habit of making up strange fictions about the pagan gods in those dialogues of his, finished up losing his wits and his faith, and turned in real life from a Christian into a diabolical Epicurean.') This curious legend concerning Lucian's apostasy is also recorded in French sources: see Robinson, 'The Reputation of Lucian', p. 390 and n. 26.

47 Some idea of the relative frequency of documentary and fictional forms of dialogue may be had by consulting the first section of the bibliography of the present study, where documentary dialogues are indicated with an asterisk. The great exception to the rule proposed here is the religious dialogue production of the Cinquecento, which shows a very marked preference for postclassical fictional models of dialogue, over classical and humanistic documentary forms. For a detailed and comprehensive typology of Cinquecento Italian religious dialogues, see Girardi, *La società del dialogo*, pp. 189–270, esp. pp. 201, 222 and 243, on continuities with patristic and medieval tradition. Where secular dialogues are concerned, 'serious' non-documentary dialogues are relatively uncommon, in Italy, though a number of dialogues on technical and scientific subjects took this form (see, for example, Paolo Pino, *Dialogo della pittura* (Venice, 1548), Giambattista Vimercato, *Dialogo della descrittione teorica e pratica de gli horologi solari* (Ferrara, 1565) and Alessandro Puccinelli, *Dialoghi sopra le cause della peste universale* (Lucca, 1557)). For a rare example of a serious fictional dialogue on a more conventionally humanistic theme, see Daniele Barbaro's *Della eloquenza* (1557), in *Trattati di poetica e*

retorica del Cinquecento, ed. Bernard Winberg (Bari, 1970–4), vol. II: a dialogue between Nature, Art and the Soul and (from p. 378), 'Dinardo' – man (a joint creation of DIO, NAtura and ARte).

48 On the aims and methods of the new literary theory of the late sixteenth century, see Bernard Weinberg, *A History of Literary Criticism in the Italian Renaissance* (Chicago, 1961) and Baxter Hathaway, *The Age of Criticism: The Late Renaissance in Italy* (Ithaca, N.Y., 1962). On the place of this phenomenon within broader developments in Italian culture in the Cinquecento, see Dionisotti, *Geografia e storia*, esp. pp. 197–203; also Andrea Battistini and Ezio Raimondi, 'Retoriche e poetiche dominanti', in Alberto Asor Rosa (ed), *Letteratura italiana. III. Le forme del testo. I. Teoria e poesia* (Turin, 1984), pp. 82–98.

49 This parallel is drawn explicitly in the dialogue which forms the third book of Claudio Corte's *Il Cavallerizzo* (1562), where, replying to the accusation that he has transgressed the Aristotelian rule of unity of theme in the first two books of the treatise, Corte defends himself by referring to the practice of Castiglione and Ariosto, neither of whom, he claims, adhered rigorously to the subject announced in the title (*Il Cavallerizzo*, 2nd edition (Venice, 1573), p. 119r). The passage reveals an awareness of contemporary critical dispute, and Corte justifies his position by referring to the 'galant' huomini' who have argued in defence of Ariosto's practice. For a discussion of Corte's rather eccentric dialogue, see below, chapter 4, pp. 38–9.

50 It should be noted, however, that Sigonio's place in the development of Aristotelian literary theory is a problematic one: as a recent critic has noted, his commitment to the methods of the new Aristotelian poetics is compromised by a '(barely) submerged vein of rhetorical thinking', more characteristic of the previous, humanistic tradition (Snyder, *Writing the Scene of Speaking*, p. 76); see also pp. 39–41 of the same volume, Dionisotti, *Geografia e storia*, p. 199 and Girardi, 'Elegans imitatio et erudita', pp. 321–7.

51 The *Giunta* to the first book of Bembo's *Prose* was published for the first time in Basle, in 1572, along with a *Correttione d'alcune cose del Dialogo delle lingue di Benedetto Varchi*. It was written earlier, however, probably at some time between 1549 and 1563: see Giorgio Patrizi, 'Lodovico Castelvetro', in *Dizionario biografico degli italiani*, vol. XXII, p. 16.

52 See Castelvetro, *Giunta alle prose del Bembo* in *Correttione d'alcune cose del Dialogo delle lingue di Benedetto Varchi, et una giunta al primo libro delle Prose di M. Pietro Bembo dove si ragiona della vulgar lingua* (Basle, 1572), pp. 121–3. At p. 121, Castelvetro claims that no one believes the conversation recounted by Bembo to have actually taken place ('io non so se si truovi persona, che creda, che il ragionamento, il quale scrive il Bembo essere stato tra questi quattro huomini, sia stato vero') and suggests that it was 'imaginato, e trovato tutto da lui [Bembo] per poter honorare in questa guisa questi suoi amici insieme co 'l fratello' ('invented by Bembo in its entirety, to commemorate his friends and his brother'). Among the reasons he cites for this assumption, two are of interest in the present context: the improbability of Carlo Bembo's being able to remember with such accuracy the 'proposte' 'riposte' and 'atti' of three days of discussion, and the gulf between the level of linguistic knowledge displayed by Bembo's protagonists in the dialogue and in real life.

Castelvetro's criticisms must be seen in the context of his eccentric and controversial theory of the dialogue and, in particular, his conception of the narrated dialogue as a species of history (see his *Poetica d'Aristotele volgarizzata e sposta* (1570), ed. W. Romani (Bari, 1978), vol. I, pp. 35–9, esp. p. 38; also Baldassari, 'L'arte del dialogo in Torquato Tasso', pp. 7–8 and Mulas, 'La scrittura del dialogo', pp. 247–50).

53 See *La Varchina*, in *L'Ercolano di M. Benedetto Varchi . . . Colla correzzione ad esso fatta da M. Lodovico Castelvetro; e colla Varchina di Messer Girolamo Muzio*, ed. Antonfrancesco Seghezzi (Padua, 1744), vol. III, p. 8; also p. 7, where Muzio ironizes about the fact that Varchi has his speakers dispatch an entire dinner between one *battuta* of the dialogue and the next. Also of interest, for the light they throw on the level of circumstantial accuracy demanded in dialogue, are Muzio's comments, at p. 9, on Bembo's more plausible handling of time in the *Prose*: 'Il terzo Dialogo del Bembo può esser grande quanto i due primi insieme: ma egli accortosi della soverchia lunghezza, come fu al mezzo del ragionamento, fece apparire i lumi, e cosí fu seguitato il parlare infino ad ora di cena. E istato essendo di Decembre, e cenandosi in Vinegia tardissimo, il Dialogo al tempo venne ad essere proporzionato.' ('The third dialogue of the *Prose* may be as long as the first two together: but, realizing that it was getting too long, when he got to the middle of the conversation, he had [the speakers] have lamps brought in, so that their dialogue could continue until dinner-time. And, since the dialogue is set in December, and it is the custom, in Venice, to dine very late, the dialogue works out to correspond with the time allocated to it.')

54 *La Varchina*, p. 9. Tasso's most explicit statements on the level of verisimilitude required in the dialogue are contained in his *Risposta alla lettera di Bastiano de' Rossi, Academico della Crusca, indifesa del suo dialogo del Piacere honesto* (1586), in *Prose diverse*, ed. Cesare Guasti, (Florence, 1875), vol. I, p. 405 where he states of the historical 'occasione' represented in the *Nifo* that 'I' ho rinnovato non come storico ma come scrittore di dialogo, il quale . . . più tosto s'obbliga al verisimile, che al vero' ('I have revived it not as a historian would, but in the manner of a writer of dialogues, who should observe the criterion of verisimilitude, rather than factual accuracy'). For a discussion of Tasso's remarks on dialogue in the *Risposta*, see below, chapter 7, p. 77.

55 See, for example, the introduction to Niccolò Granucci's *La piacevol notte e lieto giorno* (Venice, 1574), p. 5r–v, where the author, perhaps ironically, attempts to deflect possible criticisms of his dialogue on the grounds of factual inaccuracy, by laying the blame at the hands of the unnamed and evidently fictional friar, who is his source for the conversation: 'piacciavi di darne la colpa al Frate, se i nomi che si contengono nell'opera fussero aerei, e fantastichi, e se i Benci ancora non havessero Ville a Troiano: perche send'io male in gambe, e poco pratico in quel paese, non ho voluto durar più fatica in ricercarne il vero [. . .] basta ch'io habbia scritto ciò ch'egli mi raccontò fidatamente' ('if the names contained in this work are ghostly and fantastic, and if the Benci do not possess villas at Troiano, kindly lay the blame at the Friar's door; because, since I am not very robust and do not know the area well, I did not wish to weary myself overmuch in researching the truth [. . .] Let it suffice that I have faithfully recorded what he told me'). Note as well that

even the determinedly 'fantastic' Antonfrancesco Doni, in a passage from his introduction to *I Marmi* (1552–3) (cited above, chapter 2, n. 55) feels the need to deflect possible criticisms on the grounds of verisimilitude.

56 Landino's dialogue has two ideal figures, 'Aretophilus' and 'Philotimus', comfortably interacting with historical figure like Leon Battista Alberti, Angelo Poliziano, Marsilio Ficino and Lorenzo de' Medici: see Maria Teresa Liaci's edition of the dialogue (Florence, 1970), p. 20; also pp. 16–17, for a list of the most conspicuous anachronisms in the dialogue. As a contrast – from a much later period, of course – see the introduction to Sforza Pallavicino's *Del bene* (1644), where the author announces his intention to mark with a marginal note those occasions on which he has been tempted to introduce 'any notion elaborated after the death of the speakers portrayed' ('qualche pensiero [. . .] nato dopo la morte de' favellatori introdotti') (*Del bene, libri quattro*, in *Opere edite e inedite* (Rome, 1844–5), vol. II, p. xviii). It is interesting to note that Pallavicino goes on to relate the imperative of verisimilitude, explicitly, to the Ciceronian tradition: 'Questa licenza, ch'io chieggio avanti, penso che mi assolverà da qual biasimo, con cui M. Tullio derise la smemoraggine usata in questa parte da Curione in alcuni suoi dialoghi.' ('I hope that this advance warning will absolve me of the blame Cicero apportioned to Curio for his negligence in this respect.') The reference is to Cicero's *Brutus*, lix 281–19.

57 For a detailed discussion of the censorship of the *Cortegiano*, and the expurgated edition of 1584, see Guidi, 'Reformulations de l'idéologie aristocratique', pp. 162–82.

58 *Apologia de' dialoghi*, p. 275: 'le persone in due modi sogliono intrare nelli dialoghi a ragionare. E l' uno è quando l' autore istesso cortesemente, quasi loro oste, par che le meni con esso seco nel suo dialogo; e però scrive, il tal disse ed il tal rispose: il qual modo solea tener Senofonte e Ciceron molte volte; e non è comica imitazione, perciocchè pura non è, ma è meschiata delle persone e dello scrittore . . .; ben sente alquanto dello epico, onde abbia forse non so che più di onestà, che non si trova nelle commedie. Che così come non di ogni fatto si scrive istoria, ma solamente di quel che è degno e notevole; così l'autor del dialogo quei soli detti delle persone da lui condotte dee riferire, che gli sia onore il parlarne, e dee tacer tutti gli altri.' ('There are two different ways of introducing the speakers into dialogues. One is when the author himself leads them into his dialogue, courteously, in the manner of a host, and writes "so-and-so says this" and "so-and-so says that": a manner frequently employed by Xenophon and Cicero. This is not dramatic imitation, as one finds in comedy, because it is not pure, but a mixture of the characters' voices and the author's . . . It does have something in common with epic, however, and this makes it somehow more respectable than comic drama. For, just as, in historical narratives, one does not record every happening, but only what is noteworthy and merits being recorded, so the author of a dialogue should only relate those sayings of the speakers he has introduced which it would do them honour to relate, and he should suppress all the rest.') For the context of the passage, in the *Apologia* and, more broadly, within sixteenth-century dialogue theory, see below, chapter 7, pp. 73–4; also Snyder, *Writing the Scene of Speaking*, pp. 106–10.

59 ('I have never come across a man who used Scriptural citations more crudely

than you do, or who was quite so eager to cut his own throat . . .') The passage
is from Tahureau's *Les dialogues non moins profitables que facetieux* (1565), ed.
Max Gauna (Paris, 1981), p. 165; and is cited by Kushner in 'Reflexions sur le
dialogue', p. 489.

60 I am thinking here of Patrizi's early *Dialogo d'honore, detto il Barignano*
(Venice, 1553) and the twenty dialogues collected in the *Della historia* (Venice,
1560) and the *Della retorica* (Venice, 1562): his later, unpublished *Amorosa
filosofia* (1577) is more conventional in this respect. An important passage in
the introduction of the *Dialogo d'honore*, pp. 20v–21r, makes explicit Patrizi's
polemical intent in his dialogues, his proud consciousness of their novelty and
his debt to 'il divino Platone': 'essendo questa materia secondo il mio parere
nuova e d'altri per avanti non trattata, io non mi sono potuto imaginar
miglior modo . . . di farla venire a luce, che quello il quale il divino Platone, ne'
suoi dialoghi usa, che tentativi overo litigiosi si chiamano; ne' quali confu-
tando egli le false altrui opinioni passo passo per interrogatione . . . fa apparire
la verità. Il qual modo, da lui in poi, non ho ancor veduto usato da scrittor
alcuno, né greco, né latino, né volgare, essendo però bello e comodo molto.'
('since this subject-matter is entirely original, I could imagine no better way to
present it than that used by the divine Plato in his polemical or litigious
dialogues; in which he gradually brings the truth to light by means of a
step-by-step refutation of the false opinions of others. This is a type of
dialogue I have not seen used by any subsequent writer, Greek, Latin or
Italian, even though it is extremely elegant and useful.') On the origins of the
division of Plato's dialogues into 'didactic', 'dialectical', 'polemical' and
'sophistic' types, see my 'Rhetoric and Politics in Tasso's *Nifo*', p. 21, n. 59. On
Patrizi's use of the dialogue form, see Lina Bolzoni, '*L'Universo dei poemi
possibili*': *Studi su Francesco Patrizi da Cherso* (Rome, 1980), p. 64 and D.
LaRusso, 'A Neo-Platonic Dialogue: *Is Rhetoric an Art?* An Introduction and
a Translation', *Speech Monographs*, vol. 32, no. 4 (1969), pp. 398–9.

61 Even where the speakers are identifiable historical figures, like the Fracastoro
of *De l' infinito, universo e mondi* or the Tansillo of *De gli eroici furori*, Bruno's
dialogue is quite alien from the commemorative and decorous tones of the
neo-Ciceronian tradition. Indeed, the *Proemiale Epistola* to his satirical *Cena
de le ceneri* contains a passage which it would be possible to interpret as an
explicit rejection of that tradition: 'in che versa questo convito, questa cena?
Non già in considerar l'animo et effetti del molto nobile et ben creato sig[nor]
Folco Grivello, alla cui onorata stanza si convenne. Non circa gli onorati
costumi di que' signori civilissimi, che . . . vi furono presenti. Ma circa un voler
veder quantunque può natura, in far due fantastiche befane, doi sogni, due
ombre e due febbri quartane' ('What is the object of this symposium, this
banquet? It is not a study of the mind and attributes of that most noble and
courteous lord, Fulke Greville, whose honoured home it graced; nor of the fine
manners of those exquisitely courteous lords who were present at it; but rather
an investigation of what Nature can achieve when she puts her mind to it: two
fantastic crones, two dreams, two shadows, two quartan fevers [the two
Oxford doctors, Nundinio and Torquato]') (*La Cena de le ceneri*, in *Dialoghi
italiani*, ed. Giovanni Aquilecchia (Florence, 1958), pp. 9–10.

62 On the two historical figures portrayed, Filippo Salviati and Giovan France-

sco Sagredo, see Stillman Drake, *Galileo at Work; His Scientific Biography* (Chicago and London, 1978), pp. 465–6. Simplicio, named for an early commentator on Aristotle, voices arguments close to those of contemporary Aristotelians like Cesare Cremonini and Lodovico delle Colombe: see Drake, p. 219 and p. 355; also, on Cremonini, Charles B. Schmitt, *Cesare Cremonini. Un aristotelico al tempo di Galilei* (Venice, 1980), esp. p. 20. Another good example of a dialogue in which the choice to suppress the names of the speakers has clearly been made on prudential grounds is the attack on Speroni's tragedy, *La Canace*, probably written by Giambattista Giraldi Cinzio, but published anonymously, in Lucca, in 1550. It is striking that, while the anonymous speakers of the dialogue are more than happy to tear Speroni's tragedy to shreds, the only named interlocutor, Giangiorgio Trissino, discreetly refuses to comment, on the grounds that the author is a friend, and he would only wish to communicate his criticisms directly to him: see *Giudizio d'una tragedia di Canace e Macareo*, in Sperone Speroni, *Canace e Scritti in sua difesa* – Giambattista Giraldi Cinzio, *Scritti contro la Canace. Giudizio ed Epistola latina*, ed. Christina Roaf (Bologna, 1982), p. 110.

4 THE USES OF THE DIALOGUE IN SIXTEENTH-CENTURY ITALY: COMMERCE AND COURTESY

1 ('These days, almost all of us are out to get the best deal for ourselves') cited in Girardi, *La società del dialogo*, p. 67.

2 See Jane P. Tompkins, 'The Reader in History: the Changing Shape of Literary Response', in Jane P. Tompkins (ed.), *Reader-Response Criticism from Formalism to Post-Structuralism* (Baltimore and London, 1980), pp. 206–8; also Lauro Martines, *Society and History in English Renaissance Verse* (Oxford, 1985), pp. 18–20.

3 See Tompkins, 'The Reader in History', p. 208; also, on the implications of this change for the theory and practice of rhetoric in sixteenth-century Italy, my 'Rhetoric and Politics in Tasso's *Nifo*', esp. pp. 62–86.

4 Tompkins, 'The Reader in History', p. 208.

5 The term is J. L. Austin's: see his *How To Do Things With Words* (Oxford, 1975), esp. p. 109 and pp. 118–19.

6 See Pallavicino, *Trattato dello stile e del dialogo*, p. 355 (at the beginning of the chapter entitled 'Duo vantaggi che comporta lo scriver in Dialogo le dottrine'): '[il Dialogo] si col divisato colloquio di moderni Letterati, si col premesso racconto della lor condizione, apre un' illustre campo ad onorar le memoria di quei defonti la cui dottrina onorò il secol nostro mentre fur vivi . . .' ('As a depiction of a conversation between modern men of letters, prefaced by an account of their qualities, the dialogue offers a splendid opportunity for honouring the memory of those men, now deceased, who honoured the world with their learning while they lived.')

7 Pallavicino, *Trattato dello stile e del dialogo*, pp. 355–6: 'è . . . giovevole che ciascuno a poter suo s' argomenti d' accrescere i guiderdoni e gli stimoli alla Virtù; e che à que' Benemeriti della sapienza, i quali per umana sciagura non potranno allungar la vita del nome negli scritti proprij, rimanga a sperarla dalla gratitudine degli altrui' ('one should always do one's utmost to increase

the number of incentives and encouragements to virtue; and it is only right that those learned men who have not been able to prolong the memory of their name in their own writings, because of some misfortune, should be able to hold out some hope of seeing their memory preserved through the gratitude of others'). See also Pallavicino's introduction to his own dialogue, *Del bene*, pp. 12–14, where he argues that 'i moderni defonti' – recently deceased speakers – are the most suitable choice for interlocutors, and that to choose living figures makes the writer vulnerable to accusations of flattery.

8 It would be naïve, of course, to imply that the choice of deceased figures as speakers necessarily guarantees the disinterestedness of a writer. For a cynical view of the utility of praising 'i moderni defonti', as a means of flattering their living relatives, see Tasso's letter to Curzio Ardizio of 28 June 1584, in *Lettere*, ed. Cesare Guasti (Florence, 1854–5), vol. II, pp. 211–16, esp. p. 213; discussed in my article, 'Rhetoric and Politics in Tasso's *Nifo*', pp. 50–6. Tasso's point is illustrated by those dialogues, like his own *Nifo, overo del piacere onesto* (1585) or Lionardo Salviati's *Dialoghi dell'amicizia* (1564), which take as their interlocutors the fathers of their dedicatees: see *Il Nifo*, in *Dialoghi*, ed. Ezio Raimondi (Florence, 1958), vol. II, p. 157 and Peter M. Brown, *Lionardo Salviati* (Oxford, 1974), p. 18; also Tasso, *Lettere*, vol. II, p. 467, for a letter to Angelo Grillo of 1586, mentioning a proposal for a dialogue – never written – featuring Grillo's father as protagonist.

9 ('to increase the fame of our friends') *Della dedicatione dei libri, con la Correttion dell'Abuso in questa materia introdotto, Dialoghi*, (Venice, 1590), pp. 22r–v. Fratta practises what he preaches: *Della dedicatione* takes the form of a dialogue between three of his friends, written as a 'dimostratione di cara amicizia' (p. 2r); two further, entirely superfluous 'auditori' join them half-way through (p. 11r) and Fratta caps his list of great writers of dialogue at p. 22r – Plato, Xenophon, Fracastoro, Speroni – with his close friend Cesare Campana, the historian, author of such renowned dialogues as *I Synarmofili overo della vera nobiltà* (Vicenza, 1586) and *L'Agostini, overo della liberalità* (Verona, 1588).

10 On Bandello's public relations work in his dedications, see Fiorato, 'Bandello et la règne du père', pp. 98–102. Two examples of dialogues which exploit to the full the potential of the genre for giving honorary mention to acquaintances are Giacomo Lanteri's *Due dialoghi . . . del modo di disegnare le piante delle fortezze* (Venice, 1557) and Giuseppe Malatesta's *Della nuova poesia, overo delle difese del Furioso* (Verona, 1589). Lanteri dedicates his two dialogues to separate dedicatees, includes an afterword and a dialogue within the first dialogue in praise of the Counts of Arco (pp. 3–6) and terminates his second dialogue (pp. 77–93) with a long list of Brescian acquaintances. Malatesta laments the fact that, for reasons of space, he will not be able to name all the members of Cardinal d'Este's court who deserve mention (p. 3), but he nevertheless manages to start with a cast of seventeen interlocutors (pp. 4–8), who are then supplemented at p. 10 by the arrival of a further 'drapello' ('herd').

11 ('A treasure which one can keep spending for ever, without it ever running out') letter of 6 June 1537, in *Lettere. Il primo e il secondo libro*, ed. Francesco Flora (Milan, 1960), p. 173. The tone of the letter is ironic – Aretino is alluding

to the Roman courtesan Tullia d'Aragona's delight at what he considers an
overly flattering portrayal of her, in Speroni's *Dialogo d'Amore* – but the irony
is directed purely at Tullia and does not detract from the sincerity of the
compliment to Speroni. On the context of the letter, see Fournel. *Les dialogues
de Sperone Speroni*, p. 55 and p. 281, n. 39.

12 ('How it must rejoice the souls of those who have passed from this life – and,
much more, those who are still living – to see themselves immortalized by such
a man – nay, not a man, but a demi-god, a superhuman . . . What lovelier
statue, what finer trophies or tributes to their virtue could they possibly wish
for?') *Discorsi sopra i dialoghi di M. Sperone Speroni, ne' quali si ragiona della
bellezza e della eccellenza de' lor concetti* (Venice, 1561), p. 6v. There is further
evidence of the gratifications a mention in Speroni's dialogues could give in a
letter of 22 July 1564 from Annibale Caro to Torquato Conti, congratulating
Conti on his inclusion in Speroni's *Del giudicio di Senofonte*: 'Il Sig. Sperone si
raccomanda a V. S. E. le fo fede, che l'osserva molto: E. per segno di ciò, ha
fatto un dialogo, dove sopra alcune dispute di guerra, l'introduce a parlar
come uno de' più periti Signori d'Italia: Cosa che le deve esser molto cara da
un suo pari: Gli scritti del quale vanno a la volta de l'immortalità.' ('Signor
Speroni asks to be remembered to you, and I can assure you that he thinks a
great deal of you. And, as a sign of it, he has written a dialogue, in which, in a
discussion of warfare, he shows you as one of the most knowledgeable
Gentlemen in Italy – something which must give you great pleasure, since it
comes from one whose writings fly to the vaults of immortality.') (*De le lettere
Familiari del Commendatore Annibale Caro* (Venice, 1597), vol. II, p. 227) (I
am grateful to Professor C. Fahy for calling my attention to this passage.) On
Conti's role in the dialogue, see Fournel, *Les dialogues de Sperone Speroni*,
pp. 165–6; on his military career, I. Polverini Fosi's entry in *Dizionario biblio-
grafico degli italiani*, vol. xxviii, pp. 479–80.

13 Early critics' canons of great writers of dialogue often show a certain eccentricity, but they are almost unanimous in their inclusion of Speroni. Benedetto
Varchi, for example, in *L'Ercolano* (Venice, 1570), p. 279, lists Leone Ebreo,
Bernardino Tomitano, Speroni, Giambattista Giraldi Cinzio and Giambattista Pigna; Giovanni Fratta, *Della dedicatione dei libri*, p. 22 has Girolamo
Fracastoro, Speroni and Cesare Campana (on whom see above, n. 9); Agostino Michele, *Discorso in cui contra l'opinione di tutti i piu illustri scrittori del
arte poetica chiaramente si dimostra come si possono scrivere con molto lode le
comedie e le tragedie in proso* (Venice, 1592), p. 19 (cited in Hathaway, *The Age
of Criticism* p. 108) mentions Pontano and Speroni, while Sforza Pallavicino,
Trattato delo stile e del dialogo, p. 326 cites Bembo, Speroni, Cesare Bargagli
and 'sopra tutti la chiarissima penna di Torquato Tasso'. See also chapter 6,
n. 20, below. For an account of the energetic, if unsuccessful, campaign
conducted by the historian Giuliano Gosellini to win a place in Speroni's
dialogues, see Marco Forcellini, *La Vita di Sperone Speroni degli Alvarotti,
Filsofo e Cavalier Padovano*, in Speroni, *Opere*, edited by Marco Forcellini and
Natal dalle Laste, 5 volumes (Padua, 1740), vol. V, p. xli and note 373. On
Antonino Costantini's rather more successful attempt to win a place in Tasso's
dialogues, see Marcantonio Foppa's *Argomento* to the *Costantino* or *Costante*
in his edition of Tasso's *Opere non più stampate* (Rome, 1666), vol. I, p. 413.

14 An interesting, more downbeat testimony to the prestige value of a mention in dialogue is Girolamo Muzio Giustinopolitano's introductory letter to Tullia d'Aragona, *Dialogo dell'infinità di amore*, in Pozzi (ed.), *Trattati d'amore del Cinquecento*, pp. 246–7. The speakers in the dialogue, as published, are Tullia herself, Benedetto Varchi and Lattanzio Benucci, but, as Muzio records, in the manuscript she first circulated, the writer had, through modesty, replaced her own name with that of 'Sabina'. For Muzio, the resulting mixture of 'nomi finti' and 'veri' was unsatisfactory ('o tutti finti o tutti veri dovrebbono essere'), and the solution of a fully fictional dialogue unfair to the other speakers ('se . . . avessi mutati gli altri [nomi], averei fatto ingiuria a que' nobilissimi spiriti, a' quali vi era piaciuto dar vita nelle vostre carte'); he therefore decided to publish the text in its documentary form. Though too interested to be entirely reliable, Muzio's letter is worthy of note, as one of the few criticial comments on a dialogue in this period to show a consciousness of the distinction between fictional and documentary dialogues.

15 *Della dedicatione dei libri*, p. 22v. On being refused payment, the author substituted the names of the speakers in question with fictional names ('cancellò . . . il nome de gli interlocutori, e sotto persone supposite, corresse l'avidità del suo pensiero').

16 See Lodovico Castelvetro, *Correttione d'alcune cose del Dialogo delle lingue di Benedetto Varchi* (Basle, 1572), pp. 85–6, where Castelvetro accuses Varchi of having transformed a pre-existing treatise on language into dialogue form 'in order to honour many people whom he mentions in it and, in particular Cesare Ercolani' ('per poter onorare . . . molte persone delle quali vi fa menzione e spetialmente Cesare Hercolani da Bologna'). At the same time, he claims, Varchi re-dedicated several sonnets to Ercolani, which had in fact been composed much earlier, 'per accattare la gratia e per acquistare l'amore d'altri giovanetti a' quali, poi che erano fatti huomini, ritoglieva senza rossore niuno quello, che loro in altra età e forma aveva liberamente donato' ('with the aim of gaining the good graces and affection of other boys, whom he then, as soon as they grew to adulthood, quite shamelessly deprived of what he had previously given them so freely').

17 On the criteria which determined the degree of prominence accorded to the various interlocutors in successive drafts of the *Cortegiano*, see José Guidi, '"festive narrazioni", "motti" e "burle" ("beffe"): l'art des facéties dans *Le Courtisan*', in André Rochon (ed.), *Formes et significations de la 'beffa' dans la littérature italienne de la Renaissance* (Paris, 1972–5), vol. II, p. 180. On the changes of emphasis in the presentation of the political figures mentioned in the dialogue, see Guidi, 'L'Espagne dans la vie et dans l'œuvre de B. Castiglione: de l'équilibre franco-hispanique au choix impérial', in Rochon (ed.), *Présence et influence de l'Espagne dans la culture italienne de la Renaissance* (Paris, 1978), pp. 185–90. Interesting as testimony of the sort of capital which could be made out of such mentions is a letter of Castiglione's letter to Ippolito d'Este of 23 June 1520, where he assures the Cardinal that the *raison d'être* of the entire treatise is the passage in praise of him in the first book: see *Le lettere*, ed. Guido La Rocca (Milan, 1978), vol. I, pp. 546–7 and, for the passage in question, *La seconda redazione del 'Cortegiano'* (*c.* 1518–20), ed. Ghino Ghinassi (Florence, 1968), pp. 24–5.

18 The nature of Alessandro Pocaterra's favours to Tasso is indicated in a letter to Guido Coccapanni of 12 March 1581 (*Lettere*, vol. II, p. 496) where he begs Coccapanni to intervene to have his own 'few rags' ('poche robicciuole') restored to him and complains that 'questi panni che mi manda il Pocattera, me li manda sempre fuor di tempo, e per farmi dispetto' ('the linen which Pocaterra sends me is always sent at the wrong time, just to annoy me'). On Tasso's inclusion of Pocaterra's son Annibale in his dialogue *Il Romeo, overo del giuoco* (1581), dedicated to Alessandro, see Ezio Raimondi's introduction to his edition of the *Dialoghi* (Florence, 1958), vol. I, pp. 35–6.

19 See the letter to Curzio Ardizio of 27 June 1584, in *Lettere*, vol. II, pp. 206–11, where Tasso outlines his project for a commemorative dialogue set in the court of Guidobaldo II della Rovere, stating that 'il buon duca Guidobaldo . . . in guisa col suo testimonio m'onorò, ch'io al valor di lui non debbo alcun testimonio negare' ('the good Duke Guidobaldo so honoured me with his testimony that I cannot grudge him any testimony I can give to his valour') (p. 208).

20 See the letter to Guido Coccapanni, cited above, n. 18, where Tasso protests that Alessandro Pocaterra should be happy enough that he has given them such an honourable place in his dialogues, without insisting on celebration in verse ('si dovrebbe contentare ch'io tenessi cosi onorata menzione di lui e di suo figliuolo ne' miei dialoghi . . . Ma la casa di Pocaterra, per non ingannarlo, non voglio celebrare in versi . . .'). It appears that some years later, Tasso's debt with the family was still weighing on him: in a letter to his publisher, of 16 June 1586 (*Lettere*, vol. II, pp. 542–3), Tasso asks whether it might be possible to reprint a few pages of the dialogues *De la nobiltà* and *De la dignità* 'perché . . . è necessario ch'io faccia qualche onorata menzione del signor Pocaterra' ('because I need to include some honourable mention of Signor Pocaterra').

21 For examples, see below, p. 43.

22 *Della dedicatione dei libri*, p. 22v.

23 *Della nuova poesia overo delle difese dell' Ariosto* (Verona, 1589), p. 26. Speroni is replying to a request from Ercole Tassoni and Francesco Bandini Piccolomini, Archbishop of Siena, that he undertake the defence of Ariosto. Accepting, he clarifies that 'se qualcuno mi sentisse dir qualche cosa diversamente da quello che, o scrivendo, o ragionando ho detto altre volte in altri luoghi, sappia pur che, in questa giornata, io accetto come buone sol quelle opinioni, che conferiscono a mostrar quello che per obligo impostomi da questi Signori, io devo mostrare dell'Ariosto' ('in case I should be heard to say anything which differs from what I have said or written on other occasions, let it be known that, for today, I am accepting as valid only those opinions which support the case about Ariosto which these Gentlemen have ordered me to make'). On the discrepancies between Speroni's views on Ariosto and those attributed to him by Malatesta, see Forcellini, *Vita di Speroni*, p. 50, n. 428. It should be noted, however, that Malatesta's unusual argumentational strategy is carried through with a self-consciousness and ingenuity Forcellini's unsympathetic reading does not do justice to: see, for example, *Della nuova poesia*, pp. 66–7, where Speroni's antagonist, Scipione Ammirato (himself, to complicate matters further, an enthusiast of Ariosto's poetry) accuses him of surreptitiously attacking Ariosto while pretending to defend him, and see also Marsh,

The Quattrocento Dialogue, pp. 30–1, p. 40 and pp. 60–1, on classical and humanist precedents for a calculated use of ethical irony.

24 ('I do not intend to tie myself down entirely to what I have expressed in writing') Bartolomeo Meduna, *Lo Scolare* (Venice, 1588), p. 4r. A further example of this kind of strategy is to be found in Scipione Bargagli's *La prima parte dell' imprese*, 2nd edition (Venice, 1589), pp. 25–6, where, ironically, the speaker, Lelio Maretti (the 'Attonito Intronato'), is explaining away the discrepancy between his statements here and the views attributed to him by the author's brother, Girolamo Bargagli, in his *Dialogo de' giuochi che nelle vegghie sanesi s' usano di fare* (1572). For another example of the same kind of awkward disclaimer, see Bernardino Tomitano, *Quattro libri della lingua thoscana* (Padua, 1570), p. 36r, where Sperone Speroni is made to argue that the element of pleasure ('diletto') in rhetoric is compatible with – even inseparable from – the element of teaching ('insegnamento'), even though he has argued to the contrary on another occasion ('come che in altro tempo, da me sia stato difeso, che il diletto sia più tosto de la elocutione oratoria compagno, che scolare di philosophia'). The work Tomitano is referring to here is Speroni's *Dialogo della Retorica* (1542): for the problem at issue, see my 'Rhetoric and Politics in Tasso's *Nifo*', pp. 89–91.

25 Whigham, 'Interpretation at court', pp. 624–5.

26 ('all those subject areas which have a rather common flavour to them') Orazio Toscanella, *Alcune avvertenze del tesser Dialoghi*, in *Quadrivio* (Venice, 1567), p. 63v. 'Grave' subjects, to be treated in the high style, are 'Dio, Angelo, Cielo, Anima, e cose simili; con le scienze, e dottrine, e discipline, e arti specialmente considerate in astratto' ('God, Angels, Heaven, the Soul, etc.; also the sciences and arts and all branches of learning, considered in the abstract') (p. 63r). 'Mediocre' subjects are defined, in a faintly surrealistic formula, as 'Huomo, Leone, Elementi e cosi fatte creature, che sono sotto il cerchio della Luna; con le scienze, dottrine, discipline, e arti considerate in concreto' ('Man, Lions, Elements and other such created beings, beneath the circle of the Moon; along with the arts and sciences considered concretely'). Toscanella's downmarket and theoretically unsophisticated, but occasionally revealing collection of tips on dialogue composition has been understandably ignored by historians of sixteenth-century dialogue theory. On the author's life and works, see Di Filippo Bareggi, *Il mestiere di scrivere*, pp. 86–7.

27 Another, rather better-known example is Niccolò Tartaglia's *Quesiti et inventioni diverse* (1546), a structurally highly idiosyncratic work, consisting of a series of short dialogues between the author himself and various readers of his earlier treatise, the *Nova scientia* (1537), who are given the chance to air doubts and queries arising from that work, mainly concerning practical problems of ballistics. One motive for Tartaglia's choice of the dialogue form is to advertise the interest shown in his work by influential figures like Francesco Maria della Rovere, Duke of Urbino and Diego Hurtado da Mendoza, the Imperial Ambassador: see his dedication, to Henry VIII, in *Opera* (Venice, 1606), p. 5, where he draws attention to the eminence of his interlocutors, and note that, for the most part, only those interlocutors whose rank could reflect some glory onto their queries are identified by name in the dialogues, while the others are referred to simply by their professions ('Bombardiere', 'Scioppettero'). On

Tartaglia's other motives for writing in dialogue, see Girardi, *La società del dialogo*, pp. 293–303 and Luisa Cozzi, 'Il lessico scientifico nel dialogo del Rinascimento', in Davide Bigalli and Guido Canziani (eds.), *Il dialogo filosofico nel 500 europeo. Atti del convegno internazionale di studi, Milano, 28–30 maggio, 1987* (Milan, 1990), pp. 60–6 and p. 80.

28 A letter appended to the revised edition of 1573 (retitled *Il Cavallerizzo*), explaining the transfer into dialogue, reveals Corte's awareness of the apparent breach of decorum involved in using the dialogue form for such a 'mechanical subject': note particularly his insistence that the dialogue form is 'attissimo a trattar tutte le cose in qual si voglia genere, che elle si sieno' ('extremely well-suited for any kind of subject-matter whatsoever') (*Il Cavallerizzo*, 2nd edition (Venice, 1573), p. 115r). Subsequent references will be to this edition.

29 For the phrase 'manifold digressions', see Thomas Bedingfield, *The Art of Riding . . . Written at lunge in the Italian toong, by Maistre Claudio Corte . . . Here briefelie reduced into certain English discourses* (London, 1584), p. Aii.

30 ('per nominare alcuni patroni, e amici miei') *Il Cavallerizzo*, p. 115r. See also, as evidence of Corte's pragmatism, p. 118v of the same edition, where he discusses the financial rewards which can be gained through well-calculated dedications.

31 ('an extremely beautiful place, and most appropriate for a conversation of this kind') *Il Cavallerizzo*, p. 115v.

32 For Corte's comments on one aspect of the form of the *Cortegiano* – the lack of unity in its argument – see above, chapter 3, n. 49.

33 See especially the initial scene (*Il Cavallerizzo* pp. 116r–v), describing the elaborate procedure of electing an entirely superfluous 'judge'. In Corte's description of Prospero's late arrival (p. 116r), there may be an allusion to the scene in *Cortegiano*, IV iii, where Ottaviano Fregoso arrives late for the last evening's discussions.

34 The speakers divide into two categories which, to adapt the distinction in Floriani, *I gentiluomini letterati*, pp. 25–6, might be termed 'gentiluomini cavallarizzi' and 'cavallarizzi gentiluomini'. An example of the former – noblemen versed in the art of horsemanship – would be Giambattista Pignatello, 'gentilhuomo Napolitano, e veramente non meno faceto, e cortese, che nel mestier del cavalcare molto raro'. Typical of the second group – professional equerries showing a mastery of the social graces – is Roberto Mantuano, 'cavallerizzo molto eccellente, e persona molto affabile, e piacevole' (*Il Cavallerizzo*, p. 116r).

35 See *Il Cavallerizzo*, p. 121r, for Corte's stipulations concerning the education of the *cavallerizzo*.

36 See *Il Cavallerizzo*, pp. 125v–126v, on the desirability of nobility in the *cavallerizzo*; pp. 126v–127v, on physical beauty; and pp. 128r–v, on accomplishments like skill in music and dancing. For the description of the *cavallerizzo* as brother to Castiglione's courtier, see p. 129r.

37 Sir Philip Sidney, *An Apology for Poetry*, ed. G. Shepherd (London, 1963), p. 95.

38 On Lanteri's attitude to the status of architects and architecture – 'complesso e non immediatamente leggibile' – see G. Vivenza, 'Giacomo Lanteri da

Paratico e il problema delle fortificazioni nel secolo XVI', *Economia e storia*, vol. 22, fasc. 4 (1975), p. 522. Vivenza points out that, while Lanteri is adamant that all civilized men should take an interest in the theory of architecture, he considers it indecorous for a gentleman to practise the art 'manualmente', and especially 'a prezzo' (see Lanteri, *Due dialoghi*, p. 48) – this despite the fact that Lanteri, who prided himself on his noble descent (Vivenza, 'Giacomo Lanteri', p. 504, n. 6) had himself made a highly successful career as a military architect.

39 See Girardi, *La società del dialogo*, pp. 303–10; also, more generally, on the essentially monological nature of the Cinquecento scientific dialogue tradition, pp. 273–303. Lanteri makes several allusions to the intractable nature of his subject-matter: see, for example, *Due dialoghi*, p. 44, where the 'figure d'Euclide' which occupy the first dialogue are described as 'fastidiose' and 'intricate'. Similar anxieties are expressed by other authors of 'technical' dialogues. Giovanni Maria Memmo, for example, divides his *L'Oratore* (1545), into two parts: the first, a straight didactic dialogue between Memmo himself and Niccolò Querini, dealing with the technical matter of rhetoric – the 'necessary foundations' of the art, which the author acknowledges to be 'none too pleasant to hear' (p. 38) – the second, a more elegant discussion between more distinguished interlocutors, dealing with the more elevated subject of the education of the orator.

40 On the use of the term 'mechanic' as an insult, see Filippo Pigafetta's introduction to the Italian translation of Guidobaldo del Monte, *Mechanicorum libri* (1577), cited in Paolo Rossi, *I filosofi e le macchine (1400–1700)* (Milan, 1962), p. 62, n. 96: also, more generally, on the status of the 'mechanical' arts in late-Cinquecento Italy, Rossi, pp. 62–7.

41 It is interesting to note that Lanteri's second vernacular work, *Due libri del modo di fare le fortificazioni* (1559) – addressed, unlike the present one, to an audience of *addetti ai lavori* – eschews dialogue altogether, and presents its teachings more economically, as a didactic treatise: see Vivenza, 'Giacomo Lanteri', p. 524.

42 See *Due dialoghi*, pp. 3–6, and, on Lanteri's and Cattaneo's relations with the Counts of Arco, L. Olivato, 'Girolamo Cattaneo', in *Dizionario biografico degli italiani*, vol. XXII, pp. 471–73. For the phrase 'ignorante vulgo', see *Due dialoghi*, p. 47, where Lanteri's point about the social status of military architecture is made more explicitly.

43 ('To see their works pass through the hands of a hundred thousand readers, bringing them fame and immortality') *Dialoghi piacevoli* (Venice, 1586), p. 2r. On the 'stigma' which appears to have attached to publication in the Tudor court, and on the strategies developed to avoid it, see J. W. Saunders, 'The Stigma of Print: a Note on the Social Bases of Tudor Poetry', *Essays in Criticism*, vol. 1, no. 2 (1951), pp. 139–64. Steven W. May, who criticizes Saunders's thesis on the grounds that many Tudor courtiers were in fact only too eager to publish their works, seems to have failed to realize that Saunders is talking about a *convention*, a matter of etiquette: see May, 'Tudor Aristocrats and the Mythical Stigma of Print', *Renaissance Papers* (1980), pp. 11–18; also the comments of Whigham, *Ambition and Privilege*, p. 216, n. 38.

44 See, for example, Mary Louise Pratt, *Towards a Speech-Act Theory of Literary Discourse* (Bloomington, Indiana and London, 1977), esp. pp. 100–51.

45 This sense of literary activity as an extension of courtly behaviour is particularly marked in George Puttenham's *Arte of English Poesie* (1589): see Javitch, *Poetry and Courtliness in Renaissance England*, pp. 50–75.

46 On the dynamics of performance in the exasperatedly rhetorical and self-conscious culture of the Renaissance court, see Whigham, 'Interpretation at Court' and *Ambition and Privilege*, pp. 32–62; also Wayne A. Rebhorn, *Courtly Performances. Masking and Festivity in Castiglione's 'Book of the Courtier'* (Detroit, 1978), pp. 117–50. But the best guide remains, perhaps, Castiglione himself: see, in particular, on the etiquette of literary production, *Cortegiano*, I xliv, p. 162, where it is recommended that the courtier should practise writing verse and prose, if only to provide entertainment for the ladies of the court, but that 'se, o per altre faccende o per poco studio, non giungerà a tal perfezione che i suoi scritti siano degni di molta laude, sia cauto in sopprimergli, per non far ridere altrui di sé' ('if, through lack of application, or some other reason, he does not reach such perfection in the art that his writings are genuinely excellent, then he should be prudent enough to keep them under guard, so as not to provoke ridicule').

47 Pettie, *A petite Pallace of pettie his pleasure* (1576), ed. I. Gollancz (London, 1908), vol. I, p. xx. Pettie's phrasing perhaps deliberately echoes Castiglione's famous definition of *sprezzatura*, in *Cortegiano*, I xxvi: 'Ma avendo io già più volte pensato onde nasca questa grazia . . . trovo una regula universalissima, la qual mi par valer circa questo in tutte le cose umane che si facciano o dicano più che alcuna altra: e ciò è fuggir quanto più si po, e come un asperissimo e periculoso scoglio, la affettazione; e, per dir forse una nova parola, usar in ogni cosa una certa sprezzatura, che nasconda l'arte, e dimostri, ciò che si fa e dice, venir fatto senza fatica e quasi senza pensarvi.' ('But, having given some thought to this question of how to be graceful . . ., I find that there is one absolutely universal rule, which applies, more than any other, to everything we say or do. And that is to strive at all costs to avoid affectation, as though it were a jagged and perilous reef, and to perform one's every action with what we might call – to coin a new word – a certain *sprezzatura*, concealing the care and study which goes into one's actions, and appearing to do and say things effortlessly, and quite without thought.') For a discussion of the term, see Eduardo Saccone, '"Grazia", "sprezzatura", "affettazione" in the *Courtier*', in Robert W. Hanning and David Rosand (eds.), *Castiglione: the Ideal and the Real in Renaissance Culture* (New Haven and London, 1983), esp. pp. 55–64; also Whigham, *Ambition and Privilege* pp. 93–5.

48 Pratt, *Towards a Speech-Act Theory*, esp. pp. 100–16.

49 *Galateo, ovvero de' costumi*, ed. Bruno Maier (Milan, 1971), p. 102: 'dal troppo favellare, conviene che gli uomini costumati si guardino . . . perché . . . pare che colui che favella soprastia in un certo modo a coloro che odono, come maestro a' discepoli; e perciò non istà bene di appropriarsi maggior parte di questa maggioranza che non ci si conviene' ('well-mannered men do well to keep from talking too much, because the man who is speaking takes a position of dominance over his listeners, rather like a teacher with his pupils; and it is not well to appropriate for oneself a greater share of this dominance than is fair').

50 For the analogies with tennis and tyranny, see Guazzo, *La civil conversazione*,

p. 95v; also p. 88r, for the warning that 'come del vino, cosi de' ragionamenti hanno da essere tutti partecipi' ('all the guests must have their share in the conversation, just as they do of the wine'). On Guazzo's prescriptions on conversational etiquette and, in particular, on his insistence on the need to cultivate the art of *listening*, see Girardi, *La società del dialogo*, pp. 73–9.

51 Guazzo, *La civil conversazione*, p. 95v: 'un tacere a tempo avanza ogni bel parlare . . . Onde haverà ciascuno a procurare, che la sua lingua dimostri più tosto necessità, che volontà di ragionare' ('a well-timed silence is better than the finest speech . . . so it is advisable to ensure that one's tongue is seen to be stirred into action by necessity, rather than the desire to speak').

52 Rebhorn, *Courtly Performances*, pp. 134–6. Rebhorn's analysis of the inter-action between the speakers in the *Cortegiano* draws on the work of Erving Goffman: see especially, on deference rituals, 'The Nature of Deference and Demeanour', in *Interaction Ritual* (New York, 1967), pp. 47–96.

53 The most polished example occurs at the beginning of Book I (*Cortegiano*, I xiii, p. 101), when Count Lodovico da Canossa is called on by Emilia Pio to embark on the description of the perfect courtier: 'Signora, molto volontier fuggirei questa fatica, parendomi troppo difficile e conoscendo . . . ch' io non sappia quello che a bon cortegian si conviene . . . Pur, essendo cosi che a voi piaccia che io abbia questo carico, non posso né voglio rifiutarlo, per non contravenir all'ordine e giudicio vostro.' ('Madam, I would very happily escape from this duty, as it strikes me as too difficult and I am aware of how little I know about what a good courtier should be like . . . But, if it is your pleasure to give me this task, then I cannot and will not refuse it, so as not to contravene the rules of the game or go against your decision.') For other examples, see Federico Fregoso's *escusazioni* at I lv, p. 184, II xvii, pp. 215–16 and II xlii, p. 255; Bernardo Bibbiena's at II xliv–v, p. 259, Giuliano de' Medici's, at II c, p. 332, and III ii, p. 337 and Pietro Bembo's, at IV l, p. 513. Even when a speaker volunteers himself, instead of waiting to be asked, like Cesare Gonzaga, in III xl, p. 394, he is careful to present his motives as entirely disinterested – here, the duty of a 'bon cavaliero' to defend the truth and his desire to take some of the 'fatica' of the evening from Giuliano de' Medici's shoulders.

54 For this term, see Daniele Barbaro's *Della eloquenza* p. 444, where Barbaro states that a 'modesta forma del parlare', calculated to create an impression of 'gran bontade appresso chi ode', is one where the speaker 'le proprie cose abbassando innalza le altrui, e quasi cede e togliersi lascia del suo' ('disparages his own views and . . . those of others and, as it were, yields and allows the other to take advantage of him'). More generally, on tropes of self-depreci-ation in court culture, see Whigham, *Ambition and Privilege*, pp. 102–12.

55 *Il Turamino, ovvero del parlare e dello scrivere sanese* (1602), ed. Luca Serianni (Rome, 1976), p. 5: 'altra cosa si è l'appiccar ragionamento là dove talor altri è allettato dalla conversatione e dall' occasione spronato . . . altro si è l'entrare a ragionarne e discorrerne e trattarne come cosa di propria professione'.

56 *Cortegiano*, I xiii, p. 102: [Cesare Gonzaga] 'forse bon sarà differir questo ragionamento a domani e darassi tempo al Conte di pensar ciò ch'egli s'abbia a dire, ché in vero di tal subietto parlare improviso è difficil cosa.' [Canossa] 'Io non voglio far come colui, che spogliatosi in gioppone saltò meno che non avea

fatto col saio . . . 'l non avervi pensato mi escuserà, talmente che mi sarà licito dir senza biasimo tutte le cose che prima mi verranno alla bocca.' ([C.G.] 'Perhaps it would be better to put this discussion off until tomorrow, in order to give the Count time to think over what he has to say, because to improvise on a subject such as this is indeed difficult.' [L.C.] 'I would not like to finish up like the man who strips down to his shirt and then does not manage to jump any further than he would do with his coat on . . . The fact that I have not had time to think will be a good excuse, as no one will be able to blame me for saying the first thing which comes into my head.')

57 Saunders, 'The Stigma of Print', pp. 143–50. Of course, the Renaissance writer's modesty *topoi* are, in formal terms, descendents of the similar *topoi* of classical and medieval rhetoric, on which see Ernst Robert Curtius, *European Literature and the Latin Middle Ages*, trans. Willard R. Trask (New York, 1953), pp. 83–5. Saunders makes the point, however (p. 148 and n. 1), that the use of these traditional devices on the part of Tudor writers must be interpreted in the light of the very different cultural economy within which they are working.

58 See, for example, *Cortegiano*, p. 68 (dedicatory letter to Don Miguel de Silva), for Castiglione's claim that the work was written 'in pochi giorni', after the death of Guidobaldo da Montefeltro (1508) and that he has not had time since to correct it as he would wish. On the long and exhaustive revision to which the dialogue was in fact subject, see Guidi, 'Reformulations de l'idéologie aristocratique', pp. 123–37 and Ghino Ghinassi, 'Fasi dell'elaborazione del *Cortegiano*', *Studi di filologia italiana*, vol. 25 (1967), pp. 159–96. Another of Castiglione's claims in the letter, that his decision to publish the work was precipitated by Vittoria Colonna's rashly circulating a manuscript of the work, has some foundation in fact: see Guidi, 'L'Espagne dans la vie et dans l'œuvre de B. Castiglione', p. 191, n. 359. However, Guidi is surely right to suggest that Vittoria Colonna's indiscretion 'semble n'avoir fait . . . que precipiter une decision déjà arretée de longue date' ('Reformulations', pp. 133–4) and, in any case, the issue here is not the fact itself, but the manner in which this fact is incorporated into Castiglione's strategy of self-presentation.

59 ('a scribe, writing to the dictation of others') the phrase is from Sforza Pallavicino's *Trattato dello stile e del dialogo*, p. 331. The context is a deconstruction of the writer's pretence at transcription and an implicit critique of those theorists, like Lodovico Castelvetro, who took this pretence at face value.

60 See *Cortegiano*, I xxiv, p. 121, where Cesare Gonzaga describes grace – 'la grazia' – as 'un condimento d'ogni cosa'.

61 Letter of December 1594, in Guarini, *Opere*, ed. Marziano Guglielminetti (Turin, 1971), p. 48: 'Non vede ella che 'l mio *Segretario* porta nella fronte il suo nome, ch' è quasi un marchio che notifica il possessore? E se 'l mio [nome] si leva, l' opera non patisce alterazione di sorte alcuna, ma non può già levarsi quello di Vostra Signoria clarissima senza che la medesima tutta s' alteri e si contamini . . .' ('Do you not see that my *Segretario* carries your name on its cover [the Italian also means 'brow'], like a brand indicating its owner? And, if *my* name were to be removed, the work would not suffer any kind of deterioration, but the removal of that of Your Lordship would leave it impoverished

and contaminated.') For another good example of this *topos*, see Giovanni Maria Memmo's *Dialogo nel quale si forma un perfetto Prencipe*, p. 21; also, for a rather curious variant, see the letter from Pietro Gritio to Antonio Beffa Negrini, appended to the former's dialogue, *Il Castiglione, overo dell'arme della nobiltà* (Mantua, 1586), where Gritio insists that the work – in which the author himself appears as principal speaker – should be named after Count Camillo Castiglione, son of the 'famosissimo' Baldassare, because 'quantunque a parlar nel Dialogo esso Signor Conte non sia introdotto, sono nondimeno dal suo giudicio, e dalla sua bocca tolti i principali punti dell'opera' ('although the Count does not appear as a speaker in the dialogue, the principal points the work makes originated in his mind and his mouth').

62 *Il Cesano, de la lingua toscana* (1525), in Mario Pozzi (ed.), *Discussioni linguistiche del Cinquecento*, p. 189. Tolomei goes on, on the same page, to describe himself as a kind of loud-speaker: a 'trombetta' proclaiming to the world 'la sentenzia altrui'. An interesting contrast with Tolomei's authorial strategy in the *Cesano* is provided by his other vernacular dialogue, *Il Polito* (1525), which was published under a pseudonym: here, where Tolomei's own image is not at stake, he is far more straightforward about his didactic intent and does not insist on the reality of the conversation portrayed. Note that Tolomei's *modestia* may reflect a genuine reluctance to publish: for an expression of his distaste for the mercenary attitude of publishers ('questa ingordigia degli stampatori'), see *De le lettere familiari di M. Claudio Tolomei* (Venice, 1547), p. 2v; also Alberto Castelvecchi's introduction to his edition of Giangiorgio Trissino, *Scritti linguistici* (Rome, 1986), pp. xxxvivii.

63 Dedicatory letter to Ippolita Scaravella, in *Dialoghi del matrimonio e vita Vedovile* (Turin, 1578): 'Si come i figliuoli nobilmente nati, ma da povere contadine vilmente nudriti, riescono si rozzi, che l'istessa Balia si vergogna d'appresentarli alla generosa madre. Così questi Dialoghi, nati da V[ostra] S[ignoria] Ill[ustrissima] per la cagione principale, che n'è stata, e per la buona parte, che vi hanno i suoi bellissimi discorsi: appresso di me si grossamente si sono allevati, e cresciuti ... che da me stesso mi vergognai di lasciarglieli comparire avanti.' ('Just as children who are nobly born but basely nursed by poor peasant-women turn out so uncouth-looking that the nurse herself is ashamed to present them to their splendid mother, so these dialogues – which are the offspring of your Ladyship, since you inspired them, and a great part of them is made up by your eloquent discourses – have been so crudely raised and brought up by me, that I was myself ashamed to allow them to appear before you.')

64 ('I am more fitted to listen than to speak ... I should really be silent.') *Apologia dei dialoghi terza parte* p. 371. It is possible that the episode may reflect an actual trait in the speaker's behaviour: see Speroni's *Dialogo della istoria*, in *Opere*, vol. II, p. 265, for another allusion to Antoniano's habit of modestly attributing his own ideas to others. Speroni's examination of the tropes of *modestia* here is not without a certain irony, however: note that Antoniano's elaborate and rather ostentatious disclaimer follows immediately on Speroni's depiction of his own more genuinely modest refusal to speak, and that Antoniano's *excusatio* is applauded by his listeners as a *tour de force* of wit.

65 ('In recounting to you things I have heard others say – as though my memory
were dictating the words to me – I shall not feel as though I am speaking
myself, as you have asked me to, but rather as though I were still hearing and
listening, as is my custom . . . Thus I shall be able to obey you, by accepting to
speak; yet, as is my privilege, even as I speak, I shall remain silent.') *Apologia
dei dialoghi*, pp. 371–2. There are numerous other examples of the same device
in Cinquecento dialogues: see, for example, Trotto, *Dialoghi del matrimonio*,
pp. 54–5, where Trotto's spokesman, 'Astemio', reluctant to speak before a
woman of such learning as his interlocutor, Ippolita Scaravella ('Io adunque
signora Hippolita, portarò l'acqua al Mare, e le Nottole ad Atene?'),
announces his intention to preserve his modesty by recounting a dialogue in
which he had no part.

66 See also the similar episode in Speroni's *Dialogo delle lingue*, in *Trattatisti del
Cinquecento*, ed. Mario Pozzi (Milan and Naples, 1978), vol. I, pp. 617–19,
where an anonymous 'Scolare', asked for his opinion on the subject under
discussion, opts instead to recount a dialogue between Pietro Pomponazzi and
Giovanni Lascaris. I do not intend to imply here, of course, that Speroni's
reasons for adopting the dialogue form so consistently in his writings can be
reduced simply to a question of etiquette. On the philosophical motives
underlying Speroni's predilection for the dialogue form, see below, chapter 6,
n. 21. Note also that, in the case of Speroni, as in that of Claudio Tolomei (on
whom see above, n. 62), the choice of the dialogue form appears to reflect a
genuine reluctance to publish his work: see Maria Rosa Loi and Mario Pozzi,
'Le lettere familiari di Sperone Speroni', *Giornale storico della letteratura
italiana*, vol. 163, fasc. 523 (1986), p. 385 and pp. 411–12 and n. 149, but also
Giacomo Moro, 'Appunti sulla preistoria editoriale dei *Dialogi* e della
Canace', *Filologia veneta. Lingua, letteratura, tradizioni*, vol. 2, (1989),
pp. 197–200.

67 See Tasso's dedicatory letter to *La Cavaletta overo de la poesia toscana*, in
Dialoghi, vol. II, p. 613: 'Ma pur fra tutti gli altri modi estimo questo usato nel
dialogo il più dilettevole e 'l meno odioso: perch' altri non v' insegna il vero
con autorità di maestro, ma il ricerca a guisa di compagno.' ('But of all modes
[of exposition or discussion], I consider this dialogue mode to be the
pleasantest and least irksome: because the writer of a dialogue does not teach
you the truth with the authority of a master, but joins companionably with you
in the search for the truth.') See also Sperone Speroni, *Apologia dei dialoghi*,
p. 284, where Speroni states that he wrote his works as dialogues '[perché] si
accorgesse il lettore, che io in tal caso non sapiente o maestro, ma disputante
più tosto e condiscepolo seco insieme volessi essere riputato' ('to make it
apparent to the reader that I did not want to present myself as an authority or
a [school]master, but rather as a disputant, a fellow-pupil, learning alongside
him').

68 Dedicatory letter to *La Cavaletta*, p. 613: 'E come i cacciatori mangiano più
volentieri la preda ne la quale ebber parte de la fatica, così quelli che insieme
investigaron la verità participano con maggior diletto de la commune laude, e
gli altri leggono e ascoltano più volentieri una amichevole contesa d'ingegni e
d'opinioni, massimamente coloro che possono darne giudicio . . . e metter la
sua insieme con quella de gli altri.' ('And, just as hunters take particular

pleasure in eating the prey which they had a part in catching, so those who have participated in the search for the truth [ie. the interlocutors in a dialogue] feel a greater pleasure in the shared praise, while the others [the readers] read or listen with particular pleasure to a friendly contest of minds and opinions, especially those who are qualified to judge the contest . . . and add their own opinions to those of the speakers.') For another instance of a use of hunting imagery to describe the appeal of the dialogue form, see below, chapter 7, n. 51.

69 See Plato, *Phaedrus* 275d; also *Protagoras*, 329a. On the implications of Plato's critique of writing for his use of the dialogue form, see, for example, Griswold, 'Plato's Metaphilosophy', p. 161; K. Seeskin, 'Socratic Philosophy and the Dialogue Form', *Philosophy and Literature*, vol. 8, no. 2 (1984), pp. 181–91 and Steven Rendall, 'Dialogue, Philosophy and Rhetoric: the Example of Plato's *Gorgias*', *Philosophy and Rhetoric*, vol. 10, no. 3 (1977), pp. 171–2.

70 On the dynamics of the 'literary speech situation', see Pratt, *Towards a Speech-Act Theory*, pp. 100–16, esp. pp. 114–16. Particularly interesting, in this context, are those dialogues which actually stage authors in conversation with their readers: see, for example, Niccolò Tartaglia's two dialogues, *Quesiti et inventioni diverse* (on which see n. 27 above) and *Ragionamenti sopra la sua travagliata inventione* (Venice, 1551); also, for a particularly self-conscious example, Claudio Corte's *Il Cavallerizzo*, discussed above, pp. 38–9: see esp. p. 123v, where, in a bizarrely Pirandellian moment, Corte's interlocutor, Prospero, realizes that he is a character in a dialogue which has already been printed ('Questo ragionamento nostro adunque è un dialogo, e un libro?').

71 See *Cortegiano*, IV lxxi (p. 541): 'Avendo il Bembo insin qui parlato con tanta veemenzia, che quasi pareva astratto e fuor di sé, stavasi cheto e immobile, tenendo gli occhi verso il cielo, come stupido; quando la signora Emilia . . lo prese per la falda della robba e scuotendolo un poco disse: – Guardate, messer Pietro, che con questi pensieri a voi ancora non si separi l'anima dal corpo.' ('Bembo had been speaking up to this point with such vehemence that he seemed almost rapt, or possessed, and now he was silent and immobile and looked heavenwards, as though in a trance, when Emilia took him by the hem of his robe and, shaking him a little, said "Be careful, Messer Pietro, lest with these thoughts your soul too becomes released from your body."') Of course, Emilia's reminder of the need to reconcile the ideal with reality is very far from the kind of vulgar debunking attempted earlier by Morello da Ortona (IV lxiii, p. 529) and Castiglione makes it clear that she, like the others, has been listening 'extremely attentively' to his speech.

72 *Cortegiano*, III xi–xvii (pp. 350–9). The passage is discussed in detail below, chapter 8, p. 87.

73 See *Cortegiano*, III xvii, (p. 350), where, in an unprecedented breach in the fiction of his dialogue, Castiglione has Giuliano de' Medici remark that his technical terminology is directed beyond the immediate audience of the discussions, at a potential *literary* audience: 'se per sorte qui fusse alcuno che scrivesse i nostri ragionamenti, non vorrei che poi in loco dove fossero intese queste "materie" e "forme", si vedessero senza risposta gli argomenti che 'l signor Gasparo contra di voi [donne] adduce' ('if, by any chance, it turned that someone here was recording our discussions, I would not wish Signor Gasp-

are's arguments against women to be seen to be uncontended, in some place where terms like "matter" and "form" were understood'). For the context of the dispute on women, see Ian Maclean, *The Renaissance Notion of Women; a Study in the Fortunes of Scholasticism and Medical Science in European Intellectual Life* (Cambridge, 1980), esp. pp. 8–9 for the Aristotelian, biological arguments for women's inferiority to men which are being addressed in this passage of the dialogue.

74 Bembo shows a clear awareness of the potential indignity of Strozzi's position: see especially the beginning of the more didactic section of the dialogue, in Book II, where Carlo Bembo expresses his embarrassment at teaching Strozzi 'le minute cose . . . più tosto agli orecchi di nuovo scolare che di dottissimo poeta convenevoli, e già da voi, mentre eravate fanciullo, ne' latini sgrossamenti udite' ('these trivia . . . more suited to the ears of a schoolboy than to those of a most learned poet: things which you learnt in your first Latin lessons, as a child') (*Prose e rime di Pietro Bembo*, p. 142). In compensation for this demolition, Strozzi's expertise in Latin and his 'rarissimo e felicissimo ingegno' (II iii, p. 134) are continually stressed. Models for this kind of *escusazione*, frequent in Renaissance dialogues, are to be found in Cicero: see, for example, *Academica*, I v 18, where Varro alludes to the proverbial 'pig teaching Minerva' to express his embarrassment at finding himself lecturing to Atticus.

75 The most self-conscious example is the *Nifo overo del piacere onesto* (1581), in Tasso, *Dialoghi*, vol. II, which portrays the philosopher, Agostino Nifo, in conversation with the young nobleman, Cesare Gonzaga, the son of one of Charles V's most trusted advisors. Nifo makes explicit his awareness of the social distance which separates him from his 'pupil', in an important passage (p. 212), justifying his adoption of the Socratic method of questioning: 'signor Cesare, quantunque a l'alta vostra condizione paresse più convenevole ch'io così ragionassi come è mio costume di fare a le volte per dare onesto trattenimento a' gran principi, nondimeno il vostro bello ingegno e 'l'inclinazione ch'avete a le lettere m'invitava a favellar con esso voi non altrimente ch'io soglio con gli scolari e con gli amici miei' ('my lord Cesare, even though, bearing in mind your breeding and position, it might have seemed more fitting for me to talk to you in the way that I do when entertaining great princes, nonetheless your fine mind and your liking for literature have tempted me to speak to you in the same way as I might with my own students and friends'). For further discussion of this passage, see my article, 'Rhetoric and Politics in Tasso's *Nifo*', pp. 25–8 and, more generally, on the relationship between the interlocutors in Tasso's dialogues, see below, chapter 8, pp. 93–6.

76 *Ragionamenti di M. Agostino da Sessa all'illustrissimo S. Principe di Salerno sopra la filosofia morale di Aristotele* (Verona, 1554), p. 11.

77 Another good example of this stratagem is found in Annibale Romei's *Discorsi* (1585), set in the court of Ferrara: see Angelo Solerti, *Ferrara e la corte estense nella seconda metà del secolo decimosesto e i Discorsi di Annibale Romei*, 2nd edition (Città di Castello, 1900), p. 197, where the philosopher Francesco Patrizi asks Ercole Varano to clarify a point in ethics, and Varano replies: 'Son ben sicuro, signor Patrizio . . . che fingete di non intendere, acciochè altri meglio intendano . . . Per satisfar dunque a questa vostra buona intenzione,

fingerò d'insegnar a voi, acciocchè altri imparino . . . ('I am quite certain, Signor Patrizio, that you are pretending not to understand, in order that others present should have a chance to understand . . . To satisfy this good intention of yours, then, I shall pretend to teach you, in order that others shall have a chance to learn.') For further examples, see Lanteri *Due dialoghi*, p. 52 and Torquato Tasso, *Il Gonzaga overo del giuoco*, in *Dialoghi*, vol. II, p. 21.

5 CASTIGLIONE'S *CORTEGIANO*: THE DIALOGUE AS A DRAMA OF DOUBT

1 ('It is a great mistake to speak of the things of this world in general and absolute terms and, as it were, by the rule.') *Ricordo 6*, in *Ricordi*, ed. Raffaele Spongano (Florence, 1951), p. 11.

2 *Cortegiano*, I xiii, p. 103. For a translation, see n. 4 below.

3 Of course, the distinction proposed here between 'diplomatic' and 'methodological' motives for the use of the dialogue form is an artificial one, adopted simply to facilitate exposition. As a reading of the *Cortegiano* makes clear, a single, unified vision of the nature of 'conversation' (in the broad, sixteenth-century sense) underlies both the stipulations about social interaction detailed in the last chapter and the epistemological convictions which will be discussed in the present one.

4 ('I shall not attempt to persuade you that my opinion is better than yours, for not only may you and I think different things, but I may myself think one thing at one moment, and quite another the next') *Cortegiano*, I xiii, pp. 102–3. The description of Canossa's task as that of 'forming a perfect courtier with words' ('formar con parole un perfetto cortegiano') comes from Federico Fregoso's original proposal for the 'game', at I xii (p. 100).

5 *Cortegiano*, I i, pp. 80–1 (dedicatory letter to Alfonso Ariosto): 'Noi in questi libri non seguiremo un certo ordine o regula di precetti distinti, che 'l più delle volte nell'insegnare qualsivoglia cosa usar si sòle; ma alla foggia di molti antichi, rinovando una grata memoria, recitaremo alcuni ragionamenti, i quali già passarono tra omini singularissimi a tale proposito.' ('We shall not adhere to any strict order, in these books, or give a series of precepts, as the usual practice of those who are teaching something. Instead, in the manner of many ancient writers, and reviving a pleasant memory, we shall recount a series of discussions on the subject which took place between some remarkable men.') Eduardo Saccone, comparing this passage to its source in the *De oratore* (I vi 22–3), has pointed out that, in Castiglione, the 'evacuazione del testo . . . della figura dell'autore' is far more complete and consistent than it had been in Cicero ('Trattato e ritratto', p. 4, n. 10); see also, by the same critic, 'The Portrait of the Courtier in Castiglione', pp. 4 and 8, for some illuminating comments about the reasons for Castiglione's choice of the dialogue form.

6 See *Cortegiano*, I i (letter to Ariosto), p. 80, where Castiglione explains his reluctance to accept the task of defining the perfect courtier by pointing out 'come difficil cosa sia, tra tante varietà di costumi che s'usano nelle corti di Cristianità, eleggere la più perfetta forma e quasi il fior di questa cortegiania, perché la consuetudine fa a noi spesso le medesime cose piacere e dispiacere; onde talor procede che i costumi, gli abiti, i riti e i modi, che un tempo son stati

in pregio, divengono vili, e per contrario i vili divengon pregiati' ('how difficult it is, amid all the different varieties of behaviour in the various courts of Christendom, to pick the perfect form and, as it were, the flower of courtiership; for the laws of custom are such that we may often approve of something at one moment and disapprove the next; so that those habits, fashions, conventions and manners which used to be valued become despised, while those which were once despised become valued'). He concludes that 'si vede chiaramente che l'uso più che la ragione ha forza d'introdur cose nove tra noi e cancellar l'antiche', so that 'chi cerca giudicar la perfezione [delle cose], spesso s'inganna' ('it is custom, rather than reason, which introduces new habits among us and cancels the old . . . anyone who tries to judge what is right absolutely is very likely to be mistaken'). The point resurfaces later in the book, when Castiglione takes issue with those who fail to accept the full logic of the laws of custom and seek to arrest aesthetic or moral values at some artificial point of stasis: see I xxviii–xxxix, esp. I xxxvi, p. 145, on those who favour archaic forms in literary language and II i–iv, esp. II iii, pp. 193–4, on old men who champion the customs of their youth as objectively better than those of the present day.

7 *Cortegiano*, II i, p. 189 and II xxxv, p. 246.

8 The fullest exploration of the distortions which affect human judgment occurs in Book II of the treatise: see especially II i–iii (pp. 187–95), on the effect of nostalgia on judgment; II vi (p. 197), on self-love (on which see also I viii (pp. 91–2)); II vii (p. 198), on the way in which men's judgments can be affected by 'una certa innata malignità'; and II xii (p. 207), on how satiety can affect our judgments. In II xxxii (p. 240), Federico Fregoso provides an apt climax to the discourse on error, in his suggestion that 'la fortuna, come in molte altre cose, così ancor abbia grandissima forza nelle opinioni degli omini' ('fortune, as over so many other things, also holds sway over men's judgment'). For a fine discussion of the *Cortegiano*'s 'antropologia dell'errore', see Giulio Ferroni, 'Sprezzatura e simulazione', in Carlo Ossola (ed.) *La corte e il 'Cortegiano'. 1. La scena del testo*, (Rome, 1980), esp. pp. 122–35.

9 *Cortegiano*, I xiii, p. 102: [Canossa] '. . . io estimo in ogni cosa esser la sua perfezione, avvenga che nascosta; e questa potersi con ragionevoli discorsi giudicar da chi di quella tal cosa ha notizia' ('I believe that everything does have its perfection, even if it is concealed, and that this perfection can be identified by experts in the field, through rational argument'). Canossa hastily goes on to explain that he has no illusions about possessing the requisite knowledge himself ('io non mi vanto aver questa cognizione').

10 See, most famously, *Cortegiano*, I viii, p. 91, where Cesare Gonzaga reminds the company that 'a tutti ci pare essere molto savi, e forse più in quello in che più siamo pazzi' ('we all believe ourselves to be completely sane, perhaps all the more so in those areas of our life in which we are most mad'); also II vi, p. 197 and – for a brilliantly narrated cautionary tale on the discrepancy between our own vision of ourselves and that of others – II lxxxvii, pp. 316–18.

11 The vital role played by contradiction and questioning in the search for the truth is constantly stressed in the metadialogic of the *Cortegiano*: in addition to the negotiations surrounding Canossa's acceptance of the role as main speaker, discussed above, see also I xv, p. 106, where Gaspare Pallavicino first

takes advantage of 'l'autorità dataci del contradire' ('the right of contradiction which we have been granted'); I xxiii, pp. 119–20, where Cesare Gonzaga negotiates the right to ask questions as well as contradicting the speaker and, especially, II c, pp. 332–3, where Giuliano de' Medici accepts the task of forming the perfect court lady, only on condition that 'sia almen con quei patti che hanno avuto quest' altri signori: cioè che ognun possa dove gli parerà contradirmi, ch'io questo estimarò non contradizione, ma aiuto; e forse col correggere gli errori mei, scoprirassi quella perfezion della donna di palazzo, che si cerca' ('it will be on the same terms as these gentlemen have enjoyed: that is, that you should all be able to contradict me whenever you like, for I will consider it not as a contradiction, but a helping hand; and perhaps, as you correct my errors, the perfect image of the court lady which we are looking for will be revealed').

12　Letter to De Silva, in *Cortegiano*, p. 77 ('. . . even if [the multitude] may not have a complete understanding of things, it nevertheless has an instinctive feel for what is good and bad').

13　This theme is developed in Luciana Borsetto, 'Il *Libro del Cortegiano*; una codificazione del 're-citare', un emblema della scrittura', in Ossola (ed.), *La corte e il 'Cortegiano'*, pp. 271–90, esp. pp. 278–9; see also Ferroni, 'Sprezzatura e simulazione', and Giorgio Patrizi, *Il 'Libro del Cortegiano' e la trattatistica sul comportamento*, in Alberto Asor Rosa (ed.), *Letteratura italiana. III. Le forme del testo. II. La prosa* (Turin, 1982), esp. pp. 862–3.

14　The image is, of course, Ariosto's: see *Orlando furioso*, XIII, 81, 1–2; 'Di molte fila esser bisogno parme/ A condur la gran tela ch'io lavoro' ('Many threads are needed to bring to completion the great canvas on which I am working').

15　*Riposta al Valdés*, in *Il Cortegiano, con una scelta delle Opere minori*, ed. Bruno Maier, 2nd edition (Turin, 1964), p. 671: 'E se mi diceste che voi non lodate né questa né il resto, ma narrate il ragionamento di due che parlano in contradizione l'uno dell'altro, dico che a noi altri ancora è nota la maniera academica dello scrivere in dialogo e che sappiamo che il costume de' platonici era sempre il contradire e non affermar mai cosa alcuna.' ('You might claim that you are not praising this [an act of iconoclasm during the Sack of Rome, cited approvingly in the *Dialogo*] or any of the rest yourself, but simply recounting the conversation of two men disputing with one another. But I too am acquainted with the Academic convention of writing in dialogue and I am aware that it was the custom of the Platonic school to argue against the opinions of others, without ever affirming anything oneself.') It is tempting to try to identify the Ciceronian echoes in the last sentence: see, for example, *De fato*, ii 4 and *Academica*, I iv 16, and xii 44–6. Specific allusions apart, however, Castiglione's identification of the dialogue genre with the philosophical tradition of Academic scepticism is of considerable interest, in the light of his own use of the form in the *Cortegiano*. On the presence of Cicero's *Academica* in Renaissance culture, see Charles B. Schmitt, *Cicero scepticus. A Study of the Influence of the 'Academica' in the Renaissance* (The Hague, 1972).

16　('You are not sufficiently cautious in your writing for it not to be apparent which is the speaker in the dialogue whose opinion you subscribe to, and which is the one you feed stupid lines to, to make him easier to refute. And it is plain that Lattanzio's opinions are your opinions and that you are Lattanzio;

and so it will be quite deserved if, from here on, I change your name and start calling you Lattanzio.') *Cortegiano*, p. 671.

17 Compare Canossa's views on the appropriate form for the literary vernacular, in *Cortegiano*, I xxviii–xxxix (pp. 129–53, esp. pp. 141–4), with those expressed by Castiglione *in propria persona* in the dedication to De Silva (pp. 72–6). On the background to the dispute, see Mario Pozzi (ed.), *Discussioni linguistiche del Cinquecento*, pp. 9–29; also, on Castiglione's position in the contemporary debate on language, Giancarlo Mazzacurati, *Misure del classicismo rinascimentale* (Naples, 1967), pp. 35–131 and Mario Pozzi, 'Il pensiero linguistico di B. Castiglione', *Giornale storico della letteratura italiana*, vol. 156 (1979), pp. 179–202.

18 The 'feminist' speakers in Book III are Giuliano de' Medici, the officially appointed 'champion' of women and Castiglione's cousin, Cesare Gonzaga, who takes over from Giuliano between chapters xl and lii (pp. 394–412). Although there is no explicit declaration of the author's sympathies within the book, as there is in the case of the language question, the presentation of the dispute is distinctly slanted in favour of the 'feminist' speakers; and what external evidence there is of Castiglione's views on the question suggests that his contemporaries would have been able to identify his views unproblematically with those of Giuliano de' Medici and Cesare Gonzaga: see Ghinassi, 'Fasi dell'elaborazione', pp. 189–96, on the letter from Castiglione to Niccolò Frigio, undated, but apparently written well before the first draft of the *Cortegiano*, expressing views which Castiglione would later attribute to Cesare Gonzaga in the dialogue.

19 *Cortegiano*, II xviii (p. 216): [Fregoso] 'Voglio adunque che 'l cortegiano . . . si volti con tutti i pensieri e forze dell'animo suo ad amare e quasi adorare il principe a chi serve sopra ogni altra cosa; e le voglie sue e costumi e modi tutti indrizzi a compiacerlo.' [Pietro da Napoli] 'Di questi cortegiani oggidì troverannosi assai, perché mi pare che in poche parole ci abbiate dipinto un nobile adulatore.' [(F] 'I would have the courtier dedicate his every thought and his every energy to loving and almost worshipping the prince he serves, above all other things; and that he should calculate all his desires and habits and manners to please the prince.' [P] 'There should be no problem in finding such a courtier in the present times, because it seems to me that you have just sketched us a portrait of a prize flatterer.') Almost nothing is known of Pietro da Napoli, a courtier of Julius II; his only other invention in the dialogue is a *motto*, in I xlvi, p. 168.

20 *Cortegiano*, II xviii, p. 217: '. . . 'l compiacere e secondar le voglie di quello a chi si serve si po far senza adulare, perché io intendo delle voglie che siano ragionevoli ed oneste, ovvero di quelle che in sé non sono né bone né male, come saria il giocare, darsi più ad uno esercizio che ad un altro.' ('It is possible to indulge the desires of one's master without being a flatterer, because I am only talking about those desires which are reasonable and decent, or those which are morally indifferent, like a preference for one kind of game or activity over another.')

21 ('There is no surer way to gain princes' favour than to deserve it.') *Cortegiano*, II xx, p. 221.

22 ('Experience shows us very clearly that the contrary is true . . . these days,

hardly anyone is favoured by princes, except the most grasping.') *Cortegiano*, II xxi, p. 222.

23 ('The courtier must always be guided by what is right and he must never seek grace or favour by vicious or dishonest means.') *Cortegiano*, II xxii, p. 224.

24 *Cortegiano*, II xxii, p. 224. [Calmeta] 'Io v'assicuro che tutte l'altre vie son molto più dubbiose e più lunghe, che non è questa che voi biasimate; perché oggidì, per replicarlo un'altra volta, i signori non amano se non que' che son volti a tal camino.' ('I assure you that all other routes [to the prince's favour] are far longer and less direct that the one which you are criticizing [i.e. the 'via viciosa' of Fregoso's speech, cited in my previous note]; because, to repeat it once more, these days, princes have no time for anyone who is not prepared to tread that path.') On Calmeta's somewhat turbulent career, see, besides M. Pieri's entry in the *Dizionario biografico degli italiani*, vol. XXVII, pp. 49–52, Cecil Grayson's introduction to his edition of Calmeta's *Prose e lettere edite e inedite* (Bologna, 1959), esp. pp. xvi–xxii, on his service with Borgia; also pp. xxiv–v and xxviii–ix, on his notorious outspokenness – another biographical detail of obvious relevance to his portrayal in the *Cortegiano*. I find no evidence in the text or outside it to justify Piero Floriani's dismissal of Calmeta's role in the dialogue as that of a 'dispettoso portavoce di qualunquistiche lagnanze cortigiane' (*I gentiluomini letterati*, p. 66): his role is a minor, but by no means an unimportant one, and – very differently from the other figures with whom Floriani groups him, like Morello da Ortona and the Unico Aretino, on whom see below, n. 44 – he is taken seriously by the other speakers, and there is no attempt to undermine his authority by deconstructing his motives.

25 *Cortegiano*, II xxii, p. 224. [Fregoso] 'Non dite così . . . perché questo sarebbe troppo chiaro argumento che i signori de' nostri tempi fossero tutti viciosi e mali; il che non è, perché pur se ne trovano alcuni di boni. Ma se 'l nostro cortegiano per sorte sua si troverà essere a servicio d'un che sia vicioso e maligno, sùbito che lo conosca, se ne levi, per non provar quello estremo affanno che senton tutti i boni che serveno ai mali.' ('Do not say that, for to say that would be a clear admission that the princes of our time are all vicious and evil; which is not true, since there are some who are good. But if our courtier should find himself by chance in the service of a vicious and ill-intentioned prince, as soon as he realizes it, he should leave, in order not to suffer that anguish which afflicts any good man who finds himself in the service of the wicked.') The flustered obliqueness of the first sentence of Fregoso's reply is a fine dramatic touch: compare his earlier attempt at the same task of defending modern princes, at the beginning of the chapter (p. 223): 'Non voglio già comportar, messer Vincenzio, che voi questa nota diate ai signori de' nostri tempi; perché pur ancor molti sono che amano la modestia.' ('Messer Vincenzo, I would not have you attach this slur to the princes of our day; for there are many who appreciate modesty in their courtiers.')

26 *Cortegiano*, II xxii, p. 224: [Calmeta] 'Bisogna pregar Dio che ce gli dia boni [signori], perché quando s'hanno è forza patirgli tali, quali sono; perché infiniti rispetti astringono che è gentilomo, poi che ha cominciato a servire ad un patrone, a non lasciarlo; ma la disgrazia consiste nel principio; e sono i cortegiani in questo caso alla condizione di que' malavventurati uccelli, che

nascono in trista valle.' ('We must pray God to give us good masters, because once we have them it is necessary to put up with them as they are; because there are countless factors which prevent a gentleman, once he has begun to serve a prince not to leave his service. The mistake is to enter a bad prince's service in the first place; and courtiers in this position are like those unfortunate birds, who are born in an evil vale.') Vittorio Cian, in his commentary on *Il Cortegiano*, 2nd edition (Florence, 1916), p. 170, relates Calmeta's last phrase to a Tuscan proverb, 'trist'a quell'uccellino che nasce in cattiva valle'. For Castiglione's extremely problematic relationship with Francesco Gonzaga, after leaving his service in 1504 for that of Guidobaldo da Montefeltro, see J. R. Woodhouse, *Baldesar Castiglione. A Reassessment of 'The Courtier'* (Edinburgh, 1978), pp. 14–15 and p. 17; also Stephen Kolsky, 'Before the Nunciature: Castiglione in Fact and Fiction', *Rinascimento*, vol. 29 (1989), pp. 339–40.

27 *Cortegiano*, II xxii, pp. 224–5: [Fregoso] 'A me pare, che 'l debito debba valer più che tutti i rispetti; e purché un gentilomo non lassi il patrone quando fosse in su la guerra o in qualche avversità . . . credo che possa con ragion e debba levarsi da quella servitù, che tra i boni sia per dargli vergogna.' ('It seems to me that duty should outweigh all other considerations; and, as long as a gentleman does not leave his master during a war, or some other calamity . . . I believe that he can legitimately leave a post which would bring him shame in the eyes of right-thinking men, and, indeed, that he should leave it.')

28 *Cortegiano*, II xxiii, p. 225: [Pio] 'Should a courtier obey every command his prince gives him, even if he is ordered to do immoral and reprehensible things?' [Fregoso] 'We are not obliged to obey anyone, where it involves immoral action.'

29 *Cortegiano*, II xxiii, p. 225: [Pio] 'E come, s'io starò al servizio d'un principe il qual mi tratti bene, e si confidi ch'io debba far per lui ciò che far si po, commandandomi ch'io vada ad ammazzare un omo, o far qualsivoglia altra cosa, debbo io rifiutar di farla?'

30 ('You should obey your lord in all those things which will bring him profit and honour, and not in those which will bring him only disadvantage and shame . . . But it is true that there are many things which appear right, at first sight, which are in fact wrong, and many things seem wrong and yet are right. And so it can sometimes be justifiable to kill not one man but ten thousand in the service of one's masters, and to do many other things which, to someone who was not looking at them in the right light, would appear wrong, and yet which are not wrong.') *Cortegiano*, II xxiii, pp. 225–6. For examples, from Castiglione's own career, of the kind of moral problems he may have been thinking of here, see Kolsky, 'Before the Nunciature', pp. 346–7.

31 See *Cortegiano*, II i–iii, pp. 187–95, esp. p. 191, for the admission that the present age is more 'copiosa di vicii' than that immediate past. Of course, Castiglione's main point in this supremely subtle meditation is that the old are misled by nostalgia in their assessment of the present; and he finishes up by defending his own age as more copious in virtue as well as vice (pp. 191–4). It is important for our interpretation of what follows, in Book II, though, to note that Castiglione does explicitly acknowledge that many of the more serious criticisms levelled at his generation by older men are justified.

32 Diomede Carafa, *Dello optimo cortesano* (1479), ed. G. Paparelli (Salerno, 1971), p. 96: 'Per tucti li modi et vie conosce uno servitore possa fare et dire ben de suo signore lo deve fare: dico siano de natura non sia despregio de Idio lo quale ei primo signore di tucti: et non solamente cosa che se ne offende a Dio non la deve cercare di fare uno servidore per compiacerne nè ad signore nè ad altro, ma quando ce fosse comandata, non la facia: che Idio non permette may bene per fare male ... Et quando ben a tuo signore li dispiacesse quando non lo facessi, non te ne curare: che repusato lo animo, te tenerà per bono homo et li verrà voglia più farte bene et acomandarte soy cose: che per tristo sia uno signore li piace soy cose li siano fidelmente tenute.' ('A courtier should employ all the means at his disposal to further his lord's interests: all the means, that is, which do not offend God, who is the supreme Lord of all men. And not only should the courtier never do anything offensive to God of his own accord, in order to please his lord or anyone else, but even if he is commanded to do such a thing, he should not do it: for God never permits good to result from evil-doing. And even if your lord is displeased when you do not obey, you should not be concerned about it, for, when he has calmed down, he will recognize you as an upright man, and will be all the more inclined to favour you and to entrust his affairs to you: for, however wicked a prince may be, he likes his goods to be faithfully administered.') Another interesting point of comparison with Castiglione is Giambattista Giraldi Cinzio's much later *Discorso intorno a quello che si conviene a giovane nobile e ben creato nel servire un gran principe* (1569), recently edited by Walter Moretti as *L'uomo di corte*: see pp. 12–15, esp. p. 13: 'E posto che sia comune opinione che in alcune corti si ritrovino più mali uomini che buoni, e in alquante sia forse così in fatto, e si vegga spessissime volte che a questi si diano le dignità e gli onori di maggiore importanza ... dee nondimeno per ogni modo il Giovane di non essere annoverato fra quelli che malvagi sono tenuti: ma dee egli sempre servare una bontà ferma, salda, costante ... Perché, quando il Signore usa il giudicio sano, se per qualche rispetto tolera gli uomini di che abbiam detto, al fine esalta quelli che da ben sono ... E quando pure delle due cose devesse esser l'una, egli è meglio per la virtù e per la bontà sua ricever qualche dispiacere, che per essere malvagio giungere a qualche grado: perché ... il vizioso non può esser felice.' ('It is commonly reputed that in some courts there are more evil men than good ones, and it is perhaps true that this is so in certain courts, and that the highest dignities and honours do go to unprincipled men ... However, the aspiring courtier should on no account allow himself to be counted with the wicked; rather, he should always maintain a firm, steadfast and constant goodness ... For, when the Prince is judging soundly, even if, for some reason of the moment, he tolerates the evil men we have been talking about, in the long run, he will favour those who are good ... And, if it comes down to hard choices, it is better to suffer a setback because of one's virtue and goodness, than to achieve success through evil-doing: because the vicious man can never be truly happy.')

33 *Cortegiano*, II xxiii, p. 226: [Pallavicino] 'Deh, per vostra fé, ragionate un poco sopra questo, ed insegnateci come si possan discerner le cose veramente bone dalle apparenti.' [Fregoso] 'Perdonatemi, ... io non voglio entrar qua, ché troppo ci saria che dire, ma il tutto si rimetta alla discrezion vostra.'

34 I refer, of course, to Machiavelli's famous statement of intent, at the beginning of his treatment of political ethics, in chapter XV of *The Prince*: see *Il Principe*, in *Opere*, ed. Mario Bonfantini (Milan and Naples, 1954), p. 34. For a deliberately overstated, but thought-provoking 'Machiavellian' reading of Castiglione, see Sydney Anglo; *The Courtier's Art. Systematic Immortality in the Renaissance* (Swansea, 1983).

35 *Cortegiano*, II xxiv, p. 226: [Pallavicino] 'Vorrei sapere, essendomi imposto da un mio signor terminatamente quello ch' io abbia a fare in una impresa o negocio di qualsivoglia sorte, s'io, ritrovandomi in fatto, e parendomi con l'operare più o meno o altrimenti di quello che m'è stato imposto, poter fare succedere la cosa più prosperamente o con più utilità di chi m'ha dato tal carico, debbo io governarmi secondo quella prima norma senza passar i termini del comandamento, o pur far quello che a me pare esser meglio?' ('I should like to know what to do if my lord has given me precise orders about how to perform some kind of enterprise or task, and, when I am on the spot, it strikes me that, by doing something less or something more or something other than what I was told to do, I could bring about a better and more profitable result for the prince who commissioned me. Should I follow instructions, without exceeding my original brief? Or should I do what seems best to me?')

36 *Cortegiano*, II xxiv, pp. 226–7.

37 ('leave to one side this problem of how to deal with princes') *Cortegiano*, II xxiii, p. 229.

38 The Mucianus episode is introduced by Fregoso as evidence of the need to adjust one's behaviour to the character of one's prince. If the prince is 'di natura austera', like '*molti che se ne trovano*' (*Cortegiano*, p. 228, my italics), then the courtier would do well to resist any temptation to take an initiative.

39 My allusion here is to the *incipit* of one of Francesco Guicciardini's most-quoted *Ricordi*, number 35: 'Quanto è diversa la practica dalla teorica!' (*Ricordi*, p. 42).

40 Fregoso's precise task, as formulated by Emilia Pio when she gives him the commission, in *Cortegiano*, I lv (pp. 183–4), is to '[dechiarare] in qual modo e maniera e tempo il cortegiano debba usar le sue bone condizioni, ed operar quelle cose che 'l Conte ha detto che se gli convien sapere' ('to explain how and in what manner and when the courtier should put into action all those good qualities of his and all those skills which the Count has said he must acquire').

41 See *Cortegiano*, I lv, p. 184, where Fregoso replies to Emilia Pio's command (cited in the previous note) by claiming that 'volendo voi separare il modo e 'l tempo e la maniera dalle bone condizioni e ben operare del cortegiano, volete separar quello che separar non si po' ('if you propose to separate the question of how and when and in what manner the courtier should use his good qualities from those qualities themselves, then you are trying to separate the inseparable'). Pure and applied courtiership are aspects of the same subject and, by rights, it is Canossa who should continue the discussion. See also II vii (p. 198) for Fregoso's assurance, at the outset of his speech, that 'per farmi participe più ch'io posso della sua laude [di Canossa] . . . non gli contradirò in cosa alcuna' ('in order to assure myself some of the Count's reflected glory . . . I shall not dispute anything he has said').

42 *Cortegiano*, II xi, p. 206.

43 It should be noted that the 'framing' of Fregoso's speech is more complex than I have suggested here. A full analysis would have to take into account other pointers, introduced to counterbalance Fregoso's calculatedly self-deprecating presentation of his contribution; like the preface to his speech by the Duchess – the most authoritative speaker of the group, whose interventions are all the more crucial because they are so rare – calling attention to the importance of his task (*Cortegiano*, II v, p. 196). For a methodologically interesting example of how to analyse the 'frames' of the discussion, see Rebhorn, *Courtly Performances*, esp. pp. 177–80 on Ottaviano Fregoso's careful stage-management of his appearance in Book IV.

44 *Cortegiano*, II vi, p. 197. The speaker is the poet and extemporizer Bernardo Accolti, known as the Unico Aretino: a speaker whose dignity has already been subtly undermined in I ix and whose only subsequent appearance of any importance in the dialogue will be in III lx–lxiv, where he came off the worse in a bout of love casuistry with Emilia Pio. The function of Accolti's intervention here – like that of the similarly 'unreliable' Morello da Ortona at II viii (p. 200) – is simply to underline the importance of Fregoso's contribution, by offering the latter a pretext for explaining at some length the utility of the rules he is setting out to teach.

45 *Cortegiano*, I xvii, p. 109: [Canossa] 'Estimo che la principale e vera profession del Cortegiano debba esser quella dell'arme; la qual sopra tutto voglio che egli faccia vivamente e sia conosciuto tra gli altri per ardito e sforzato e fidele a chi serve.' ('I consider the courtier's principal and true profession to be that of warfare; and I desire him to cultivate this art above all others and to make a name for himself as daring and bold and faithful to his prince.')

46 *Cortegiano*, II viii, p. 200: [Fregoso] 'Se ben vi ricorda, volse ierisera il Conte che la prima profession del cortegiano fosse quella dell'arme e largamente parlò di che modo far la doveva; però questo non replicaremo più.' ('If you remember, the Count stated last night that the courtier's principal profession was warfare and he spoke at length on how this profession should be practised; so I shall not go over the same ground again.')

47 *Cortegiano*, II viii, pp. 200–1 ('Yet my rule [i.e. the rule of paying attention to time and place] can teach us something new: that, when the courtier finds himself in a skirmish, or a clash or a pitched battle, or something of the sort, he should attempt to withdraw discreetly from the main body of troops and to accomplish those bold and striking deeds he proposes to perform with as little company as possible and within sight of the most noble and respected men in the army and, above all, in the presence of and, if possible, under the very eyes of his king, or the lord he is serving; for it is entirely justified to capitalize on one's good actions. And I consider that, just as it is wrong to seek out false and undeserved glory, it is also wrong to cheat oneself of the honour which is one's due and not to seek out that acclaim which is the only true prize of virtuous deeds.')

48 ('even when they think they are not being watched, or observed, or noticed') *Cortegiano*, I xvii, p. 110; my italics. The point is insisted on throughout the chapter: see, for example, p. 109, where Canossa insists that ''l nome di queste bone condicioni [i.e., courage, daring and loyalty] si acquisterà facendone l'opere in ogni tempo e loco, imperò che non è licito in questo mancar mai,

senza biasimo estremo' ('and to gain this reputation, he will need to exercise these qualities in every place and on every occasion, for, where these virtues are concerned, it is impossible to lapse without bringing on oneself the most severe opprobrium'). The distance between Fregoso and Canossa's perspectives is also apparent in their differing views on the wisdom of exercising one's valour in minor skirmishes. Canossa (p. 110) insists that 'molte volte più nelle cose piccole che nelle grandi si conoscono i coraggiosi' ('it is often in minor episodes, rather than major ones, that men's bravery is best judged') and he is disparaging about those who screw their courage to the sticking-point for major actions, but 'nelle cose che poco premono e dove par che possano senza esser notati restar di mettersi a pericolo, volentier si lasciano acconciare al sicuro' ('in unimportant matters, when they feel they can avoid exposing themselves to danger without it being noticed, thankfully remain in safety'). Fregoso, on the other hand, is almost equally disparaging about soldiers he has known who 'metteano la vita a pericolo per andar a pigliar una mandra di pecore, come per esser i primi che montassero le mura d'una terra' ('put their lives at risk as willingly to capture a herd of sheep as to be among the first to scale the walls of a beseiged town)' (p. 201).

49 ('But because fortune holds sway over men's judgment, as over so many other things, it sometimes happens that a gentleman, for all his fine accomplishments and pleasing graces, may not please his prince; that, for no discernible reason, they will simply not, as people say, "hit it off". And, since all the other courtiers will go along with the prince's judgment, this means that he will get nowhere and become a figure of fun, even if he is the worthiest man in the world. And, on the contrary, if the prince happens to take to some clumsy and inarticulate imbecile, his manners, however stupid and awkward, will often start attracting extravagant praise from all around him, and the entire court will admire and respect him . . ') *Cortegiano*, II xxxii, pp. 240–1.

50 ('Besides his actual worth, I would have the courtier draw on his wits and his skill.')

51 See above, chapter 4, n. 3.

52 On the debate on the moral status of rhetoric in classical and Renaissance culture, see my 'Rhetoric and Politics in Tasso's "Nifo"', pp. 81–3, and the bibliography cited there.

53 The moral dangers involved in Fregoso's recommendation that the courtier should cultivate appearances are dramatized in the discussion: see, for example, *Cortegiano*, II xxvii–xxviii, pp. 232–4, where Fregoso's contention that 'le cose estrinseche spesso fan testimonio delle intrinseche' ('outward things are often a testimony to what is inside') is contested by Gaspare Pallavicino and Cesare Gonzaga; also II xl, p. 252, where Pallavicino responds to Fregoso's teachings on the art of cultivating an image that 'questa a me non par arte ma vero inganno; né credo io che si convenga, a chi vuol esser omo da bene, mai lo ingannare' ('this sounds to me less like art than outright deception; and I do not believe that a decent and upright man should ever stoop to deceit').

54 *Cortegiano*, IV v and IV ix–x. The relation between the fourth book of the dialogue and the preceding three is one of the aspects of the book which has aroused most debate among critics: see Lawrence V. Ryan, 'Book IV of

Castiglione's *Courtier*: Climax or Afterthought?', *Studies in the Renaissance*, vol. 19 (1972), pp. 156–79, Rebhorn, *Courtly Performances*, pp. 177–204, Woodhouse, *Baldesar Castiglione*, esp. pp. 142–50, and, most recently, Edvardo Saccone, 'The Portrait of the Courtier in Castiglione', *Italica*, vol. 61, no. 1 (Spring 1987), esp. pp. 9–17. Crucial to this discussion is, of course, the question of the changes the dialogue underwent during the long process of its revision: it was only in the final *redazione*, of 1521–4, that Bembo's disquisition on Neoplatonic love was added and the fourth book took on the form it has in the published version: see Ghinassi, 'Fasi dell'elaborazione', and, for briefer accounts of the emergence of the themes of Book IV, Ferroni, 'Sprezzatura e simulazione', pp. 135–6 and José Guidi, 'Le jeu de cour et sa codification dans les différentes rédactions du "Courtisan"', in Centre Interuniversitaire de Recherche sur la Renaissance Italienne, *Le pouvoir et la plume. Incitation, contrôle et répression dans l'Italie du XVIème siècle* (Paris, 1982), pp. 107–14.

55 Martines, *Power and Imagination*, p. 465. The most vivid representation of princely corruption in Book IV is in chapters vi–viii, pp. 452–6; esp. p. 454, for Ottaviano's striking comparison of the princes of his day to the enormous puppets ('colossi') paraded in Roman festivals: impressive on the outside, but inside stuffed with bits of old rag and straw. For other allusions to the unreality of Ottaviano's vision, see *Cortegiano*, IV xxvi (p. 479), xxxv (p. 495), xlii (pp. 500–1) and xlviii (p. 510).

56 See Anglo, *The Courtier's Art*, pp. 5–6, on the approval of Ascham and other moralists; pp. 7–15 on later developments in manuals on behaviour at court.

57 See *The Advancement of Learning*, II xvii 2–4, pp. 134–5, also, for a discussion of this distinction in Bacon, Lisa Jardine, *Francis Bacon: Discovery and the Art of Discourse* (Cambridge, 1974), pp. 174–5.

6 THE CHANGING FORM OF THE ITALIAN RENAISSANCE DIALOGUE

1 ('It will be assumed that whoever is the main speaker in the dialogue will be expressing views of the author') *De dialogo, c.* 457A.

2 Recent studies on aspects of Cinquecento Italian dialogue production are listed above, chapter 3, n. 3.

3 For overviews of Quattrocento humanistic dialogue production, see Tateo, *Tradizione e realtà*, pp. 221–421, Marsh, *The Quattrocento Dialogue* and De Caprio, 'I cenacoli umanistici'.

4 See Marsh, *The Quattrocento Dialogue*, pp. 6–8 for a summary of the various classical forms of dialogue revived by Quattrocento humanists. Tateo, *Tradizione e realtà*, pp. 223–4 stresses that it is impossible to speak of the existence of a 'genere dialogo formalmente e sostanzialmente omogeneo' in a period before the prescriptive theoretical initiative of the mid-Cinquecento.

5 For discussion of these three dialogues, see Marsh, *The Quattrocento Dialogue*, pp. 24–37 (on Bruni), pp. 38–49 (on Bracciolini) and pp. 55–77 (on Valla). See also, on the latter, Marsh's 'Struttura e retorica nel *De vero bono*', in Ottavio Besomi and Mariangela Regoliosi (eds.), *Lorenzo Valla e l'umanesimo italiano. Atti del convegno internazionale di studi umanistici (Parma, 18–19 ottobre, 1984)* (Padua, 1986), pp. 311–26; also Letizia A. Panizza, 'Lorenzo

Valla's *De vero falsoque bono*. Lactantius and Oratorical Scepticism', *Journal of the Warburg and Courtauld Institutes*, vol. 41 (1978), pp. 76–107.

6 On the value of disputation, see, for example, the famous speech of Coluccio Salutati's in the first of Leonardo Bruni's *Dialogi ad Petrum Histrum*, in *Prosatori latini del Quattrocento*, ed. Eugenio Garin (Milan and Naples, 1952), pp. 46–8. On the dialogue as *provocatio*, see Marsh, *The Quattrocento Dialogue*, p. 11; also pp. 51–2 and p. 111.

7 On the prevalence of Ciceronian influences in the dialogue in this period, see Tateo, *Tradizione e realtà*, p. 224, n. 3 and p. 228.

8 Marsh, *The Quattrocento Dialogue*, p. 48; see also pp. 10–11 on the differences between humanist and Ciceronian practice in this respect. An important factor to be taken into account in explaining the tendencies towards 'closure' in the humanist dialogue is the influence of Augustine: see Marsh, pp. 42–3, 49–50, 56–7 and 60.

9 See, for example, Marsh, *The Quattrocento Dialogue*, p. 49, on Bracciolini's *De avaritia*, also Tateo, *Tradizione e realtà*, p. 256, on the clarity with which the authorial position emerges in this and Bracciolini's other moral dialogues, despite his keen exploitation of the dramatic potential of dialectical conflict.

10 See, for example, Tateo, *Tradizione e realtà*, pp. 240–2, on Bartolomeo Fazio. De Caprio, 'I cenacoli umanistici', p. 803, has suggested the same of Lorenzo Valla, though other critics disagree: see, for example, Marsh, *The Quattrocento Dialogue*, pp. 76–7 and 'Struttura e retorica'.

11 The observation is Vincenzo De Caprio's: see his 'I cenacoli umanistici', p. 804.

12 That the sophistication of the audience condones a certain licence in the practice of argument *in utramque partem* is explicitly stated by Valla in *De bono*, when Antonio da Rho defends Maffeo Vegio's praises of Epicurean doctrine as an exercise in the rhetorical genre of the paradoxical encomium: 'I suspect that you spoke not in earnest but in jest . . . You spoke feignedly, which you would not have done (at least not rightly) with a different audience. But you had no need to fear corrupting such worthy men with your speech. . .' (*De vero falsoque bono*, ed. M. De Panizza Lorch (Bari, 1970), p. 106; translated by David Marsh, in *The Quattrocento Dialogue*, p. 62). On the limitations on expression in the humanist dialogue, see also, however, Marsh, *The Quattrocento Dialogue*, p. 31.

13 It is noteworthy that an early exception to this rule is the most famous of the relatively rare vernacular dialogues of the Quattrocento, Alberti's *Della famiglia* (1433/4 and 1443), a substantial part of which is occupied by uncontested exposition. This is not to suggest, of course, that *Della famiglia* is entirely 'monological': see, for example, Tateo, *Tradizione e realtà*, pp. 279–318, esp. pp. 280–1, on the intimately 'dialogical' character of the work.

14 See above, chapter 2, p. 15.

15 The definition of the first half of the sixteenth century as a period of literary 'hedonism' orginates in Cesare Segre, 'Edonismo linguistico nel Cinquecento', in *Lingua, stile e società* (Milan, 1974), pp. 369–96. On the breakdown of humanist ideals, in this period, and the emergence of a new conception of literature as autotelic, see Mazzacurati, 'La formazione della letteratura' and Lionello Sozzi, *Retorica e umanesimo*, in Corrado Vivanti (ed.), *Storia d'Italia. Annali 4. Intellettuali e potere* (Turin, 1981), pp. 65–73.

16 Giangiorgio Trissino, *Dialogo intitulato il Castellano nel quale si tratta de la lingua italiana* (1529), in Pozzi (ed.), *Discussioni linguistiche del Cinquecento*, p. 172. Trissino's patently manipulative exploitation of Sannazaro's authority appears to have caused some unease to at least one reader: Torquato Tasso, in his generally laconic marginal notes on the *Castellano*, was moved at this point to exclaim, 'che fa in questo dialogo il Sannazaro! o che dice!' ('What on earth is Sannazaro doing in this dialogue? What is he saying?') (Anna Maria Carini, 'Le postille del Tasso al Trissino', *Studi tassiani*, vol. 7 (1957), p. 73.)

17 I quote from an interesting letter from Girolamo Muzio to Renato Trivulzio, of 31 December 1541, containing Muzio's assessment of the as yet unpublished *Cesano*. For the text, see Muzio, *Lettere* (Florence, 1590), pp. 143–51; for the circumstances of the letter, Pozzi (ed.), *Discussioni linguistiche del Cinquecento*, p. 179. Of particular interest, in the present context, is the passage near the beginning of the letter (pp. 144–5), where Muzio points out that, despite the fact that the work purports to be an impartial representation of a 'disputa . . . fra alcuni dotti huomini', the author nevertheless shows his hand quite unashamedly, in his own prefatory matter, right from the very title of the work (*Il Cesano, Della lingua Toscana*). He concludes that, 'parlando come parla, . . . [Tolomei] si leva la fede di dover fedelmente esporre quanto per ciascuna delle parti si possa dire. Oltra che egli riserbi l'ultimo luogo a colui, che parla per la Toscana [lingua]; e fa che egli disputa contra le opinioni de gli altri, e niuno contra la sua . . .' ('by speaking as he does [in favour of Tuscan], Tolomei loses our trust that he is going to record faithfully all that might be said in support of each of the different positions in the dispute. Besides which he reserves the last place for the speaker who is putting the case for Tuscan, and lets him argue against the others' views, while no-one gets a chance to argue against his . . .').

18 *Dialogo della volgar lingua*, in Pozzi (ed.), *Discussioni linguistiche del Cinquecento*, p. 93.

19 Recent critical discussions of the two dialogues which pay due attention to their formal complexity and sophistication include (on Valeriano), Floriani, *I gentiluomini letterati*, esp. pp. 87–90 and (on Speroni), Mazzacurati, *Il Rinascimento dei moderni*, pp. 261–95, Fournel, *Les dialogues de Sperone Speroni*, pp. 119–30 and Antonio Daniele, 'Sperone Speroni, Bernardino Tomitano e L'Accademia degli Infiammati', *Filologia veneta. Lingua, letteratura, tradizioni*, vol. 2: *Sperone Speroni* (1989), pp. 22–4.

20 On the differences between the two traditions, see above, chapters 2 and 3. Speroni's dialogue production does include some experiments with overtly fictional forms: his *Dialogo dell'usura* is a conversation between the comic actor and playwright Ruzante (Angelo Beolco) and a personification of Usury, while the unfinished *Dialogo dell'amicizia* is a dialogue between Socrates, Timon and Criton. The majority of his dialogues, however, are conversations between well-known contemporary figures, often portrayed with an irony which would be unimaginable in the more reverent tradition of the courts: see, for example, Fournel, *Les dialogues de Sperone Speroni*, pp. 61 and pp. 64–5, on Speroni's characterization of Bernardo Tasso, in the *Dialogo d'amore* and pp. 166–7, pp. 237 and 241–5, on his portrayal of the Venetian humanist and publisher Paolo Manuzio, in the later *Dialogo del giuditio di Senofonte* and

Dialogo della Istoria. It is interesting to note that the dedicatory letter of Rocco Cataneo's edition of Cicero's *Partitiones oratoriae* (Venice, 1545) locates Speroni firmly within the Lucianic tradition, praising him alongside Lucian, Erasmus and Aretino as one of the supreme exponents of the dialogue form of ancient and modern times: see Moro, 'Appunti sulla preistoria editoriale', p. 209, n. 69.

21 As Jean-Louis Fournel has stressed in his recent monograph, the notion of dialogue assumes a complex significance in Speroni's thought and in his intellectual praxis which sets his use of the literary form of the dialogue apart from that of his contemporaries: 'avant d'être une catégorie technique de l'écriture le dialogue est pour lui une pratique sociale, une conception de la transmission du savoir, une mise au point des modalités et des instruments de cette transmission, une réflexion active et apliquée sur les formes de la parole et même . . . une utopie personelle et l'aporie d'une recherche existentielle' ('[For Speroni], rather than just a technical literary category, dialogue is a social practice, a way of thinking about how knowledge can be communicated, a refinement of the modalities and instruments of this communication, an active and applied reflection on the forms language takes – even a personal utopia, and the aporia of an existential investigation') (*Les dialogues de Sperone Speroni*, p. 15; see also pp. 115–51, esp. pp. 135–6 and 147–8). See also, for a very interesting discussion of Speroni's use of the dialogue form and the peculiar brand of relativism which informs it, Mario Pozzi, 'Sperone Speroni e il genere epidittico', in *Filologia veneta. Lingua, letteratura, tradizione*, vol. 2: *Sperone Speroni* (1989), pp. 55–88, esp. pp. 85–8.

22 My evidence for this assertion is provided by a copy of the 1547 Manuzio edition of the *Cortegiano* in the Biblioteca Marciana, Venice (Mss. Italiani Classe II, Cod. CXIV, Coll. 5251), once owned by Alessandro Tassoni and containing, besides his own marginal notes, a series of annotations by Speroni, transcribed, as Tassoni informs us, from Speroni's own copy of the work. These annotations – if we can trust their accuracy – constitute precious evidence of how one of the greatest writers of dialogue in the Cinquecento read the work of another. Immediately apparent, especially when Tassoni's notes are used as a control, is Speroni's interest in the *form* of the dialogue, independent of its content. Some of the most densely annotated passages are, indeed, those which dramatize the distribution of conversational turns in the *Cortegiano*: see especially pp. 10r–v (*Cortegiano*, I xiii, where Emilia Pio gives the charge of speaking on the courtier to Canossa, and he replies with an important programmatic speech on the status of his teaching as pure opinion); p. 42r (*Cortegiano*, I liv, where Canossa concludes his speech with a further disclaimer); p. 62r (*Cortegiano*, II xvii, where Federico Fregoso modestly attempts to curtail his speech by protesting his ignorance); p. 74v (*Cortegiano*, II xliv, where Speroni notes that Castiglione has imitated Cicero's *De oratore* (II lvii 234) in his handling of the changeover between Federico Fregoso and Bibbiena); p. 102v (*Cortegiano* II, xcvi, where Bibbiena concludes his speech with a final *escusazione*) and, finally, p. 194v (*Cortegiano*, IV lxxiii, where, with the coming of the dawn, Castiglione achieves a purely 'dramatic' resolution of his dialogue, obverting the need for any argumentational resolution). Speroni's annotations are unrevealing in themselves, consisting as they do, for the

most part, simply of highlighting words from the text. But the repeated selection of words like 'gioco'; 'ignoranza'; 'openione' (pp. 10r–v), which would become key terms in Speroni's theory of the dialogue (discussed below, in chapter 7), confirms our impression that what Speroni appreciated about Castiglione's handling of moments such as those listed above in his use of the dialogue to dramatize a probabilistic attitude to truth.

23 Alessandro Citolini, *La tipocosmia* (Venice, 1561), dedicatory letter to Carlo Perinotti, Bishop of Aras. The entire passage is of interest: Citolini explains that he had originally started writing the work 'in filo continuato', as a treatise, 'ma perché, per rispondere a le tante tacite domande, ed obiezzioni, che far mi si poteano, mi era necessario far troppe digressioni, per levar via cotale impedimento, mi risolsi di dimostrarlo in dialogo. E per levar parimente ogni impedimento del dialogo, io do ad un solo tutto il carico de 'l ragionamento, e in luogo de le digressioni servono gli altri interlocutori.' ('But to respond to the many tacit questions and objections which could be put to me, I had to include too many digressions; so, in order to get rid of this obstacle, I resolved to cast my argument in the form of a dialogue. And to remove any obstacles within the dialogue, I give the entire burden of the discussion to a single speaker, letting the other speakers take the place of the digressions.') Citolini's commitment to demystifying the genre apparently extends to the conventional fiction that the dialogue is recording an actual historical conversation: he concludes his dedication with the statement that 'vedendo io ogni introduttor di dialogo, a più potere ingegnarsi, cercare e porre ogni fatica, in mostrare, che altrimenti stia il fatto, di quello, che veramente sta, e non di meno volere, che il fatto altrimenti s'intenda di quello, che egli medesimo lo descrive, io senza altro fare, entrerò semplicemente ne 'l Dialogo mio, non fingendo senon quanto mi sforza la presente necessità.' ('I see that whenever anyone introduces a dialogue he always tries his utmost and puts every possible effort into showing that things are otherwise than they actually are, while still hoping that the reader will understand them to be otherwise than he claims them to be. [But] I will present my dialogue quite simply, without any further introduction and without inventing anything beyond what present circumstances compel me to.')

24 ('just ask questions, without disputing or contradicting anything, so that the person replying simply trots out his opinion, or gives instruction in some discipline or skill') *Poetica d'Aristotele volgarizzata e sposta* (1570), p. 38. The examples Castelvetro cites are the second and third books of Bembo's *Prose* and Cicero's *Partitiones oratoriae*.

25 Visdomini's comments on the *Turamino* are contained in a manuscript in the Biblioteca Comunale, Siena: see Luca Serianni's introduction to his edition of the dialogue (Rome, 1976), pp. xii–xv; esp. p. xv, for the comment cited here.

26 ('though very sceptical at first, later became as docile as a lamb, and not only believed everything that was said to him, but expressed his approval after every other word') *L'Hercolano*, p. 261. The reference is to a semi-fictional 'Signor Licenziato' who appears in Carlo Lenzoni's dialogue *In difesa della lingua fiorentina e di Dante* (Florence, 1557). Varchi's allusion here may reflect his awareness that his own practice might be open to similar criticism: an awareness he betrays openly elsewhere (see especially p. 276, where Cesare

Ercolani, about to cede an argument to Varchi, declares that 'io non mi curerò, che voi mi tenghiate il signor Licenziato' ('I don't care whether you think me another Signor Licenziato')).

27 See *Discorso dell'arte del dialogo*, pp. 128–9. It should be noted that Tasso himself was not exempt from criticism where this question of 'monologism' was concerned: Lionardo Salviati, in a polemical reply to Tasso's *Apologia in difesa della sua Gierusalemme Liberata* (1585), suggests 'Signor Eco' as a more appropriate name for the figure of a 'Segretario' who appears in the dialogical section of the treatise: see Salviati's *Infarinato primo ovvero Risposta dell'Infarinato all'Apologia di Torquato Tasso* (1585), in *Opere di Torquato Tasso, con le controversie sulla Gerusalemme Liberata*, ed. G. Rosini (Pisa, 1827–32), vol. XIX, p. 333.

28 *Discorso*, p. 128. For a discussion of the significance of this passage in Tasso's theory of the dialogue and its implications for his own practice, see my 'Rhetoric and Politics in Tasso's *Nifo*', pp. 22–3.

29 The reference to 'Lattanzio' is an allusion to Castiglione's letter to Alfonso de Valdés, discussed above, chapter 5, p. 50. Classical authorities for the practice of portraying oneself as *princeps sermonis*, in a dialogue, were Aristotle (in his lost dialogues) and Cicero: see Ruch, *Le préambule dans les œuvres philosophiques de Cicéron*, pp. 40–1; Sigonio, *De dialogo liber*, *c*. 457C. Though never common, it did become more frequent in the Italian dialogue as the sixteenth century progressed: see, for example, Niccolò Tartaglia, *Quesiti et inventioni diverse* (1546); Paolo Giovio, *Dialogo delle imprese militari ed amorose* (Rome, 1555); Marco Mantova Benavides, *Discorsi sopra i dialoghi di M. Sperone Speroni* (Venice, 1561); Antonio Minturno, *L'arte poetica* (Venice, 1563); Benedetto Varchi, *Ercolano* (Venice, 1570); Pietro Gritio, *Il Castiglione, overo dell'arme di nobilità* (Mantua, 1586) and Ciro Spontone, *Il Bottrigaro, overo del nuovo verso enneasillabo* (Verona, 1589). A rather more modest solution was to portray the author in a lightly disguised form: Tasso, in a number of his *Dialoghi* (1579–94), depicts himself in the Platonic guise of a 'Forestiere Napoletano' (though, in others, like the *Costante*, and the *Cataneo overo de le conclusioni amorose*, he appears under his own name) and Cristofano Bronzini, in the dedication to the second part of his mammoth *Della dignità, e nobilità delle donne* (1625), explains that his *princeps*, Onorio, is in fact 'il Bronzini d'Ancona' and that Onorio is a 'nome finto da Lui per ragionevole rispetto'. Comparable – though here, obviously, there are more complex motivations at work – is the case of dialogues featuring as *princeps sermonis* a close relative of the author. This solution seems to have been particularly favoured by Venetian writers, whose choice of speakers perhaps reflects the importance of the fraternal bond in Venetian family structure: Pietro Bembo feature his dead brother, Carlo, in the *Prose della volgar lingua*, while Giacomo Gabriele, in his *Dialogo de la sphera* (Venice, 1545) and Giovanni Maria Memmo, in his *Tre libri della sostanza del mondo* (Venice, 1545), both portray an uncle of the writer – in Gabriele's case, the renowned critic, Trifon Gabriele.

30 *De dialogo liber*, *c*. 457A, cited above, as epigraph to this chapter; also *c*. 435C of the same work, discussed in Snyder, *Writing the Scene of Speaking*, pp. 48–9. Note, however, that Sigonio is aware of the dangers of heavy-handedness: he goes on to warn (*c*. 457D) that the *adversantes* in a polemical

dialogue should be given strong enough arguments to prevent their defeat from being attributed to sheer incompetence.

31 ('the speaker who sustains the main argument in the dialogue must be graver, more learned and more expert than the other speakers') Toscanella, *Alcune avvertenze del tesser Dialoghi*, p. 66r. On the relation of this work to the conventional dialogue theory of the period, see above, chapter 4, n. 26.

32 *Annotationi nel libro della Poetica d'Aristotele* (Venice, 1575), p. 33, cited below, chapter 9, n. 16. It is the merit of Raffaele Girardi to have called attention to Piccolomini's interesting discussion of dialogue in this work, and to have identified it as a response to Castelvetro's attack on the genre in his *Poetica* (1570): see *La società del dialogo*, pp. 45–54, esp. p. 53, for the passage referred to here.

33 *Del Dialogo: Trattato del Marchese della Villa*, in appendix to *Erocallia ovvero dell'Amore e della Bellezza, dodici dialoghi* (Venice, 1628), p. 1049. Within this basically didactic model, Manso allows for more or less authoritarian variants of dialogue: the 'student' may simply 'domandare' and the *princeps* 'rispondere', or the former may 'dubitare e impugnare', forcing the latter to 'affermare e confermare' (p. 1050). Manso's scheme also allows for a distinction between 'active' and 'passive' secondary interlocutors. The latter – the examples given are Plato's Hippothales (in the *Lysis*), Cicero's Catulus (in the *De oratore*) and the son in Tasso's *Padre di famiglia* – 'poco più fanno ch'ascoltare o dar opportunità a' ragionamenti'. For a discussion of Manso's theory of dialogue, see Snyder, *Writing the Scene of Speaking*, pp. 185–97.

34 ('When a speaker has once assumed the *persona* of a master, he must not, in the same dialogue, be demoted to a pupil.') *Trattato del dialogo*, p. 1058.

35 ('the appropriateness of the speakers' behaviour to their roles in the dialogue') *Trattato del dialogo*, p. 1058.

36 See the comments of Wayne A. Rebhorn, *Courtly Performances*, pp. 154–5.

37 Very clear examples of this sort of role-division are to be found in Paolo Paruta's *Della perfettione della vita politica* (Venice, 1579) and Bartolomeo Meduna's *Lo Scolare* (Venice, 1588). An interesting transitional example is Valerio Marcellino's *Il Diamerone* (Venice, 1564): a dialogue clearly modelled on *Il Cortegiano*, which includes a group of superficially irreverent young speakers, who nevertheless, essentially, respect their status as pupils (see pp. 7–9 and p. 101 and, for a discussion for the dialogue, see below, chapter 7, pp. 82–3).

38 I am thinking particularly of Girolamo Zabarella, in the *Dialogo della Istoria* (1585–8), who, though he behaves, at least initially, with the modesty appropriate to a young unknown in the company of a scholar as celebrated as Paolo Manuzio, in fact finishes up by dominating the discussion. On Zabarella's role in the dialogue, see Fournel, *Les dialogues de Sperone Speroni*, pp. 232–47.

39 A keen sense of the novelty represented by his imitation of Plato is apparent in a passage of the preface to Patrizi's *Dialogo d'honore* (1553), cited above, chapter 3, n. 60. Besides the *Dialogo d'honore*, Patrizi published two *deche* of dialogues, *Della istoria* (Venice, 1560) and *Della retorica* (Venice, 1562); see also his two unpublished dialogues *L'amorosa filosofia* (1577), ed. John Charles Nelson (Florence, 1963) and *Il Delfino overo del bacio*, in *Lettere ed opuscoli inediti*, ed. Danilo Aguzzi Barbagli (Florence, 1975), pp. 135–64.

40 ('completely given up to writing dialogues, inspired by his reading of Plato')
   Scipione Ammirato, *Il Rota overo de l'imprese*, in *Scritti d'arte del Cinquecento*, ed. Paola Barocchi (Milan and Naples, 1971–7), vol. III, p. 2783.
   Ammirato's other dialogues, both also written around 1560, and both very
   self-consciously Platonic in style, are *Il Maremonte overo de l'ingiurie* and *Il
   Dedalione o ver del poeta*.
41 See the passage from the *Discorso dell'arte del dialogo*, pp. 127–9, cited below,
   chapter 8, n. 59.
42 On the social advantage of the Platonic model of dialogue, see below, chapter
   8, p. 94.
43 *Dell' ordine de' libri di Platone* (1590), pp. 177–8. This claim must be understood in the context of Patrizi's account of the genre's Hermetic origins: see
   p. 175 of the same work, for his assertion that the dialogue was not invented by
   the Greeks, 'as they would have us believe', but by Hermes Trismegistus. It is
   interesting to note that Giambattista Manso follows Patrizi in this account of
   the prehistory of the genre (*Trattato del dialogo*, p. 1041), though whether the
   influence is direct or mediated – perhaps through Tasso – is open to question.
44 For a particularly explicit statement on the subject, see Giambattista Manso,
   Erocallia overo dell'amore e della bellezza, pp. 272–3, where, after noting
   Plato's skill in representing the various opinions of his speakers 'così accon-
   ciamente . . . che si possa le più volte qual sia d'essa la miglior dubitare' ('so
   scrupulously . . . that one is often left in doubt about which is the better
   opinion'), he concludes nevertheles that 'fra queste molte opinioni ch'egli suol
   rapportare, qual ne sia la vera e da lui la più ricevuta, vien nella maggior parte
   de' suoi dialogi dalla persona di Socrate dimostrato' ('among the many
   opinions that he generally records, the true opinion, and the one Plato himself
   favours, is, in most of the dialogues, given to Socrates'). It should be noted that
   this reflects a general tendency in Renaissance Platonism: see Schmitt, *Cicero
   scepticus*, pp. 51–3, on the tendency, in the Renaissance, to suppress the
   'critical, quasi-sceptical and probabilistic elements in the teaching of Socrates',
   in favour of the 'dogmatic, metaphysical and mystical side' developed by the
   Neoplatonists. A notable exception to this rule is Speroni, whose comments on
   Plato interestingly prefigure modern critics' 'discovery' of the dialogue character of the dialogues (on which see above, chapter 1, p. 2 and n. 7): see his
   Apologia dei dialoghi, pp. 269 and 284, for explicit statements of the 'comic'
   and poetic nature of Plato's dialogues; also p. 371, for an interesting insight
   into the practical implications of this fact for our interpretation of Platonic
   dialogue: one of the speakers in the dialogue on sophism which concludes the
   third part of the *Apologia*, called on by his host to remind the company of
   Plato's definition of the sophist in the dialogue of that name, refuses to do so,
   on the grounds that 'la definizione del sofista, benché sia breve, vien dietro a
   tanti ragionamenti fatti da Socrate, da Melisso, da Teodoro e da Teeteto,
   ognun de' quali vuol dir la sua; e non ho a mente ogni cosa' ('the definition of
   the sophist, although it is short in itself, comes at the end of a whole sequence
   of arguments, from Socrates, [the Stranger], Theodorus and Theaetetus, each
   of whom wants to have his say; and I cannot recall them all').
45 The distinction is Francis Bacon's: see above, chapter 5, p. 59. Manso's
   'monological' conception of the dialogue is well illustrated by the fact that he

starts his *Trattato* with a comparison between the dialogue and the treatise, intended to ascertain which 'maniera' is 'più acconcia ad insegnare' ('more suitable for teaching purposes') (*Trattato del Dialogo* (p. 1034)).

46 ('someone to direct the disputants, and to point out and explain what should be believed') *Costituzioni della Compagnia di Gesù*, IV vi 10, in *Il pensiero politico della Controriforma*, ed. L. Volpicella (Florence, 1960), p. 535.

47 On the dialogue in this period, see Guido Baldassari, 'Interpretazioni del Tasso'; also Altieri Biagi, 'Forme della communicazione scientifica', pp. 919–23.

48 See Michael Caesar, 'Leopardi's *Operette morali* and the Resources of Dialogue', *Italian Studies*, vol. 43 (1988), p. 26 and n. 18.

49 See Orazio Lombardelli's criticism of Bembo's *Prose*, in *I fonti toscani* (Florence, 1598), p. 23, cited below, as an epigraph to chapter 8; also Sforza Pallavicino, *Trattato del dialogo*, p. 347, where Pallavicino alludes to a common contemporary criticism of the dialogue form as a waste of the reader's time: 'Molto [tempo] se ne consuma nel proemio del Dialogo, molto in formar a poco a poco una girevole strada onde i proposti favellatori conducansi ad entrare nella destinata questione: e poi non meno or in parole di cortesia, o di scherzo, or in episodij che vannosi perpetuamente intrallacciando; si che l'albero al fine riesce bensi ornato di molte foglie e di molti fiori . . . ma fertile di pochi frutti.' ('A great deal of time is wasted in the introduction to the dialogue, a great deal more in tracing a winding path to lead the speakers gradually towards the question that they are supposed to be dealing with: and then still more in words of courtesy or jest, and in the digressions which endlessly weave into one another; so that the tree finishes up laden with abundant flowers and leaves, but with very little fruit.') For testimonies to this critical attitude, in the same period, in France, see Le Guern, 'Sur le genre du dialogue', pp. 145–6 and Maurice Roelens, 'Le dialogue philosophique, genre impossible?', *Cahiers de l'Association Internationale des Etudes Françaises*, no. 24 (1972), pp. 48–9.

7 THE THEORY AND PRACTICE OF THE DIALOGUE IN COUNTER-REFORMATION ITALY

1 ('Since every intellectual discipline is burdened with an infinite swarm of falsehoods, every possible care must be taken to protect the intellect from them, as from an infectious disease.') *Apologia dei dialoghi*, p. 345.

2 For the circumstances which led to the composition of the *Apologia*, see Speroni's letter to Matteo Macigni, of 9 October 1574, in *Opere*, vol. V, pp. 209–10; also Snyder, *Writing the Scene of Speaking*, pp. 88–90, and Fournel, *Les dialogues de Sperone Speroni*, pp. 191–5.

3 Snyder, *Writing the Scene of Speaking*, p. 91. Mario Pozzi's edition of the first part of the *Apologia* is at pp. 683–724 of the first volume of his anthology *Trattatisti del Cinquecento* (Milan and Naples, 1978).

4 Since Mario Pozzi's edition, a number of critics have made use of the *Apologia* in interpreting Cinquecento dialogue practice: see, for example, Floriani, *I gentiluomini letterati*, pp. 40–9; Ordine, 'Il dialogo cinquecentesco italiano', pp. 171–2 and Giorgio Patrizi, *Il 'Libro del Cortegiano' e la trattatistica sul*

comportamento, in Alberto Asor Rosa (ed.), *Letteratura italiana. III. Le forme del testo. II. La prosa* (Turin, 1982), p. 859. In addition, the past few years have seen several important new readings of the *Apologia*: Snyder, *Writing the Scene of Speaking*, pp. 87–133; Girardi, *La società del dialogo*, pp. 81–103 and, most recently, Fournel, *Les dialogues de Sperone Speroni*, pp. 187–223. Of the critics cited, only Girardi and Fournel have made a serious attempt to take on board the contradictions between the first two, and the two subsequent parts of the *Apologia*.

5 See especially the letter to Matteo Macigni of 9 October 1574, in Speroni, *Opere*, vol. V, pp. 209–10, where Speroni describes the *Apologia* as 'conditissima'; written 'in uno stile non più veduto, e con tale arte formata, che voi direte ella è sua. Non sarà manco Cristiana, che sia Roma, né manco gentile, che fussero le genti istesse, né manco accorta e semplice che qual si voglia serpe Affricana o colomba Assiria.' ('in a style the modern world is unaccustomed to, and constructed with such skill that you will say: it must be his! It will be as Christian as Rome itself, as genteel as the Gentiles [the pun is untranslatable], and as worldly-wise and innocent as any African serpent or Assyrian dove.') The last phrase contains a wry allusion to Matthew 10.16: 'Behold, I send you forth as sheep in the midst of wolves: be ye therefore wise as serpents, and harmless as doves.' The construction of almost all of Speroni's works testifies to his delight in paradox and argument *in utramque partem*: the techniques he describes, on one occasion, as 'l'arte di fare il contrario' (*Sommarii e frammenti di lezioni in difesa della 'Canace'* (post 1550), in *Opere*, vol. IV, p. 184). On Speroni's fascination with the classical tradition of the paradoxical encomium, see Pozzi, *Trattatisti del Cinquecento*, p. 686, n. 4 and 'Speroni e il genere epidittico', pp. 84–5. For his interest in the complementary tradition of the Stesichorean palinode – particularly relevant to the *Apologia* – see his *Dialogo primo sopra Virgilio* (post 1560), in *Opere*, vol. II, p. 183 and his *Sommario per la vita sobria* (*c.* 1560), in Emilio Lippi, *Cornariana. Studi su Alvise Cornaro* (Padua, 1983), p. 42 and n. 28.

6 *Apologia*, pp. 421–2.

7 The first papal Index was issued by Paul IV, in 1559; a revised version, sanctioned by the Council of Trent, in 1564. In 1571–2, the Congregation of the Index was founded and, as Rotondò notes ('La censura ecclesiastica e la cultura', p. 1407), it was from this period that censorship and surveillance began to make their mark on the whole of Italian culture, rather than simply religious speculation; see also Delio Cantimori, 'Galileo e la crisi della Controriforma', in *Storici e storia* (Turin, 1971), esp. pp. 663–5. The position on censorship argued by Speroni in the *Parte quarta* was not without its adherents in this period: see Weinberg, *A History of Literary Criticism in the Italian Renaissance*, pp. 346, 305–8 and 335–8; also, for a particularly extreme example, Rotondò, pp. 1439–40.

8 The elusiveness of the *Apologia* is well illustrated by the sharp discrepancy between the interpretations of the only two critics to date who have attempted complete readings of the text: contrast Fournel, *Les dialogues de Sperone Speroni*, pp. 208–23, who interprets the palinodes of the third and fourth parts as complementary and entirely sincere, with Girardi, *La società del dialogo*, pp. 94–103, who emphasizes the discontinuities between the two palinodes,

and interprets the final, religious renunciation as a paradoxical continuation of the first part's defence of the autonomy of art.

9 The term 'annihilation' is Shaftesbury's: see chapter 1, p. 4.

10 *Apologia*, p. 276: 'io non parlo specialmente de' miei dialoghi, parlo ben della idea dei miei dialoghi e degli altrui, nè cose dico . . . volgari . . .' ('I am not talking about my dialogues in particular, rather, I am talking about the idea of my dialogues and dialogues in general, and what I am saying is not common knowledge.')

11 See *Apologia*, pp. 267–8, 276–8 and 280–1. Speroni draws here on two distinct, though associated, traditions within thought on the arts of discourse: the ultimately Platonic view of literary and figurative art as 'gioco' (see Snyder, *Writing the Scene of Speaking*, pp. 124–5 and Francesco Bruni, 'Sperone Speroni e l'Accademia degli Infiammati', *Filologia e letteratura*, vol. 13, fasc. 1, no. 49 (1967), p. 53 and n. 61) and the Aristotelian conception of rhetoric and dialectic as morally neutral arts (see my 'Rhetoric and Politcs in Tasso's *Nifo*', pp. 81–3.) The phrase 'the point from which my defence derives, as the circumference of a circle from its centre', is at p. 289.

12 See *Apologia*, pp. 273–4, for a distinction between the 'strada utile Aristotelica, la qual conduce al sapere; ed è tenuta per tutta Europa generalmente da' studiosi delle dottrine' and the 'sentiero delli dialogi, per lo quale noi camminiamo anzi a' giardini e alle vigne che a' buoni campi contemplativi' ('the useful Aristotelian way, which leads us to knowledge, and which is the way generally followed by scholars in all exact disciplines throughout Europe' and 'the by-way of dialogue, which takes us to pleasure-gardens and vineyards, rather than the useful farmlands of philosophy'). As he goes on to point out, the fact that he himself chose to write 'dialogizzando', is a clear indication that 'anzi a giuoco, che per ver dire, io . . . ragionassi' ('I was writing to amuse, rather than to convey truths'). See also p. 284, where Speroni rather engagingly states that 'se di quello che ci si tratta, avessi avuto certa scienzia, non ne faceva dialoghi; ma arei scritta ogni cosa alla maniera Aristotelica' ('if I had possessed certain knowledge of the problems under discussion, I would not have written dialogues; instead, I would have written everything in the Aristotelian manner'). On Speroni's epistemology and its historical context, see Bruni, 'Sperone Speroni e l'Accademia degli Infiammati'.

13 *Apologia*, pp. 280–1; also Snyder, *Writing the Scene of Speaking*, pp. 121–30 and Mulas, 'La scrittura del dialogo', p. 258. Speroni distinguishes three levels of certitude in human knowledge: the 'certain and invariable knowledge' generated by the demonstrative syllogism, the 'opinion' generated by the 'probable syllogism' (in which the premises are only considered probably, not demonstrably true), and the, finally, weaker brand of opinion produced by the rhetorical techniques of enthymeme and example. The relation between these three levels is expressed in terms of imitation: the probable syllogism is an 'imagine della perfetta dimonstrazione'; the enthymeme an 'effigie imperfetta del sillogismo probabile'. Dialogues, which characteristically employ dialectical and probabilistic reasoning, thus occupy the middle ground in Speroni's hierarchy of modes of argument, between Aristotelian scientific discourse, on the one hand, and Ciceronian oratory, on the other. For this implications of this positioning for dialogue practice, see below, p. 73.

14 *Apologia*, p. 284. The point is supported by the *exemplum* of Plato: see esp.
    pp. 284 and 269 for allusions to Plato's *Second Letter* (314c), where the
    philosopher asserts that he 'has never written anything' and that 'there is not
    and will not be any written work of Plato's own' (trans. L. A. Post, in Plato,
    The Collected Dialogues, including the Letters, ed. Edith Hamilton and
    Huntingdon Cairns (Princeton, 1961), p. 1567; see also the *Seventh Letter*,
    344c). For an analysis of the use made by Speroni of the figure of Plato, in the
    first part of the *Apologia*, see Snyder, *Writing the Scene of Speaking*,
    pp. 110–17.
15 *Apologia*, p. 274.
16 *Apologia* p. 283: '[Le persone del dialogo] non a insegnare maestrevolmente
    ma si a contendere s'introducono. Nel quale caso cotai persone introdotte non
    son diverse al fucile, con ciò sia cosa che nel contrasto, che elle hanno insieme
    intorno a qualche materia, l'una batta con sue ragioni la opinione dell'altra,
    non altrimenti in un certo modo che faccia il ferro la pietra, o la pietra il ferro.
    Il che facendosi disputando, quantunque intiera ed aperta non salti fuora la
    verità ricercata, nondimeno scintillando per sua natura la verità, siccome fa
    sempremai, forza è talora che se ne vedano le faville. Queste, in principio
    piccole e poche, se buona è l'esca che le riceve [ie. i lettori di umano ingegno e
    non maligno intelletto], non molto dopo chiara e gran fiamma suol secondare.'
    ('The speakers are introduced not to teach authoritatively, but rather to
    contend with one another. These speakers are rather like a tinder-box, since, in
    the course of their dispute, one of them will use his or her arguments to batter
    away at the opinion of the other, just as the iron strikes against the flint, or the
    flint against the iron. And as this happens, and they argue away, even though
    the truth does not leap out fully-formed and plain to be seen, nonetheless, it is
    inevitable that a few sparks of truth will appear, especially since truth is
    sparkling by nature. And these sparks, even if they are few and small at first, if
    they fall on to good kindling [ie. readers with well-disposed minds and
    intellects not tainted with malice] will quickly fan into a clear and steady
    flame.') The source of Speroni's imagery here is, perhaps, ultimately Platonic:
    see Plato's *Seventh Letter*, 341d.
17 *Apologia*, pp. 275 and 278–9. One of the delights of comedy cited in the latter
    passage is 'il por fin facilmente a una difficile impresa; provedere al bisogno
    con li rimedii non preveduti' ('bringing a difficult enterprise to an easy
    conclusion, or solving a problem by the most unexpected means'). The dia-
    logue translates this pattern into argumentation (p. 282) when 'le persone
    ignoranti [. . .] non sappiendo [. . .] rispondere agli argomenti delli adversarii e
    non volendo tacere né confessar la ignoranzia; vengono a' motti e colle arguzie
    delle parole pongono fine alle lor contese' ('ignorant speakers, not knowing
    how to respond to their opponents' arguments and not wishing to give in or
    confess their ignorance, have recourse to wit and put an end to the dispute
    through ingenious word-play'). A good example of this in Speroni's practice
    are the Cortigiano's retorts to Lazzaro Bonamico's arguments in his *Dialogo
    delle lingue*; see, for example, esp. pp. 591, 594 and 598.
18 ('Ignorance, which cannot make its own choices, must never be equated with
    virtue') *Apologia*, p. 292.
19 *Apologia*, p. 281; see above, n. 13.

20 *Apologia* p. 281. This harsh judgment of Ciceronian oratory is not unique to this passage: see also, for example, *Apologia* pp. 343 and 359 and *Dell'arte oratoria*, in *Opere*, vol. V, esp. pp. 537–8.

21 *Della imitazione*, in *Opere*, vol. V, p. 559: 'Platone . . . non fu men di [Aristotele] sapiente, ma non ne scrisse scientemente, ma probabilmente; se non forse quando divide e diffinisce: nel resto è oratore, o al più dialettico.' ('Plato was no less wise than Aristotle, but he did not write scientifically, but probabilistically, except perhaps when he is practising definition and division; for the rest, he remains a rhetorician or, at most, a dialectician.')

22 On the classical sources and the Renaissance *fortuna* of this distinction, see Pignatti, 'I *Dialoghi* di Torquato Tasso', pp. 10–13. Exhumed by Sigonio (*De dialogo liber, c.* 450C–E), this division is cited by most subsequent theorists of the dialogue: see, for example, Castelvetro, *Poetica d'Aristotele volgarizzata e sposta*, pp. 35–6; Alessandro Piccolomini, *Annotationi nel libro della Poetica d'Aristotele*, pp. 30–1; Tasso, *Discorso dell'arte del dialogo*, pp. 121–2; Manso, *Trattato del dialogo*, pp. 1051–2; Pallavicino, *Trattato dello stile e del dialogo*, p. 331. By the time Speroni was writing, theoretical discussion of the narrative/ dramatic distinction had become complicated by the controversy excited by Castelvetro's polemical intervention, which denied legitimacy to both dramatic and narrative forms of dialogue, on the grounds that they did not meet the requirements for true drama or true history. On Castelvetro's theory of dialogue, and the reactions it excited, see Baldassari, 'L'arte del dialogo in Torquato Tasso', pp. 7–14; Girardi, *La società del dialogo*, pp. 45–54 and Snyder, *Writing the Scene of Speaking*, pp. 134–80, esp. pp. 153–5.

23 *Apologia*, p. 275, cited above, chapter 3, p. 32 and n. 58.

24 See above, chapter 2, p. 18. It is interesting to note that Speroni's only known attempt at a Ciceronian narrated dialogue – the *Dialogo della fortuna* (*c.* 1539–42) – was abandoned after a few pages (see *Opere*, vol. II, pp. 336–44, and Fournel, *Les dialogues de Sperone Speroni*, pp. 96–7). The only one of his published dialogues which approaches this model – the *Dialogo della vita attiva e contemplativa*, with its narrative introduction – was recognized by Tasso as a model for honorific dialogue: see his letter of 13 February 1593, to Antonio Costantini in *Lettere*, vol. V, p. 139.

25 The *Parte seconda* – a detailed analysis of those dialogues and passages which Speroni's accuser had particularly objected to – may be left out of my consideration here, as it is really no more than a practical application of the theory outlined in the *parte prima*. It is discussed in some detail in Fournel, *Les dialogues de Sperone Speroni*, pp. 203–8.

26 For the term 'l'arte privata', see *Apologia*, p. 346.

27 For Speroni's distinction between the various decorums, see *Apologia*, pp. 330–1. On the 'decoro dello scrittore', see pp. 333–41, especially p. 334, on the moral danger involved in immersing oneself in imitation and especially 'imitazione de' peggiori'. At p. 340, Speroni analyses the components of the writer's 'decoro particolare': he must write as is fitting to his 'grado', his 'costumi', his 'professione' and 'le leggi della città'.

28 See *Apologia*, p. 347, where Speroni states that 'le nostre arti particolari dalla civile son regolate'; also pp. 346 and 348 for the implications of this statement for the practice of dialogue. On this critical trend, see Weinberg, *A History of*

Literary Criticism in the Italian Renaissance, pp. 297–348, especially the balanced summary at pp. 345–6; also pp. 27–31 and pp. 672–6, on the controversy between Battista Guarini and Giason de Nores, over Guarini's *Pastor fido*, which brought these issues to the forefront of cultural debate in the last decade of the century. The difficulty of establishing Speroni's true position on the issue is well illustrated by the fact that both sides in the Guarini–de Nores dispute claimed the recently deceased Speroni as authority for their views: see Fournel, *Les dialogues de Sperone Speroni*, p. 343, n. 105.

29 See especially *Apologia*, pp. 407 and 410.

30 *Apologia*, p. 345, cited above, chapter 3, n. 46.

31 ('in a manner befitting his status as a civilized and respectable person') *Apologia*, pp. 331 and 334.

32 ('I should not, when writing, have let my eyes and tongue stray from my own character and condition, but rather I should have constructed the characters in my dialogues in my own image, correcting them and putting them on the right path') *Apologia*, p. 335.

33 The letter is published in Loi and Pozzi, 'Le lettere familiari di Sperone Speroni', pp. 386–7. For Speroni's defence of the *Dialogo dell'usura* as a paradoxical encomium, see the second part of the *Apologia*, pp. 308–9 and 312. On the revised version of the dialogue, composed after 1574, in which Ruzante does answer the goddess Usury's arguments, see Fournel, *Les dialogues de Sperone Speroni*, pp. 205–6. It is interesting to note that there is evidence that, in its original form, the *Dialogo dell'usura* was read as a defence of usury: see Giambattista Gelli's *I capricci del bottaio* (1548), in Pozzi, *Trattatisti del Cinquecento*, vol. I, p. 940, where the *Dialogo dell'usura* is coupled with Aretino's *Cortigiana*, 'l'una . . . sufficiente a corrompere l'onestà di Lucrezia Romana, e l'altra la liberalità d'Alessandro Magno' ('the one sufficient to corrupt the chastity of Lucretia, the other the liberality of Alexander the Great'); also Annibale Romei, *Discorsi*, (1585), p. 106, where a speaker refers to 'un dialogo d'un gran letterato' – later explicitly identified as Speroni – 'nel quale egli prova che l'usura è necessaria al bene e beato vivere' ('a dialogue by a great writer, in which usury is proved to be necessary to the well-being of society'). Modern commentators have tended to agree: see Fournel, pp. 86–90; also Pozzi, p. 499, where it is noted that Speroni 'gives such credibility' to the words of the goddess Usury that 'sembra di leggere una spregiudicata difesa del capitalismo'.

34 A good example is Valerio Marcellino's *Il Diamerone* (Venice, 1564), discussed below, pp. 82–3; but see also, for example, Marco de la Frata et Montalbano's *Discorsi de' principii della nobiltà*, 2nd edition (Venice, 1549).

35 For contrasting readings of the dialogue, see Fournel, *Les dialogues de Sperone Speroni*, pp. 216–20, who particularly stresses the originality of Speroni's rehabilitation of sophism, and Girardi, *La società del dialogo*, pp. 96–7.

36 The protagonists of the dialogue on sophism are the Venetian ex-ambassador and cardinal Marcantonio da Mula; the brilliant young humanist, Silvio Antoniano, himself a future cardinal; the publisher and humanist, Paolo Manuzio; the poet, Bernardo Cappello and a lesser-known figure, Costantino Ralli.

37 *Apologia*, p. 369.

38 ('It is only reasonable that we should conclude it in a manner which is more appropriate to Lent') *Apologia*, p. 389.

39 For Speroni's association of dialogue and carnival, see Loi and Pozzi, 'Le lettere familiari di Sperone Speroni', p. 386: 'era tale alli antichi dotti nel loro ocio onorato questa maniera di scrivere, quale è il giuoco alla nostra plebe oggi e forse maschera il carnevale' ('for the learned men of antiquity, in their respectable leisure, this manner of writing was what card-playing is to the lower classes today, and perhaps the same as disguising oneself for carnival').

40 *Risposta alla lettera di Bastiano de' Rossi*, p. 405: 'I' ho rinovata [l'occasione] non come istorico ma come scrittore di dialogo, il quale . . . più tosto s'obbliga al verisimile, che al vero' ('I have evoked the circumstances of the dialogue not in the manner of a historian but as a writer of dialogues does, aiming at verisimilitude rather than a strict allegiance to the truth'). On the circumstances of composition of the *Risposta*, see Margaret W. Ferguson, *Trials of Desire, Renaissance Defences of Poetry* (New Haven and London, 1983), p. 79; also, more generally, on the *Risposta* pp. 70–98.

41 See *Risposta alla lettera di Bastiano de' Rossi*, p. 408, where Tasso points out that, if de' Rossi's description of the *Nifo* as a trifle (a 'giuoco di bagatelle') was acccurate, it would absolve him from responsibility, since calumny can only occur in 'things intended seriously' ('le cose dette senza scherzo'). In fact, however, 'chiamandolo giuoco, . . . gli dà nome sconvenevole; percio ch'egli è ragionamento di cose gravi' ('he is wrong to call it a trifle, since it is a discussion of serious issues'). Tasso's unstated antagonist here is probably, beyond de' Rossi, Lodovico Castelvetro, who had claimed that, as poetry, the dialogue has no right to deal with serious subjects: see Castelvetro, *Poetica*, p. 37 and, on the relation of Tasso's theory of dialogue to Castelvetro's, Baldassari, 'L'arte del dialogo in Torquato Tasso', pp. 7–10 and Snyder, *Writing the Scene of Speaking*, pp. 150–6.

42 ('Truth has as great a place in my dialogues as is consistent with respecting the decorum of the speakers') *Risposta alla lettera di Bastiano de' Rossi*, p. 408. The phrase recalls Tasso's much-quoted definition of the writer of dialogue, in the *Discorso dell'arte del dialogo*, p. 129, as 'quasi mezzo fra 'l poeta e 'l dialettico' ('as it were, half-way between the poet and the dialectician'). I have omitted any reference of the *Discorso* here, since Tasso makes no direct mention there of the problem of authorial accountability in the dialogue, but much of his treatment of the relation between poetry and dialectic in the dialogue is relevant to my arguments here. For a discussion of these issues, see Snyder, *Writing the Scene of Speaking*, pp. 146–80, esp. pp. 158–66.

43 See, for example, *Risposta alla lettera di Bastiano de' Rossi* p. 396: '. . . il parer di mio padre [Bernardo Tasso, cited at length in the dialogue] . . . fu . . . quasi il medesimo con quel del Sessa [Agostino Nifo da Sessa, the *princeps sermonis* of the dialogue] . . . e soggiungo appresso, che fu buono assolutamente' ('my father's opinion almost coincided with that of Nifo – and, I might add, it was the right opinion, in absolute terms').

44 There is, to my knowledge, only one recent study which deals with Pallavicino's discussion of the dialogue form, in the *Trattato dello stile e del dialogo* (1662), in any depth or detail: Snyder, *Writing the Scene of Speaking*, pp. 197–213. More generally, on Pallavicino's career and writings, see Mario

Scotti's introduction to his edition of the *Storia del Concilio di Trento ed altri scritti* and the bibliography cited there; also, on his importance as a literary critic and theorist, Franco Croce, *Tre momenti del barocco letterario* (Florence, 1966), pp. 161–220.

45 The *Trattato* was first published, under the title *Considerazioni sopra l'arte dello stile e del dialogo*, in 1646, thirteen years after the condemnation of Galileo's *Dialogo sui massimi sistemi* (1632), and two years after the publication of Pallavicino's own dialogue, *Del bene*. On Galileo's trial and its aftermath, see Maurice A. Finocchiaro, *The Galileo Affair. A documentary History* (Berkeley, Los Angeles and London, 1989); also, more specifically, on the effects of Galileo's 'strategically unhappy' use of the dialogue form on the reputation of the genre in Italy, Altieri Biagi, 'Forme della comunicazione scientifica', pp. 919–23. On Pallavicino's own involvement in the affair – his known sympathies with Galileo appear to have led him into difficulties, in 1632 – see Scotti's introduction to the *Storia del Concilio di Trento*, p. 34 and Pietro Redondi, *Galileo eretico* (Turin, 1983), pp. 332–3.

46 *Trattato dello stile e del dialogo*, pp. 343–4: 'contro alle composizioni in Dialogo suole allegarsi, che da essi mal si può ricogliere il sincero della dottrina: tutte impiegandosi in apportar con eloquenza molte ragioni fra sé opposte per una e per altra parte; e qui terminando: quasi una contesa di litiganti senza decreto di Giudice' ('a frequent allegation against works in dialogue form that it is difficult to extract any doctrine from them in a pure form, since they devote all their energies to presenting many conflicting arguments, on both sides of an issue, as eloquently as possible, and then just stop, like a courtroom battle without any final sentence').

47 ('[dialogues which] leave the reader unsure of which side the author is on') *Trattato dello stile e del dialogo*, p. 344.

48 ('what is recorded in favour of both points of view in the Acts of nature and the mind') *Trattato dello stile e del dialogo*, p. 344.

49 ('the urge to look into things more closely and subtly') *Trattato dello stile e del dialogo*, pp. 344–5.

50 *Trattato dello stile e del dialogo*, p. 345.

51 This sympathy is expressed more fully, outside the apologetic context of the *Trattato*, in a letter to Virgilio Malvezzi, of 27 October 1646, which contains an acute psychological analysis of the appeal of the dialogue form: see *Storia del Concilio di Trento ed altri scritti*, pp. 644–6, esp. p. 645, where Pallavicino compares the 'probable arguments' of dialogues like his *Del bene* to 'quei cacciatori che non prendon la fiera, ma la discuoprono al lor signore, acciocché egli goda l'onore di seguirla e di prenderla' ('those huntsmen who do not catch the prey themselves, but simply beat it out of cover, leaving the honour of the chase and the kill to their masters').

52 *Trattato dello stile e del dialogo*, p. 346. The 'perfection' of the examples cited is said to lie in the fact that 'in essi con gran chiarezza riluce l'opinione dello Scrittore e 'l suo fondamento' ('in them, the Author's opinions and their foundations are very clearly revealed').

53 ('modestly, as private citizens, [so that], having recognized their merits, the intellect will spontaneously call on them to take over the government') *Trattato dello stile e del dialogo*, pp. 345–6.

54 Galileo's *Dialogo sui massimi sistemi* does not, of course – as its censors realized – genuinely fall into Pallavicino's category of dialogues which leave the reader unsure of where the author's sympathies lie. For reasons of prudence, however, it *was* presented as such: the full title of the work – imposed on Galileo, at a late stage, by Pope Urban VIII – stresses that the dialogue presents the arguments for both the Ptolomaic and Copernican systems with complete impartiality ('indeterminatamente . . . tanto per l'una, quanto per l'altra parte'), while the preface – again, added just prior to publication, on the Pope's orders – insists that the author's intention was simply to demonstrate to critics of the 1616 condemnation of Copernicanism that the Church's decision was not motivated by ignorance and that it had acted in full awareness of the scientific arguments on both sides. For the text of the preface, see Finocchiaro, *The Galileo Affair*; pp. 214–16; also p. 213 and notes 56 and 57, on the circumstances of its composition.

55 *Cortegiano*, I xiii, discussed above, chapter 5, p. 47.

56 For the term 'closed dialectical dialogue', see Le Guern, 'Sur le genre du dialogue', p. 144.

57 *Trattato dello stile e del dialogo*, p. 355. At the beginning of his treatment here of the 'vantaggi' of the dialogue, Pallavicino states that 'saremo più brevi per tralasciar molte cose che nella . . . *Apologia* dello Speroni havrà per avventura vedute il nostro lettore' ('we will deal with this briefly, omitting many things which the reader will already, perhaps, have seen in Speroni's *Apologia*').

58 ('whatever Speroni alleged to the contrary') *Trattato dello stile e del dialogo*, p. 328.

59 ('the discovery of the truth of the matter and of arguments to prove it') *Trattato dello stile e del dialogo*, p. 329. Pallavicino's account of the process of dialogic composition rests on the division of the creative process in classical rhetorical theory into the three stages of 'inventio', 'dispositio' and 'elocutio'.

60 ('expressing the truth in words appropriate to speakers of speculative mind, in an informal setting') *Trattato dello stile e del dialogo*, p. 329. The examples Pallavicino cites of other 'prose writings' involving this basic level of imitation are 'le lettere' and 'le istorie'. It is interesting to note that, outside an apologetic context, Speroni expresses similar reservations about the status of the dialogue as an imitative genre. In a fascinating, though frustrating and fragmentary passage of a draft of his essay, *Dell' imitazione* in vol. XVI of his manuscripts, in the Biblioteca Capitolare, Padua, Speroni suggests that 'forse il dialogo, nel quale si parla e risponde è cosa loica disputante perché imita il poema quanto le persone parlanti, ma non per vero, essendo ciò loicale professione, dunque non ogni sembianza è imitazione poetica, la quale è delle persone operanti et registranti et parlanti et delli affetti di esse persone, non della dottrina, della quale si tratta logicalmente' ('perhaps the dialogue, in which people talk and answer one another, is a product of disputational logic, because it may be like a poem in that [it imitates] people speaking, but not in any real sense, since [imitating a dispute] is the task of the logician. So not all appearances count as poetic imitation, which should be reserved for [imitations of] people acting and reacting and speaking, and their emotions. But doctrine is dealt with by logic'). I am indebted to Jean-Louis Fournel for calling my attention to this passage.

61 ('of benefit in the acquisition and progress of knowledge') *Trattato dello stile e del dialogo*, p. 330. Interestingly, in the passage which precedes this statement (p. 328), Pallavicino discounts the possible counter-example of Plato, frequently cited by theorists in support of the dialogue's status as poetry (see, for example, Tasso, *Discorso dell'arte del dialogo*, pp. 132–4). For Pallavicino, the 'forme spiritose e sfoggiate' ('spirited and exuberant forms') of Plato's dialogues are an exception which proves his rule: while, in Plato's case, the reader might be lead to doubt 'se il prossimo fine dello Scrittore fosse l'insegnamento o 'l diletto' ('whether the author's immediate intention was to instruct or to entertain'), in most cases, in dialogue, 'diletto' is purely incidental to teaching.

62 Trattato dello stile e del dialogo, pp. 356–7.

63 See above, p. 72.

64 See above. p. 75.

65 For Galileo's attempt to use arguments drawn from what Speroni would call 'l'arte privata' to defend himself against the accusation of having favoured the heretical Copernican thesis in his *Dialogo sui massimi sistemi*, see his depositions at his trial, especially the second, of 30 April 1633, in A. Favoaro (ed.), *Opere* (Florence, 1890–1909), reprinted, 1964–6, vol. XIX, p. 343, where he confesses that, re-reading his dialogue, he sees that it would be possible for a reader 'non consapevole dell'intrinseco mio' ('unaware of my real feelings'), to get the impression that he was sympathetic to 'la parte falsa, ch'io intendevo di confutare' ('the [Copernican] side, which I intended to confute'). One of the reasons he gives for this unfortunate flaw in his work is that he was acting on the principle that 'nel recitar gli argomenti della parte avversa, quando s'intende di volergli confutare, si debbono portare (e massime scrivendo in dialogo) nella più stretta maniera, e non pagliargli a disavvantaggio dell'avversario' ('when one is stating the arguments for the opposing side, with the intention of confuting them, it is necessary (especially when one is writing a dialogue) to give them in the most convincing way possible, and not to pad them out with straw, in order to put the adversary at a disadvantage').

66 ('It is forbidden to the author, under any pretext whatsoever, and whatever the nature of the speaker represented, ever to allow these serpents to appear in an honourable guise, masquerading as truth or virtue.') *Trattato dello stile e del dialogo*, pp. 357–8. Pallavicino's insistence here on the need for self-censorship on the part of writers is matched by his conviction of the necessity for institutional censorship: see his defence of the Index, directed against Paolo Sarpi, in his *Storia del Concilio di Trento* (1656) pp. 442–7; also Rotondò, 'La censura ecclesiastica e la cultura', pp. 1478–9.

67 ('Both charity and prudence dictate that no one should use his art to lend an enticing disguise to these snakes; even if he is doing it with the intention of later laying them ignominiously bare.') *Trattato dello stile e del dialogo*, p. 358. It is interesting to note that one of the criticisms levelled at Galileo by the commission constituted to examine his *Dialogo* was that his retraction at the end of the dialogue – 'la medicina del fine' – was too rushed and lukewarm to perform its intended function: see the report of September 1632 in Favaro (ed.), *Opere*, vol. XIX, p. 326; also Finocchiaro, *The Galileo Affair* p. 221 and, for the passage in question, pp. 216–18.

68 Giovanni Pietro Bellori, *Ai lettori*, in Foppa (ed.), *Opere non più stampate del*

Signor Torquato Tasso: 'Quanto all'intentione dell'Autore, si avverte, che debba haversi particolar riguardo ... all'arte e al costume dello scriver' i Dialoghi ... In essi alcune volte si disputa di propositioni non vere, ma probabili, o verisimili, e si recano ancora alcune opinioni de gli antichi Filosofi, riprovate dalla verità della nostra Fede, o d'alcuni di esse problematicamente si quistiona, o si portano dubitativamente, o conditionalmente, e non per affermarle, anzi per modo di semplice racconto, e finalmente in essi, non per far noto esattamente il vero, ma per dimostratione d'ingegno, e per vaghezza d'eloquenza ... fra coloro, che vi s'introducono, variamente si discorre. Però, leggendosi ne' presenti Dialoghi ... alcune cose somiglianti, e parlandovisi della Fortuna, o del Fato, o del Destino, o de' giuditij dell'Astrologia, o d'altro, secondo la dottrina de' Platonici, e de' Peripatetici, non dovrà nascer dubbio in alcuno, della mente di quest' Autore, che in tant' altre sue Opere mostrò, e professò sempre la sua pietà, e la fermezza nella Cattolica Chiesa.' ('To discern the author's intention in these works, the reader is advised that it is necessary to pay close attention to the art and conventions of writing dialogues ... It is not uncommon for dialogues to include discussions of propositions which are not true, but simply probable, or plausible; and they may also contain the opinions of ancient philosophers, which the revealed truth of our Faith has proved false. These ancient opinions may be disputed about, in dialogues, or stated hypothetically or conditionally, but no claims are made for their validity; they are simply recounted. And, to conclude, the various discussions which take place in dialogues, are not intended to reveal the truth, but simply to display the speakers' wit and eloquence. So, when any such dubious opinions are encountered in the present dialogues; when one comes across talk of Fortune, or Fate, or Destiny, or Astrology, or suchlike subjects, discussed in the manner of the Platonic or Peripatetic schools, this should not arouse any suspicion about the intentions of this author, who displayed, and openly professed his piety and orthodoxy, in so many of his other works.')

69 Granucci, *La piacevol notte e lieto giorno*, pp. 60r–v ('the Inquisitor does not wish anyone to debate, or to write, on this question'). The speaker who interrupts is Agniolo Benci, described (p. 8r) as a 'professor di Leggi, e della sacra scrittura'. According to Benci, the only correct line on the issue is that women are inferior to men ('la donna sia nel secondo grado'); any other position is in clear contradiction of St Paul. His interlocutor, Giulio Petrucci, a student of 'humanità, e filosofia' at Padua (p. 7r), objects that the ban is only on asserting women's *superiority* to men: allowing women as equals is permissible.

70 See Quondam, '"Mercanzia d'onore" / "mercanzia d'utile"', pp. 73, 90 and 103; also Grendler, *The Roman Inquisition and the Venetian Press*, pp. 129–34.

71 Marcellino's fear of alienating his potential audience by the grimness of his subject is dramatized, within the fictional exchange of the dialogue, when one of the interlocutors threatens to boycott these 'funesti ragionamenti': see *Il Diamerone, ove con vive ragioni si mostra la morte non esser quel male, che 'l senso si persuade*, (Venice, 15644), p. 7. A similarly self-conscious approach to the problem of accommodating sacred subject-matter to a worldly and humanistically educated audience is apparent in another dialogue of the same period,

also published by Giolito, Bonaventura Gonzaghi's *Ragionamenti sopra i Sette peccati mortali* (Venice, 1567), discussed in Girardi, *La società del dialogo*, pp. 264–70, esp. pp. 268–9.

72 See *Diamerone*, pp. 2–3 for the introduction of Veniero (compare *Cortegiano*, I iii, pp. 83–4); and pp. 126–7 for Speroni's rapture (clearly modelled on Bembo's in *Cortegiano*, IV lxxi, p. 541). Other reminiscences of the *Cortegiano* include the detail of the interlocutors' arrangement in a circle (p. 4; compare *Cortegiano*, I vi, p. 89) and the mention of the younger interlocutors' game of teasing out the hidden seeds of madness in their companions (p. 4; compare *Cortegiano*, I viii, pp. 91–3). On Venier, see Alvise Zorzi, *Cortigiana veneziana. Veronica Franco e i suoi poeti* (Milan, 1986), chapter V, esp. p. 77, on the illness which had left him semi-paralysed and p. 79 on the theme of death in his poetry.

73 On Atanagi's career, see C. Mutini's entry in the *Dizionario biografico degli italiani*, vol. IV, pp. 503–6. For the tradition of this sort of 'ethical irony' in the humanist dialogue, see Marsh, *The Quattrocento Dialogue*, p. 30–1, p. 40 and pp. 60–1. Here the factor of the interlocutor's reputation outside the dialogue is particularly crucial since Atanagi is made to express doubts on doctrines as fundamental as the immortality of the soul (*Diamerone*, pp. 27–8) and the resurrection of the flesh (p. 78).

74 *Diamerone*, p. 10. See also p. 35, where, after an eloquent refutation by Speroni of his insinuation that the arguments of reason may conflict with the tenets of faith, Atanagi admits that his suggestion was intended 'anzi ad eccitarlo [Speroni] che ad altro' ('rather to excite him [to further discussion] than for any other reason'), and congratulates himself on having provoked 'si gran copia di ragioni in così alto soggetto' ('such abundant arguments, on such an important subject'). At pp. 80–1, in a similar episode, Marcellino interjects an authorial aside to the effect that 'disputando è lecito dire ogni cosa, spetialmente in ragionamento si fatto, nel quale, io mi aviso, che molti paradossi si sian difesi etiandio contra la mente di coloro, che li hanno presi a difendere' ('it is legitimate to say anything in an argument, and particularly in an argument like this in which, I warrant, many paradoxes have been defended, which even those defending them did not believe in').

75 For the phrase 'parte giusta', see *Diamerone*, p. 10. For the scene of the capitulation of Speroni's listeners – a travesty of its model, the deliberately inconclusive last scene of the *Cortegiano* – see p. 127 of the dialogue.

76 On the function of these devices in the *Cortegiano*, see Rebhorn, *Courtly Performances*, pp. 134–6 and pp. 138–41.

77 For Speroni's initial protestations of his reluctance to speak, see *Diamerone*, pp. 8–9 and compare Canossa's 'deference ritual' in *Cortegiano*, I xiii, discussed above, chapter 4, p. 41 and n. 53, and chapter 5, pp. 47–8. Unlike Canossa, however, who ends his formation of the courtier in the same modest spirit as he began it (*Cortegiano*, I liv, p. 182), Speroni is speaking confidently, by the end of the first book, of his desire to 'recare a perfettione il ragionamento' ('to bring the discussion to completion').

78 Wit, in the *Diamerone*, is the exclusive province of the younger, more light-weight interlocutors. It has a purely decorative function – defined at p. 101 as that of 'sweetening' what would otherwise be a somewhat grim debate – and it

is not allowed any resonance in the argument itself. We are always *told* when someone is joking (see, for example, p. 9, or p. 77) and reminded that their comments have no bearing on the truth.

79 *Diamerone*, p. 10.

80 *Diamerone*, p. 78.

81 See above, chapter 3, n. 47.

82 On the censorship of the *Cortegiano* and the expurgated edition of 1584, see Guidi, 'Reformulations de l'idéologie aristocratique', pp. 162–82. On the second part of Speroni's *Apologia*, and on the 'correction' of his early dialogues, see Fournel, *Les dialogues de Sperone Speroni*, pp. 203–8.

83 I am thinking of passages like that in the *Gonzaga overo del piacere onesto* (1579) (*Dialoghi*, vol. III, p. 228), where Agostino Nifo, after explaining the Aristotelian concept of a 'tirannide legittima', notes that 'allora era in uso tra' barbari, ma s'or sia in uso o non sia, voglio che mi giovi sotto silenzio trapassare' ('then [i.e. in Aristotle's day] such a thing did exist, among barbarous nations, but whether it exists today or not is something I would prefer to pass over in silence'). Another instance – again, significantly, from the first version of a dialogue later corrected – is in *Il Forno overo della nobiltà* (1579) (*Dialoghi*, vol. III, p. 10), when Antonio Forno, after listing classical examples of princely vices, states that 'mi giova di non istender la lingua ne' principi e ne' cavalieri cristiani' ('it is better for me not to let my tongue stray on to the subject of Christian princes and knights'). On Tasso's awareness of the problems involved in any direct denunciation of contemporary abuses, see my 'Rhetoric and Politics in Tasso's *Nifo*', esp. pp. 50–7, and, for readings of two of his dialogues which stress his use of the form as a vehicle for dissimulated social and political criticism, see Lord, 'The Argument of Tasso's *Nifo*' and Trafton, 'Tasso's Dialogue on the Court'.

8 FROM THE 'GIREVOLE STRADA' TO THE STRAIGHT AND NARROW PATH

1 ('They demand a reader who is well-grounded in the subject, attentive, committed and energetic: someone capable of salvaging those treasures which are almost drowned in the dialogue and in a rather eccentric manner of exposition.') Orazio Lombardelli, *I fonti toscani* (Florence, 1598), p. 23.

2 *Trattato dello stile e del dialogo*, p. 357. For the context in which these terms occur, see above, chapter 7, p. 80.

3 *Trattato dello stile e del dialogo*, p. 346, discussed above, chapter 7, p. 78. See also Castelvetro, *Poetica*, vol. I, p. 38, where the *Prose* are again cited as an example of didactic dialogue, though this time in a more hostile context.

4 The term 'girevole strada' is from a passage in Sforza Pallavicino's *Trattato dello stile e del dialogo*, p. 347, cited above, in chapter 6, n. 49.

5 *Cortegiano*, I i, p. 80 ('a strict order, or a series of precepts . . ., as is the usual practice of those who are teaching something'): see above, chapter 5, p. 48.

6 ('to follow Aristotelian method entirely') Guazzo, *Civil conversazione*, dedicatory letter to Claudio Peschiera (unnumbered).

7 ('the order and method of Aristotelian doctrine' . . . 'the charm of Platonic dialogue') *Civil conversazione*, letter to the author from Gabriello Frascati

(unnumbered). Note, however, that neither the *Civil conversazione*, nor the dialogues in Guazzo's later volume of *Dialoghi piacevoli* (Venice, 1586), are, strictly speaking, 'ordered', in the sense outlined in this and the following chapter.

8 Bacon, *The Advancement of Learning*, II xvii 11–12.

9 *Cortegiano*, IV, esp. chapters iv–x (pp. 449–58) and lxvii (p. 507–10), where the courtier's new role is defined as that of 'institutor del principe.' For the critical debate on this much discussed transition, see the bibliography cited above, in chapter 5, n. 54.

10 *Cortegiano*, IV viii, p. 456: 'se ad alcuni de' nostri principi venisse innanti un severo filosofo . . ., il qual apertamente e senza arte alcuna volesse mostrar loro quella orrida faccia della vera virtù . . . son certo che al primo aspetto lo aborririano come un aspide, o veramente se ne fariano beffe come di cosa vilissima' ('if one of our modern day princes were to be approached by a stern philosopher, wanting to reveal the awful face of true virtue to him openly and quite without art, I am quite certain that he would shrink from the sight of him as from a snake, or perhaps jeer at him, as something despicable'). See also IV vii (pp. 453–4), on the depravity of modern princes; and IV xlvii (p. 509) for the cautionary tale of Callisthenes, who came to an untimely end at the court of Alexander the Great, 'per voler esser puro filosofo e [. . .] austero ministro della nuda verità, senza mescolarvi la cortegiania' ('because [unlike Aristotle, to whom he is being contrasted], he wanted to be a pure philosopher, an austere minister to the naked truth, without any admixture of courtly manners').

11 *Cortegiano*, IV x (p. 457). Little practical advice is given on the way in which the courtier should go about framing his guidance to the prince, but one important indication (IV ix, p. 457) is that the courtier should concentrate on offering incitements to virtue, in the form of examples of 'celebrati capitani' and 'omini eccellenti'.

12 *Cortegiano*, III i (p. 336), for the identity of Castiglione's projected audience; IV x (p. 458), for his comparison of the courtier's gentle presentation of harsh truths to a doctor's sweetening of sick children's medicine-cups with 'some sweet liquor'. The image, very frequent in the Renaissance, originated in Lucretius (*De rerum natura*, I 936–50).

13 Sidney, *An Apology for Poetry*, p. 109: 'the philosopher teacheth, but he teacheth obscurely, so as the learned only can understand him; that is to say, he teacheth them that are already taught. But the poet is food for the tenderest stomachs . . .'; also p. 113: 'The philosopher showeth the way . . . But this is to no man, but will read him, and read him with attentive studious painfulness.'

14 This is the case, for example, with the discussion of language, in Book I, which arises when Lodovico da Canossa, attempting to exemplify 'affectation', chooses as one of his examples the use of ancient Tuscan words (*Cortegiano*, I xxviii, p. 129). Federico Fregoso objects to this, and the two men wrangle on this point for a while until a group of their listeners persuade Canossa to undertake a more formal treatment of the subject (I xxxi–xxxii, pp. 134–6). The same pattern may be observed, on a rather grander scale, in the discussion of women, in Book III: the subject of women's moral and intellectual equality with men arises half-jokingly out of a discussion of practical jokes, in Book II

xc–xci, p. 321–2; and it is only in the following book that the root questions begin to be discussed.

15 The most striking example is, perhaps, that at *Cortegiano*, I xxiv–vi, pp. 120–5, where Canossa's crucial definition of *sprezzatura* (cited above, chapter 4, n. 47) arises out of Cesare Gonzaga's request for a clarification of a concept which has been recurring, unexplained, through the Count's exposition, of a 'grace' or 'gracefulness' (*grazia*) which appears to be acquired, rather than innate.

16 *Cortegiano*, I xxviii–xxxix (pp. 129–53). On the background to the dispute, see above, chapter 5, n. 17.

17 *Cortegiano*, I xxxviii, pp. 151–2.

18 *Cortegiano*, I xxxix, pp. 152–3. The episode of Emilia's 'censorship' is protracted: the participants attempt to continue the dispute – with Fregoso forgetting his manners so far as to rise to his feet – and she is forced to intervene a second time, at the end of I xxxix.

19 See, for example, *Cortegiano*, III xii (p. 352) and III xviii (p. 359), where Giuliano expresses his reservations about entering into the discussion of 'queste suttilità'; also III xv (p. 356), where Gaspare gives a characteristically misogynistic twist to the same scruple: 'Io non vorrei . . . che noi entrassimo in tali suttilità, perché queste donne non c'intenderanno' ('I would prefer not to enter into such technical matters, because these women will not be able to follow us').

20 ('leave all this talk about "matter" and "form" and "the masculine" and "the feminine" and talk in a comprehensible manner') *Cortegiano*, III xvii (p. 358). The passage is discussed, in another context, in chapter 4, p. 45; see also Luisa Mulas, 'Funzione degli esempi: funzione del Cortegiano', in Carlo Ossola (ed.), *La corte e il Cortegiano. Vol. I. La scena del testo* (Rome, 1980), esp. p. 101.

21 For contemporary consciousness of the indecorousness of one speaker dominating a discussion, see above, chapter 4, p. 41.

22 For the phrase 'gran pelago' ('great ocean'), see *Cortegiano*, I xxxviii, p. 151.

23 On the 'anti-humanism' of Accademia degli Infiammati and its influence on the culture of the later Cinquecento, see the two fundamental articles by Francesco Bruni, 'Sperone Speroni e l'Accademia degli Infiammati', already quoted, and 'Ideologia e pubblico della cultura anitiumanistica', in *Sistemi critici e strutture narrative (ricerche sulla cultura fiorentina del Rinascimento)* (Naples, 1967), pp. 11–42; but also, for a useful reconsideration of the Accademia's relation to humanism, Maria Rosa Davi, 'Filosofia e retorica nell'opera di Sperone Speroni', *Filologia veneta. Lingua, letteratura, tradizione*, vol. 2: *Sperone Speroni*: (1989), esp. p. 109. For more details on the activity of the Academy, see Daniele, 'Sperone Speroni' and R. S. Samuels, 'Benedetto Varchi, the *Accademia degli Infiammati*, and the Origins of the Italian Academic Movement', *Renaissance Quarterly*, vol. 29 (1976), pp. 599–634.

24 The concept of 're-feudalization' originated in economic history and has been widely adopted by cultural historians: see Girardi, 'Elegans imitatio et erudita', p. 324, n. 9 for an account of the use of the term. For general statements on the effects of 're-feudalization' on Italian cultural life and on the status of the intellectual, see Gaeta, 'Dal comune alla corte rinascimentale', esp. pp. 241–55, Rosa, 'Chiesa e stati regionali nell'età dell'assolutismo', esp.

pp. 266–7, and Battistina and Raimondi, 'Retoriche e poetiche dominanti', pp. 77–8. On the more specific subject of the rejection, during this period, of the humanistic ideal of rhetoric, see – apart from the works by Francesco Bruni cited in the previous note – Sozzi, 'Retorica e umanesimo' and Mazzacurati, *Il Rinascimento dei moderni*, esp. pp. 237–57.

25 I use the term 'dialectic' to refer to the humanistic logic popularized in the sixteenth century in the textbooks of writers like Agricola and Sturm. One distinguishing characteristic of this dialectic is its closeness to the rhetorical tradition, and it would be misleading to propose any absolute and watertight distinction between dialectical and rhetorical argumentation in this period. Some kind of distinction between the two is, however, detectable in contemporary usage (see, for example, the passage from Tasso's *Discorso dell'arte del dialogo*, cited in the following note), and it appears justified to distinguish, within the repertory of argumentational strategies available to the sixteenth-century writer of dialogues, a 'rhetorical' procedure, inspired by Cicero and characterized by the use of *oratorio continuens* and argument *in utramque partem*, and a more technical, 'dialectical' procedure, based on Plato's method in his dialogues. For a useful overview of developments in the arts of discourse in this period, see Lisa Jardine, 'Humanistic logic', in Quentin Skinner and Charles B. Schmitt (eds.), *The Cambridge History of Renaissance Philosophy* (Cambridge, 1988), pp. 173–98; (though see also John Monfasani 'Lorenzo Valla and Rudolph Agricola', *Journal of the History of Philosophy*, vol. 28 (1990), pp. 181–200); also, for more detail, Vasoli, *La dialettica e la retorica dell'umanesimo* and Walter J. Ong, *Ramus, Method and the Decay of Dialogue* (Cambridge, Mass., 1958). For a brief but thought-provoking attempt to relate the Agricolan dialectic tradition to the study of the structure and argumentation of Renaissance dialogues, see Armstrong, 'The Dialectical Road to Truth: the Dialogue'.

26 *Discorso dell'arte del dialogo*, p. 129: 'Cicerone . . . volle forse assomigliarsi a Platone; nondimeno nelle quistioni e nelle dispute alcuna volta è più simile a gli oratori ch'a' dialettici' ('Cicero perhaps wanted to write like Plato; however, [his treatment of] discussions and disputations, is sometimes more reminiscent of an orator than a dialectician'). See also p. 131, for a criticism of Cicero's 'oratorical' (and, by implication, somewhat Asiatic) style in his dialogues; and, more generally, pp. 125–7, on the primacy of dialectic in dialogue.

27 Bruni, 'Ideologia e pubblico della cultura antiumanistica', p. 27.

28 Perelman and Obrechts-Tyteca, *The New Rhetoric: A Treatise on Argumentation* (Notre-Dame and London, 1969), pp. 193–5, esp. 194, on the way in which 'quasi-logical' arguments depend, for their effect, on their exploitation of 'the prestige of rigorous thought'.

29 For descriptions of the political, social and cultural life of Alfonso d'Este's court, see Solerti, *Ferrara e la corte estense*, and, more recently, Alain Godard, 'La première représentation de l'*Aminta*: la cour de Ferrare et son double', in André Rochon (ed.), *Ville et campagne dans la littérature italienne de la Renaissance. Vol. II. Le courtisan travesti* (Paris, 1977), esp. pp. 187–208; Giovanni Da Pozzo, *L'ambigua armonia. Studio sull''Aminta' del Tasso* (Florence, 1983), pp. 13–75. Also useful, though focused on an earlier period, is

Guy Lebatteux, 'Idéologie monarchique et propagande dynastique dans l'œuvre de Giambattista Giraldi Cinthio', in André Rochon (ed.), *Les écrivains et le pouvoir en Itali à l'époque de la Renaissance (deuxième série)* (Paris, 1974), pp. 243–342.

30 On Tasso's brief residence at the court of Urbino, from 1557–9 see Angelo Solerti, *Vita di Torquato Tasso* (Turin, 1895), vol. I, pp. 23–37. On Romei's presence there, see Solerti, *Ferrara e la corte estense*, p. xxv and Francesco Erspamer, *La biblioteca di don Ferrante. Duello e onore nella cultura del Cinquecento* (Rome, 1982), p. 104.

31 ('those things which generally occupy the conversations of well-bred ladies and gentlemen in the courts') dedication to Lucrezia d'Este, Duchess of Urbino, in Annibale Romei, *Discorsi*, in appendix to Solerti, *Ferraro e la corte estense*, p. 3. All subsequent references to the *Discorsi*, unless otherwise stated, will be to this edition. A recent reading of the *Discorsi* is Werner Gundersheimer, 'Burle, generi e potere: i *Discorsi* di Annibale Romei', *Schifanoia*, vol. 2 (1986), pp. 9–21. On Romei's considerable debt to Castiglione, where both the form and substance of his argument are concerned, see Danilo Aguzzi Barbagli, 'La difesa di valori etici nella trattatistica sulla nobiltà del secondo Cinquecento', *Rinascimento*, vol. 29 (1989), p. 414, and n. 181.

32 See Tasso, *Lettere*, vol. II, p. 208, for a letter of 27 June 1584, to Curzio Ardizio, in which Tasso speaks of his gratitude to Guidobaldo II, and his desire to return his compliments by writing something in his honour: 'E volentieri il farei co 'l formar un Cortegiano, s'egli già non fosse stato così ben formato, che presunzion sarebbe la mia s'io volessi ritrattar cosa ben trattata. Non mancherebbon nondimeno altri soggetti di ragionamento, perioché molti ne furono fatti veramente; ed a tutti, o a la maggior parte di loro, si trovò presente il signor conte Camillo, così degno del padre, com'alcun altro figliuolo d'onorato padre nascesse giamai.' ('And I would willingly do this by constructing a perfect courtier, if it were not for the fact that it has already been done so well that it would be presumptuous of me to attempt to go over the same ground again. However, there would be no lack of other subjects for a dialogue, because many discussions did in fact take place; and at all of them, or the majority of them, Count Camillo [Castiglione] was present: a man as worthy of his father, as any son ever was.') On Camillo Castiglione (1517–98) – at the time of Tasso's writing, a trusted courtier of the Duke of Mantua and a man worth cultivating in his own right – see G. De Caro's entry in the *Dizionario biografico degli italiani*, vol. XXII, pp. 75–6.

33 Tasso's dialogues were written as occasional works, over a period of some fifteen years (1579–94), but the existence of a project, on the author's part, to publish them together as a volume of his proposed collected works seems to justify viewing them together, as a collection: see Raimondi's introduction to his edition of the *Dialoghi* (Florence, 1958), vol. I, p. 4.

34 A recent reading of the *Dialoghi* which stresses Tasso's departures from the Castiglionesque model of courtly dialogue is Pignatti, 'I *Dialoghi* di Torquato Tasso'.

35 It cannot be proved that the form of Romei's dialogue is a deliberate homage to the *Cortegiano*, but there is evidence that Romei was aware of the existence of more 'contemporary' models of dialogue in his unpublished dialogue

Sull'anima umana (Biblioteca Ariostea, Ferrara (CL.I 482)). This work – extremely interesting, by virtue of its controversial subject – is markedly more technical than the *Discorsi* and takes a form reminiscent of the dialogues of Tasso or Francesco Patrizi: it contains only three interlocutors, Enofilo, Cintio and Teodoro, and follows Platonic models, taking first a 'tentative', then a didactic form. See also Romei's other published dialogue, the *Dialogo del Terremoto* (Ferrara, 1587), which has the same fictional interlocutors as his dialogue on the soul, but is more unvariedly didactic in form.

36 Romei, *Discorsi*, pp. 5–7.

37 Preface to J[ohn] K[epers], *The Courtiers' Academie* (London, 1598). Kepers's description is accurate: for examples of Romei's speakers' reference to Aristotle ('il Filosofo') and Plato ('il divin Filosofo') as absolute authorities for assertions not otherwise proved, see *Discorsi*, pp. 40, 50, 57, 64, 83, 90, 94–5, 96, 102, 107, etc.

38 See, for example, *Cortegiano*, II xxxix (p. 251), and II lxxi (p. 294), for anecdotes concerning, respectively, Paolo Nicola [Nicoletto] Vernia (1420–99) and Nicolò Leonico Tomeo (1456–1531), both Aristotelians and both, in their time, professors at the *Studio* of Padova. Note that, while Tomeo, consistent with his urbane *ethos* in life, makes a flattering appearance as author of a *motto*, Vernia – long dead, of course, at the time of composition – is presented as a warning example of uncouthness and vanity.

39 Tassoni and Gualengo were both prominent members of the Ferrarese nobility, who held important offices at court: see Solerti, *Ferrara e la corte estense*, pp. lxv and lxviii and Godard, 'La première représentation de l'*Aminta*', p. 207, n. 83. On Patrizi's employment at the Ferrarese Studio, from 1577/8 to 1591/2, see Lina Bolzoni, *L'universo dei poemi possibili. Studi su Francesco Patrizi da Cherso* (Rome, 1983), pp. 173–83.

40 See *Cortegiano*, I xii, p. 100, where Federico Fregoso, in his suggestion of the 'game' of defining the perfect courtier, stipulates that 'in quelle cose che non pareranno convenienti sia licito a ciascun contradire, come nelle scole de' filosofi a chi tien conclusioni' ('[when the main speaker says] things which do not seem right, anyone who wishes to should have the right to contradict him, just like in schools of philosophy, when someone is defending a thesis'); also I xii (p. 101), where Emilia Pio underlines the importance of the right to contradict; I xv (p. 106), where Gaspare Pallavicino becomes the first to exercise this right and I xxiii (pp. 119–20), where Cesare Gonzaga negotiates the right for the audience to ask questions as well as intervening to contradict, referring explicitly to the 'libertà ch'io ho di parlare' ('my freedom to speak').

41 See above, p. 87; also chapter 4, p. 45.

42 *Discorsi*, p. 28 and p. 57. Tarquinia Molza, daughter of the Modenese poet Francesco Maria, and a frequent visitor to the Este court, was, of course, famed for her learning: besides Romei's *Discorsi*, she figures in Tasso's dialogue, *La Molza overo de l'amore* (1585), and, most significantly, in Francesco Patrizi's *L'amorosa filosofia* (1577), where she takes the role of Diotima to Patrizi's Socrates. For further evidence of an interest in philosophy among the women of the Este court, see the introduction to the first edition of Romei's *Discorsi* (*Discorsi*, p. 7, n. 1), which mentions the pleasure the Duke's cousin, Marfisa d'Este, took in discussing 'li alti concetti di filosofia' with Antonio

Montecatini; also Solerti, *Vito di Torquato Tasso*, p. 129, note 3 and p. 130, on women's participation in public philosophical disputes in the academies of Ferrara and Mantua.

43 *Discorsi*, p. 87. Compare the similar incident in Tasso's *Gonzaga overo del giuoco* (1581–22), pp. 486–7, where Margherita Bentivoglio asks the meaning of the terms 'per sé' and 'per accidente'. In both instances, the presence of a female interlocutor is a pretext for explaining technical terminology for the benefit of readers without a formal philosophical training. In Tasso, as in Romei, however, in strong contrast with the passage in *Cortegiano*, III xxxviii, discussed above, p. 87, the listener – and by implication the reader – is presumed to have at least an informed interest in philosophy. In the *Gonzaga*, it is even suggested that Margherita is merely feigning ignorance to test her interlocutor's expository skills.

44 See *Discorsi*, p. 23, where Battista Guarini is complimented for having spoken 'molto sottilmente e dottamente'; p. 259 for Patrizi's taxonomy of forms of argumentation.

45 The term occurs in the preface to Romei's *Dialogo del Terremoto*, in an interesting passage expressing his hope that the work – far more technical than the *Discorsi*, of course – will be of interest not merely to 'idioti' and 'semidotti', but to 'i dotti' as well.

46 On Giraldi Cinzio's choice of an academic career as 'la voie la plus sûre pour s'approcher au pouvoir', and, more generally, on the peculiarly close relations between Court and Studio in Ferrara, see Lebatteux, 'Idéologie monarchique', pp. 249–53. On Antonio Montecatini, professor of philosophy at the Studio and, from 1574, Ducal Secretary, see Solerti, *Ferrara e la corte estense*, pp. lxxii–iii. See also, for the social status of university employment, Romei, *Discorsi*, pp. 200–1, where it is agreed that a paid academic post is a decorous employment for a man of noble birth.

47 A subsequent performance of fifty theses on love, by Tasso, was given as a carnival entertainment and attended by the Duke and his whole court, wearing masks: see Solerti, *Vita di Torquato Tasso*, vol. I, pp. 127–31. On Montecatini's precedent, see Solerti, *Vita*, p. 129, n. 1 and *Ferrara e la corte estense*, pp. lxxii–iii; also p. lxxii, on the previous tradition of informal extra-mural teaching established by his predecessor as Ducal Secretary, Giambattista Pigna.

48 The second term of this equation is taken from Tasso's *Il Forno overo de la nobilità* (1585–7 version), in *Dialoghi*, vol. II, p. 13, where the philosopher Antonio Bucci talks of 'quello onore che i valorosi cavalieri sogliono apportare a' maestri' ('that honour which worthy knights bring to their teachers').

49 See *Il Forno overo de la nobilità* (1580), in *Dialoghi*, vol. III, p. 8: [Antonio Forni] 'Voi mi fate violenza e mi rapite quasi a forza dalla corte all'Academia, ov'io non entrai giamai. Piacciavi dunque come cortegiano con cortegiano o pur come filosofo con cortegiano di favellare.' ('This is an assault – you are trying to kidnap me from the court and carry me off to the Academy, where I have never been before. Do me the kindness of speaking to me as one courtier to another, or at least as a philosopher speaking to a courtier.') See also pp. 25–6 of the same dialogue, where Forni teases Bucci about his sect's fetishistic regard for Aristotle and p. 40, for another, more general, attack on

'authority'. On the *ethos* of the 'Cortigiano' in Speroni's *Dialogo delle lingue*, whom Forni in some ways resembles, see Mazzacurati, *Il Rinascimento dei moderni*, pp. 215 and 267–75.

50 See Baldassari, 'L'arte del dialogo in Torquato Tasso', pp. 29 and 42.

51 *Il Forno* (1587), p. 22: [Bucci] 'molti stimano che 'l ragionar de la nobilità sia ufficio de [sic] cortigiano più tosto che di filosofo.' [Forni] 'Peraventura può esser ufficio di cortigiano non men che di filosofo, ove tale sia il cortigiano quale da alcuni è formato . . .' ([Bucci] 'many people think that to discourse on nobility is a task for the courtier, rather than the philosopher.' [Forni] 'It may indeed be the task of the courtier as much as the philosopher – when the courtier is such a man as certain writers have described him as . . .') That Forni's sarcasm is directed at Castiglione there can be little doubt: besides the verbal echo of Castiglione's description of his aim in the *Cortegiano* as to 'formare con parole un perfetto cortegiano' (*Cortegiano*, I xii, p. 100), such a criticism would be consistent with Tasso's reservations about the idealism of Castiglione's treatise, as expressed elsewhere in his work (see my 'Rhetoric and Politics in Tasso's *Nifo*', pp. 40 and 51–2). It is interesting to compare Forni's docility in this passage with the combative attitude he adopts, in a similar situation, in the first version of the dialogue: see *Il Forno* (1580), pp. 22–4, especially the following outburst at p. 22: [A. F.] 'se voi negate che ne' bambini possa esser nobilità, negate quello che tutti confessano, o parlate in un vostro modo ch'io per me non intendo, né curo d'intendere; perché, se ben io vorrei sillogizzare come filosofo, mi giova nondimeno favellar come favellano gli uomini civili.' ('if you deny that children can be noble, then you are denying something which everyone else holds to be true. Either that, or you are speaking in some manner of your own, which, for my part, I neither understand nor wish to understand, for, even if I would like to be able to talk in syllogisms like a philosopher, in reality, I have to speak in the manner of a normal citizen.')

52 On Ruscelli's career as an editor and *poligrafo*, see Di Filippo Bareggi, *Il mestiere di scrivere*, pp. 78–80 and Amedeo Quondam, *Petrarchismo mediato; per una critica della forma 'antologia'. Livelli d'uso nel sistema linguistico del petrarchismo* (Rome, 1974), pp. 221, 227–8 and 230–1. On his *ethos* in the *Minturno*, see my 'Rhetoric and Politics in Tasso's *Nifo*', pp. 47–8.

53 See esp. *Il Gonzaga secondo overo del giuoco*, in *Dialoghi*, vol. II, p. 454, where Giulio Cesare Gonzaga's informal education, accumulated in the course of 'domestici ragionamenti', is contrasted with Annibale Pocaterra's formal academic training. For examples of Gonzaga's adept use of Socratic questioning in the dialogue, see pp. 462–4 and 469–70.

54 See *Il Principe* (Venice, 1561), pp. 59v–60r, where Pigna warns of the unsuitability for court employment of 'un infelice dottore che non si sia mai tolto de' suoi libri'. The ideal court philosopher is 'colui, che con la dottrina habbia congiunto l'uso de la Corte' ('someone who combines learning with a familiarity with court manners'): someone who possesses the *savoir-faire* to 'eleggere quelle scientie che sono le più importanti, o che più si confanno con la dispositione del Signore ch'egli serve, o che recano dilettatione maggiore delle altre' ('to select those areas of knowledge which are most important, or which are most to the taste of the Prince whom he serves, or which bring the greatest

pleasure'). On Pigna's own success in this role – he rose from humble origins to the highest honours of the court – see Solerti, *Ferrara e la corte estense*, pp. 70–2 and Godard, 'La première représentation de l'*Aminta*', esp. p. 247, n. 204.

55 *Orazione fatta nell'aprirsi dell'Accademia ferrarese* (1570), in *Prose diverse*, vol. II, p. 22: 'Questi [the 'studi' to be pursued in the Academy] tanto saranno più seguiti da coloro che 'l negozio o la milizia si prescrivono per fine, quanto hanno maggior somiglianza con lo stile cortigiano e cavalleresco; che già il nome solo di scuole o di dottori suona in non so che modo spiacevole a 'l'orecchie di molti nobili.' ('For these lectures to be popular with those who have chosen to pursue an active or military life, they must be couched in a courtly and chivalrous style; for the very name of schools and academics has something vaguely offputting about it for many noblemen.') On Tasso's awareness of the problems of accommodating school philosophy to this sort of audience, see Baldassari, *L'arte del dialogo in Torquato Tasso*, pp. 14–16.

56 Marsilio Ficino (1433–99) was, of course, a friend and courtier of Lorenzo de' Medici. Agostino Nifo (1469/70–1538) was made Count Palatine by Leo X, in 1520, and spent the last years of a highly successful career as an advisor to Ferrante Sanseverino, Prince of Salerno. He alludes frequently to his own experiences as a courtier in his eccentric and fascinating treatise on the court, *De re aulica* (1525). Simone Porzio (1496–1554) was an intimate of Cosimo I of Tuscany, who lured him from Naples to teach in the Studio of Pisa. There are brief biobibliographies of all three in Charles B. Schmitt and Quentin Skinner (eds.), *The Cambridge History of Renaissance Philosophy* (Cambridge, 1988), pp. 817, 828 and 834. On Bucci, who was attached to the court of the Duke of Savoy, see Solerti, *Vita di Torquato Tasso*, vol. I, p. 180 and p. 304. On Tasso's presentation of himself in the dialogues, see my 'Rhetoric and Politics in Tasso's *Nifo*', pp. 36–7 and pp. 96–7.

57 For the phrase 'lo stile cortigiano e cavalleresco', see the *Orazione fatta nell'aprirsi dell'Accademia ferrarese*, p. 22, cited above, no. 55. Tasso's most explicit statement on the need to accommodate one's argumentation to the audience one is addressing is found in *Il Malpiglio overo della corte*, p. 561, where the Forestiere Napoletano warns that 'chi disputa ne le corti e aspira in tutti i modi a la vittoria e con tutte le persone egualmente senza risguardo e senza considerazion di tempi e di luoghi, è più tosto vago de la gloria che desidera il dialettico, che de l'onor cercato dal cortigiano' ('those who seek victory at all costs, when debating at court, without regard for the time and the place and the people they are speaking to, show themselves to be eager for the logician's laurels, rather than the honour due to the courtier').

58 ('Courtiers might start finding it a mite irritating, if someone were to claim to know nothing and then to come out on top in every discussion, by refuting everyone else's opinion.') *Dialoghi*, vol. II, p. 561. It is possible that Tasso is deliberately taking his distance here from Giambattista Giraldi Cinzio's recommendation of Socrates as a role-model for the courtier: see *L'uomo di corte*, pp. 20 and 24.

59 Tasso's preference for the Socratic method is clearly stated in the *Discorso dell'arte del dialogo*, pp. 127–9, in a passage which also provides some clue to the reasons for this preference, in its insistent – and untranslatable – play on

the different meanings of the word 'artificio': 'L'*artificio* della quale [i.e. of the dialectical manner of dialogue] consiste principalmente nella dimanda usata con molto *artificio* da Socrate ne' libri di Platone . . . Ma da questo *artificio* si dipartì M. Tullio, il quale nelle *Partizioni oratorie* pone la dimanda in bocca non di quel ch'insegna ma di colui ch'impara . . . Laonde pare che la dimanda fatta dal discepolo sia derivata da Cicerone, e l'*artificio* sia proprio de' Romani, il quale s'usò dal Possevino [Giambattista Possevino, author of a *Dialogo d' honore* (Venice, 1553)] e da altri nella dottrina peripatetica, perché forse è più facile, ma non è così lodevole . . . E nella nostra lingua, coloro c' hanno scritto dialogi, per la maggior parte hanno seguita la maniera meno *artificiosa*: nella quale quale dimanda quel che vuole imparare, non quel ch'insegna. E s'alcuno s' è dipartito da questo modo di scrivere, merita lode maggiore.' ('The real art of dialectic dialogue lies mainly in questioning, practised with great skill by Socrates in the dialogues of Plato. But then Cicero departed from this technique, and, in the *Partitiones oratoriae*, he puts the questions in the mouth of the pupil rather than the teacher . . . So it seems that [the kind of dialogue in which] the question [is] asked by the pupil derives from Cicero, and is a Roman invention. This is the form used by Possevino and other Aristotelians, perhaps because it is easier than the alternative, even though it is not so deserving of praise . . . Those who have written dialogues in Italian have, for the most part, chosen this less sophisticated manner, in which the person who does the asking is the person who wants to learn, rather than the teacher. So anyone who has departed from this manner deserves all the higher praise.') On the way in which Tasso uses the Socratic method in his dialogues, see Pignatti, 'I *Dialoghi* di Torquato Tasso', pp. 37–9 and my 'Rhetoric and Politics in Tasso's *Nifo*', esp. pp. 21–8. On the impoverished nature of Tasso's conception of Socratic maieutic – which is, in effect, reduced from a means of discovering new truths to a mere technique for the exposition of old ones – see Baldassari, 'L'arte del dialogo in Torquato Tasso', pp. 39–40.

60 *Il Forno* (1580), p. 10.

61 *Il Gonzaga secondo*, p. 462. On the increasing importance accorded to the process of definition in dialogues in the second half of the sixteenth century, see below, chapter 9, pp. 99–100.

62 *La Molza overo de l'amore* (1585), in *Dialoghi*, vol. II, p. 746: 'Userò un artificio . . . che sogliono usare in corte ne le feste, ne le quali le vecchie molte fiate sono le prime a baciarsi, mentre le giovinette s'adornano.' ('I will use a convention often seen on social occasions at court, when the older women are very often the first to greet one another, while the young girls are still getting dressed.')

63 'L'arte del dialogo in Torquato Tasso', pp. 28–36. In this otherwise admirable analysis of the 'openness' of Tasso's dialogues, Baldassari does not mention the possible influence of Speroni's theory and practice, which is surely germane to an understanding of Tasso's 'art of dialogue'. On the contacts between the two men see Luigi Firpo's introduction to Tasso. *Tre scritti politici*, pp. 26–9 and Fournel, *Les dialogues de Sperone Speroni*, pp. 182–5.

64 On Tasso's relations with Pocaterra, see Tasso, *Dialoghi*, vol. I, pp. 35–6.

65 *Due dialoghi della vergogna* (Ferrara, 1592), pp. 18–20. On the Montagnuola, see Solerti, *Ferrara e la corte estense*, pp. xiii–xiv; also p. civ, on plans to stage

the *Aminta* there and pp. clxxviii–clxxx, on its use as a setting for court masques.

66 *Due dialoghi della vergogna*, p. 21. On Alessandro Guarini (1563–1636), see A. Di Benedetto, 'Alessandro Guarini, trattatista e critico letterario', in *Tasso, minori e minimi a Ferrara* (Pisa, 1970), pp. 195–223. On Orazio Ariosto (1555–93), great-nephew of the poet, see P. Todini's entry in *Dizionario biografico degli italiani* (Rome, 1960–), vol. IV, pp. 192–3. I have not been able to discover any biographical information on the third speaker, Ercole Castello.

67 For the phrase 'sottile questionare', see *Due dialoghi della vergogna*, p. 30. The best translation for 'sottile' here might be something like 'philosophically sophisticated': see above, notes 19 and 44 for instances of the use of this adjective to indicate an academic and technical register of argumentation.

68 See *Due dialoghi della vergogna*, p. 53, for an acknowledgement of Ariosto's dominant role, and pp. 33, 55 and 63 for accusations that Guarini is playing devil's advocate. On the first of these occasions (p. 33), it is established that Guarini's motive for contradicting Ariosto is not genuine disagreement, but a desire to assist in the process of educating Ercole Castello, described at p. 85 as a 'giovinetto inesperto' (see also p. 42). The term 'insegnatore del vero' is from Sforza Pallavicino's *Trattato dello stile e del dialogo*, discussed above, chapter 7, p. 80.

69 *Due dialoghi della vergogna*, p. 191. This moment of oedipal defiance is, though, it should be noted, anything but characteristic of the *Dialoghi*: Aristotle's lapse is excused on the grounds that he was following different criteria in different works, and he is referred to with great reverence throughout the dialogue as the supreme philosophical authority (see for example pp. 30, 90, 98, 191).

70 *Due dialoghi della vergogna*, pp. 192–203. Pocaterra is obviously a little uneasy about the implausibility of Orazio Ariosto's improvization of a seven-page summary of the various *persone* who can inspire shame in us, and he attempts to maintain an air of verisimilitude by having him ask for a moment to think before he embarks on his *divisione* (p. 192), and by having Castello then summarize his summary in order to fix it in his mind (pp. 199–200).

71 See, for example, *Due dialoghi della vergogna*, p. 31, where he objects that opposites must fall under the same genre, so that, for shame to be a species of 'timore', shamelessness would also have to be one. At p. 33, Ariosto describes his objections as 'dialettiche saette' ('dialectical arrows').

72 See *Due dialoghi della vergogna*, pp. 128–43, where Castello – the youngest and least authoritative of the interlocutors – delivers an oration in praise of *vergogna*, which is applauded by his listeners as a pure exercise in *eloquenza*, and which has no effect whatever on the progress of the discussion.

73 ('any opinion, whether true, or plausible, or simply believed without good reason' . . . 'to determine the truth of the matter') *Due dialoghi della vergogna*, p. 54. Dante, interestingly, as a 'poeta filosofo', seems to be excluded from this ban (p. 116).

74 *Cortegiano*, I xiii, p. 102; discussed above, chapter 5, p. 47.

75 See, for example, the first day of discussions, which ends with Patrizi suspending his judgement over the priority of form or colour as the prime constituent

of beauty (Romei, *Discorsi*, p. 32); also the last day, where a discussion of the traditional debating-point of the relative nobility of arms and letters is given a compromise solution (p. 286).

9 FROM THE OPEN DIALOGUE TO THE CLOSED BOOK

1 Bacon, *Advancement of Learning*, II xvii 1.

2 On the controversy over method in the Renaissance see Ong, *Ramus, Method and the Decay of Dialogue*, pp. 225–69 and N. W. Gilbert, *Renaissance Concepts of Method* (New York, 1960); also, for a brief overview, Jardine, 'Humanistic Logic', pp. 187–92.

3 Rather confusingly, writers of dialogue not infrequently identify these quasi-Platonic procedures as 'il metodo d'Aristotile' (see, for example, the passage from Lodovico Domenichi's *Dialogo d'amore*, cited below, n. 8). This sort of confusion is already present in the treatment of method of humanist dialecticians like Agricola and Melancthon: see Gilbert, *Renaissance Concepts of Method*, pp. 124–5.

4 As an example of Ammirato's very self-conscious attitude to method, see, for example, the following exchange in his *Il Maremonte overo de l'ingiurie* (1560), in *Opuscoli* (Florence, 1637–42), vol. III, p. 240: [Ferrante Raino] 'Ma in prima che venghiamo a favellare del rimettimento dell' ingiurie, bisogna veder che cosa sia ingiuria, appresso in quanti modi ... riceviamo l'ingiurie.' [Giuseppe Maremonte] 'Voi procedete da buon Filosofo.' ([F. R.] 'But before we go on to talk about how to repair a slight to one's honour, first we should see what a slight is, and then in how many different ways we can receive them.' [G. M.] 'You are going about things like a true philosopher.') A notable exception to the chronology sketched out here is Giangiorgio Trissino's dialogue on language, *Il Castellano* (1529), anomalous for its period in what a recent editor has called its 'ostentazione di schematicità' (Alberto Castelvecchi, introduction to Trissino, *Scritti linguistici*, p. xl; see also pp. 44–53 of the same volume, for a good example of the kind of ostentatious ordering he is referring to). Various biographical reasons have been suggested for Trissino's departure from the norms of dialogue in his age (see, for example, Floriani, *I gentiluomini letterati*, pp. 96–7 and Amadeo Quondam, introduction to Trissino, *Rime (1529)* (Vicenza, 1981), pp. 10–11), but perhaps the best way to see the *Castellano* is not as an isolated aberration, but rather as a precocious example of what would later become a significant trend.

5 ('First, one must define the subject-matter one is dealing with; then it must be divided, or distributed into its various parts; then discussed, according to the opinions held by the various different schools, or authorities') *Alcune avvertenze del tesser Dialoghi*, p. 66r. On the rather anomalous position of the *Avvertenze* in Cinquecento dialogue theory, see above, chapter 4, p. 38. In view of his insistence on the need for 'order' in the dialogue, it is interesting to note that, in the same year as the *Avvertenze* (1567), Toscanella produced a translation of Rudolf Agricola's *De inventione dialectica*, while the following year, he produced an 'ordered' edition of Cicero's *Partitiones oratoriae*. *Il dialogo della partitione oratoria di Marco Tullio Cicerone; tirato in tavole da Orazio Toscanella* (Venice, 1568).

6 Romei, *Discorsi* p. 188. The 'authorities' Romei refers this dictum to are Cicero and Plato: see *De officiis*, I ii 7, and the fundamental and much-disputed passage in the *Phaedrus*, 263a–264a.

7 See *Il Malpiglio overo de la corte*, p. 552 and contrast Castiglione's treatment of definition, discussed above, chapter 8, p. 86.

8 *Dialogo d'amore*, in *Dialoghi*, p. 29: [Ercole Rangone] 'Noi habbiamo tutto hoggi ragionato d'Amore, . . . e per anchora non si è diffinito, che cosa sia Amore, tal che se questi nostri ragionamenti . . . per avventura capitassero mai all'orecchie d'alcuno di questi Filosofi selvatichi, i quali cercano il pelo nel uovo, senza un rispetto al mondo ci leverebbe a cavallo e darebbecene parecchi delle buone [sic]: tassandoci, che noi non havessimo trattato di questa materia secondo il Methodo d'Aristotile, il quale . . . usa cominciare sempre dalla diffinitione.' ('We have been talking about love all day, and we have not yet defined what love is; so that, if these discussions of ours should ever fall into the hands of one of these fierce philosophers, who love nothing more than splitting hairs, he would haul us up and give us a good talking-to, and accuse us of not dealing with the question according to Aristotelian method, which always starts off from a definition.') Rangone's attempt to introduce a more 'ordered' argumentation fails, and the company soon turns to 'materia più dilettevole' (p. 33). On the courtly ambience of the *Dialogo d'amore* – unique in this respect among Domenichi's dialogues – see above, chapter 2, p. 19.

9 *Il Rota overo de l'imprese*, pp. 2771–2. For a distinction between 'la diffinitione esquisita, e sustantiale' appropriate in philosophy and the less rigorous variety permissible in rhetoric, see Bartolomeo Cavalcanti, *La retorica* (Pesaro, 1559), p. 127.

10 Giovio's only concession to 'order' is his statement that he will deal with the 'universals' of his subject before moving on to particular emblems (see *Dialogo delle imprese militari ed amorose* (1555), ed. Maria Luisa Doglio (Rome, 1978), p. 37). Of course, my chronology of the adoption of 'method' in the dialogue is not intended to be understood too rigidly: a good example of a self-consciously 'ordered' dialogue, dating from not much later than Giovio's *Dialogo*, is Benedetto Varchi's *Ercolano*, which was written around 1560, though first published in 1570. For Varchi's preoccupation with order, see *Ercolano*, p. 105, where he criticizes previous works on language which have not proceeded from 'i primi principi', first defining, then dividing the subject in hand; also notes 66, 68 and 70 below.

11 I have consulted the second edition, *La prima parte dell'imprese di Scipione Bargagli* (Venice, 1589). The process of definition takes no less than sixty pages (pp. 21–81); the author's own definition is at pp. 39–40. Note that Bargagli self-consciously aims at a strict definition, rejecting the looser 'rhetorical' formulations favoured by his predecessors: see p. 22 for his criticism of Ammirato's use of a metaphor in his definition of the emblem; also p. 21, where, in implicit polemic with Quintilian (*Institutio oratoria*, V x 55), he states his objection to the use of etymology in definition.

12 *Il Conte overo de l'imprese* (1594), in *Dialoghi*, vol. II, pp. 1052–61. Tasso's main departure from Aristotle (*Topics* 139b 32–8) is his greater tolerance of the use of 'parole traslate' in definition: see esp. p. 1053, where he shows that

both Aristotle and Plato used metaphors themselves in definition (a point also made in the first version of *Il Forno* (1580), pp. 27 and 107).

13 See the passage from the prefatory letter to Guazzo's dialogue, by Gabriello Frascati, cited above, chapter 8, p. 85.

14 Prefatory letter, *Ai lettori* in *Dialogo nel quale si ragiona delle qualità, diversità e proprietà de i colori* (Venice, 1565), p. 4v: 'Né [l'autore] ha serbato molto ordine, ma detto ciò secondo, che ne' veri ragionamenti alla memoria può sovenire.'

15 Giovio, *Dialogo dell'imprese*, p. 96.

16 Piccolomini, *Annotationi nel libro della Poetica d'Aristotele*, p. 33: 'Et molto meno ancora è fuora del verisimile che fra coloro che sono introdotti a ragionare uno o più ve ne siano che come principali et quasi maestri degli altri abbian in pronto le cose scientifiche, che dicono o insegnano con tutte quelle minute divisioni, diffinitioni et argomentationi, che fresco studio et maturo pensamento pare che ricerchino.' ('And still less is it implausible that, among those who are introduced as speakers, there should be one or more who, like leaders and, as it were, teachers of the others, have scientific knowledge at their fingertips, and speak or teach with all those precise divisions, definitions and arguments, which recent study and a long habit of thought appear to demand.') The passage concludes on a less convinced note, with an appeal to poetic licence: 'oltra che molti talmente dotti et risoluti nelle dottrine si trovano, ch'all'improvista parlan delle cose non men dottamente ch'a pensarvi suso, ci s'aggiugne che questa ancora è una di quelle cose che s' hanno da conceder nella poesia et nell' arte dell'imitare in questo gener dei dialoghi, si come altre se ne concedono nell' altre spetie di poesia' ('and not only is it the case that many people do exist who are so learned and so fully in possession of their learning, that they can improvise on a subject in just as erudite a manner as if they had thought it through, but it should also be added that this is another of those things which must be conceded to the art of poetic imitation in dialogue, just as other things must be conceded in other kinds of poetry'). On the context of the passage, see Girardi, *La società del dialogo*, pp. 45–54, esp. p. 53.

17 ('In a conversation like the present one, it is impossible to maintain order, with each individual speech following smoothly on from the last, so that one finishes up with what gets called "method", in well-constructed writings. [Because] written works proceed from a single mind and a single pen, [while] conversation arises out of several different tongues and several different minds. And all the relevant notions about a given subject do not occur to these different minds at precisely the same point in time.') *Il Turamino*, pp. 94–5.

18 See above, chapter 7, p. 72.

19 *Dialogues concerning Natural Religion*, p. 143. Hume goes on to explain the dilemma faced by the 'dialogue-writer', that 'if he carries on the dispute in the natural spirit of good company, by throwing in a variety of topics and preserving a proper balance between the speakers: he often loses so much time in preparations and transitions that the reader will scarcely think himself compensated, by all the graces of dialogue, for the order, precision and brevity which are sacrificed to them'.

20 See Ong, *Orality and Literacy*, pp. 80 and 105.

21 On the 'residual orality' of chirographic and early print culture, see Walter J. Ong, *The Presence of the Word. Some Prolegomena for Cultural and Religious History* (New Haven and London, 1967), pp. 54–63, esp. pp. 61–2. For a more detailed study of its manifestations in a particular area, that of prose style, see Ong's *Rhetoric, Romance and Technology. Studies in the Interaction of Expression and Culture* (Ithaca and London, 1971), pp. 23–47. On the reflections of this residual orality in the humanist dialogue, see Peter Burke, 'The Renaissance Dialogue', *Renaissance Studies*, vol. 3, no. 1 (1989), p. 7.

22 On the oral roots of rhetorical culture, see Ong, *Orality and Literacy*, pp. 108–9. Scholastic logic is described as 'written' only in relation to humanist rhetoric, of course: as Ong has argued (*The Presence of the Word*, pp. 58–60), compared with modern formal logic, it still bears very clearly the marks of 'oral' habits of mind.

23 Sidney, *Apology for Poetry*, p. 113: '[The poet] beginneth not with obscure definitions, which must blur the margent with definitions and load the memory with doubtfulness; but he cometh to you with a tale . . . which holdeth children from play and old men from the chimney-corner.'

24 See the passage in *Cortegiano*, III xvii, p. 358, discussed above, chapter 4, p. 45 and chapter 8, p. 90. Emilia's protest there ushers in a long series of *exempla* of female virtue (*Cortegiano*, III xxii–lii, pp. 366–414), solicited from Giuliano de' Medici and Cesare Gonzaga by their female listeners. For an analysis of the role of *exempla* in the argumentation of the *Cortegiano*, see Mulas, 'Funzione degli esempi: funzione del *Cortegiano*'.

25 On analogy, metaphor and *exemplum* as associated modes of argumentation, see Perelman and Obrechts-Tyteca, *The New Rhetoric*, p. 399; also p. 393 on the intrinsic 'instability' of such modes. On the use made of these forms of argumentation by Tasso, in his dialogues, see my 'Rhetoric and Politics in Tasso's *Nifo*', pp. 15–21.

26 ('Examples are always equally willing to prove two quite opposite points.') *Il Maremonte overo de l' ingiurie*, p. 266; also Scipione Bargagli, *La prima parte delle Imprese*, p. 21 and Giambattista Guarini, *Il Segretario* (Venice, 1594), pp. 45–6, for similar accusations levelled at another notoriously imprecise technique of argumentation, argument by etymology.

27 ('All arguments which depend on analogy are limping arguments . . .; example is the most trivial argument there is') *Ercolano*, p. 141; see also p. 319: 'Gli exempli non mancano mai, ma furono trovati per manifestare le cose, non per provarle.' ('One can always find examples [by implication, for any argument, good or bad], but examples are meant to illustrate points, not to prove them in the first place.')

28 See Ong, *Ramus, Method and the Decay of Dialogue*, esp. pp. 307–18.

29 Ong, *The Presence of the Word*, pp. 54–63; *Orality and Literacy*, pp. 108–16.

30 See, for a very clear exposition of the differences between Ramus' and Descartes' logic in this respect, Wilbur Samuel Howell, *Logic and Rhetoric in England, 1500–1700* (Princeton, 1956), pp. 346–7. On Ramist logic as a precocious manifestation of the split between thought and discourse which would be realized by Descartes, see Ong, *Ramus, Method and the Decay of Dialogue*, pp. 288–92 and p. 318.

31 ('In order not to waste time, I shall initially propose the following six queries:

THE FIRST, What speaking is; THE SECOND, Whether speaking is unique to human beings; THE THIRD, Whether speaking is natural to human beings . . .') *Ercolano*, p. 28. Another, more extreme, example of the use of a numbered list in a dialogue occurs in Francesco Sansovino's tourist-guide, *Delle cose notabili che sono in Venetia* (Venice, 1561), p. 33r, where the main speaker launches into a numbered list of all the doges in Venetian history.

32 ('Speech, or exterior human communication, is nothing else than revealing the thoughts of the mind to another person through the medium of [spoken] words.') *Ercolano*, p. 28.

33 See *Ercolano*, pp. 28–30, for Varchi's explanation of his definition (and see also pp. 106–8), and, for his answers to Ercolani's doubts, pp. 109, 112, 121, 124, etc. Another dialogue which employs *maiuscoli* in a similarly disconcerting way is Scipione Bargagli's *La prima parte dell'imprese*: see esp. pp. 39–40 of the 1589 edition for the capitalization of Bargagli's definition of the emblem.

34 See, for example, p. 224 of the 1570 edition, where Ercolani refers to a passage in Castelvetro's *Poetica* 'a carte 94 di quella in quarto foglio che si stampò prima, e 144 di quella in ottavo che si stampò ultimamente' ('at page 94 of the old edition, in quarto, and page 144 of the more recent octavo edition'). For other, similar 'footnotes', see also, for example, pp. 183 and 225. Another example of this kind of typographic interference in the dialogue of the *Ercolano* is the presence of long, acknowledged citations from other works, apparently quoted from memory: see, for example, pp. 122, 130–1, 160, 316, 318, 320, 322, etc.

35 See *Ercolano*, pp. 116 and 271, and (for the table of pronouns), pp. 196–204. On the diagrammatic presentaton of dichotomies in Ramist textbooks, and its implications for the shift to a visual culture, see Ong, *Ramus, Method and the Decay of Dialogue*, pp. 199–201 and p. 311. As Elizabeth Eisenstein has stressed, there are precedents for Ong's 'Ramist' phenomena in manuscript culture and the incunabular phase of printing (*The Printing Press as an Agent of Change*, vol. I, p. 52 and p. 92, n. 54). However, since I am concerned here not with the general question of their genesis, but with the particular issue of the chronology of their introduction into the quasi-oral form of dialogue, this point does not touch on my argument here.

36 For the first, see Altobello Meloni [Ercole Bottrigari], *Il Desiderio, overo de' Concerti Musicali di varij Instrumenti*, 2nd edition (Milan, 1601), pp. 31 and 37; see also the musical notaton at pp. 20–1 and 26–8. For Lanteri's diagrams, see *Del modo di disegnare le piante delle fortezze*, pp. 9, 13, 17–19, 25, 28–9 etc.; for Galileo's, *Dialogo sui massimi sistemi*, pp. 4, 6, 15–16, 18, 20, 73, 199, 211 etc. An interesting contrast is provided by Machiavelli's *Arte della guerra* (1521) – the earliest dialogue illustrated with diagrams I have come across – which relegates the diagrams most modern editions incorporate in the text to a separate section at the back of the book, *outside* the fictional dialogue. On the innovativeness of Machiavelli's use of diagrams in this work, see J. R. Hale, 'A Humanistic Visual Aid. The Military Diagram in the Renaissance', *Renaissance Studies*, vol. 2, No. 2 (October 1988), p. 283. For other examples of dialogues which incorporate diagrams, see Memmo, *Tre libri della sostanza del mondo*, Tartaglia, *Quesiti et inventioni diverse*, Vimercato, *Dialogo della descrittione tecnica e pratica de gli horologi solari*.

37 See, for example, *Dialogo sui massimi sistemi*, p. 4: [Salviati] 'Per più facile intelligenza piglieremo carta, e penna, che già veggio qui per simili occorrenze apparecchiate, e ne faremo un poco di figura' ('To make it easier to under-stand, let's draw a few figures – I can see there's a pen and some paper here, ready, in case we needed them'); also p. 287 of the same dialogue, where Galileo attempts a naturalistic introduction of twenty-five pages of mathemati-cal calculations by having Giovan Francesco Sagredo jokingly question how Filippo Salviati has managed to produce such a volume of work overnight. For Bottrigari's mention of the clavichord, see *Il Desiderio*, p. 16. Another example of this kind of concern for verisimilitude is found in Tartaglia, *Quesiti et inventioni diverse*, pp. 38–9, where a long recital of technical details is 'dramatized' by having Tartaglia's interlocutor dictate them to him, after having sent a servant to his house to pick up the list where he has written them down.

38 On the new perception of the book as object, see Ong, *Orality and Literacy*, pp. 125–6; also pp. 130–5, on the social, psychological and literary effects of this development.

39 Ong, *Orality and Literacy*, p. 133.

40 Ong, *Orality and Literacy*, p. 135.

41 Ong, *Orality and Literacy*, pp. 43 and 134.

42 See Lombardelli, *I fonti toscani*, p. 23: 'Richiedon leggitore introdotto bene, attento, assentito e valoroso, che ne sappia cavar que' tesori che vi son quasimente affogati nel dialogo, ed in una maniera di trattarli anzi strava-gante, che no: per lo che all'improviso non vi si può ritrovar cosa che altri voglia, se non si ricorre a quella tavola che alcuni valentuomini fiorentini vi fabbricaron dattorno, perché venissero lette più volentieri.' ('They demand a reader who is well-grounded in the subject, attentive, committed and energetic: someone capable of salvaging those treasures which are almost drowned in the dialogue and in a rather eccentric manner of exposition. For it is impossible immediately to locate what one wants, in the *Prose*, unless one has recourse to the index which some Florentine gentlemen constructed for them, to make them easier to read.') Lombardelli is probably referring to Benedetto Varchi's edition of 1548, which contains a very thorough 47-page 'tavola', also used by subsequent Venetian editors. On the *index locorum* as a symptom of the visual culture ushered in by typography, see Ong, *Ramus, Method and the Decay of Dialogue*, p. 313 and *Orality and Literacy*, pp. 123–6. A further, and even more ambitious, attempt to transform Bembo's *Prose* into a more user-friendly form, is Marcantonio Flaminio's *Le prose di Monsignor Bembo ridotte a metodo* (Naples, 1569), on which see P. Sabbatino, *Il modello bembiano a Napoli nel Cinquecento* (Naples, 1986), pp. 125–71.

43 The last, and most lavish of Dolce's editions of the *Cortegiano* was published posthumously by Domenico Farri (Venice, 1574). For a detailed account of his interventions, see Guidi, 'Reformulations de l'idéologie aristocratique au XVIe siècle', pp. 143–51.

44 For this distinction, see Ong's discussion of the difference between early and later editions of Ramus' works, in *Orality and Literacy*, p. 311.

45 See Guidi, 'Reformulations de l'idéologie aristocratique au XVIe siècle', pp. 148–50.

46 See Ossola, *Dal 'Cortegiano' all''Uomo di mondo'*, pp. 56–8, esp. p. 57, for a comparison between the wariness with which Castiglione's speakers characteristically express their behavioural recommendations ('Qual di voi è che non rida quando . . .'; 'Ma sia il cortegiano, quando gli vien in proposito . . .'; 'Parmi che chi s'impone altra legge non sia ben sicuro di non incorrere in [quella affettazione tanto biasimata . . .]' ('Which among you does not laugh when . . .'; 'But the courtier should perhaps, if need be . . .'; 'It seems to me that whoever does not follow this rule may not be entirely safe from the deadly risk [of appearing affected]')) and Dolce's far more forthright transcriptions of these 'rules' ('Come si dee . . .'; 'Deesi fuggire . . .'; 'Donna non dee . . .' ('How one should . . .'; 'One should on no account . . .'; 'A woman should never . . .')).

47 I refer here, of course, to the passage in *Cortegiano*, I i, pp. 80–1 (discussed above, chapter 5, p. 48), in which Castiglione gives his reasons for choosing the form of a dialogue, rather than the more usual didactic form of a 'certo ordine di precetti distinti'.

48 For the genesis of the *Segretario*, see Guarini's letter to Bartolomeo Zucchi of 3 August 1594, cited in Vittorio Rossi, *Battista Guarini e il 'Pastor Fido'* (Turin, 1886), p. 111, where he states that he originally wrote a 'lettera sulle lettere', which he then 'converted' into dialogue. It seems probable that the original *Lettera* coincided more or less with the detailed treatment of epistolography identified, in two marginal notes in the second edition of the dialogue, as 'il trattato dell'arte di scriver lettere' (*Il Segretario*, 2nd edition (Venice, 1600), pp. 74 and 78. All subsequent references will be to the first edition, of 1594). Guarini wrote *Il Segretario* in temporary retirement, after leaving Alfonso d'Este's service under something of a cloud, and one of the dialogue's intended functions was undoubtedly to clear its author's name from this slur: see, for example, *Segretario*, p. 79, where it is insisted that the secretary's reputation depends entirely on the whim of his patron and that, if his prince takes against him, 'not even the finest of men could avoid seeming a poor secretary'.

49 On the use of the dialogue as an instrument of public relations, see above, chapter 4, esp. n. 61, on Guarini. On Contarini, see M. Tafuri, *Venezia e il Rinascimento: religione, scienza, architettura* (Turin, 1985), pp. 197–208. On the other speakers in the dialogue, Francesco Morosini and Sebastiano Venier, see Gaetano Cozzi, *Paolo Sarpi, tra Venezia e l'Europa* (Turin, 1979) passim; also, on Venier, Aguzzi Barbagli, 'La difesa di valori etici', pp. 422–3; and, on Morosini, Cozzi, *Il doge Nicolo Contarini. Ricerche sul patriziato veneziano agli inizi del Seicento* (Venice and Rome, 1958), p. 303 and n. 1. I have not been able to identify the fourth interlocutor, Girolamo Zeno.

50 See, for example, *Il Segretario*, p. 81, where Girolamo Zeno, on hearing an account of the secretary's relations with his patron, exclaims: 'Ringrazio Dio [. . .] che ci habbia fatti nascer in libertà da poter comandare, e non da dover servire.' ('Thank God that we were born in freedom, to rule, rather than to serve.') On Guarini's complex and fluctuating attitude to the court, see Luisa Avellini, '"Pelago" e "porto": la corte e il cortigiano nell'epistolario del Guarini', in Giuseppe Papagno and Amedeo Quondam (eds.), *La corte e lo spazio. Ferrara estense* (Rome, 1982), pp. 683–96.

51 ('as a narrator' . . . 'as a participant') *Il Segretario*, p. 6. The device of having the interlocutors 're-enact' a previous dialogue is not unique to *Il Segretario* (see, for example, Lanteri, *Del modo di disegnare le piante delle fortezze*, p. 6, or Speroni, *Dialogo del giudicio di Senofonte*, pp. 47–50): what is of interest here is the critical *use* to which Guarini puts this device.

52 ('the heat and the freedom') *Segretario*, p. 6.

53 I am quoting from John Florio's translation of the essay, *On the Art of Conferring*: see *The Essayes of Michael, Lord of Montaigne, translated into English by John Florio*, ed. D. MacCarthy (London and Toronto, 1928), vol. III, p. 158. The criterion of 'heat' in dialogue criticism seems to refer explicitly to the degree of 'contention' involved: see, for example, *Cortegiano*, I xiii, where Emilia states that, without the possibility of contradiction, 'il gioco saria freddo' ('the game [of 'forming' a perfect Courtier] would be "cold"'). Sperone Speroni, in a draft of the first part of his *Apologia dei dialoghi* in volume II of his manuscripts, in the Biblioteca Capitolare of Padua, comments that the use of the Socratic method would have given 'vita' to Cicero's strictly didactic *Partitiones oratoriae*, 'il quale è morto di freddo' ('which is dead from the cold').

54 On this function of the dialogue in Plato, see Rendall, 'Dialogue, Philosophy and Rhetoric', esp. pp. 171–2.

55 On the function of combat imagery in a dialogue like the *Cortegiano*, as a safety-valve for the aggression generated by dissent, see Rebhorn, *Courtly Performances*, pp. 138–40. On its purely decorative function in 'monological' dialogues like the *Diamerone*, see above, chapter 7, p. 83. For examples in Guarini's use of this imagery, see *Segretario*, pp. 15, 17, 24, 26–7, 37, 47 and 52–3, where Girolamo Zeno, understandably enough, exclaims: 'Non vorrei più sillaba d'arme.' ('I don't want to hear another syllable about arms.')

56 See, for example, *Segretario*, pp. 1–2, 9, 62, 78, for Contarini's reluctance to take the floor, and pp. 34–5 and p. 73 for his consultation of his companions. At p. 35, Contarini draws on Socratic obstetric imagery to define his purely ancillary role in the dialogue.

57 *Segretario*, p. 48: [Zeno] 'finalmente voi siete il nostro padre e 'l nostro maestro' ('when it comes down to it, you are our father and our teacher'). Note that Zeno produces this explicit acknowledgment of Contarini's dominance at a point of particular tension, when the speakers have divided into two camps. For a further statement of Contarini's authority and the others' unquestioned assent, see the conclusion of the controversial part of the dialogue at pp. 72–3; also the beginning of the technical discussion of epistolography (p. 78), where the pretence of equality is dropped and it is established that Contarini will do the 'deciding' and 'teaching' ('dicidere' and 'insegnare'), while the others' role becomes simply to 'ask questions, express doubts and learn' ('richiedere, dubitare e imparare').

58 For Speroni's use of the image of a tinder-box to describe the workings of the open dialogue, see the passage from the first part of his *Apologia dei dialoghi*, cited above, chapter 7, n. 16.

59 *Segretario*, p. 3: [Contarini] 'Ricorrete alla regola de' filosofi, se volete rammemorarvi, conciosia che dall'ordine voi havrete le circostanze, e queste v'additeranno le cose, e l'un per l'altro vi porgeranno i concetti.' ('You should have

recourse to the rule of the philosophers, if you want to remember the dialogue. Think of the order [or the argument] first, and that will give you the circumstances; the circumstances will lead you to the substance of what was said, and the sequence of ideas.')

60 *Segretario*, p. 4: [Zeno] 'Se non vi serve l'ordine di natura, prendete quello del caso, e cominciando da capo narrate l'occasione della contesa, e poi di mano 'n mano quel che fù detto, quel che risposto.' ('If natural order is no use to you, why not just adopt the order of chance, and, starting from the beginning, tell us how and where the dispute arose and then what was argued and what was replied, just as it happened.') For the concept of 'natural order' in humanist dialectic, see Lisa Jardine, *Francis Bacon: Discovery and the Art of Discourse* (Cambridge, 1974), pp. 33–4. An awareness of the difficulty of reconciling the two 'orders' Guarini is referring to here is apparent in Orazio Toscanella's *Alcune avvertenze del tesser Dialoghi*, p. 66r where, after advising the writer to structure his dialogue according to the exigencies of method, he notes that he should do this, '*se possibile e*' (my italics), in accordance with 'l'ordine delle circostanze, e specialmente . . . de i tempi e de i luoghi' ('the order of the circumstances, and especially time and place').

61 This narrative principle is generally tacitly assumed in those parallel episodes in earlier dialogues where a narrator is called on to recount a dialogue within the dialogue. In Pierio Valeriano's *Dialogo de la volgar lingua* (*c.* 1524), p. 55, the 'riferente', Angelo Colocci, presents the problem of narrating a dialogue purely as one of representing the *ethos* and delivery of the protagonists with sufficient *enaergia*. At the beginning of Giangiorgio Trissino's *I Ritratti* (Rome, 1524) (no page numbers), Luca Pompilio insists on the need for 'order' and 'clarity', when recounting a dialogue. But, as the context makes clear, the 'order' he is referring to is narrative, rather than argumentational: effectively, a detailed and accurate account of 'nomi', 'tempi' and 'luoghi'.

62 An interesting parallel with the opening of the *Segretario*, formally less complex but similar in function, is the 'false start' of Vitale Zuccolo's *Dialogo delle cose metereologiche* (Venice, 1590); see esp. p. 10, where Zuccolo's *princeps sermonis*, Stefano Viari, abruptly interrupts the discussion of meteorology he has casually launched into to apologize for having started out 'così inordinatamente' and to announce his intention to start again, this time from first principles. For an interesting comparison between the attitude to order implicit in Zuccolo's *Dialogo* and the far more casual attitude of an earlier scientific dialogue, Giacomo Gabriele's *Dialogo de la sphera* (1545), see Girardi, *La società del dialogo*, p. 290, n. 30 and pp. 286–7.

63 *Segretario*, p. 5. The term 'proposizione contenziosa' is Contarini's. Michele's proposed *questione* is: 'a quale delle due facoltà, o politica, o retorica, l'ufficio del Segretario subordinar si dovesse' ('which of the two disciplines of politics and rhetoric a Secretary's work belongs to').

64 ('Then all the men present started piling in with their opinions on the subject, until, just as the dispute was at its most heated and its most enjoyable, it came to an end, without any solution.') *Segretario*, p. 5.

65 See, for example, *Segretario*, p. 72, where a comparison between rhetoric and music is described as 'forse non men dilettevole, che proprio, et efficace' ('perhaps no less delightful than it is appropriate and effective'); also p. 73, for

Contarini's description of another analogy – between the Secretary's function and that of the rational soul – as the 'sugello' (the 'seal') on his argument. Note that both analogies occur *after* the 'questione' of the dialogue has been resolved.

66 For this distinction, see Perelman and Obrechts-Tyteca, *The New Rhetoric*, pp. 357–8; also Benedetto Varchi, *Ercolano*, p. 319, 'Gli esempi . . . furono trovati per manifestare le cose, non per provarle . . .' ('Examples were invented as a means of illustrating points, not proving them in the first place.') In the 1600 edition of *Il Segretario*, where *esempi* are labelled as such in the marginal notes (see pp. 72 and 74), the division between 'real' argument and illustration is even more clearly marked.

67 See, for example, *Il Segretario*, pp. 20–1, where Contarini criticizes Veniero's attempt to argue from a metaphor of Aristotle's; also p. 54, for Contarini's own, very cautious, essay in an argument by analogy.

68 See *Il Segretario*, p. 12, where Veniero quibbles that an example of Contarini's 'non giung[e] all'efficacia di quella pruova, che richiede il bisogno. . . . essendo egli molto diverso dalla materia, che noi trattiamo' ('is not as efficient a proof as is needed at this point, since it is very different from the question under discussion'); compare Benedetto Varchi's theoretical statement (*Ercolano*, p. 141) that 'tutti gli argomenti del *sicut* . . . zoppicano, perche in tutti si truova alcuna diversità' ('all arguments which depend on analogies are limping arguments, because in all of them there is some discrepancy [between the two things being compared]').

69 See above, chapter 5.

70 ('appetisers and *hors d'œuvre* of time-wasting and modest words') *Il Segretario*, p. 25. For similar episodes, see pp. 2, 9, 47, 73 etc. This censorship of 'ceremonie' is a very common feature in dialogues of the second half of the Cinquecento: see, for example, Varchi, *Ercolano*, p. 28; Meduna, *Lo Scolare*, pp. 3v–4r; Scipione Bargagli, *La Prima parte dell'imprese*, pp. 8, 21 etc.; Bernardino Tomitano, *Quattro libri della lingua thoscana* (Padua, 1570), pp. 54r–v and Ciro Spontone, *Hercole difensore d'Homero, Dialogo* (Verona, 1595), p. 5. Of course, one role of such passages is to establish an informal tone and their increased incidence in later dialogues may be explained in part as a reaction to the more ceremonial Spanish-influenced etiquette of the day. Besides this social role, however, the rejection of 'ceremony' has a *structural* function in the dialogue – that of calling attention to the integrity and unity of the argument.

71 For this terminology, see Claudio Corte, *Il Cavallerizzo*, p. 115r: 'ho voluto scrivere in Dialogo per venirmi assai più facile il mettere de gli essempi, de' discorsi, e delle digressioni' ('I chose to write in dialogue, because it would make it a great deal easier for me to include examples, discourses and digressions'). See also the passage from the dedicatory letter of Alessandro Citolini's *La tipocosmia*, cited in chapter 6, n. 23; also, for a more systematic discussion of the advantages of this looseness of structure, see Sforza Pallavicino, *Trattato dello stile e del dialogo*, pp. 362–7, especially the interesting distinction at p. 362: 'quando l'Autor di dottrina scrive in persona sua, il decoro gli vieta di traviare; aspettando i lettori di lui parole ben meditate ne l'intelletto, e gastigate poi dalla lima, co' riciderne quanto vi fusse d'ambizioso

e di straniero . . . Ma lo Scrittore del Dialogo assume la persona d'huomini che tra sé parlin familiarmente: il perché tutte le digressioni le quali non disconvengano al sermone familiare degli introdotti parlatori, non disconverranno quivi al decoro.' ('when the author of didactic works is writing *in propria persona*, it would be wrong for him to wander off the subject, since the reader is expecting words from him which have been thoroughly pre-meditated, and carefully revised, with all that is ill-founded or irrelevant pared away . . . But the writer of dialogue assumes the persona of men engaged in informal conversation, so that any digressions which would not be out of place in the speakers' conversation will not be out of place in the dialogue.')

72 *Trattato dello stile e del dialogo*, p. 348: see above, chapter 6, n. 49.

73 The clearest statement of this is Torquato Tasso's, in *Discorso dell'arte del dialogo*, p. 125: 'quale è favola nel poema, tale è nel dialogo la quistione . . . Però s'uno è la favola, uno dovrebbe esser il soggetto del quale si propongono i problemi.' ('What the plot is to a poem, the issue to be debated is to a dialogue. So, if the plot of a poem must be a single one, so too must the subject under discussion in a dialogue.') For a discussion of the passage in the context of contemporary Aristotelian thought, see Snyder, *Writing the Scene of Speaking*, pp. 158–60. For the analogy between digressions and the 'episodi' of an epic, see Tasso, *Discorso dell'arte del dialogo*, p. 30; Manso, *Trattato del dialogo*, p. 1062 and Pallavicino, *Trattato dello stile e del dialogo*, pp. 363–5; Pallavicino and Manso, in particular, stress the importance of not allowing digressions to impinge on the clear unfolding of the principal argument. Scipione Bargagli, unusually, compares a digression in his dialogue, *Il Turamino*, to the *intermezzo* of a comedy (*Il Turamino*, p. 180).

74 ('for us lovers of philosophical frugality' . . . 'limit our palates to a single food') *Segretario*, p. 52; see also Marco Mantova Benavides, *Discorsi sopra i dialoghi di M. Sperone Speroni*, p. 3, where the same image of a strict diet of 'un solo cibo' ('a sole foodstuff') is used to describe a methodical dialogue, again in implicit contrast with the traditional imagery of the dialogue as a banquet ('un convito'). In Mantova Benavides's dialogue, however, the *princeps sermonis* rejects this alternative in favour of a looser structure: 'una cosa . . . confusa e varia, propriamente da Villa' ('a jumbled thing, a hotch-potch – just right for an informal setting').

75 It is interesting to note that Sforza Pallavicino couples metaphor and example ('la similitudine di qualch'effetto della Natura o dell'Arte poco notato' or 'l'esempio di qualche istoria curiosa'), along with substantive digressions, as wanderings from the 'argomento principale' (*Trattato dello stile e del dialogo*, p. 365).

76 ('of no use whatsoever in bringing us nearer a real conclusion') *Segretario*, p. 45, referring to a digression on the history of the secretarial profession; see also pp. 88–9 for another instance of a digression being clearly labelled as such.

77 At a theoretical level, Contarini admits that it is as impossible to divide 'la parola, e 'l concetto' ('word and thought') as it is 'l'anima, e 'l corpo' ('body and soul') (*Segretario*, p. 51). In practice, however, as it emerges in the discussion of the Secretary's rule, *inventio, dispositio* and *elocutio* are all too separable. In fact, the conceptual content of the Secretary's writings – 'il

midollo, e la sostanza di tutto quello ch'egli ha a spiegare' ('the heart and the substance of what he is to express') – proceeds entirely from his master, 'non havendo egli altro di proprio, che lo spiegare, et dettare' ('while his only function is to explain and express it') (p. 57).

78 On the Secretary's relations with his patron, see *Il Segretario*, pp. 65–8 and 79–81. M. Guglieminetti, in the introduction to his edition of Guarini's *Opere*, pp. 59–60, suggests that Guarini's whole insistence on the secretary's slavish obedience and lack of autonomy can be explained as a bitter recantation of his earlier illusions about the role of the secretary being 'quello glorioso del cancelliere umanistico fiorentino, alla Leonardo Bruni'. Closer targets are undoubtedly Francesco Sansovino and Torquato Tasso who, in their respective treatises on the role of the secretary (*Del Segretario, Libri VII* (Venice, 1564) and *Il Segretario*, (Ferrara, 1587)), had allowed their subject a rather greater margin of creative autonomy than Guarini.

79 On the political background of the decline of the status of rhetoric in the later sixteenth century, see Sozzi, 'Retorica e umanesimo'; Mazzacurati, *Il Rinascimento dei moderni*, pp. 237–57 and Marc Fumaroli, 'Rhetoric, Politics and Society; from Italian Ciceronianism to French Classicism', in James J. Murphy (ed.), *Renaissance Eloquence. Studies in the Theory and Practice of Renaissance Rhetoric* (Berkeley, Los Angeles and London), pp. 253–73. On the acknowledged status of Venice as the last refuge of political rhetoric, see my 'Rhetoric and Politics in Tasso's *Nifo*', p. 70, n. 204. Guarini's analysis of the standing of rhetoric in absolutist regimes gains considerable depth from the presence of a Venetian political perspective: see pp. 98–9 for Contarini's spirited and outspokenly republican history of the art and p. 58 for an implied contrast between the practice of political oratory in Venice and elsewhere.

80 Ong, *Ramus, Method and the Decay of Dialogue*, p. 288.

81 See Eisenstein, *The Printing-Press as an Agent of Change*, vol. I, pp. 230–1, where she relates the form of Montaigne's *Essais* and the new sense of self they express to the new conditions of reading and habits of mind created by print.

82 *Trattato dello stile e del dialogo*, pp. 353–4 (the passage forms part of Pallavicino's defence of the dialogue against accusations of timewasting and didactic inefficiency): 'Quanto più tempo costa l'ire alla scuola, e l'udir le voci del Maestro, che se le medesime cose fossero lette nella propria sua camera dallo studiante? Quell' ascoltar il suono delle parole, quel vedere il volto e i gesti di chi le proferisce, sono tante martellate che scolpiscono . . . le immagini delle cose insegnate nell'animo de' discepoli. Simigliante efficacia è quella del Dialogo . . .' ('How much more time it takes for students to go to school and hear the voice of the teacher, than it would do for them to read the same things for themselves, in their own rooms! And yet the results show that this expense of time is well worth it. The sounds of the words, and the expression and gesture of the person speaking are like so many hammer-blows, sculpting the images of the things being taught onto the pupils' minds.')

83 *De dialogo liber*, c. 439A–B.

84 Girardi, 'Elegans imitatio et erudita', pp. 337–8.

Bibliography

I. PRIMARY WORKS

ITALIAN DIALOGUES 1500–1650

Note: An asterisk before the title of a dialogue in this section indicates that the interlocutors of the work are historically identifiable contemporary or near-contemporary figures, portrayed in a realistic setting. In equivocal cases (as, for example, when a dialogue mixes historical and fictional figures, or when a volume of collected dialogues contains both 'documentary' and fictional works), the work has been placed in the category considered most appropriate.

Amadi, Francesco. *Dialogo de la lengua italiana*, edited by Daria Perocco, *Studi e problemi di critica testuale*. Vol. 26 (1983), pp. 117–50

Ammirato, Scipione. *Il Dedalione o ver del poeta*. In Bernard Weinberg (ed.), *Trattati di poetica e retorica del Cinquecento*, 4 volumes. Bari, 1970–4. Vol. II

Il Maremonte overo de l'inguirie. In *Opuscoli*, 3 volumes. Florence, 1637–42. Vol. III

Il Rota overo de l'imprese. In Paola Barocchi (ed.), *Scritti d'arte del Cinquecento*, 3 volumes. Milan and Naples, 1971–7. Vol. III

Aretino, Pietro. *Le carte parlanti*. Venice, 1543

Ragionamento della Nanna e della Antonia. Dialogo nel quale la Nanna insegna alla Pippa. In *Sei giornate*, edited by Giovanni Aquilecchia. Bari, 1969

Ragionamento nel quale M. Pietro Aretino figura quattro suoi amici che favellano delle Corti del Mondo, e di quelle del Cielo. Novara, 1538

Barbaro, Daniele. *Dell'eloquenza, dialogo*. In Bernard Weinberg (ed.), *Trattati di poetica e retorica del Cinquecento*, 4 volumes, Bari, 1970–4. Vol. II

Bargagli, Girolamo. *Dialogo de' giuochi che nelle vegghie sanesi s'usano di fare*, edited by P. d'Incalchi Ermini. Siena, 1982

Bargagli, Scipione. *La prima parte dell'imprese di Scipione Bargagli dove, dopo l'opere così a penna, come a stampa, ch'egli ha potuto vedere di coloro che della materia dell'Imprese hanno parlato, della vera natura di quelle si ragiona*. 2nd edition. Venice, 1589

Il Turamino, ovvero del parlare e dello scrivere sanese, edited by Luca Serianni. Rome, 1976

Bembo, Pietro. *Volgarizzamento des dialogs de Guido Ubaldo Feretrio deque Elisabetha Gonzagis Urbini ducibus*, edited by M. Lutz. Geneva, 1980

Gli Asolani. *Prose della volgar lingua.* In *Prose e rime di Pietro Bembo,* edited by Carlo Dionisotti. 2nd edition. Turin, 1960

Berni, Francesco. *Dialogo contra i poeti.* In *Poesie e prose,* edited by Ezio Chiòrboli. Geneva and Florence, 1934

Betussi, Giuseppe. *Dialogo amoroso.* Venice, 1543

  Il Raverta, nel quale si ragiona d'Amore e degli effetti suoi. *La Leonora, ragionamento sopra la vera bellezza.* In Giuseppe Zonta (ed.), *Trattati d'amore del Cinquecento,* reprinted, with an introduction by Mario Pozzi. Bari, 1975

Bottazzo, Giovanni Iacopo. *Dialoghi maritimi di M. Gioan Iacopo Bottazzo, et alcune rime maritime di M. Nicolò Franco, et d'altri diversi spiriti, dell'Accademia de gli Argonauti.* Mantua, 1547

Borri, Girolamo. *Dialogo del flusso e reflusso del mare d'Aleseforo Talascopio. Con ragionamento di Telifilo Filogenio della perfettione delle donne.* Lucca, 1561

Bottrigari, Ercole. *Il Desiderio, overo de' Concerti Musicali di varij Instrumenti.* 2nd edition, Milan, 1601 (published under the name of Altobello Meloni)

Bronzini, Cristofano. *Della dignità, e nobiltà delle donne, dialogo . . . Diviso in Quattro Settimane; E ciascheduna di esse in Sei Giornate. Settimana Prima, e Giornata Quarta* [in fact, Days Four to Six]. Florence, 1625

Brucioli, Antonio. *Dialogi.* Venice, 1526

  Dialogi. 2nd edition. Venice, 1537

  Dialogi. 3rd edition. Venice, 1544–5

Bruno, Giordano. *La cena de le ceneri. De la causa, principio e uno. De l'infinito, universo e mondi. Spaccio della bestia trionfante. Cabala del Cavallo Pegaseo. De gli eroici furori.* In *Dialoghi italiani,* edited by Giovanni Gentile. 2nd edition, by Giovanni Aquilecchia. Florence, 1958

Bursati, Lucrezio. *La vittoria delle donne: nella quale in sei dialoghi si scopre la grandezza Donnesca e la bassezza Virile.* Venice, 1621

Castiglione, Baldassare. *La seconda redazione del 'Cortegiano',* edited by Ghino Ghinassi. Florence, 1968

  Il libro del Cortegiano. In *Il libro del Cortegiano con una scelta delle Opere minori,* edited by Bruno Maier. 2nd edition. Turin, 1964

Cebà, Ansaldo. *Il Gonzaga overo del poema heroico, dialogo.* Genova, 1621

Citolini, Alessandro. *La tipocosmia.* Venice, 1561

Corte, Claudio. *Il Cavallerizzo . . . nel quale si tratta della natura de' Cavalli, delle Razze, del modo di governarli, domarli e frenarli, et di tutto quello, che a Cavalli, e a buon Cavallerizzo s'appartiene.* 2nd edition. Venice, 1573

Dalla Torre, Giovanni. *Dialogo della giostra fatta in Trivigi l'anno MDXCVII, dove s'hanno diverse ingeniosi, e piacevoli Discorsi intorno alla Dechiaratione e Interpretatione delle Livree, Imprese, e Motti di ciascuno de' Cavalieri.* Treviso, 1598

Da Canal, Cristoforo. *Della Milizia marittima,* edited by Mario Nani Mocenigo. Rome, 1930

D' Aragona, Tullia. *Dialogo dell'infinità di amore.* In Giuseppe Zonta (ed.), *Trattati d'amore del Cinquecento,* reprinted, with an introduction by Mario Pozzi. Bari, 1975

Degli Oddi, Nicolò. *Dialogo di Don Nicolò degli Oddi Padovano, In difesa di Camillo Pellegrino Contra gli Academici della Crusca.* Venice, 1587

Di Forte, Angelo. *Opera nuova molto utile e piacevole, ove si contiene quattro Dialoghi*. Venice, 1532

Dolce, Lodovico. *Dialogo della institution delle donne, secondo li tre stati, che cadono nella vita humana*. Venice, 1545

*Dialogo della pittura intitolato l'Aretino, nel quale si ragiona della dignità di essa Pittura, e di tutte le parti necessarie, che a perfetto Pittore si acconvengono. Venice, 1557

Dialogo in cui si parla di che qualità si dee tor moglie e del modo che vi si ha a tenere in *Paraphrasi nella sesta satira di Giuvenale, nella quale si ragiona delle miserie de gli huomini maritati. Dialogo in cui si parla . . . Lo Epithalamio di Catullo nelle nozze di Peleo e di Theti*. Venice, 1538 [1539]

Dialogo nel quale si ragiona del modo di accrescere e conservare la memoria. Venice, 1562

Dialogo nel quale si ragiona delle qualità, diversità e proprietà de i colori. Venice, 1565

*Dialogo piacevole, nel quale M. Pietro Aretino parla in difesa d'i male avventurati mariti. Venice, 1542

Domenichi, Lodovico. **Dialoghi; cioè, d'Amore, de' Rimedi d'Amore, Dell'Amor Fraterno, Della vera Nobiltà, Dell'Imprese, Della Corte e Della Stampa*. Venice, 1562

*La nobiltà delle donne. Venice, 1549

Dondi dell'Horologio, Giuseppe. **L'inganno, dialogo*. Venice, 1562

Doni, Anton Francesco. *I Marmi*, edited by Ezio Chiòrboli. Bari, 1928

Ebreo, Leone [Jehudah Abarbanel]. *Dialoghi d'amore*, edited by Santino Caramella. Bari, 1929

Firenzuola, Agnolo. *Ragionamento. Dialogo delle bellezze delle donne*. In *Opere*, edited by Delmo Maestri. Turin, 1977

Florimonte, Galeazzo. **Ragionamenti di M. Agostino da Sessa all'illustrissimo S. Principe di Salerno sopra la filosofia morale di Aristotele*. Verona, 1554

Fonte, Moderata [Modesta da Pozzo]. *Il merito delle donne . . . ove chiaramente si scuopre quanto siano elle più degne, e più perfette de gli huomini* (1600), edited by Adriana Chemello. Venice, 1988

Franco, Niccolò. *Dialoghi piacevoli*. 2nd edition. Venice, 1541

*Dialogo . . . dove si ragiona delle Bellezze. 2nd edition. Venice, 1542

Il Petrarchista, edited by Roberto L. Bruni. Exeter, 1979

Frata et Montalbano, Marco de la. **Discorsi de' principii della nobiltà et del governo che ha da tenere il nobile, et il principe nel reggere se medesimo, la famiglia et la Republica, partiti in sei Dialoghi*. 2nd edition. Venice, 1549

Fratta, Giovanni. **Della dedicatione dei libri, con la Corettion dell'Abuso in questa materia introdotto, Dialoghi*. Venice, 1590

Gabriele, Giacomo. **Dialogo nel quale de la sphera, et degli orti et occasi de le stelle, minutamente si ragiona*. Venice, 1545

Gaci, Cosimo. **Dialogo nel quale passsati in prima alcuni ragionamenti . . . d'intorno all'eccellenza della Poesia, si parla poi delle valorose operationi di Sisto V, P. O. M. et in particolare del trasportamento dell'Obelisco del Vaticano*. Rome, 1586

Galilei, Galileo. **Dialogo dove ne i congressi di quattro giornate si discorre sopra i due massimi sistemi del mondo*. Florence, 1632

212 Bibliography

Gelli, Giambattista. *I capricci del bottaio. La Circe.* In Mario Pozzi (ed.), *Trattatisti del Cinquecento.* Milan and Naples, 1978
  Ragionamento intra M. Cosimo Bartoli e Giovan Battista Gelli sopra le difficultà del mettere in regola la nostra lingua. In *Opere,* edited by A. Corona Alesina. Naples, 1969
Giambullari, Pier Francesco. *Il Gello.* Florence, 1546
Giannotti, Donato. *Della Repubblica de' Viniziani.* In *Opere politiche,* edited by Furio Diaz. Milan, 1974
  Dialogo dei giorni che Dante consumò nel cercare 'l Inferno e 'l Purgatorio, edited by Deoclecio Redig de Campos. Florence, 1939
Giovio, Paolo. *Dialogo delle imprese militari ed amorose,* edited by Maria Luisa Doglio. Rome, 1978
Giraldi Cinzio, Giambattista. *Giudizio d'una tragedia di Canace e Macareo,* in Sperone Speroni, *Canace e Scritti in sua difesa* – Giambattista Giraldi Cinzio, *Scritti contro la Canace. Giudizio ed Epistola latina,* edited by Christina Roaf. Bologna, 1982
  Dialoghi della vita civile. In *La seconda parte de gli hecatommithi nella quale si contengono tre Dialoghi della vita civile.* Mondovi, 1565
Gonzaghi, Bonaventura. *Ragionamenti sopra i Sette peccati mortali, et sopra i Sette Salmi Penetentiali del Re David ridotti in sette Canzoni, et Parafrasticati dal medesimo.* Venice, 1567
Gottifredi, Bartolomeo. *Specchio d'amore.* In Giuseppe Zonta (ed.), *Trattati d'amore del Cinquecento,* reprinted, with an introduction by Mario Pozzi. Bari, 1975
Granucci, Niccolò. *La piacevol notte e lieto giorno, Opera morale.* Venice, 1574
Grimaldi Robio, Pelegro de. *Discorsi ne' quali si ragiona di quanto far debbono i gentilhuomini ne' servigi de' lor signori per acquistarsi la gratia loro.* 2nd edition. Venice, 1544
Gritio, Pietro. *Il Castiglione, overo dell'arme della nobiltà.* Mantua, 1586
Guarini, Giambattista. *Il Segretario, dialogo.* Venice, 1594
Guazzo, Stefano. *La civil conversazione.* 6th edition. Venice, 1579
  Dialoghi piacevoli. Venice, 1586
Guicciardini, Francesco. *Dialogo del reggimento di Firenze.* In *Opere,* edited by Emanuella Scarano Lugnani. Turin, 1970–81. Vol. I
Guicciardini, Luigi. *Del Savonarola, ovvero dialogo tra Francesco Zati e Pieradovardo Giachinotti il giorno dopo la battaglia di Gavinana,* edited by Bono Simetta. Florence, 1959
Lanteri, Giacomo. *Due dialoghi . . . del modo di disegnare le piante delle fortezze secondo Euclide e del modo di comporre i modelli e torre in disegno le piante delle città.* Venice, 1557
Lenzoni, Carlo. *In difesa della lingua fiorentina e di Dante.* In Mario Pozzi (ed.), *Discussioni linguistiche del Cinquecento.* Turin, 1988
Lionardi, Alessandro. *Due dialoghi dell' invenzione poetica.* In Bernard Weinberg (ed.), *Trattati di poetica e retorica del Cinquecento.* Bari, 1970–4. Vol. II
Luigini, Federico. *Il libro della bella donna.* In Giuseppe Zonta (ed.), *Trattati del Cinquecento sulla donna.* Bari, 1913
Machiavelli, Niccolò. *Dialogo o discorso intorno alla nostra lingua,* edited by Bartolo Tommaso Sozzi. Turin, 1976

*L'Arte della guerra. In Opere, edited by Sergio Bertelli and Franco Gaeta. Milan, 1960–5. Vol. II

Malatesta, Giuseppe. *Della nuova poesia overo delle difese del Furioso. Verona, 1589

Manso, Giambattista. *Erocallia ovvero dell'Amore e della Bellezza, dodici dialoghi, con gli argomenti a ciascun dialogo del Cavalier Marino et nel fine un Trattato del Dialogo dello stesso autore. Venice, 1628

*I Paradossi. Venice, 1608

Mantova Benavides, Marco. *Discorsi sopra i dialoghi di M. Sperone Speroni. Venice, 1561

Marcellino, Evangelista. Della vanità del mondo, dialoghi dodici ... Con un Dialogo della Povertà. Camerino, 1580

Marcellino, Marco Valerio. *Il Diamerone. Venice, 1564

Mazzarelli, Domenico. Dialogo della filosofia. Venice, 1568

Meduna, Bartolomeo. *Lo Scolare. Venice, 1588

Memmo, Giovanni Maria. *L'Oratore. Venice, 1545

*Tre libri della sostanza et forma del Mondo. Venice, 1545

*Dialogo nel quale dopo alcune filosofiche dispute, si forma un perfetto Prencipe, e una perfetta Republica, e parimente un Senatore, un Cittadino, un Soldato, e un Mercatante. Venice, 1563

Minturno, Antonio Sebastiano. *L'arte poetica, reprinted Munich, 1971

Modio, Giambattista. *Il Convito overo del Peso della Moglie. In Giuseppe Zonta (ed.), Trattati del Cinquecento sulla donna. Bari, 1913

Muzio Giustinopolitano, Girolamo. Il gentilhuomo. Venice, 1571

Nenna, Giambattista. *Il Nennio, nel quale si ragiona di nobiltà. Venice, 1542

Ochino, Bernardino. Dialogi sette. In I 'dialogi sette' e altri scritti, edited by U. Rozzo. Turin, 1985

Pallavicino, Sforza. *Del bene, libri quattro. In Opere edite e inedite. 4 volumes. Rome, 1844–5. Vol. II

Paruta, Paolo. *Della perfettione della vita politica, libri tre. Venice, 1579

Patrizi, Francesco. *Dialogo dell'honore, detto i Barignano. Venice, 1553

*Della historia, dieci dialoghi. Venice, 1560

*Della retorica, dieci dialoghi. Venice, 1562

*L'amorosa filosofia (1577), edited by John Charles Nelson. Florence, 1963

Il Delfino overo del bacio. In Lettere ed opuscoli inediti, edited by Danilo Aguzzi Barbagli. Florence, 1975

Pellegrini, Antonio. *I segni de la natura ne l'huomo. Venice, 1545

Pellegrino, Camillo. *Dialogo dell'epica poesia. In Degli Accademici della Crusca, difesa dell' 'Orlando Furioso' dell'Ariosto contra 'l Dialogo di Camillo Pellegrino. Stacciata prima. Florence, 1584

Piccolomini, Alessandro. Dialogo della bella creanza delle donne. In Giuseppe Zonta (ed.), Trattati del Cinquecento sulla donna. Bari, 1913

Pino, Paolo. Dialogo di pittura. Venice, 1548

Pocaterra, Annibale. *Due dialoghi della vergogna. Ferrara, 1592

Possevino, Giambattista. *Dialogo dell'honore. Venice, 1553

Puccinelli, Alessandro. Dialoghi sopra le cause della peste universale. Lucca, 1577

Ringhieri, Innocenzo. Dialoghi della vita, et della morte. Bologna, 1550

Romei, Annibale. Dialogo ... diviso in due giornate. Nella prima delle quali si *tratta delle cause universali del Terremoto, e di tutte le impressioni, e apparenze, che, con stupor del volgo, nell'Aria si generano. Nella seconda, del Terremoto, della Salsedine del Mare, della via Lattea, e del flusso, e reflusso del mare, s'assegnano cause particolari, diverse da Aristotele, e da qualunque Filosofo sin 'ad hora ne habbi scritto.* Ferrara, 1587

Dialogo sull'anima umana. Ms., Biblioteca Ariostea, Ferrara, Cl. 1 482

*Discorsi. In Angelo Solerti, *Ferrara e la corte estense nella seconda metà del secolo decimosesto e i Discorsi di Annibale Romei.* 2nd edition. Città di Castello, 1900

Sansovino, Francesco. *Delle cose notabili, che sono in Venetia, libri due.* Venice, 1561

Ragionamento nel quale brevemente s'insegna a' giovani la bella arte d'amore. In Giuseppe Zonta (ed.), *Trattati d'amore del Cinquecento*, reprinted, with an introduction by Mario Pozzi. Bari, 1975

Simeoni, Gabriele. *Dialogo pio e speculativo.* Lyons, 1560

Speroni Sperone. *Dialogo dell'usura.* In *Opere*, edited by Marco Forcellini and Natal dalle Laste. 5 volumes. Padua, 1740. Vol. I. Reprinted, with a foreword by Mario Pozzi, Rome, 1989

Dialogo dell'amicizia (fragment). **Dialogo sopra la fortuna. *Dialogo della vita attiva e contemplativa. *Dialogo del giudicio di Senofonte. *Dialogo primo sopra Virgilio. * Dialogo della istoria.* In *Opere*, edited by Marco Forcellini and Natal dalle Laste. 5 volumes. Padua, 1740. Vol. II

*Dialogo d'amore. *Dialogo delle lingue. *Dialogo della retorica. In Mario Pozzi (ed.), *Trattatisti del Cinquecento.* Milan and Naples, 1978

Spontone, Ciro. **Il Bottrigraro, overo del nuovo verso enneasillabo.* Verona, 1589

*Hercole difensore d'Homero. Dialogo nel quale, oltre ad alcune nobilissime materie, si tratta de' Tiranni, delle congiure contro di loro, della Magia naturale, e dell'Officio Donnesco. Verona, 1595

Tartaglia, Niccolò. **Quesiti et inventioni diverse.* In *Opere.* Venice, 1606

*Ragionamenti sopra la sua travagliata inventione. Venice, 1551

Tasso, Torquato. **Il Forno overo de la nobiltà* (1587). **Il Gonzaga secondo overo del giuoco. *Il Nifo overo del piacere onesto. *Il Malpiglio overo de la corte. *Il Malpiglio secondo overo del fuggir la moltitudine. *La Cavaletta overo de la poesia toscana. *La Molza overo de l'amore. *Il Cataneo overo de le conclusioni amorose. *Il Ficino overo de l'arte. *Il Minturno, overo della bellezza. *Il Porzio overo de le virtù. *Il Conte overo de l'imprese.* In *Dialoghi*, edited by Ezio Raimondi. 3 volumes. Florence, 1958. Vol. II

*Il Forno overo de la nobiltà (1580). **Il Gonzago overo del piacere onesto. *Il Romeo overo del giuoco.* In *Dialoghi*, edited by Ezio Raimondi. 3 volumes. Florence, 1958. Vol. III

Tolomei, Claudio. **Il Cesano de la lingua toscana.* In Mario Pozzi (ed.), *Discussioni linguistiche del Cinquecento.* Turin, 1988

*Il Polito. In Brian Richardson (ed.), *Trattati sull'ortografia del volgare (1524–6).* Exeter, 1984

Tomitano, Bernardino. **Quattro libri della lingua thoscana.* Padua, 1570

Trissino, Giangiorgio. **I Ritratti.* Rome, 1524

*Dialogo intitolato il Castellano nel quale si tratta de la lingua italiana. In Mario Pozzi (ed.), *Discussioni linguistiche del Cinquecento.* Turin, 1988

Trotto, Bernardo. *Dialoghi del matrimonio e vita vedovile. Turin, 1578

Valeriano, Pierio [Giovanni Pietro Bolzani Dalle Fosse]. *Dialogo della volgar lingua (c. 1524). In Mario Pozzi (ed.), Discussioni linguistiche del Cinquecento. Turin, 1988

Varchi, Benedetto. *L'Hercolano, dialogo di M. Benedetto Varchi. Venice, 1570

Vimercato, Giambattista. Dialogo della descrittione tecnica e pratica de gli horologi solari. Ferrara, 1565

Vito di Gozze, Niccolò. *Dialogo della bellezza, detto Antos, Secondo la mente di Platone. Venice, 1581

*Dialogo d'Amore, detto Antos, Secondo la mente di Platone. Venice, 1581

Zabata, Cristofano. Ragionamento di sei nobili fanciulle genovesi, le quali con assai bella maniera di dire, discorrono di molte cose allo stato loro appartenenti. Pavia, 1583

Zuccolo, Vitale. *Dialogo delle cose Metereologiche. Venice, 1590

OTHER PRIMARY WORKS

Aretino, Pietro. Lettere. Il primo e il secondo libro, edited by Francesco Flora. Milan, 1960

Ariosto, Lodovico. Orlando Furioso. In Tutte le opere, edited by Cesare Segre. 5 volumes. Milan, 1964–76. Vol. I

Aristotle. On Poetics, translated by I. Bywater, in The Works of Aristotle, edited by W. D. Ross. 3rd edition. Chicago, 1955. Vol. II

Topics, translated by W. A. Pichard-Cambridge, in The Works of Aristotle, edited by W. D. Ross. 3rd edition. Chicago, 1955. Vol. I

Ascham, Roger. Toxophilus. In English Works of Roger Ascham, edited by William Aldis Wright. Reprinted Cambridge, 1970

Badouin, Jean. Les morales de Torquato Tasso. Paris, 1612

Les œuvres de Lucien, de nouveau traduites en francois. Paris, 1613

Bedingfield, Thomas. The Art of Riding . . . Written at lunge in the Italian toong, by Maistre Claudio Corte, a man most excellent in this Art, Here briefelie reduced into certain English discourses. London, 1584

Bellori, Giovanni Pietro. Ai lettori. In Opere non più stampate del Signor Torquato Tasso, raccolte e publicate da Marc'Antonio Foppa, con gli argomenti del medesimo. Rome, 1666

Boccaccio, Giovanni, Decameron, edited by Vittorio Branca. Turin, 1980

Bracciolini, Poggio. De avaritia. In Eugenio Garin (ed.), Prosatori latini del Quattrocento. Milan and Naples, 1952

Bruni, Leonardo. Dialogi ad Petrum Paulum Histrum. In Eugenio Garin (ed.), Prosatori latini del Quattrocento. Milan and Naples, 1952

Bryskett, Lodovico. A Discourse of Civill Life. In Literary Works, edited by J. H. P. Pafford. Farnborough, 1972

Buchanan, George. The Art and Science of Government Among the Scots, translated by D. H. MacNeill. Glasgow, 1964

Calmeta [Vincenzo Colli]. Prose e lettere edite e inedite, edited by Cecil Grayson. Bologna, 1959

Carafa, Diomede. Della optimo cortesano, edited by G. Paparelli. Salerno, 1971

Caro, Annibale. De le lettere Familiari. Venice, 1597

Castelvetro, Lodovico. *Giunta alle prose del Bembo.* In *Correttione d'alcune cose del Dialogo delle lingue di Benedetto Varchi, et una giunta al primo libro delle Prose di M. Pietro Bembo dove si ragiona della vulgar lingua.* Basle, 1572
Poetica d'Aristotele volgarizzata e sposta, edited by W. Romani. Bari, 1978
Castiglione, Baldassare. *Le lettere,* edited by Guido La Rocca. Milan, 1978
Cavalcanti, Bartolomeo. *La Retorica.* Pesaro, 1559
Chapelain, Jean. *Lettere inedite a corrispondenti italiani,* edited by P. Ciureanu. Genoa, 1964
Cicero. *Academica.* In *De natura deorum. Academica,* translated by H. Rackham. 2nd edition. Cambridge, Mass. and London, 1951
De amicitia, in *De senectute, De amicitia, De divinatione,* translated by W. A. Falconer. Cambridge, Mass. and London, 1923
Brutus, translated by G. L. Hendrickson. 2nd edition. Cambridge, Mass. and London, 1962
De fato. In *De oratore. De fato, Paradoxa stoicorum, De partitione oratoria,* translated by H. Rackham. Cambridge, Mass. and London, 1948
De natura deorum. In *De natura deorum. Academica,* translated by H. Rackham. 2nd edition. Cambridge, Mass. and London, 1951
De officiis, translated by W. Miller. 2nd edition. Cambridge, Mass. and London, 1968
De oratore, translated by E. W. Sutton and H. Rackham. 2nd edition. Cambridge, Mass. and London, 1967–8
De Brués, Guy. *Dialogues contre les nouveaux Académiciens.* In P. P. Morphos, *The Dialogues of Guy de Brués: a Critical Edition with a Study in Renaissance Scepticism and Relativism.* Baltimore, 1953
De Nores, Giasone. *Discorso . . . intorno a que' principii, cause et accrescimenti che la comedia, la tragedia ed il poema eroico ricevono dalla philosophia morale e civile e da' governatori delle republiche.* Padova, 1587
Della Casa, Giovanni. *Galateo, ovvero de' costumi,* edited by Bruno Maier. Milan, 1971
Pseudo-Demetrius. *De elocutione,* translated by G. M. A. Grube. Toronto, 1961
De Tyard, Pontus. *Les discours philosophiques . . . Premier Solitaire. Second Solitaire. Mantice. Premier Curieux. Second Curieux. Scève, ou discours du temps.* Paris, 1587
De Valdés, Juan. *Diálogo de la lengua,* edited by C. Barbolani. Madrid, 1982
Alfabeto Christiano che insegna la vera via d'acquistare il lume dello spirito santo. Venice, 1546
Diogenes Laertius. *Life of Plato.* In *Lives of Eminent Philosophers,* translated by R. D. Hicks. 2nd edition. Cambridge, Mass. and London, 1965–6. Vol. I
Dolet, Étienne. *Dialogus de imitatione Ciceroniana adversus Desiderium Erasmum Roterodamum.* In Émile V. Telle, *L''Erasmianus sive Ciceronianus' d' Étienne Dolet.* Geneva, 1974
Doni, Antonfrancesco. *La libraria,* edited by Vanni Bramanti. Milan, 1972
Dryden, John. *Life of Lucian.* In *The Works of Lucian. Translated from the Greek by Several Eminent Hands. The first Volume with the Life of Lucian, a Discourse on his Writings and a Character of some of the present Translators, written by John Dryden Esq.,* London, 1711

Elyot, Sir Thomas. *Of the Knowledge Which Maketh a Wise Man*, edited by Edwin Johnston Howard. Oxford, Ohio, 1946

Erasmus, Desiderius. *Ciceronianus*, translated and edited by A. Gambaro. Brescia 1965

The Colloquies of Erasmus, edited by Craig R. Thompson. Chicago and London, 1965

Estienne, Henri. *Deux dialogues du Nouveau Langage François Italianizé et autrement desguizé principalement entre les Courtisans de ce temps*, edited by P. Ristelhuber. Paris, 1885

Foppa, Marcantonio. *Argomenti* to *Il Ficino overo dell'arte, Il Portio overo delle virtù, Il Minturno overo della Bellezza, Il Cataneo overo delle conclusioni, Il Malpiglio secondo overo del fuggir la moltitudine* and *Il Costantino overo della clemenza*. In *Opere non più stampate del Signor Torquato Tasso, raccolte e publicate da Marc'Antonio Foppa, con gli argomenti del medesimo*. 2 volumes. Rome, 1666

Galilei, Galileo. *Second Deposition*. In A. Favaro (ed.), *Opere*. 20 volumes. Florence, 1890–1909; reprinted, 1964–6. Vol. XIX

Giraldi Cinzio, Giambattista. *L'uomo di corte. Discorso intorno a quello che si conviene a giovane nobile e ben creato nel servire un gran principe*, edited by Walter Moretti. Modena, 1989

Guarini, Giambattista. *Opere*, edited by Marziano Guglielminetti. Turin, 1971

Guicciardini, Francesco. *Ricordi*, edited by Raffaele Spongano. Florence, 1951

Heywood, Ellis. *Il Moro*, edited by Roger L. Deakins. Cambridge, Mass., 1972

Hume, David. *Dialogues concerning Natural Religion*. In *The Natural History of Religion and Dialogues concerning Natural Religion*, edited by A. Wayne Colver and John Vladimir Price. Oxford, 1976

K[epers], J[ohn]. *The Courtiers' Academie*, London, 1598 (translation of *I Discorsi di Annibale Romei* (1585))

Landino, Cristoforo. *De vera nobilitate*, edited by Maria Teresa Liaci. Florence, 1970

Disputationes camaldulenses. In Eugenio Garin (ed.), *Prosatori latini del Quattrocento*. Milan and Naples, 1952

Lombardelli, Orazio. *I fonti toscani*. Florence, 1598

Lucian. *The Double Indictment*. In *Works*, translated by A. M. Harman, K. Kilburn and M. D. MacLeod. 2nd edition. 8 volumes. Cambridge, Mass., 1960–5. Vol. III

To One Who Said 'You're a Prometheus in Words'. In *Works*, translated by A. M. Harman, K. Kilburn and M. D. MacLeod. 2nd edition. Cambridge, Mass., 1960–5. Vol. VI

Machiavelli, Niccolò. *Il Principe. Discorsi sopra la prima deca di Tito Livio*. In *Opere*, edited by Mario Bonfantini. Milan and Naples, 1954

Lettere, edited by Franco Gaeta. Milan, 1961

Manso, Giambattista. *Vita di Torquato Tasso*. Venice, 1621

Trattato del Dialogo. In *Erocallia ovvero dell'Amore e della Bellezza, dodici dialoghi, con gli argomenti a ciascun dialogo del Cavalier Marino et nel fine un Trattato del Dialogo dello stesso autore*. Venice, 1628

Marino, Giambattista. *La galeria*, edited by Marzio Pieri, Padua, 1979

Michele, Agostino. *Discorso in cui contra l' opinione di tutti i piu illustri scrittori dell'arte poetica chiaramente si dimostra come si possono scrivere con molto lode le comedie e le tragedie in prosa.* Venice, 1592

Montaigne, Michel de. *The Essayes of Michael, Lord of Montaigne, translated into English by John Florio,* edited by D. MacCarthy. London and Toronto, 1928

More, St Thomas, *Utopia,* edited by Edward Surtz, S.J., and J. H. Hexter, in *The Complete Works of St. Thomas More.* New Haven and London, 1963–. Vol. IV

Muzio Giustinopolitano, Girolamo. *La Varchina.* In *L'Ercolano di M. Benedetto Varchi . . . Colla correzzione ad esso fatta da M. Lodovico Castelvetro; e colla Varchina di Messer Girolamo Muzio,* edited by Antonfrancesco Seghezzi. 2 volumes. Padua, 1744. Vol. II

Lettere. Florence, 1590

Nifo, Agostino. *De re aulica.* In *Opuscula moralia et politica,* edited by Gabriel Naudé, Paris, 1645. Vol. II

Pallavicino, Sforza. *Storia del Concilio di Trento ed altri scritti,* edited by Mario Scotti. Turin, 1962

Trattato dello stile e del dialogo. 3rd edition. Rome, 1662

Palissy, Bernard. *Recepte véritable par laquelle tous les hommes de la France pourront apprendre à multiplier et augmenter leurs thresors* (1563), edited by Keith Cameron. Geneva, 1988

Parabosco, Girolamo. **I Diporti.* In *Novellieri minori del Cinquecento. G. Prabosco – S. Erizzo,* edited by Giuseppe Gigli and Fausto Niccolini. Bari, 1912

Patrizi, Francesco. *Dell'ordine de' libri di Platone.* In *Lettere ed Opuscoli morali,* edited by Danilo Aguzzi Barbagli. Florence, 1975

Peletier du Mans, Jacques. *Dialogue de l'Ortografe et Prononçiation Françoese.* Poitiers, 1550

Pettie, George. *A petite Pallace of Pettie his pleasure; containing many pretie histories by him set forth in comely colours and most delightfully discoursed,* edited by I. Gollancz. London, 1908

Piccolomini, Alessandro. *Annotationi nel libro della Poetica d'Aristotele, con la traduzione del medesimo libro in lingua volgare.* Venice, 1575

Pigna, Giambattista. *Il principe.* Venice, 1561

Plato. *The Collected Dialogues, including the Letters,* edited by Edith Hamilton and Huntingdon Cairns. Princeton, 1961

Poliziano, Angelo. *Commento inedito alle selve di Stazio,* edited by Lucia Cesarini Martinelli. Florence, 1978

Shaftesbury, Anthony Ashley Cooper, 3rd Earl of. *Characteristics of Men, Manners, Opinions, Times, etc.,* edited by J. M. Robertson. London, 1900

Sidney, Sir Philip. *An Apology for Poetry,* edited by G. Shepherd. London, 1963

Sigonio, Carlo. *De dialogo liber.* In *Opera omnia,* edited by F. Argelati. 6 volumes. Milan, 1732–7. Vol. VI

Speroni, Sperone. *Apologia dei dialoghi.* In *Opere,* edited by Marco Forcellini and Natal dalle Laste. 5 volumes. Padua, 1740. Vol. I

Sommarii e frammenti di lezioni in difesa della 'Canace'. In *Opere,* edited by Marco Forcellini and Natal dalle Laste. 5 volumes. Padua, 1740. Vol. IV

Dell'arte oratoria. Della imitazione. In *Opere,* edited by Marco Forcellini and Natal dalle Laste. 5 volumes. Padua, 1740. Vol. V

Sommario per la vita sobria. Sommario contra la vita sobria. In Emilio Lippi, *Cornariana. Studi su Alvise Cornaro.* Padua, 1983

Marginal notes to Baldassare Castiglione, *Il Libro del Cortegiano* (Venice, 1547). Biblioteca Marciana, Mss. Italiani, Cl.II, N° 114, Coll. 5251

Starkey, Thomas. *A dialogue between Reginald Pole and Thomas Lupset,* edited by Kathleen M. Burton. London, 1948

Tahureau, Jacques. *Les dialogues non moins profitables que facetieux,* edited by Max Gauna. Paris, 1981

Tasso, Torquato. *Discorso dell'arte del dialogo.* In Guido Baldassari, 'Il discorso tassiano *Dell'arte del dialogo'. La rassegna della letteratura italiana.* Vol. 75, series 7, nos. 1–2 (1971), pp. 93–134

Lettere, edited by Cesare Guasti. 5 volumes. Florence, 1852–5

Riposta alla lettera di Bastiano de' Rossi, Academico della Crusca, in difesa del suo dialogo del Piacere honesto. In *Prose diverse,* edited by Cesare Guasti. 2 volumes. Florence, 1875. Vol. I

Il Segretario. Ferrara, 1587

Lettera del Signor Torquato Tasso nel quale paragona l'Italia alla Francia. In *Tre scritti politici,* edited by Luigi Firpo. Turin, 1980

Tolomei, Claudio. *De le lettere familiari. Con una breve considerazione in fine di tutto l'ordin de l'ortografia di questa opera.* Venice, 1547

Toscanella, Orazio. *Alcune avvertenze dell tesser Dialoghi.* In *Quadrivio, il quale contiene un trattato della strada, che si ha da tenere in scrivere istoria. Un Modo, che insegna a scrivere epistole latine, e volgari . . . Alcune avvertenze del tesser Dialoghi. Et alcuni Artificii delle Ode di Oratio Flacco.* Venice, 1567

Il dialogo della partitione oratoria di Marco Tullio Cicerone; tirato in tavole da Orazio Toscanella. Venice, 1568

Trissino, Giangiorgio. *Scritti linguistici,* edited by Alberto Castelvecchi. Rome, 1986

Rime (1529), edited by Amedeo Quondam. Vicenza, 1981

Valla, Lorenzo. *De vero falsoque bono,* edited by M. De Panizza Lorch. Bari, 1970

Villalón, Cristobal de, *El Scholástico* (1535–6 version), edited by M. Menéndez y Pelayo. Madrid, 1911

El Scholástico (1538–9 version), edited by R. J. A. Kerr, Madrid, 1967

Wilson, Thomas. *A Discourse on Usury,* edited by R. H. Tawney. London, 1925

II. SECONDARY WORKS

Aguzzi Barbagli, Danilo. 'La difesa di valori etici nella trattatistica sulla nobilità del secondo Cinquecento', *Rinascimento.* Vol. 29 (1989), pp. 377–427

Altieri Biagi, Maria Luisa. 'Forme della communicazione scientifica'. In Alberto Asor Rosa (ed.), *Letteratura italiana. III. Le forme del testo. II. La prosa.* Turin, 1984

Anglo, Sydney. 'The Courtier. The Renaissance and Changing Ideals'. In A. G. Dickens (ed.), *The Courts of Europe. Politics, Patronage and Royalty, 1400–1800.* London, 1977

The Courtier's Art. Systematic Immortality in the Renaissance. Swansea, 1983

Armstrong, C. J. R. 'The Dialectical Road to Truth: the Dialogue'. In Peter

Sharratt (ed.), *French Renaissance Studies 1540–1570: Humanism and the Encyclopedia.* Edinburgh, 1976

Austin, J. L. *How to Do Things with Words.* 2nd edition. Oxford, 1975

Avellini, Luisa. '"Pelago" e "porto". La corte e il cortigiano nell'epistolario del Guarini'. In Guiseppe Papagno and Amedeo Quondam (eds.), *La corte e lo spazio. Ferrara estense.* Rome, 1982

Baldassari, Guido. 'L'arte del dialogo in Torquato Tasso'. *Studi Tassiani.* Vol. 20 (1970), pp. 5–46

'Interpretazioni del Tasso. Tre momenti della dialogistica di primo Seicento'. *Studi Tassiani.* Vol. 37 (1989), pp. 65–86

Barberis, Walter. 'Uomini di corte nel Cinquecento'. In Corrado Vivanti (ed.), *Storia d'Italia. Annali. 4. Intellettuali e potere.* Turin, 1981

Barocchi, Paola (ed.), *Scritti d'arte del Cinquecento.* 3 volumes. Milan and Naples, 1971–7

Battistini, Andrea and Ezio Raimondi. 'Retoriche e poetiche dominanti'. In Alberto Asor Rosa (ed.), *Letteratura italiana. III. Le forme del testo. I. Teoria e poesia.* Turin, 1984

Biondi, Albano. 'La giustificazione della simulazione nel Cinquecento'. In Luigi Firpo and Giorgio Spini (eds.), *Eresia e riforma nell'Italia del Cinquecento. Miscellanea I.* Florence and Chicago, 1974

Bolgar, Robert Ralph. *The Classical Heritage and its Beneficiaries.* Cambridge, 1954

Bolzoni, Lina. *'L'Universo dei poemi possibili': studi su Francesco Patrizi da Cherso.* Rome, 1984

Borsellino, Nino. 'Morfologie del dialogo osceno: la *Cazzaria* dell'Arsiccio Intronato'. In Giulio Ferroni (ed.), *Il dialogo. Scambi e passaggi della parola.* Palermo, 1985

Borsetto, Luciana. 'Il *Libro del Cortegiano*; una codificazione del "re-citare", un emblema della scrittura'. In Carlo Ossola and Adriano Prosperi (eds.), *La corte e il 'Cortegiano'.* 2 volumes. Rome, 1980. Vol. I

Bragantini, Renzo. 'La novella del Cinquecento: rassegna di studi, 1960–1980'. *Lettere italiane.* Vol. 33, no. 1 (1981), pp. 77–114

Brown, Peter M. *Lionardo Salviati.* Oxford, 1974

Bruni, Francesco. 'Ideologia e pubblico della cultura antiumanistica'. In *Sistemi critici e strutture narrative (ricerche sulla cultura fiorentina del Rinascimento).* Naples, 1967

'Sperone Speroni e l'Accademia degli Infiammati'. *Filologia e letteratura.* Vol. 13, fasc. 1, no. 49 (1967), pp. 24–71

Burke, Peter. 'The Renaissance Dialogue', *Renaissance Studies.* Vol. 3, no. 1 (1989), pp. 1–12

Caesar, Michael. 'Leopardi's *Operette morali* and the Resources of Dialogue'. *Italian Studies.* Vol. 43 (1988), pp. 21–40

Cairns, Christopher. *Pietro Aretino and the Republic of Venice; Researches on Aretino and his Circle in Venice 1527–1556.* Florence, 1985

Cantimori, Delio. 'Galileo e la crisi della Controriforma'. In *Storici e storia.* Turin, 1971

Carini, Anna Maria. 'Le postille del Tasso al Trissino'. *Studi tassiani.* Vol. 7 (1957), pp. 31–73

Casadei, Alberto. 'L'esordio del canto XLVI del *Furioso*: strategia compositiva e varianti storico-culturali'. *Italianistica*. Vol. 15, no. 1 (1986), pp. 53–93

Centre Interuniversitaire de Recherche sur la Renaissance Italienne, *Le pouvoir et la plume*. Paris, 1982

Réécritures. Commentaires, parodies, variations dans la littérature italienne de la Renaissance. 2 volumes. Paris, 1983–4

Cian, Vittorio. *Un illustre nunzio pontificio. Baldessare Castiglione*. Vatican City, 1951

Clough, Cecil H. 'Francis I and the Courtiers of Castiglione's *Courtier*'. In *The Duchy of Urbino in the Renaissance*. London, 1981

'La "famiglia" del Duca Guidobaldo da Montefeltro ed il *Cortegiano*'. In Cesare Mozzarelli (ed.), *'Famiglia' del Principe e famiglia aristocratica*. Rome, 1988

Cox, Virgina. 'Rhetoric and Politics in Tasso's *Nifo*'. *Studi secenteschi*. Vol. 30 (1989), pp. 3–98

Cozzi, Gaetano. *Il doge Nicolò Contarini. Ricerche sul patriziato veneziano agli inizi del Seicento*. Venice and Rome, 1958

Paolo Sarpi, tra Venezia e l'Europa. Turin, 1979

Cozzi, Luisa. 'Il lessico scientifico nel dialogo del Rinascimento'. In Davide Bigalli and Guido Canziani (eds.), *Il dialogo filosofico nel '500 europeo. Atti del convegno internazionale di studi, Milano, 28–30 maggio, 1987*. Milan, 1990

Croce, Benedetto. 'L'arte del dialogo secondo il Tasso'. In *Poeti e scrittori del pieno e tardo Rinascimento*. 2 volumes. Bari, 1945. Vol. I

'Sulle traduzioni e imitazioni dell' *Elogio* e dei *Colloqui* di Erasmo'. In *Aneddoti di varia letteratura*, 2nd edition. Bari, 1953–4. Vol. I, pp. 411–24

Croce, Franco. *Tre momenti del barocco letterario*. Florence, 1966

Curtius, Ernst Robert. *European Literature and the Latin Middle Ages*, translated by Willard R. Trask. London, 1953

Da Pozzo, Giovanni. *L'ambigua armonia. Studio sull' 'Aminta' del Tasso*. Florence, 1983

Daniele, Antonio. 'Sperone Speroni, Bernardino Tomitano e l'Accademia degli Infiammati'. *Filologia veneta. Lingua, letteratura, tradizioni*. Vol. 2: *Sperone Speroni* (1989), pp. 1–53

Davi, Maria Rosa. 'Filosofia e retorica nell'opera di Sperone Speroni'. *Filologia veneta. Lingua, letteratura, tradizioni*. Vol. 2: *Sperone Speroni* (1989), pp. 89–112

De Caprio, Vincenzo. 'I cenacoli umanistici' in Alberto Asor Rosa (ed.), *Letteratura italiana. I. Il letterato e le istituzioni*. Turin, 1982

De Caro, G. 'Camillo Castiglione'. In *Dizionario biografico degli italiani*. Rome 1960–. Vol. XXII

Deakins, Roger L. 'The Tudor Prose Dialogue: Genre and Anti-Genre'. *Studies in English Literature 1500–1900*. Vol. 20, no. 1 (1980), pp. 5–24

Desjardins, R. 'Why Dialogues? Plato's Serious Play'. In Charles L. Griswold (ed.), *Platonic Writings, Platonic Readings*. London and New York, 1988

Di Benedetto, Arnaldo 'Alessandro Guarini, trattatista e critico letterario'. In *Tasso, minori e minimi a Ferrara*. Pisa, 1970

Di Filippo Bareggi, Claudia. *Il mestiere di scrivere: lavoro intellettuale e mercato libraio a Venezia nel Cinquecento*. Rome, 1988

Dionisotti, Carlo. *Geografia e storia della letteratura italiana.* Turin, 1967
    Machiavellerie. Turin, 1980
Drake, Stillman. *Galileo at Work; His Scientific Biography.* Chicago and London,
    1978
Eisenstein, Elizabeth L. *The Printing Press as an Agent of Change: Communi-
    cations and Cultural Transformations in Early-Modern Europe.* 2 volumes.
    Cambridge, 1979
Erspamer, Francesco. *La biblioteca di don Ferrante. Duello e onore nella cultura del
    Cinquecento.* Rome, 1982
Ferguson, Margaret W. *Trials of Desire. Renaissance Defences of Poetry.* New
    Haven and London, 1983
Ferreras, Jacqueline. *Les dialogues espagnols du XVIème siècle, ou l'expression
    littéraire d'une nouvelle conscience.* Paris, 1985
Ferroni, Giulio. 'Sprezzatura e simulazione'. In Carlo Ossola and Adriano Pros-
    peri (eds.), *La corte e il 'Cortegiano'.* 2 volumes. Rome, 1980. Vol. I
Finocchiaro, Maurice A. *Galileo and the Art of Reasoning: Rhetorical Foundations
    of Logic and Scientific Method.* Dordrecht, 1980
    The Galileo Affair. A Documentary History. Berkeley, Los Angeles and
    London, 1989
Fiorato, Adelin Charles. 'Bandello et le règne du père'. In André Rochon (ed.),
    Les écrivains et le pouvoir en Italie à l'époque de la Renaissance. 2 volumes.
    Paris, 1973–4. Vol. 2
Floriani, Piero. *I gentiluomini letterati. Studi sul dibattito culturale nel primo
    Cinquecento.* Naples, 1981
Forcellini, Marco. *La Vita di Sperone Speroni degli Alvarotti, Filosofo e Cavalier
    Padovano.* In Sperone Speroni, *Opere,* edited by Marco Forcellini and Natal
    dalle Laste. 5 volumes. Padua, 1740. Vol. V
Fournel, Jean-Louis. *Les dialogues de Sperone Speroni: libertés de la parole et
    règles de l'écriture.* Marburg, 1990
Friedrich, Hugo. *Montaigne,* translated by R. Rovini. Paris, 1968
Frye, Northrop. *Anatomy of Criticism: Four Essays.* Princeton, 1957
Fumaroli, Marc. 'Rhetoric, Politics and Society; from Italian Ciceronianism to
    French Classicism'. In James J. Murphy (ed.), *Renaissance Eloquence. Studies
    in the Theory and Practice of Renaissance Rhetoric.* Berkeley, Los Angeles
    and London, 1983
Gadamer, Hans-Georg. *Dialogue and Dialectic: Eight Hermeneutical Studies on
    Plato,* translated by P. Christopher Smith. New Haven and London, 1980
    'Reply to Nicholas P. White'. In Charles L. Griswold (ed.), *Platonic Writings,
    Platonic Readings.* London and New York, 1988, pp. 258–66
Gaeta, Franco. 'Dal comune alla corte rinascimentale'. In Alberto Asor Rosa
    (ed.), *Letteratura italiana. I. Il letterato e le istituzioni.* Turin, 1982
Garin, Eugenio. *Medioevo e Rinascimento: studi e ricerche.* Bari, 1954
Ghinassi, Ghino. 'Fasi dell'elaborazione del *Cortegiano', Studi di filologia italiana.*
    Vol. 25 (1967), pp. 159–96
Gilbert, Felix. 'Machiavelli in an Unknown Contemporary Dialogue', *Journal of
    the Warburg Institute.* Vol. 1 (1937), pp. 163–6
Gilbert, N. W. *Renaissance Concepts of Method.* New York, 1960
Gilmore, Myron P. 'Anti-Erasmianism in Italy; the Dialogue of Ortensio Lando

on Erasmus' Funeral'. *Journal of Medieval and Renaissance Studies*. Vol. 4, no. 1 (1974), pp. 1–14

'Italian Reactions to Erasmian Humanism'. In Heiko A. Oberman and Thomas A. Brady Jr (eds.), *Itinerarium Italicum. The Profile of the Italian Renaissance in its European Transformations. Dedicated to Paul Oskar Kristeller on the occasion of his 70th birthday*. Leiden, 1975

Ginzburg, Carlo. *Il formaggio e i vermi; il cosmo di un mugnaio del '500*. 2nd edition. Turin, 1977

Girardi, Raffaele. '"Elegans imitatio et erudita": Sigonio e la teoria del dialogo'. *Giornale storico della letteratura italiana*. Vol. 163, fasc. 523 (1986), pp. 321–54

La società del dialogo. Retorica e ideologia nella letteratura conviviale del Cinquecento. Bari, 1989

Godard, Alain. 'La première représentation de l'*Aminta*: la cour de Ferrare et son double'. In André Rochon (ed.), *Ville et campagne dans la littérature italienne de la Renaissance*. 2 volumes. Paris, 1976–7. Vol. II

Goffman, Erving. *Interaction Ritual*. Garden City, N.Y., 1967

Görler, W. 'From Athens to Tusculum: Gleaning the Background of Cicero's *De Oratore*'. *Rhetorica*. Vol. 6, no. 3 (1988), pp. 215–35

Gorni, Guglielmo. 'Veronica e le altre: emblemi e cifre onomatiche nelle rime di Bembo'. In *Veronica Gambara e la poesia del suo tempo nell'Italia settentrionale. Atti del Convegno (Brescia-Correggio, 17–19 ottobre 1985)*, edited by Cesare Bozzetti, Pietro Gibellini and Ennio Sandal. Florence, 1989

Greenblatt, Stephen. *Renaissance Self-Fashioning*. Chicago, 1980

Greenwood, Thomas. 'L'apologie rationelle de Guy de Bruès'. *Revue d'histoire et de philosophie religieuses*. Vol. 36 (1956), pp. 20–49

Grendler, Paul F. *Critics of the Italian World 1530–1560. Anton Francesco Doni. Nicolò Franco. Ortensio Lando*. Madison, Milwaukee and London, 1969

(with Marcia G. Grendler) 'The Survival of Erasmus in Italy'. *Erasmus in English*. Vol. 8 (1976), pp. 1–42

The Roman Inquisition and the Venetian Press, 1540–1605. Princeton, 1977

Grimal, Pierre. 'Caractères généraux du dialogue romain, de Lucilius à Cicéron'. *L'information littéraire*. Vol. 7, no. 5 (1955), pp. 192–8

Griswold, Charles L. 'Style and Philosophy: the Case of Plato's Dialogues'. *The Monist*. Vol. 63, no. 4 (1980), pp. 530–46

'Plato's Metaphilosophy: Why Plato Wrote Dialogues'. In Charles L. Griswold (ed.), *Platonic Writings, Platonic Readings*. London and New York, 1988

Gross, Alan G. *The Rhetoric of Science*. Cambridge, Mass. and London, 1990

Guidi, José. 'Baldassare Castiglione et le pouvoir politique: du gentilhomme de cour au nonce pontificiel'. In André Rochon (ed.), *Les écrivains et le pouvoir en Italie à l'époque de la Renaissance*. 2 volumes. Paris, 1973–4. Vol. I

'*Festive narrazioni, motti e burle (beffe)*: l'art des facéties dans *Le Courtisan*'. In André Rochon (ed.), *Formes et significations de la 'beffa' dans la littérature italienne de la Renaissance*. 2 volumes. Paris, 1972–5. Vol. II

'L'Espagne dans la vie et dans l'œuvre de B. Castiglione: de l'équilibre franco-hispanique au choix impérial'. In André Rochon (ed.), *Présence et infuence de l'Espagne dans la culture italienne de la Renaissance*. Paris, 1978

'Le jeu de cour et sa codification dans les différentes rédactions du

"Courtisan"'. In Centre Interuniversitaire de Recherche sur la Renaissance Italienne. *Le pouvoir et la plume. Incitation, contrôle et répression dans l'Italie du XVIème siècle.* Paris, 1982

'Reformulations de l'idéologie aristocratique au XVIe siècle: les différentes rédactions et la fortune du "Courtisan"'. In Centre Interuniversitaire de Recherche sur la Renaissance Italienne. *Réécritures. Commentaires, parodies, variations dans la littérature italienne de la Renaissance.* 2 volumes. Paris, 1988–4. Vol. I

Gundersheimer, Werner, 'Burle, generi e potere: i *Discorsi* di Annibale Romei'. *Schifanoia.* Vol. 2 (1986), pp. 9–21

Hale, J. R., 'A Humanistic Visual Aid. The Military Diagram in the Renaissance'. *Renaissance Studies.* Vol. 2, no. 2 (1988), pp. 280–98

Hall, J. *Lucian's Satire.* New York, 1981

Hathaway, Baxter. *The Age of Criticism: The Late Renaissance in Italy.* Ithaca, N.Y., 1962

Hirzel, Rudolf. *Der Dialog, ein literaturhistorischer Versuch.* Leipzig, 1895

Howell, Wilbur Samuel. *Logic and Rhetoric in England, 1500–1700.* Princeton, 1956

Innamorati, G. 'Pietro Aretino'. In *Dizionario biografico degli italiani*, Rome 1960–. Vol. IV

Jakobsen, Roman. 'Linguistics and Poetry'. In *Style and Language*, edited by T. Sebeok. Cambridge, 1960

Jardine, Lisa. *Francis Bacon; Discovery and the Art of Discourse.* Cambridge, 1974

'Humanistic logic', in Charles B. Schmitt and Quentin Skinner (eds.), *The Cambridge History of Renaissance Philosophy.* Cambridge, 1988

Javitch, Daniel. '*The Philosopher of the Court*; a French Satire Misunderstood'. *Comparative Literature.* Vol. 33, no. 2 (1971), pp. 97–124

'Rival Arts of Conduct in Elizabethan England: Guazzo's *Civile Conversation* and Castiglione's *Courtier*'. *Yearbook of Italian Studies* (1971), pp. 178–98

Poetry and Courtliness in Renaissance England. Princeton, 1978

Jordan, Mark. 'A Preface to the Study of Philosophical Genres'. *Philosophy and Rhetoric.* Vol. 14, no. 4 (1981), pp. 199–211

Kelso, Ruth. *The Doctrine of the English Gentleman in the Sixteenth Century, with a Bibliographical List of Treatises on the Gentleman and Related Subjects Published in Europe to 1625.* Urbana, 1929

Kemal Bénouis, Mustapha. *Le dialogue dans la littérature française du seizième siècle.* The Hague and Paris, 1976

Kerr, R. J. A. 'Prolegomena to an edition of Villalón's *Scholástico*'. *Bulletin of Hispanic Studies.* Vol. 32 (1955), pp. 130–9 and 203–13

Kolsky, Stephen D. 'Before the Nunciature: Castiglione in Fact and Fiction'. *Rinascimento.* Vol. 29 (1989), pp. 331–57

Kushner, Eva. 'Reflexions sur le dialogue en France au XVIe siècle'. *Revue des sciences humaines.* Fasc. 148 (1972), pp. 485–501

'Le dialogue de 1580 à 1630; articulations et fonctions'. In J. Lafond and André Stegmann (eds.), *L'Automne de la Renaissance 1580–1630.* Paris, 1981

'Le dialogue en France de 1550 à 1560'. In M. T. Jones-Davies (ed.), *Le dialogue au temps de la Renaissance.* Paris, 1984

Lang, Berel. 'Towards a Poetics of Philosophical Discourse'. *The Monist*. Vol. 63, no. 4 (1980), pp. 445–64

LaRusso, D. 'A Neo-Platonic Dialogue: *Is Rhetoric an Art?* An Introduction and a Translation'. *Speech Monographs*. Vol. 32, no. 4 (1969), pp. 398–9

Le Guern, Michel. 'Sur le genre du dialogue'. In J. Lafond and André Stegmann (eds.), *L'Automne de la Renaissance 1580–1630*. Paris, 1981

Lebatteux, Guy. 'Idéologie monarchique et propagande dynastique dans l'œuvre de Giambattista Giraldi Cinthio'. In André Rochon (ed.), *Les écrivains et le pouvoir en Italie à l'époque de la Renaissance*. 2 volumes. Paris, 1973–4. Vol. II

Levi, Albert W. 'Philosophy as Literature: the Dialogue'. *Philosophy and Rhetoric*. Vol. 9, no. 1 (1976), pp. 1–20

Levine, M. 'Cicero and the Literary Dialogue'. *The Classical Journal*. Vol. 53, no. 4 (1958), pp. 146–51

Lievsay, John L. *Stefano Guazzo and the English Renaissance (1575–1675)*. Chapel Hill, 1961

Loi, Maria Rosa and Mario Pozzi. 'Le lettere familiari di Sperone Speroni', *Giornale storico della letteratura italiana*. Vol. 163, fasc. 523 (1986), pp. 383–413

Longo, Nicola. 'La letteratura proibita'. In Alberto Asor Rosa (ed.), *Letteratura italiana. Vol. V. Le Questioni*. Turin, 1986

Lord, Carnes. 'The Argument of Tasso's *Nifo*'. *Italica*. Vol. 56, no. 1 (1979), pp. 22–45

Lowry, Martin. *The World of Aldus Manutius; Business and Scholarship in Renaissance Venice*. Oxford, 1979

MacGowan, Margaret M. *Montaigne's Deceits: the Art of Persuasion in the 'Essais'*. London, 1974

Maclean, Ian. *The Renaissance Notion of Women; a Study in the Fortunes of Scholasticism and Medical Science in European Intellectual Life*. Cambridge, 1980

Malanima, P. 'Bartolomeo Cerretani'. In *Dizionario biografico degli italiani*. Rome 1960–. Vol. XXIII

Marias, Julián. *Philosophy as Dramatic Theory*, translated by J. Parsons. University Park, Pa., and London, 1971

Marsh, David. *The Quattrocento Dialogue; Classical Tradition and Humanist Innovation*. Cambridge, Mass., and London, 1980
'Struttura e retorica nel *De vero bono*'. In Ottavio Besomi and Mariangela Regoliosi (eds.), *Lorenzo Valla e l'umanesimo italiano. Atti del convegno internazionale di studi umanistici (Parma, 18–19 ottobre, 1984)*. Padua, 1986

Martines, Lauro. *Power and Imagination. City-States in Renaissance Italy*. New York, 1979
Society and History in English Renaissance Verse. Oxford, 1985

Mattioli, Emilio. *Luciano e l'umanesimo*. Naples, 1980

May, Steven W. 'Tudor Aristocrats and the Mythical Stigma of Print'. *Renaissance Papers* (1980), pp. 11–18

Mayer, C. A. *Lucien de Samose et la Renaissance française*. Geneva, 1984

Mazzacurati, Giancarlo. *Misure del classicismo rinascimentale*. Naples, 1967
Il Rinascimento dei moderni; la crisi culturale del Cinquecento e la negazione delle origini. Bologna, 1985

McCuaig, William. *Carlo Sigonio. The Changing World of the Late Renaissance.* Princeton, 1988

Merrill, E. 'The Dialogue in English Literature', *Yale Studies in English Literature.* Vol. 42 (1911); reprinted, New Haven, 1969

Mittelstrass, Jürgen. 'On Socratic Dialogue'. In Charles L. Griswold (ed.), *Platonic Writings, Platonic Readings.* London and New York, 1988

Monfasani, John. 'Lorenzo Valla and Rudolph Agricola'. *Journal of the History of Philosophy,* vol. 28 (1990), pp. 181–200

Moro, Giacomo. 'Appunti sulla preistoria editoriale dei *Dialogi* e della *Canace*'. *Filologia veneta. Lingua, letteratura, tradizioni.* Vol. 2: *Sperone Speroni* (1989), pp. 193–218

Morphos, P. P. *The Dialogues of Guy de Brués; a Critical Edition with a Study in Renaissance Scepticism and Relativism.* Baltimore, 1953

Morrisoe, M., Jr. 'Hume's Rhetorical Strategy: a Solution to the Riddle of the *Dialogues concerning Natural Religion'. Texas Studies in Literature and Language.* Vol. 11, no. 2 (1969), pp. 963–74

'Characterization as Rhetorical Device'. *Enlightenment Essays.* Vol. 1 (1970), pp. 95–107

Mulas, Luisa. 'Funzione degli esempi, funzione del Cortegiano'. In Carlo Ossola and Adriano Prosperi (eds.), *La corte e il Cortegiano.* 2 volumes. Rome, 1980

'La scrittura del dialogo'. In Giovanna Cerina, Cristina Lavinio and Luisa Mulas (eds.), *Oralità e scrittura nel sistema letterario. Atti del convegno, Cagliari, 14–16 aprile, 1980.* Rome, 1982

Mutini, C. 'Dionisio Atanagi'. In *Dizionario biografico degli italiani.* Rome 1960–. Vol. IV

Olivato, L. 'Girolamo Cattaneo'. In *Dizionario biografico degli italiani.* Rome 1960–. Vol. XXII

Ong, Walter J. *Ramus, Method and the Decay of Dialogue: From the Art of Discourse to the Art of Reason.* Cambridge, Mass., 1958

The Presence of the Word. Some Prolegomena for Cultural and Religious History. New Haven and London, 1967

Rhetoric, Romance and Technology. Studies in the Interaction of Expression and Culture. Ithaca and London, 1971

Orality and Literacy; the Technologizing of the Word. London and New York, 1982

Ordine, Nuccio. 'Il dialogo cinquecentesco italiano tra diegesi e mimesi'. *Studi e problemi di critica testuale.* Vol. 37 (1988), pp. 155–79

Ossola, Carlo. *Dal 'Cortegiano' all''Uomo di mondo'. Storia di un libro e di un modello sociale.* Turin, 1987

Panizza, Letizia A. 'Lorenzo Valla's "De vero falsoque bono": Lactantius and Oratorical Scepticism', *Journal of the Warburg and Courtauld Institutes.* Vol. 41 (1978), pp. 76–107

Papagno, Giuseppe. 'Corti e cortigiani'. In Carlo Ossola and Adriano Prosperi (eds.), *La corte e il 'Cortegiano'.* 2 volumes. Rome, 1980. Vol. II

Patrizi, Giorgio. 'Lodovico Castelvetro'. In *Dizionario biografico degli italiani.* Rome 1960–. Vol. XXII

Il 'Libro del Cortegiano' e la trattatistica sul comportamento. In Alberto Asor

Rosa (ed.), *Letteratura italiana. III. Le forme del testo. II. La prosa*. Turin, 1982

'La "Civil Conversatione"', libro europeo'. In Giorgio Patrizi (ed.), *Stefano Guazzo e la 'Civil Conversazione'*. Rome, 1990

Perelman, Chaim, with Lucie Obrechts-Tyteca. *The New Rhetoric: a Treatise on Argumentation*, translated by John Wilkinson and Purcell Weaver. Notre-Dame and London, 1969

Phillips, Mark. *Francesco Guicciardini. The Historian's Craft*. Toronto and Buffalo, 1977

Piéjus, Marie-Françoise. 'Venus bifrons: le double idéal féminin dans *La Raffaella* d'Alessandro Piccolomini'. In *Images de la femme dans la littérature italienne de la Renaissance. Préjugés misogynes et aspirations nouvelles*. Paris, 1980

Pieri, M. 'Vincenzo Colli'. In *Dizionario biografico degli italiani*. Rome 1960–. Vol. XXVII

Pignatti, Franco. 'I *Dialoghi* di Torquato Tasso e la morfologia del dialogo cortigiano rinascimentale'. *Studi Tassiani*. Vol. 36, no. 36 (1988), pp. 7–43

Plaisance, Michel. 'Une première affirmation de la politique culturelle de Côme 1er: la transformation de l'académie des "Humidi" en Académie Florentine (1540–2)'. In André Rochon (ed.), *Les écrivains et le pouvoir en Italie à l'époque de la Renaissance*. 2 volumes. Paris, 1973–4. Vol. I

'Culture et politique à Florence de 1542 à 1551'. In André Rochon (ed.), *Les écrivains et le pouvoir en Italie à l'époque de la Renaissance*. 2 volumes. Paris, 1973–4. Vol. II

Polverini Fosi, I. 'Torquato Conti'. In *Dizionario biografico degli italiani*. Vol. XXVIII

Pozzi, Mario (ed.). *Trattati d'amore del Cinquecento*, edited by Giuseppe Zonta; reprinted with an introduction by Mario Pozzi. Bari, 1975

(ed.) *Trattatisti del Cinquecento*. Milan and Naples, 1978

'Il pensiero linguistico di B. Castiglione'. *Giornale storico della letteratura italiana*. Vol. 156 (1979), pp. 179–202

(with M. R. Loi) 'Le lettere familiari di Sperone Speroni', *Giornale storico della letteratura italiana*. Vol. 163, fasc. 523 (1986), pp. 383–413

(ed.) *Discussioni linguistiche del Cinquecento*. Turin, 1988

'Sperone Speroni e il genere epidittico'. *Filologia veneta. Lingua, letteratura, tradizioni*. Vol. 2: *Sperone Speroni* (1989), pp. 55–88

Pratt, Mary Louise. *Towards a Speech-Act Theory of Literary Discourse*. Bloomington, Indiana and London, 1977

Purpus, E. R. 'The Plain, Easy and Familiar Way: the Dialogue in English Literature 1660–1725'. *English Literary History*. Vol. 17 (1950), pp. 47–58

Quondam, Amedeo. *Petrarchismo mediato; per una critica della forma 'antologia'. Livelli d'uso nel sistema linguistico del petrarchismo*. Rome, 1974

La parola nel labirinto: società e scrittura del Manierismo a Napoli. Rome and Bari, 1975

'"Mercanzia d'onore"/"mercanzia d'utile": produzione libraria e lavoro intellettuale a Venezia nel Cinquecento'. In Armando Petrucci (ed.), *Libri, editori e pubblico nell'Europa moderna. Guida storica e critica*. Bari, 1977

'Dal "formulario" al "formulario": cento anni di "libri di lettere"'. In Amedeo

Quondam (ed.), *Le carte messaggiere. Retorica e modelli di comunicazione epistolare: per un'indice dei libri di lettere del Cinquecento.* Rome, 1981

La letteratura in tipografia. In Alberto Asor Rosa (ed.), *Letteratura italiana. II. Produzione e consumo.* Turin, 1983

Raimondi, Ezio. 'Il problema filologico e letterario dei *Dialoghi* di T. Tasso'. In *Rinascimento inquieto.* Palermo, 1966

Rebhorn, Wayne A. *Courtly Performances; Masking and Festivity in Castiglione's 'Book of the Courtier'.* Detroit, 1978

Redondi, Pietro. *Galileo eretico.* Turin, 1983

Rendall, Steven. 'Fontanelle's Art of Dialogue and His Public'. *Modern Language Notes.* Vol. 84, no. 4 (1971), pp. 496–508

'Dialogue, Philosophy and Rhetoric: the Example of Plato's "Gorgias"'. *Philosophy and Rhetoric.* Vol. 10, no. 3 (1977), pp. 165–79

Robinson, Christopher. 'The Reputation of Lucian in Sixteenth-Century France'. *French Studies.* Vol. 29, no. 4 (1975), pp. 385–97

Lucian and his Influence in Europe. London, 1979

Roelens, Maurice. 'Le dialogue philosophique, genre impossible?' *Cahiers de l'Association Internationale des Etudes Françaises.* No. 24 (1972), pp. 43–58

Rosa, S. 'Chiesa e stati regionali nell'età dell'assolutismo'. In Alberto Asor Rosa (ed.), *Letteratura italiana. I. Il letterato e le istituzioni.* Turin, 1982

Rosen, Stanley. *Plato's 'Symposium'.* New Haven and London, 1968

Plato's 'Sophist'. The Drama of Original and Image. New Haven and London, 1983

Rossi, Paolo. *I filosofi e le macchine (1400–1700).* Milan, 1962

Rossi, Vittorio. *Battista Guarini e il 'Pastor Fido'.* Turin, 1886

Rotondò, Antonio. 'La censura ecclesiastica e la cultura'. In *Storia d'Italia. Vol. V. I documenti. 2.* Turin, 1973

Ruch, Michel. *Le préambule dans les œuvres philosophiques de Cicéron: essai sur la genèse et l'art du dialogue.* Paris, 1958

Rummel, Erika. *Erasmus as a Translator of the Classics.* Toronto and London, 1985

Ryan, Lawrence V. 'Book IV of Castiglione's *Courtier*: Climax or Afterthought?' *Studies in the Renaissance.* Vol. 19 (1972), pp. 152–79

Sabbatino, Pasquale. *Il modello bembiano a Napoli nel Cinquecento.* Naples, 1986

Saccone, Eduardo. 'Trattato e ritratto: l'introduzione del *Cortegiano*'. *Modern Language Notes.* Vol. 93, no. 1 (1978), pp. 1–21

'"Grazia", "sprezzatura", "affettazione" in the *Courtier*'. In Robert W. Hanning and David Rosand (eds.), *Castiglione: the Ideal and the Real in Renaissance Culture.* New Haven and London, 1983

'The Portrait of the Courtier in Castiglione'. *Italica.* Vol. 61, no. 1 (1987), pp. 1–18

Samuels, Richard S. 'Benedetto Varchi, the *Accademia degli Infiammati*, and the Origins of the Italian Academic Movement'. *Renaissance Quarterly.* Vol. 29 (1976), pp. 599–634

Saunders, J. W. 'The Stigma of Print: a Note on the Social Bases of Tudor Poetry'. *Essays in Criticism.* Vol. 1, no. 2 (1951), pp. 139–64

Sayce, R. A. *The Essays of Montaigne. A Critical Exploration.* London, 1972

Sayre, K. M. 'Plato's Dialogues in the Light of the *Seventh Letter*'. In Charles L.

Griswold (ed.), *Platonic Writings, Platonic Readings*. London and New York, 1988

Schmitt, Charles B. *Cicero scepticus. A Study of the Influence of the 'Academica' in the Renaissance*. The Hague, 1972

Cesare Cremonini. Un aristotelico al tempo di Galilei. Venice, 1980

Scrivano, Riccardo. 'Nelle pieghe del dialogare bembesco'. In Giulio Ferroni (ed.), *Il dialogo. Scambi e passaggi della parola*. Palermo, 1985, pp. 101–9

Segre, Cesare. 'Edonismo linguistico nel Cinquecento'. In *Lingua, stile e società* (Milan, 1974)

Seeskin, K. 'Socratic Philosophy and the Dialogue Form'. *Philosophy and Literature*. Vol. 8, no. 2 (1984), pp. 181–94

Seidel Menchi, Silvana. 'Alcuni atteggiamenti della cultura italiana di fronte ad Erasmo (1520–1536)'. In Luigi Firpo and Giorgio Spini (eds.), *Eresia e riforma nell'Italia del Cinquecento. Miscellanea I*. Florence and Chicago, 1974

'La circolazione clandestina di Erasmo in Italia. I casi di Antonio Brucioli e di Marsilio Andreasi'. *Annali della Scuola Normale Superiore di Pisa (Lettere e Filosofia)*. Series III, vol. 9, no. 2 (1979), pp. 573–601

'La discussione su Erasmo nell'Italia del Rinascimento'. In *Società, politica e cultura a Capri ai tempi di Alberto III Pio. Atti del Convegno Internazionale, Capri, 19–21 maggio, 1978*. Padua, 1981

Simpson, David. 'Hume's Intimate Voices and the Method of Dialogue'. *Texas Studies in Literature and Language*. Vol. 21, no. 1 (1979), pp. 68–72

Smith, Pauline M. *The Anti-Courtier Trend in Sixteenth-Century French Literature*. Geneva, 1966

Snyder, Jon R. *Writing the Scene of Speaking: Theories of Dialogue in the Late Italian Renaissance*. Stanford, Ca., 1989

Solerti, Angelo. *Ferrara e la corte estense nella seconda metà del secolo decimosesto e i Discorsi di Annibale Romei*. 2nd edition. Città di Castello, 1900

Vita di Torquato Tasso. 2 volumes. Turin, 1895

Sozzi, Lionello. *Retorica e umanesimo*. In Corrado Vivanti (ed.), *Storia d'Italia. Annali 4. Intellettuali e potere*. Turin, 1981

Stokes, Michael C. *Plato's Socratic Conversations. Drama and Dialectic in Three Dialogues*. London, 1986

Strosetzki, Christoph. *Rhétorique de la conversation: sa dimension littéraire et linguistique dans la société française du XVIIème siècle*, translated by Sabine Seubert. Paris, Seattle and Tübingen, 1984

Tafuri, M. *Venezia e il Rinascimento; religione, scienza, architettura*. Turin, 1985

Tateo, Francesco. *Tradizione e realtà nell'Umanesimo italiano*. Bari, 1967

Tenenti, A. *Cristoforo Da Canal. La marine Vénitienne avant Lépante*. Paris, 1962

Thompson, Craig R. *The Translations of Lucian by Erasmus and St Thomas More*. New York, 1940

Tillman, J. 'Bacon's Ethos: the Modest Philosopher'. *Renaissance Papers* (1976), pp. 11–20

Todini, G. 'Orazio Ariosto'. In *Dizionario biografico degli italiani*. Rome 1960–. Vol. IV

Tompkins, Jane P. 'The Reader in History: the Changing Shape of Literary Response'. In Jane P. Tompkins (ed.), *Reader-Response Criticism from Formalism to Post-Structuralism*. Baltimore and London, 1980

Trafton, Dain A. 'Tasso's Dialogue on the Court'. *English Literary Renaissance Supplements.* No. 2 (1973)

Vasoli, Cesare. *La dialettica e la retorica dell'umanesimo: 'invenzione' e 'metodo' nella cultura del XV e del XVI secolo.* Milan, 1968

Vivenza, G. 'Giacomo Lanteri da Paratico e il problema delle fortificazioni nel secolo XVI'. In *Economia e storia.* Vol. 22, fasc. 4 (1975), pp. 503–38

Volpicelli, L. (ed.), *Il pensiero politico della Controriforma.* Florence, 1960

Weinberg, Bernard. *A History of Literary Criticism in the Italian Renaissance.* Chicago, 1961

Wheeler, K. J. 'Berkeley's Ironic Method in the *Three Dialogues*'. *Philosophy and Literature.* Vol. 4, no. I (1980), pp. 18–32

Whigham, Frank. 'Interpretation at Court: Courtesy and the Performer-Audience Dialectic'. *New Literary History.* Vol. 14, no. 3 (1983), pp. 623–39

Ambition and Privilege; the Social Tropes of Elizabethan Courtesy Theory. Berkeley and London, 1984

White, Nicholas P. 'Observations and Questions about Hans-Georg Gadamer's Interpretation of Plato'. In Charles L. Griswold (ed.), *Platonic Writings, Platonic Readings.* London and New York, 1988

Wilson, K. J. *Incomplete fictions: the Formation of the English Renaissance Dialogue.* Washington D.C., 1985

Woodhouse, J. R. *Baldesar Castiglione. A Re-assessment of 'The Courtier'.* Edinburgh, 1978

Wyss Morigi, Giovanna. *Contributo allo studio del dialogo nell'epoca dell'umanesimo e del Rinascimento.* Monza, 1950

Zonta, Giuseppe. 'Note betussiane'. *Giornale storico della letteratura italiana.* Vol. 52 (1908), pp. 321–65

Zorzi, Alvise. *Cortigiana veneziana. Veronica Franco e i suoi poeti, 1546–1591.* Milan, 1986

Index

231

Made in the USA
Middletown, DE
14 May 2018